7

The Breakdown
of
the Old Politics

THE BREAKDOWN OF THE OLD POLITICS

THOMAS A. LANE

ARLINGTON HOUSE·PUBLISHERS
NEW ROCHELLE, N. Y.

Manufactured in the United States of America

Library of Congress Cataloging in Publication Data

Lane, Thomas A   1906-
    The breakdown of the old politics.

    Includes bibliographical references.
    1. Political parties—United States. 2. United States—Politics
and government—20th century.
I.   Title.
JK2261.L35   320.9'73'09   74-11036
ISBN 0-87000-217-1

CONTENTS

PREFACE

Democracy in America is awash in a sea of troubles. Government seems incapable of preserving public order. Crime is rampant, the political parties are fragmenting. Why?

The United States has been the victim of party politics, a unique variety unknown to the parliamentary system, indigenous to America.

The American political order was inaugurated without national political parties. President Washington, the unanimous choice of the Electoral College, symbolized and maintained a national unity above factionalism. The political parties just grew. Differences of view on basic policy and interest between the industrial East and the agrarian frontier emerged in factions and then in formal party organization.

Thus, the political party is not an integral element of the American political system, as are the political parties in countries organized under the parliamentary system. The American political party has no formal role in government. It is constituted to serve its own interests.

In the first 150 years of government, the Constitution was the controlling instrument of our political order. The political parties operated as rallying points of public policy, ever respectful of the Constitution except in the brief interlude of Reconstruction.

In the past half-century, the American political scene has changed drastically. A concerted drive to change the limited character of our national government by judicial interpretation and legislative usurpation, without constitutional amendment, has succeeded. A concentration of power, authority and staff in Washington has drastically altered the balance of the federal system.

Although these political changes have been promoted as a necessary accommodation of national needs in a modern society, they seem rather to have fractured our domestic peace and concord, wasted our substance in foreign adventures and undermined our strength and resolution in foreign affairs.

The system of politics which "just grew" today loudly proclaims its service and essentiality to our national political structure. The claims are extravagant and self-serving. It may well be that escape from the political paralysis imposed by the two-party system is the most urgent need of our society.

A special characteristic of present government is its hidden character. Money rules, not openly but in ways permitted by law. The facade of popular choice is almost as phony here as it is in the Soviet Union. A first step of reform must be to put all the political cards on the table.

In this book, I have undertaken to identify the most serious errors of our political policy, domestic and foreign, in recent history and to relate those errors to changes in our political system wrought by two-party government. The process of decay has proceeded so far that courageous action by determined citizens will be required to give our country a new direction.

I express my sincere appreciation to Mrs. Julia L. Walsh and Mr. Jeremiah J. Lane for their research assistance and to Dr. A. G. B. Metcalf for perceptive criticism of a first draft of the manuscript.

McLean, Virginia
November 29, 1973

The Breakdown
of
the Old Politics

Chapter 1

THE FOUNDATION OF POLITICS

FROM THE EXPERIENCE of living, through his own powers of perception and reason, man reaches conclusions about the world and the universe of which he is part. He stores this knowledge in the accumulated wisdom of the human race. And then he disregards this wisdom to act in ways prompted by the passions of his complex being.

What does man learn from simple observation of the world about him? That he is in physical strength one of the weakest of the animals. He cannot run with the lion or leap with the deer, or climb trees with the apes. His young have an extraordinary period of helplessness before they become self-reliant. It is a mystery of nature that he survives.

He survives by his wits. He has the capacity to inquire and to understand, to learn the meaning of observed phenomena and therefore to make and to use tools. He notes a quality of intelligence in the animal kingdom and comes to realize that he has more of it than any other animal. He observes that this intelligence can be used to compensate for his physical shortcomings in the struggle for survival.

He learns the laws of nature that regulate the cycles of plant and animal life, the changing seasons, night and day. He observes the sun, moon, and stars and their changing relationship with earth.

And yet, though he has learned so much, he still knows so little. Who is he? Where did this world come from? Why is he on it? Is there no purpose in life except to live and to die? Yes, his intelligence is the greatest he can find in the animal kingdom, but it is not enough. There must be a higher intelligence, one that comprehends these fundamental questions. There must be a creator who made the universe and who understands all things.

So man set out to learn about his creator. Man found His will reflected in the laws of nature. Reason told him that these laws of a higher intelligence were to be obeyed. Man had the freedom to defy those laws but in doing so he would be asserting an inferior intelligence and courting an inferior performance. Man exercised his own intelligence to reach out to his Maker and in doing so learned much about the will of God. He learned about himself in the pursuit of philosophy.

Before man ever learned to write, he knew all these things. In the earliest history of man, we find him conversant with the laws of nature, with sun, wind and tides, with astronomy. And even among tribes living in prehistory, there is the universal recognition of man's spirit and of a spiritual order under the aegis of God or of the gods.

When we speak of humanity we must be aware of the wide range of talents encompassed in the category. Just as a dog can hear what we do not hear and an eagle can see what we do not see, some men can hear and see what others do not see and hear. So too in the realm of the mind, some men can perceive and comprehend what others neither see nor comprehend.

The generalization about the perceptions of man has many exceptions. Throughout history men insensitive or indifferent to the presence of a superior intelligence have lived for their own material aggrandizement alone. Others, postulating the non-existence of a superior intelligence, have rejected all higher restraint upon the judgments of men. Some others have conceived themselves to be the devil's disciples. But all these are a small minority of mankind. Few truths are so self-evident to everyman as the fact that man did not create this world but has been placed in it by a higher intelligence.

Who is man? The question is so basic to the human condition that plans for creating an optimum human society must depend on the answer. If man is an intermediate intelligence, a bridge between the creator and the created world, a whole philosophy of human life and purpose derives from that condition. Man then strives to know and to serve this higher wisdom. His own permissible range of action is structured by the divine law as he discerns it.

If, however, there is no divine intelligence, if man is merely an animated speck of matter, different in quality but not in essence from a cabbage, certain other conclusions follow. Human life has no value except to achieve the aims of men. Human beings who interfere with the achievements of those aims are as dispensable as the weeds in a garden.

From these different perceptions of the human condition, different systems of government emerge. In the one, man is endowed with an immortal soul destined for union with its creator; and the purpose of all human institutions is to contribute to the fulfillment of that soul's destiny. In this system, the individual person is the central value of society which must be served.

In this system, all of man's institutions are limited in power and authority by the presence of God's law and by the dignity which the individual has in his relationship with God. Government can be only a deputy, never a supreme authority. Criticism of the state is not only tolerable but necessary because the state represents only the judgments of men. As Jacques Maritain has stated:[1]

> ... one is in danger of forgetting that no human agency has by virtue of its own nature a right to govern men. Any right to power in political society, is possessed by a man or a human agency in so far as he or it is in the body politic a part at the service of the common good, a part which has received this right, within certain fixed bounds, from the people exercising their fundamental right to govern themselves.

In the opposing system, the individual is a transient force, the collectivity is the enduring force which must be served. Society is organized for the general welfare of the people as that welfare is judged by the political leaders, without restraint of any law—divine or human.

In this system, acknowledging no higher intelligence than that of man, government is the supreme authority. It is not restrained by any higher law in its judgment of what is expedient. It is God. It cannot tolerate public criticism, for such criticism would impugn its supremacy. Its logic is tyranny.

The first system postulates a self-reliant and self-sufficient citizenry needing from government only the direction of manifestly collective interests. The second system requires a citizenry subject to and obedient to the state in all things.

Throughout recorded history, the government of human communities has been based upon the recognition of a divine presence and divine law. Even the tyrant's power was limited by what he could claim before his people to be the will of God. Only in modern times have we seen the systematic rejection of God in organized government as tyrants have striven to liberate themselves from restraints of the natural and divine law.

This is the central struggle of our age. The determination of some men to destroy God shapes the conflicts of this century. Two opposing political systems stand in conflict. John Courtney Murray has noted that the opposed systems stood in stark contradiction at the founding of the American Republic:[2]

> The Jacobin tradition proclaimed the autonomous reason of man to be the first and sole principle of political organization. In contrast, the first article of the American political faith is that the political community, as a form of free and ordered human life, looks to the sovereignty of God as to the first principle of its organization.

13

But we must also be aware of cleavages within systems. In the Soviet Union, citizens live in faithful devotion to God, suffering persecution for His sake. And in the United States, citizens who reject God work for a totalitarian government that would wash the vestiges of religion from society—in blood, if necessary.

To this fundamental ideological conflict we must add the other clashes of territorial defense and conquest, of economic and scientific competition which animate the political scene. We must add those influences which enliven or shrivel the human spirit, which nurture courage or cowardice, charity or greed, honesty or casuistry. All add color to politics and direction to the fate of man.

Chapter 2

ORGANIZING SOCIETY

NATURE BRINGS KINDS together in the instincts of their common beings and in understanding of their common needs and dangers. Mankind, because of the physical weakness of the individual and the consequent necessity for group action, is impelled even in primitive conditions to the formation of tribal organization. In the tribal state, the achievements of collective action mark a beginning of civilization.

The development of civilization poses a continuing tension with barbarism, both within the community against the remnants or revivals of barbarism, and without the community in as yet uncivilized neighbors. Thus, the growth of civilization and the survival of the community require the creation of institutions broadly comprehended in "government." As one perceptive observer has described this foundation of civilization:[1]

> It is simply the human community which, in proportion as it is civilized, strives to maintain itself in some small margin of safe distance from the chaos of barbarism. For this effort the only resources directly available to the community are those which first rescued it from barbarism, namely, the resources of reason, made operative chiefly through the processes of reasonable law, prudent public policies, and a discriminatingly apt use of force.

In the necessary organization of government, the hierarchical order was both the natural order and the common order of political structure. As

15

the father was the head of the family, the chief was the head of the tribe and the king was the head of the nation. The larger social community was regarded as the larger family, and so it was.

As the numbers and the territory of political organization increased, suitable bureaucracies were created to administer the state in behalf of the king. A court surrounding the king administered national affairs. The domain was divided into duchies or other principalities to be administered by hereditary or appointed officials acting on behalf of the king. Cities grew, new economic and social classes emerged. Local forms of government were improvised. But all government was under the leadership of the king.

In man's primitive condition, the tribal preserve was the tribal lifeline. If the tribe increased in numbers, the domain had to be expanded to provide food for all. In this stage of development, man lived in perpetual warfare with his neighbors, either to protect his own tribal preserve or to seize territory which would support tribal growth.

Survival imposed a necessary discipline on man. The young African boy who had to go into the jungle, spear in hand, to challenge the lion as a demonstration of fitness as a tribal warrior, faced at that early age the hard reality of life. He knew that his intelligence and his weapon made him lord of the jungle.

As human intelligence in some climes turned from hunting to the arts of agriculture and animal husbandry, man was able to wrest greater productivity from the soil and the sea. Life was necessarily more settled. The tribal domain could support a larger population. The variety of available foods and artifacts could be expanded. The complexity of society and of personal relationships increased. The simple form of the tribal council had to be elaborated with lawmaking and law administration.

Food productivity stimulated diversity of occupation, the development of new skills and products, the organization of human work, the development of urban centers, the growth of the city-state. In the Greek city-state, pagan culture achieved its highest expression of art and culture.

But the art of war flourished too. Human ambition sought new conquests as Alexander fulfilled the dreams of Philip. However reluctantly, the world was being united.

It remained for Rome to provide not only the might of legions but the organizing genius which could bring the diverse peoples of a new empire under a rational and civilizing rule. Roman law and justice reached out to embrace the barbarians on the fringes of the Mediterranean basin. The civilizing of Europe was begun.

In the more primitive organization of the tribe, when war was a constant or recurring condition, leadership was accorded by tribal council to the warrior who had proven his superiority in battle. As pastoral living was succeeded by the agricultural economy, settled communities and greater security, the leadership of the nation became hereditary, but still with strong emphasis on the king as a warrior. As the reigning family decayed, losing its capacity to lead, lieutenants of the realm arose to seize the national leadership, sometimes after bitter civil war, sometimes by general recognition of power and excellence. New alliances were formed. New wars were waged to defend or expand the national domain.

Some of the greatest military leaders went on from building the nation to building the empire. The victorious people prospered, civilization developed. But then, the pace could not be maintained. The qualities of leadership declined. For want of that binding power, the empire disintegrated. Civilization deteriorated.

The people, softened by the luxuries of civilization, desperately wanted to believe that their possessions were the just reward of their labors and that they could retain them without fighting. Reason, they thought, would defend what was right. Demagogues arose to cultivate the illusion and to win political preferment. Civilization was ripe for the plucking by a new order of barbarism using force as an instrument of conquest and contemptuous of the pacifistic pretensions of the decadent empire. The old civilization expired and a new civilization was born.

Even as the pagan Roman empire seemed to reach its peak of power, its disintegration was assured. A civilization spread by conquest and preserved by slavery could not long satisfy the insistent quest of the human spirit for justice. The Christian spirit, stemming from the loins of Judaism, bespoke a new human order based not on power and oppression but upon submission and sanctity. And the measure of sanctity was not wealth but poverty. A new set of values seeped through the pagan world.

The conquests of empire had established a new unity of the civilized world and a receptive climate for the universality of the Christian message. St. Paul could counsel Christian slaves to serve their masters but he could not counsel Christian masters to keep their fellow Christians in slavery. Slavery, the industrial fuel of Roman civilization, simply dissolved.

Although Christianity could destroy slavery, it could not offer a substitute economy to keep the lights of civilization burning. It might convert the barbarian hordes but it could not keep them from overrunning Christendom. Europe adjusted economically and culturally to an era of feudalism from which it would be aroused when a new thrusting of the human spirit would reach out to the "new" world and would discover through science new sources of power to serve mankind.

The ferment of the Renaissance, the dissolution of the Holy Roman Empire, the sectarian division of Christendom, the emergence of new states, the wars for religion, land, and survival, all marked a new and turbulent era. With all these political conflicts, there was an accompanying flowering of political philosophy. Refreshed by the history of the Greeks, driven by the compulsions of power in their own time, men speculated

17

about the role of man in history, about the proper organization of human society for the benefit of man, about the role of excellence and the role of leadership in managing human society.

And yet, while philosophers speculated about other orders, the ancient hierarchical order persisted. The whole world, East and West, was ruled by kings and emperors. Courts of elite retainers administered kingdoms. Lands and authority were, outside the church, hereditary. The individual value and worth of man defined by Christian teaching, when confronted with the real problem of an organized society, could survive as a spiritual concept without altering the structure of society. The compunctions of existence would exert a strong influence on sons to follow in the footsteps of fathers until another age would open new avenues to all.

In Britain, the power of the king had been curbed by mutual protective action of the dukes of the realm. The Magna Carta meant little to the common man but it was a step in a process that would in time establish a rule of representative government. The struggle between kings and nobles was to take Englishmen on a long, bloody way before sovereignty of the people would be established.

The renaissance of republican government was to come in America through the revolt of the British colonies from the mother country. In their pioneering exploration of a new continent, colonists in America had developed an independence and self-reliance far surpassing the freedoms available to Englishmen on their home island. When King and Parliament asserted a purpose to bring the colonies within the onerous jurisdiction of Parliament, the colonists rebelled. They declared to the world the basis of their rebellion, raising a new standard of government drawn jointly from Christian philosophy and from the renaissance ferment of speculation on the political rights of man.

Chapter 3

THE AMERICAN REVOLUTION

THE DECLARATION OF INDEPENDENCE was much more than a severance of political connection with Mother England. It was the charter of a new political order which was to sweep the world. It would inspire a century of revolution liberating men from the authoritarianism of the ancient order and realizing dreams of self-rule. It was the most significant political document to be composed by man in a thousand years. It swept away the ancient concepts of government.

"We hold these truths to be self-evident, that all men are created equal, that they are endowed by their Creator with certain inalienable Rights, that among these are life, liberty, and the pursuit of happiness. That to receive these rights, Governments are instituted among Men, deriving their just powers from the consent of the governed." With this ringing declaration, these courageous rebels against the tyranny of a remote government defined a new political order. They proclaimed their faith in the Creator and His law, the rights of man and the proper place of government in human society. In this statement we have the foundation of the American political order.

Of this declaration, John Courtney Murray wrote:[1]

Our Fathers thought that the life of man in society under government is founded on truths, on a certain body of Truth, universal in its import, ac-

19

cessible to the reason of man, definable, defensible. If this assertion is denied, the American proposition is I think eviscerated at one stroke. It is indeed in many respects a pragmatic proposition; but its philosophy is not pragmatism.

For the pragmatist, there are, properly speaking, no truths; there are only results.

The American proposition has indeed been challenged and is challenged in our time. The elites who cultivate power in every age have no confidence in the people. They prefer the hierarchical order and a government of authority that will use the few to rule the many. The people themselves, deprived of knowledge about their own government, can weary of its corruption and turn to a Caesar for salvation.

The almost universal acceptance of the hierarchical form of government in the ancient world was thoroughly human. It was natural to take the family as the model of tribal and national organization, for these groups were merely the greater family. Moreover, the absolute necessity of unified leadership and resolute decision-making in societies fighting for survival confirmed the seeming logic of the hierarchical order. Religion, too, drawing its authority from a divine order superior to man, contributed its approval to a hierarchical order comporting with its own logical structure.

All this seeming logic was swept aside by the architects of the American Revolution. They rejected a political order modeled on the human family. They declared that no man, by taking public office, acquired the relationship to his fellow citizens that a father bore to the family. Rather, they declared, all men are politically equal and they create governments to serve man. The proper concept of government, they said, is not of a father caring for his family but of a servant working for his masters.

In one ringing declaration, they turned the concept of sovereignty upside down. A false analogy that had dominated human concepts of the political order for millennia was destroyed simply by being challenged. Sovereignty resided not in king or president but in the people.

The rightness of this new perception of human relations was immediately apparent to all men, but the consequence of its adoption was largely unforeseen and is today largely unappreciated. The miracle of production which springs from this source is often attributed to other aspects of human relations.

The hierarchical order, symbolized by the pyramid, is a static order. Authority resides at the top in the soverign. Innovation and progress are limited to ideas which reach the sovereign through his court. It is possible but difficult for a new concept to rise through the layers of bureaucracy to win approval at the top.

Wise sovereigns, aware of the weakness of the system, tried to encourage constructive contributions from the people; but they were working against the system. Their efforts could have only a temporary and limited effect. We can speculate that the millennia of limited human progress in the physical sciences reflect the paralysis which hierarchical organization imposed on the human mind and spirit.

The Declaration of Independence brushed that enduring disability aside. In declaring the sovereignty of the individual, it liberated the energy and the initiative of man. A new burst of creative activity surged through the world as the value of a new invention was judged by public acceptance in the marketplace, not by the flawed "omniscience" of government bureaucracy.

The unprecedented production of wealth in a grand diversity of forms in America has been variously attributed to the richness of soil, minerals, and climate. But these are resources not significantly different from similar resources in other parts of the world. The real motor of progress has been the political liberation of the human spirit from the bondage of government combined with a pioneer spirit which called men to a vigorous exercise of the new freedom.

President Herbert Hoover, that sage observer of our political scene, noted the high standards of excellence to which men aspire when freedom and justice encourage their endeavors:[2]

> Our American System is not alone an economic method, a definition of rights, a scheme of representative government, an organization to maintain order and justice, a release of constructive instincts and desires. It is far more than that, for it is a system of stimulation to higher standards, to higher aspirations and ideals.
>
> While we have built a gigantic organized society upon the attainment of the individual, we should not have raised a brick of it but by the stimulation to self-restraint and by drawing upon those high aspirations of men and women expressed in their standards of truth and justice and in their spiritual yearnings.
>
> These ideals are never wholly realized. Not a single human being personifies their complete realization. It is therefore not surprising that society, a collection of persons, a necessary maze of instincts of individuals, cannot realize its ideals wholly.

If the thousands of decisions made daily in the United States by businessmen using their own judgment and risking their own capital had to be approved by the governmental bureaucracy, as they are in Communist countries, our productive economy would grind almost to a halt. Yet, this is where we are headed as businessmen turn increasingly to government for favor or advantage.

The American concept of a right political order was to have far-reaching impact on all the world. It has inspired political revolutions across the world and over the centuries. It will continue to do so into the indefinite future. The world will never be the same again.

The human preference for freedom and the readiness of the working man to risk his livelihood in a fair market were demonstrated in the massive emigration from Europe to America. Just as people today show their preference for freedom by risking death to escape through the Iron and Bamboo Curtains, a century ago they showed similar daring in leaving home and family to seek a new life of freedom in a distant land.

The common man saw in the American proposition a first offering in history of that dignity, freedom, and opportunity to which all men aspire. He responded with enthusiasm. He cherished the system of law which liberated him from the whim of authoritarian government. His love affair with America has been enduring. He has rejected the blandishments of fascism and socialism. If there is disloyalty in our society, it is among the rich and powerful, not among the workingmen.

It is one thing to define a correct principle and quite another to create a political order that will effect the principle. It is this task of creating a viable political order which continues to challenge the wisdom and prudence of mankind.

We have described the paternal political order as the natural order, and so it is. Mankind seems to divide into a small element of ambitious men, motivated to lead and dominate society, and a larger component of men not only content to follow but looking for and needing leadership. Some theorists will argue that the American theory of political equality does not comport with the real talents of men.

ELITES VS. PEOPLE

The thesis for paternalistic government is sustained also by argument that government must be administered by elites specially trained for the responsibility. It is not possible, so this thesis runs, for all citizens to be fully informed on public issues and qualified to judge them. Therefore, it is said, the people must leave the great questions of public policy to government. The general public must accept the judgment of the leaders. Father knows best.

This thesis has a superficial logic, especially attractive to the elites. We hear government officials and policy-makers telling the people that the structure of policy is too complex for public explanation, that the people must have faith in their officials who have access to all the relevant facts. This is the fallacy on which nations founder. What the elites hide from the people are the bad judgments of the elites.

We must indeed select carefully and train thoroughly those who are to be trusted with high public office. Competence is even more important in war and diplomacy than in industry. We must not, however, make the mistake of supposing that these officials have a sense of the national interest superior to that of the people.

Elites have their own foibles and vulnerabilities. In official positions, they are subject to the persuasion and pressure of friend and foe, and therefore are prone to misjudgment of the national interest. In the very intensity of their education and training they are removed from contact with the common sense of the people. No one is more gullible than the self-styled sophisticate.

22

On the great issues of national survival, the judgment of a people having full access to relevant information is the best index of the true national interest:[3]

> On this popular level, the public philosophy would appear as a wisdom, possessed almost intuitively, in the form of a simple faith rather than an articulate philosophy. To this wisdom the people are heir by tradition; it is their patrimony. It gives them an identity as a people by relating them to their own history within which their identity was shaped. Even in simple form this wisdom would be adequate to its function, which is to enable the people to "judge, direct and correct" the moral bearing of courses of government (I use the famous three words of Medieval political theory).

For these reasons, the true statesman works in full harmony with his people. He has confidence in their judgment. He keeps them informed of the vital issues. He and the people are one.

Unfortunately, our elites produce few statesmen. All nations are fated in time to be ruled by lesser men who mistakenly conceive for themselves a mission to shape a higher national destiny than the people could understand or accept.

Recent history is filled with examples of superior judgments of the people rejected by our elites. One such case leading to tragedy was the decision of President Kennedy in 1963, under pressure of his sophisticated advisers, to overthrow the government of President Ngo D. Diem and replace it with a regime that would form a coalition government with the Viet Cong. This elite could see no other way to end the war. But the American people knew better. Their consistent counsel in national polls was to end the war by defeating the enemy. They had no fear of Soviet or Red Chinese intervention.

But our elite, tortured by fears of Communist intervention, pulled by futile hopes of negotiating détente with these powers, was incapable of viewing the conflict objectively. In a time when the United States held overwhelming superiority of strategic nuclear power, the proposition that the Soviet Union or Red China would risk the destruction of their growing arsenals to save North Vietnam from defeat was, of course, preposterous. Yet, precisely such irrationality was the cornerstone of the American policy contrived by our ruling elite.

The Kennedy policy was so contrary to the will and judgment of the people that it had to be concealed from public view. An elaborate campaign in the American press was contrived to represent the Diem government as an authoritarian regime, which was persecuting Buddhists and which had lost the confidence of its people. The coup was depicted as the reaction of generals who wanted to win the war and considered the removal of Diem essential to that end. Without these lies and deception, the American people would never have tolerated the Kennedy policy. They never knew what the policy was.

We have come upon an era when national policy is contrived and administered in secret. It is responsive to the interests of political and economic blocs within our society but hostile to the general sense of our people. This is why "credibility" has become a key word in national politics and why none of our recent Presidents has been credible.

Thus, the fundamental principle of our own Declaration of Independence —the sovereignty of the people—is repudiated in our national life and government. We have gone far down the road to paternalism. Not without cause did a visitor to our shores observe, "You do not have a Republic in the United States. You have an Elective Monarchy." The President is king. Through the party mechanism, the Congress is his court. And the judiciary, appointed by the President, is obedient to his mandate.

This outcome was predicted. There have always been men who considered the American concept of political equality to be utopian. They knew that the power of wealth would always rule, whether through king or parliament. They knew that wealth demands a central power which could protect its interests. They were confident that the people would not long sustain the burdens of individual responsibility under law but would implore government to assume a paternalistic concern for individual welfare. In substance if not in form, the king and his court would be restored.

This rejection of the American proposition is today dominant in our society. Both political parties sustain it. The reversion to paternalism has wrought grievous damage to our constitutional order while wheedling the people with promises of prosperity and justice. We have gone far down the path to a new tyranny.

We have made serious misjudgments in turning away from our patrimony of freedom. But we have done these things under the influence of hostile forces which have cleverly manipulated the good will of the people. There are ways to correct the errors and restore our dynamic society founded on freedom. It is time for the American people to be about their fathers' business.

*

Chapter 4

CREATING A NEW ORDER

DURING THE REVOLUTION, the Continental Congress provided a temporary union of the colonies for the purpose of prosecuting the war. With victory, the colonies became independent states, keenly aware of their sovereignty but also aware of their interdependence. Articles of Confederation defined a new attempt at cooperation expressing the general distrust of a centralized political power.

Under the Articles of Confederation, Congress was composed of delegations of varying size from the states. The delegations voted as units, each state being allowed one vote. Delegates were paid by their state governments. Important bills required a two-thirds vote for passage.

Although the Congress had nominal authority over such common interests as foreign affairs, treaties, coinage, and postal service, it had *no* power to raise funds except by requisition on the states. Because these levies were more ignored than honored, the Congress was effectively strangled, financially and practically. Under the Articles, the central authority was inadequate to perform the essential common functions. Another effort to form a more perfect union was required.

The Constitutional Convention of 1787 assembled a truly remarkable congress of delegates. They had suffered a long and destructive war; they had known the exhilaration of victory, and they had faced the challenges of peace. They shared a vision of union and a fear of tyranny. So it was that out of the differing views of able men, a consensus could be reached. A Constitution was born. America was greatly blessed in this convention, for, as Maritain was to write:[1] "The happiest circumstance for the body politic obtains when the top men in the state are at the same time genuine prophets of the people." In this Convention, they were.

The Constitution was a compact of the states designed to effect the purposes of the Declaration of Independence. The new government was to reflect the principles which had bound the colonies together in war.

The Constitution has been generously praised by great scholars and philosophers. It has been meanly criticized by the lumpen-intelligentsia. But the true measure of its excellence lies in its performance—in a record of freedom and achievement unparalleled in history.

John C. Calhoun, who worked within the constitutional framework in a time of stress and conflict, noted that[2] "this admirable federal constitution of ours is superior to the wisdom of any or all the men by whose agency it was made. The force of circumstances and not foresight or wisdom induced them to adopt many of its wisest provisions."

The times and circumstances did shape some of the Constitution's wisest provisions, but they did so through the prudent judgments of men equal to the challenge.

Jacques Maritain saw in the Constitution an expression of the moral strength and religious faith which begot it:[3]

Peerless is the significance, for political philosophy, of the establishment of the American Constitution at the end of the XVIIIth Century. This Constitution can be described as an outstanding lay Christian document tinged with the philosophy of the day. The spirit and inspiration of this great political Christian document is basically repugnant to the idea of making human society stand aloof from God and from any religious faith. Thanksgiving and public prayer, the invocation of the name of God at the occasion of any major official gathering, are, in the practical behavior of the nation, a token of this very same spirit and inspiration.

The Constitution provided a unique resolution of the question of sovereignty. The states did not cede their sovereignty to a new government of union. They ceded *a part of their sovereignty* as defined in the Constitution. They created a federal union of sovereign powers; a sovereign central government of limited and defined powers, united with sovereign states retaining powers not ceded to the central government. States and central government constituted separate sovereignties drawing their powers from the same people. The Constitution defined the division of powers between central and state governments and also defined the methods by which that division of powers might be altered to meet the needs of future generations.

There is no other government in the world so constituted. In ages past and in decades since 1787, nations have been formed with one sovereignty reposing in a central government. Constitutions have affected to limit government power, with only modest success.

The principle of subsidiarity holds that the powers of government should repose in the lowest echelon of government which can administer those powers effectively and efficiently. It is a principle much honored in theory but rarely reflected in practice. It stands in opposition to the passion of leaders to claim all power and responsibility in fulfillment of their promises to the people.

The United States Constitution makes a practical application of the principle of subsidiarity. Delegates to the Constitutional Convention had a principal task of defining what powers were appropriate to a central government and what powers should be retained by local government. Compromises were made; but a century and a half of experience demonstrated the essential wisdom of the original compact. Subsidiarity was vindicated in practice.

It is a sad commentary upon the intellectual quality of twentieth-century political science that these most prudent provisions of the Constitution are so often misunderstood and misrepresented. Consider, for example, the following comment:[4]

> In many respects the Constitution of 1787 reflects the concept of *laissez-faire capitalism* which was especially popular with many of the influential members of the Convention. According to this doctrine, government was to restrict its activities to a few though vital functions. It was to protect the people from outside enemies, maintain the public order at home, perhaps undertake a few essential public works, establish a stable monetary arrangement, and provide a fair system of courts so that, among other things, individuals would be given adequate protection of their property rights. In other words, the government was to play a negative role in respect to matters of economics.

The authors have thoroughly confounded the very different principles of subsidiarity and of free-market economics. They note in the central government the lack of those powers which are reserved to the states, as though to imply that the powers do not exist in government. But in truth they do exist, and they exist where they belong—close to the people served. The central government has all the powers required for its function. By such misleading presentation, the very strength of the constitutional order is depicted as weakness.

Convention delegates had also to design the new central government. Their chief concern was to keep it a servant of the people. They understood the temptation of such a creation to draw all power to itself.

Because tyranny is by definition the concentration of all power in one person or office, they created a central government of divided powers. There would be legislative, executive and judicial branches, each with powers defined in the Constitution.

The general temper of the Convention was expressed by James Madison:[5]

> The genius of republican liberty seems to demand on one side not only that all power should be derived from the people, but that those intrusted with it should be kept in dependence on the people by a short duration of their appointments; and that even during this short period the trust should be placed not in a few, but in a number of hands.

The mistake is often made of referring to these branches of the central government as coequal. They are equal only in being constitutional: They are quite different in powers. The constitutional architects knew that every government must have the power of decision and that coequal branches could produce stalemate. They therefore reposed the ultimate power of decision in the legislature. Congress can pass bills over a presidential veto. It can impeach and remove from office officers of the executive and judicial branches. It defines the structure and appropriates the pay of the executive and judicial branches.

There can be no question that the new central government was to be *representative* government, dominated by the Congress. But that government was hedged with checks and balances to encourage sober thought and mature decisions. The delegates knew from British history that a parliament could be as tyrannical as any king.

In designing the legislative branch, the Convention delegates had the task of balancing the interests of the large and small states. Their solution was to create a Congress of two houses, one apportioned according to population and the other with equal representation for the sovereign states. The arrangement seemed a reasonable adjustment to the interests of the states but one likely to delay or frustrate the legislative process. Delegates accepted that prospect not out of necessity but because mature deliberation on vital issues was considered appropriate to legislative process.

In a parliamentary government, the chief executive is a legislator, leader of the ruling party or coalition, who with his cabinet assumes full control of the government bureaucracy. The creation of the office of President, subject to direct election by the people and heading the bureaucracy, substantially reduced the powers of the Congress as compared with Parliament.

In a country where the qualifications of electors varied with state law and where "one man, one vote" would have been considered a silly proposition wholly lacking in merit, the method of electing the President required some attention. Delegates might have followed the parliamentary pattern by having the President elected by the Congress. Direct popular election would not allow due weight to the sovereignty of the separate states. In compromise, an Electoral College was created with each state having representation according to its combined total representation in Congress. Delegates would be elected by popular vote. For election, a candidate was required to receive a majority vote in the Electoral College. If no candidate had the requisite majority in the Electoral College, the issue would go to the House of Representatives for decision.

Thus, in the executive branch as in the legislative branch a balance of state and popular interest became the measure of political power. In the Presidency as in the Congress, the majority, as determined by this measure of political power, would rule.

The Constitution gave scant attention to the judiciary. It created a Supreme Court with a defined jurisdiction and such additional jurisdiction as the Congress might give to it. It left to the Congress the creation of such other courts as the Congress might deem necessary.

It would have been deemed superfluous at the time to specify that the judicial function was to interpret the law in cases in dispute, *giving effect to the will of the legislature.* That definition of the judicial function was so well settled in colonial practice that the prospect of judicial usurpation of the legislative power must have seemed remote. Moreover, with definition of the powers of the courts resting in the Congress, it was hardly to be anticipated that the legislature would tolerate judicial usurpation.

When the basic constitutional structure had been settled, delegates remained dissatisfied with the document. While it could readily be assumed that the new central government would have only the power specifically delegated to it, critics demanded more specific limitations on the powers of that government. Consequently, the first ten amendments to the Constitution were approved and submitted to the states with the Constitution for ratification. These amendments constitute our "Bill of Rights": the subject of so much demagoguery in recent decades as the Supreme Court has sought by interpretation to convert limitations on the central government into limitations on the states.

There was not in the first 150 years of the United States Constitution any doubt about the interpretation of the Bill of Rights. These amendments were designed to protect the states and the people from encroachment of the central government. They were not written to limit the powers of the state governments with respect to censorship of the press or the establishment of a state religion but only to deny such powers to the central government. This was the universal judgment of the courts.

There has never been an amendment of the Constitution to deny these retained powers to the states. There has never been an abuse of these powers by the states that would warrant such amendment of the Constitution. And yet, these powers have been stripped from the states by decision of the Supreme Court. The very action which the Bill of Rights undertook to prohibit—the establishment of a national rule of law in these matters—has now been taken by the Court on its own account. The Supreme Court, which was constitutionally excluded from these reserved powers, has set itself up as the supreme arbiter of these powers.

It would be difficult to find in human history a similar example of the abdication of powers by the people's elected representatives in the face of flagrant judicial usurpation. The details of the process will be analyzed in later chapters. It is important here to note the true nature and function of the Bill of Rights. For if the judiciary can by interpretation alter the distribution of powers between the central government and the state governments, the Court has substituted itself for the Constitution.

With the adoption of the Constitution, the first stage of the American Revolution was completed. The principles of human relations defined in the Declaration of Independence were given effect in practical government. The new federal system with its constitutional decentralization of power, its division of powers in the central government, and its emphasis on the sovereignty of the people seemed admirably structured to preserve individual freedom and to inhibit the growth of tyranny.

The new system had some serious defects, notably in its failure to terminate the institution of slavery. That defect would rend the union with bloody warfare in the next century. But, given the temper of the times, the failure to deal with slavery was a necessary compromise. Sentiment against the institution had not yet risen in the Atlantic world to the point of forcing national action. The states were free to terminate slavery within their jurisdiction at will. It would be forty-five years before Britain set an example by outlawing slavery.

In spite of its limitations, the Constitution of the United States was a remarkable document. It brought government into line with the best thought of the Western world on the relationship of a citizen with his government in a free society. The solution was consistent with the philosophy of Christianity, derived in full measure from Christian concepts of man's place in a world created by God. It represented a harmony of religious and political perception of human society theretofore unprecedented.

One fine appraisal of the Constitution was given by Frank S. Meyer, who exhausted the promise of communism before returning to the wisdom of the American proposition and then became at mid-century one of our best American political philosophers. He wrote:[6]

> The men who settled these shores, and established an extension of Western civilization here, carried with them the heritage of centuries of Western development. . . . In the open lands of this continent, removed from the overhanging presence of cosmological remains, they established a constitution that for the first time in human history was constructed to guarantee the sanctity of the person and his freedom. But they brought with them also the human condition, which is tempted always by the false visions of Utopianism.
>
> The establishment of a free constitution is the great achievement of America in the drama of Western civilization. The struggle for its preservation against Utopian corrosion is the continuing history of the United States since its foundation, a struggle which continues to this day and which is not yet decided.

Chapter 5

A COMPETING CONCEPT

THESE TRIUMPHS OF FREEDOM in the United States of America stirred no avalanche of imitation in the rest of the world. The same ferment of ideas which produced one effect in the pioneer societies of the new world produced a quite different effect in the old world.

In Europe, champions of the rights of man saw kings and courts as the oppressors. These entrenched and vested interests had to be smashed before the working man could share fully in the fruits of his labors. And because the churches were closely allied with the royal establishment, religion was regarded by many freedom fighters as part of the oppressive superstructure.

Viewing the problem in this way, European reformers were concerned not about a hierarchical order that supported tyranny but rather with the seizure of power. When the power of government was transferred to representatives of the people, they reasoned, that power would be administered in the public interest, not for private advantage. Their aim was to replace the king with representatives of the people and to convert the monopolies of economic power possessed by the king's retainers into public monopolies owned by the state for the people. Then, they argued, the profits of industry would accrue to the people through the government, and justice would be served.

31

This perception of government power not as the source of tyranny but as a potential source of benefit for the people was widely embraced by European freedom fighters. From the moderate social reformers on the one hand who regarded representative government as a rightful power of the people to the radical terrorists of the Marxist factions advocating dictatorship of the proletariat, there was agreement that justice required the transfer of all political and economic power to the people's representatives. This was the spectrum of socialism which in 1903 would break into Menshevik and Bolshevik (led by Lenin) branches of the movement.

In Europe, the fight for freedom erupted in the French Revolution. It started as a movement to increase the popular power in government, fell into the hands of the Jacobins, went through throes of madness into a tyranny more fearful than the scourges of Genghis Khan, and fell ultimately into the hands of a military genius, Napoleon, who, more than any democrat, could capture the confidence and devotion of the people.

In America, the barbaric excesses of the Jacobin period were regarded with horror. It seemed clear that those who denied God were possessed by the devil. Compared with the paternal concern of a king and the noblesse oblige of an hereditary court, however decadent, the monstrous zealotry of a Robespierre was not liberation but the imposition of a new, more absolute tyranny on the people.

Despite the aberrations of the French Revolution, that event came to be regarded in Europe, and in lands influenced by European philosophy, as a landmark in the fight for freedom. The socialist theory of a powerful government working for the benefit of the people was not discomfited by the lapse into tyranny. Moderate socialists admitted the excess but regarded it simply as a mistake.

The socialist camp has long been split on the issue of method. All cherish the goal of a wise government ruling in behalf of the people. One faction holds that rule of the people can be achieved only by revolutionary violence which will defeat and dispossess the capitalists. The other faction holds that socialist aims can be achieved through parliamentary process. This is the essential difference between Marxist-Leninists and the Democratic Socialists.

The twentieth century has shed new light on socialist thought, since the theories of both factions have been tested in practice. In Russia and China the Marxist-Leninists ruled, with an extermination of their own people unprecedented in history. In prior human experience, enemies were killed in internal battles for power; but when victory was won, the new leader regarded all the people as his people. He would punish rebellion but seek to unite all who accepted his rule.

It remained for the Marxist-Leninists to resort to the extermination of a whole class of the people, and not only capitalists but also simple peasants. Fifty million lives were the toll in the Soviet Union; forty million, in Red China. Lenin, Stalin and Mao made Genghis Khan and Robespierre look like pikers. These were the measures allegedly undertaken for the benefit of the people. Genghis Khan and Robespierre made the same claim. "Plus ca change, plus c'est la meme chose." The astonishing aspect of this performance is that young people in every generation continue to be persuaded that Marxism-Leninism is a force for the benefit of mankind.

The evil nature of the Marxist-Leninist conception of polity has been amply analyzed in our modern political literature. Its deification of the state—that is, the party—its oppression of the working people, its barbarism, its utter incompetence to manage human society, all have been demonstrated in great detail.

And yet, these realities are virtually unknown to the American people. The political process has thrust this reality aside as if it were too difficult to confront, and has substituted an image of the Communist powers as countries like our own, serving only their own security and willing to make mutual accommodation of interests. This false image of the Communist powers is the cornerstone of a national policy that has nurtured the steady decline of the United States and the extension of Communist hegemony in the world.

This political preference for a false image of communism stands against the repeated warnings of our best scholarship. The true nature of communism has been amply defined in recent literature.

Ludwig von Mises has shown how Communist totalitarianism exceeds in terror all the tyrannies of the past:[1]

> Totalitarianism is much more than mere bureaucracy. It is the subordination of every individual's whole life, work, and leisure, to the orders of those in power and office. It is the reduction of man to a cog in an all-embracing machine of compulsion and coercion. It forces the individual to renounce any activity of which the government does not approve. It tolerates no expression of dissent. It is the transformation of society into a strictly disciplined labor-army—as the advocates of socialism say—or into a penitentiary—as its opponents say. At any rate, it is the radical break from the way of life to which the civilized nations clung in the past. It is not merely the return of mankind to the Oriental despotism under which, as Hegel observed, one man alone was free and all the rest slaves, for those Asiatic kings did not interfere with the daily routine of their subjects. To the individual farmers, cattle breeders, and artisans a field of activities was left in the performance of which they were not troubled by the king and his satellites. They enjoyed some amount of autonomy within their own households and families. It is different with modern socialism. It is totalitarian in the strict sense of the term. It holds the individual in tight rein from the womb to the tomb. At every instant of his life the "comrade" is bound to obey implicitly the orders issued by the supreme authority. The state is both guardian and his employer. The state determines his work, his diet, and his pleasures. The state tells him what to think and what to believe in.

Communism cannot survive in competition with God. It is therefore committed to the extermination of a religious sense that supposes an authority superior to the Party. Whittaker Chambers made the point:[2]

> In *Witness* I sought to make two points which seemed to me more important

than the narrative of unhappy events which, time has compelled me to conclude, chiefly interested most readers. The first point had to do with the nature of communism and the struggle against it. The crux of this matter is the question whether God exists. If God exists a man cannot be a Communist, which begins with the rejection of God. But if God does not exist, it follows that communism, or some suitable variant of it, is right.

John Courtney Murray made the same crucial point in more detail:[3]

Communism in theory and in practice has reversed the revolution which Christianity initiated by the Gelasian doctrine, "Two there are by which this world is ruled." This new system has proposed with all logic an alternative to the basic structure of society, and a surrogate of society's spiritual substance, as these are defined in the Christian Theorem. And the question is, whether there are in the spirit of modernity as such the resources whereby the Christian revolution, with all its hopes of freedom and justice, can be reinstated in its course, and the reactionary counter-revolution halted. The issue is clear enough; two contrary views of the structure of reality are in conflict. And the issue is certainly basic—too basic to be solved either by military measures or by political techniques. Free elections, for instance, have their value. But of themselves they leave untouched the basic issue, which is joined between the clashing assertions: "Two there are" and "One there is."

The monstrous end of the Communist extermination of unoffending fellow citizens has been noted by Whittaker Chambers:[4]

Ours is the first age in history in which duly constituted governments, duly recognized by others calling themselves civilized, practice the extermination of their own people by millions, as a matter of calculated policy. Within the lifetime of young men and women who have scarcely reached the age of twenty-one, the Soviet government had exterminated so many of its people that it did not dare publish the census figures; the population, despite all official pressures and inducements to breed, had fallen too steeply below the level of a few decades before. The same government decreed, because their peasants were hiding their grain, that they should be starved to death. So they were, from three to six million of them. The statistics cannot be confirmed. But what can millions more or millions less mean to a mind when a million is a measurement of individuals, each of whom is a unit of agony.

Henry Paolucci has explained the Leninist justification of this practice: that freedom would be achieved by practicing tyranny. He writes:[5]

Lenin explained the necessity of thoroughness in annihilating the defeated classes after the power of the nation-state governments has passed into Communist hands: "When the resistance of the capitalists has been completely crushed," he wrote, "when the capitalists have disappeared, when there are no classes, i.e., when there is no difference between the members of society as regards their relation to the social means of production" only then "the state . . . ceases to exist" and it becomes possible to speak of freedom. Freedom is the ultimate object of the final solution of the Communists, to be sure; but it can come, as Lenin explains, only after the dictatorship of the inner circle of Communist Party members has effectively leveled everyone else in the world into a condition of social equality without freedom; only then will the absolute class difference between the ruling party elite and the ruled begin to fade, for by that time the people will have "gradually become accustomed," as Lenin emphasizes, "to observing the

34

elementary rules of social intercourse that have been known for centuries and repeated for thousands of years in all copybook maxims; they will become accustomed to observing them without force, without compulsion, without subordination, without the *special apparatus* for compulsion which is called the state."

The Communists do not propose, therefore, to perpetuate in their world victory the age-old practice of the mighty, which has been to oppress and exploit the defeated in perpetuity, if possible; instead, they will free themselves of the temptation to do so by exterminating the conquered.

The multiplicity of socialist political forms and programs has certainly contributed to popular confusion about the nature of communism or Bolshevism. Moreover the Marxist-Leninists of the Communist fronts have diligently sowed in the West the misconception that theirs is simply the correct version of socialism. In particular, they have succeeded in spreading the misapprehension that national socialism and fascism, because of their intense opposition to Bolshevism, are not socialism at all but a kind of antisocialism. In reality, of course, Hitler and Mussolini were disciples of Marx and admirers of Stalin, cultivating their own socialist variant of the omnipotent state. Professor Paolucci draws a parallel:[6]

Surely as a scheme for the reordering of human relations and the re-education of social feelings, the Marxist-Leninist doctrine invites comparison with Hitler's scheme for a final solution to the problem of anti-Semitism in Germany. According to the chief Nazi racist, Arthur Rosenberg, the mass of Hitler's followers, who came to believe that the German Jews were living off them parasitically, had been animated by a racial hatred analogous to the class hatred of the Communist proletariat against the capitalist classes. If the defeated Jews were permitted to survive in Germany after the Nazi victory, the Aryan community would be tempted to exploit and abuse them forever, he argued, and that would make it morally ugly. To avoid that kind of "corruption" of the Germans, Rosenberg urged that the Jews stripped of power be physically removed from Germany with the thoroughness of the Marxist proposal to obliterate the last trace of capitalist exploiters.

Ann Watson, recounting her experiences with both Nazi and Russian Communists in a conquered Vienna, wrote:[7]

The Nazis admire the Soviet system of repression, from the use of the concentration camp to the centralized power of the Communist Party. Goering, after conferring with Marshal Stalin, said: "I have the impression that something is very strong here . . . because I saw how this one man had these 200,000,000 Russian people in his hand like that." Hitler always refers admiringly to Stalin as the "great one—Genghis Khan."

Maritain made the point that these totalitarian systems are perversions of the role of the State, not a fulfillment of that institution:[8]

Let us not forget, moreover, that this trend toward supreme domination and supreme amorality, which has fully developed and is in full swing in the totalitarian states, is by no means inherent in the state in its real nature and its true and necessary functions, but depends on a perverted notion which preys upon the modern state, and of which democracy, if it is to survive, will get clear.

There is a quality of mind which communism and socialism share and in which the differences are of degree. Arthur Koestler examined its most extreme form in *Darkness at Noon*, speaking in the person of Ivanov, the Inquisitor:[9]

> We were neo-Machiavellians in the name of universal reason—that was our greatness; the others in the name of a national romanticism, that is their anachronism. That is why we will in the end be absolved by history; but not they. . . . Yet for the moment we are thinking and acting on credit. As we have thrown overboard all conventions and rules of cricket-morality, our sole guiding principle is that of consequent logic. We are under the terrible compulsion to follow our thought down to its final consequence and to act in accordance to it. We are sailing without ballast; therefore each touch on the helm is a matter of life or death.
>
> History has taught us that often lies serve her better than the truth; for man is sluggish and has to be led through the desert for forty years before each step in his development. And he has to be driven through the desert with threats and promises, by imaginary terrors and imaginary consolations, so that he should not sit down prematurely to rest and divert himself by worshipping golden calves. We have learnt history more thoroughly than the others. We differ from all others in our logical consistency. We know that virtue does not matter to history, and that crimes remain unpunished; but that every error has its consequences and venges itself unto the seventh generation. Therefore we concentrated all our efforts on preventing error and destroying the very seeds of it. Never in history has so much power over the future of humanity been concentrated in so few hands as in our case. Each wrong idea we follow is a crime committed against future generations. Therefore we have to punish wrong ideas as others punish crimes: with death. We were held for madmen because we followed every thought down to its final consequence and acted accordingly. We were compared to the Inquisition because, like them, we constantly felt in ourselves the whole weight of responsibility for the superindividual life to come. We resembled the great Inquisitors in that we persecuted the seeds of evil not only in men's deeds, but in their thoughts. We admitted no private sphere, not even inside a man's skull.
>
> "My point is this," he said, "one may not regard the world as a sort of metaphysical brothel for emotions. That is the first commandment for us. Sympathy, conscience, disgust, despair, repentance, and atonement are for us repellent debauchery."

This is the kind of ignorance and madness which destroys a man's interior balance while preserving an exterior appearance of sanity. It is a facet of the Soviet official unseen by his non-Soviet associates but deeply implanted in his psyche by indoctrination and practice. The Western mind cannot believe that such an attitude exists behind the appearance of suave decorum or Khrushchev ebullience.

If this is indeed the character of communism, the surviving totalitarianism, how can we explain the failure of the new world to comprehend and overthrow the system?

Let us note at once that the Communist system has spread not with the concurrence of its own people, as in the Mongol and Arab expansions, but in spite of their determined resistance. The nonproductivity of Soviet agriculture and Soviet industry reflects the resistance of the people to Soviet tyranny.

The Communist expansion has been facilitated and aided by Atlantic powers indifferent to their heritage of freedom and anxious to do business with the enemy for a profit. Professor Antony C. Sutton has demonstrated[10] that Soviet industry was built by American capitalists working within a political system insensitive to its own survival. Profit has blinded our capitalists and handcuffed our politicians.

Illusions about communism in the free world are fostered in the first instance by democratic socialists. On occasions and at times, the democratic socialists have taken a hard line against communism, usually when their own rule was threatened by Communist subversion or conquest. But over the long run, the democratic socialists regard communism as an errant but fundamentally valid edition of socialism. They are sympathetic to its socialist activities, to its attacks on capitalism, even as they abhor its terrorism. They carry a banner for this edition of socialism in such conflicts as the Vietnam War, and they are eternally tempted to coalition with the Communists, often combining with them as in the French elections of March 1973. In Britain and in the United States the converts to a Fabian socialism have exerted great influence to project to the people a false image of the Communist system.

Whittaker Chambers stated the difference between the Communists and the socialists:[11]

> For Communists understand, in its most cold-blooded form, the art of ruling, that is, the art of exercising power. This is precisely what, in general, socialists have never understood for reasons that go deep into the real differences between socialist and Communist, but which this is not the place to examine. Thus, socialism almost always enters into coalition with communism, dragging along a whole flutter of people who are not even as well defined as socialists. These are the vaguely humane and progressive, sometimes articulate as a rule, intellectually and politically rather genderless people that perhaps every civilization in collapse breeds as a symptom of waste product, and this one certainly does.

Although democratic socialism does not doctrinally proclaim the death of God and the omnipotence of the state, it has powerful influences of that stripe in the early and in the continuing leadership of the movement. This influence within the movement inclines it to the methods of communism and to a rejection of the principles of human freedom. As Father Murray put it, attributing to "modernity" and "secularism" what is really the contribution of socialism:[12]

> It has been specific of modernity to regard the state as a moral end in itself, a self-justifying entity with its own self-determined spiritual substance. It is within the secular state, and by appeal to secular sources, that man is to find the interpretation of his own nature and the means to his own destiny. The state itself creates the ethos of society, embodies it, imparts it to its citizens, and sanctions its observance with rewards and punishments. Outside the tradition of Jacobin or Communist dogmatism, the modern democratic sec-

ular state does not indeed pretend to be the Universe or to speak infallibly. But it does assert itself to be the embodiment of whatever fallible human wisdom may be available to man, because it is the highest school of human experience, beyond which man can find no other School and no other Teacher.

In the West, socialist leaders dissemble their rejection of God to avoid the hostility of the people. But they administer power with no respect for divine law.

The nineteenth-century materialists, of which Marx and Engels were a product, enamored of power and determined to overthrow the established political order, sought to close off man's instinctive reach for the infinite. They fashioned a new mythology that held that religion was a creation of the ruling elite to hold the peasant in subjection; or that it was the creation of a cowed mankind fearful of the calamities visited upon him by nature.

Who among the great philosophers of antiquity answers to such a description? Not one. This is sheer fiction fashioned by modern man to avoid the great questions of his presence in the universe that man, as a reasonable creature, must try to explain. It is a closing of the mind to reality, a denial of reason. In the twentieth century, playing God is the game.

The democratic socialist shares the utopian vision of a planned order dispensing justice in every phase of human activity. He rejects the use of force which Communists believe to be essential to such an order and believes that he can achieve his Utopia politically, without force. His conjoined promise of Utopia and freedom is tempting but illusory.

Democratic socialism proved more popular than Bolshevism. A small fraction of intellectual leaders in European countries embraced Marxism-Leninism but the bulk of them espoused the method of parliamentary reform. They regarded private profit as the source of evil that divided the human community and believed that state control of industry would reform society.

In Great Britain, the democratic socialists achieved power in the 1920s through the British Labour Party. They nationalized industries and demonstrated that government ownership was incompatible with efficiency. In a democratic society, government cannot maintain standards of work and production which are required for the success of competitive industry. British products could not compete with German, Japanese, and American products. British trade languished. The people asked the Conservative Party to take back the government. Socialist rule was repudiated.

In the aftermath of World War II, many of the new nations with a heritage of European politics turned to socialism. The socialist concept of an elite managing the country and the economy for the people was congenial to the ambitions of dictators as well as to the intellectuals of the industrial countries. The elites are always confident that they know best what is good for the workingman. In the developing lands, socialism showed its true role as the mother of dictatorship.

The disabilities of socialism should be obvious to all students of government. It has only two alternatives to offer. If individual freedom under representative government is preserved, socialism offers inefficiency in production and social stagnation under an insufferable bureaucracy. The alternative is dictatorship, where government tells everyone when and where to work and for what pay. In this kind of socialist rule, the bureaucracy is reinforced by the police power of the state and the workingman is reduced to the status of a serf.

The fundamental disability of socialism is its hierarchical structure. In terms of structure it is not essentially different from a monarchy, without the heart. It depends upon a central authority for planning and execution. It requires government by an elite for the "benefit" of the common people. Its claim that these powers can be better administered by ambitious politicians on the make than by an hereditary aristocracy is certainly of dubious merit.

And yet, socialism continues to be a powerful force among people who are sincerely dedicated to individual rights and freedom. It suffices to note at this point that socialism in all its forms is the chief obstacle to human freedom and prosperity in the world today. It restores the paralysis of paternalism. It offers to politicians in democratic societies a rationalization of their aggrandizement at the expense of the working man. It discourages personal ambition, individual industry and social awareness.

If this analysis of the merits of socialism, democratic and totalitarian, does not depict a formidable adversary, perhaps we have not sufficiently emphasized the forces in society which find in socialism the handmaiden of their special interests. This is, in reality, the story of politics in America which we shall develop in following chapters.

Chapter 6

OF, BY, AND FOR THE PEOPLE

IT COULD HARDLY have been foreseen by those who crafted it that the Constitution of the United States was the charter of what would become the most powerful country in the world. Conscientious men gave the best of their wisdom and experience to a compact they hoped would prove suitable and enduring. But the approximately four million* people scattered along the Atlantic Coast, facing a vast wilderness, had immediate tasks too pressing to allow time for dreaming.

The story of expansion, of taming the wilderness, of cultivating and building and praying, is a familiar one to older Americans who were nurtured on tales of pioneer skill and bravery. It is a story too of innovation, of invention, of improvisation as all citizens seemed to join in the search for a better way of doing work. Alexis de Tocqueville made a memorable personal survey of young America, recounted chiefly in *Democracy in America*, to describe the quality of life and of political institutions in the new country. Tocqueville's comment on the religious fervor of the people was perceptive:[1]

> I sought for the greatness and genius of America in her commodious harbors and her ample rivers, and it was not there; in her fertile field and boundless

---

*3, 929, 214—Census of August 2, 1790.

prairies, and it was not there; in her rich mines and her vast world commerce, and it was not there. Not until I went to the churches of America and heard her pulpits aflame with righteousness did I understand the secret of her genius and power. America is great because she is good, and if America ever ceases to be good, America will cease to be great.

Daniel Webster could say with some assurance in 1825:[2]

> Our history proves . . . that with wisdom and knowledge men may govern themselves; and the duty incumbent on us is, to preserve . . . the cheering example. . . . If, in our case, the representative system ultimately fails, popular government must be pronounced impossible. No combination of circumstances more favorable to the experiment can ever be expected to occur. The last hopes of mankind therefore rest with us . . .

The country was prospering because a fortunate concurrence of wisdom and opportunity had given the new country a sturdy charter for the liberties of its citizens. Freedom under law evoked the talents of the people and generously rewarded achievement.

The merits of various political orders are the subject of endless theory. Curiously, the theoretical arguments persist, even when their premises have been invalidated in practice. Political science has no accepted scale for measuring validity.

There are, however, indices of the quality of government that dispel the clouds of propaganda for various systems. One index is the judgment of the people. Is the tyranny so severe or the poverty so oppressive that they flee from their homeland, sometimes at the risk of their lives? Or are freedom and opportunity so attractive that the poor and oppressed peoples of other countries regard it as the promised land?

We can indeed discuss the production of wealth as an index of good political organization. Slaves can produce wealth. The proper measure of political organization is the well-being of the worker. This is, after all, what all modern political parties profess to offer.

By every rational measure of a society, the United States of America in the nineteenth century was the most advanced in the world. Immigrants flocked to it from all quarters of the world. Human innovation and resourcefulness were stirred to create new and improved products needed in a developing society. Despite the tide of immigration, wage rates remained attractive. The opportunities for self-improvement and for advancement based on merit carried an irresistible attraction for adventurous spirits.

The American concept of the citizen sovereign pursuing his heart's desire under minimal government preserving law and order proved a great success. But this was no millennium. Politics remained a lively force engaging the attention and concern of the people.

Politics of the period was animated by lively conflict, all within a solid public consensus about the purpose of life, the rights of the individual and the function of the community. In these circumstances, growth could be both turbulent and tranquil. Life in America met Maritain's definition of the common good:[3]

41

The common good is not only the collection of public commodities and services which the organization of common life presupposes: a sound fiscal condition, a strong military force; the body of just laws, good customs, and wise institutions which provides the political society with its structure; the heritage of its great historical remembrances, its symbols and its glories, its living traditions and cultural treasures. The common good also includes the sociological integration of all the civic conscience, political virtues and sense of law and freedom, of all the activity, material prosperity and spiritual riches, of unconsciously operating hereditary wisdom, of moral rectitude, justice, friendship, happiness, virtue and heroism in the individual lives of the members of the body politic. To the extent to which all these things are, in a certain measure, communicable and revert to each member, helping him to perfect his life and liberty as a person, they all constitute the good human life of the multitude.

While some of the emigration from Europe to the United States was to escape political, ethnic, or religious persecution, the chief stimulant was the attraction of economic opportunity in a new land. After this demonstration of the eagerness of people to work hard for their own economic improvement, there should have been no doubt about the effectiveness of the profit motive in promoting economic progress.

Politics in this period had a unifying premise. All citizens and all parties cherished the United States Constitution. All politicians extolled the great charter of citizen liberties, at election time and on special holidays. The competition of political parties was conducted under the umbrella of the Constitution.

In the beginning, the nascent political parties of the confederation had little impact on national affairs. George Washington was generally respected as the national leader of the Revolution. The national spirit was united around his person in a commitment that subdued latent factionalism. During his administration, all factions were accommodated within the cabinet and reconciled by his leadership.

With the retirement of President Washington, differences of perspective and interest emerged. The Federalist Party, with John Adams and Alexander Hamilton as chief spokesmen, attracted those interests desiring a strong central government. Opposition to that trend gathered about Thomas Jefferson to form the Republican Party, appealing to farmers and workingmen. This general division of political parties along economic lines was to continue through the nineteenth century.

There were conflicts of personality and interest within the parties as well as between them. John Adams and Alexander Hamilton were less than compatible.

Federalist opposition to the War of 1812 seriously discredited the party. In the aftermath of victory, the party transformed itself into the National Republican Party.

Meanwhile, the Republican Party of Thomas Jefferson was transforming itself into the Democratic Party of Andrew Jackson, taking a name which would endure for a century and a half. Andrew Jackson was the father of the modern political party, based not on issues but on a continuing interest in political power.

The National Republican Party of John Quincy Adams did not long endure. It changed its name to the Whig Party, borrowing on the fame and prestige which the Whigs had built in England. The Whigs elected William Henry Harrison in 1840 and Zachary Taylor in 1848, but failed the test provided by the growing controversy over slavery.

The Republican Party, our last successful third party movement, succeeded because the two existing parties were incapable of resolving the growing public concern about slavery. As Democrats and Whigs fought over the extension of slavery to new territories, neither party was capable of ending slavery.

When the Constitutional Convention of 1787 set a date for ending the importation of slaves, that was a significant achievement in a world where slavery was widely tolerated. By the middle of the nineteenth century, the situation had changed. The Argentine had moved against slavery in 1821, by decreeing that all persons thereafter born in the country would be free. Britain had ended slavery within its empire in 1833 at a cost of 20,000,000 pounds sterling paid to former slave owners. Northern states in the Union had abolished slavery. Pressures were building to free the slaves everywhere, but the existing political parties only temporized. The new Republican Party pledged to free the slaves.

In the slavery controversy, the Constitution, designed to preserve a sound political order, protected an anachronistic institution incorporated in that order. The difficulty of changing the Constitution favored the status quo.

There were strong pressures from abolitionists to end slavery by judicial fiat, but the sense of constitutional order, the respect of the judiciary for the legal distinction between making and interpreting law, was a barrier to judicial usurpation of the legislative authority. Chief Justice Roger Taney stated the constitutional issue in the Dred Scott decision:[4]

> . . . it speaks not only in the same words, but with the same meaning and intent with which it spoke when it came from the hands of its framers, and was voted upon and adopted by the people of the United States. Any other rule of construction would abrogate the judicial character of this court, and make it the mere reflex of the popular opinion or passion of the day.

Abraham Lincoln voiced the determination of the Republicans to arrest and ultimately to end slavery:[5]

> I believe this government cannot endure permanently half slave and half free. I do not expect the Union to be dissolved—I do not expect the house to fall—but I do expect that it will cease to be divided. It will become all one thing, or all the other. Either the opponents of slavery will arrest the further spread of it, and place it where the public mind shall rest in the belief that it is in the course of ultimate extinction; or its advocates will push it forward, till it shall become alike lawful in all the states, old as well as new—North as well as South.

43

The mere election of Abraham Lincoln was enough to precipitate secession and civil war. Success in war and the ending of slavery made the Republican Party dominant in the nation for the next seventy years. After the bitterness of Reconstruction had somewhat subsided, a Grover Cleveland could be elected to the presidency. But this turning to a Democrat was only for occasional relief from Republican rule. Not until the depression of the 1930s and the administration of Franklin D. Roosevelt would the balance of power be shifted away from the Republican Party.

The Republican Party took over the Whig interests of the industrial states in the Northeast and became the party of the new corporate power. The Democratic Party continued to represent the agrarian interests of the South and West, and the new immigrant workers in the East. As the issues of slavery and civil war faded from the political scene, economic interests emerged as the new basis of political partisanship. New waves of European immigrants, growing industrialization, corporate economic power, and the organization of labor became the problems of the late nineteenth century.

It was a time of rapid growth as the westward movement of population continued. The Indian tribes were pacified, railroads spanned the continent, and the pony express had its brief heyday. The turbulent energies of a lightly governed people were expended in a steadily widening range of human activity. Inventiveness devised new methods of farming and industry, new products to serve society and to provide the base for new industry.

It was a time too of great national pride. The rush of immigrants confirmed the American belief that the United States was the happiest land with the best government and maximum freedom and opportunity for its citizens. There were signs of radical socialism among the European immigrants but these were regarded tolerantly as the vestiges of foreign economic and political systems. Socialism might be a useful political ethic in Europe but it had no place in America.

The aggressive, pioneering spirit of the country and the growing power of the press combined at the close of the century to thrust the country into war with Spain. Sympathy for the Cuban independence movement could easily be worked into a state of belligerency. Theodore Roosevelt and his Rough Riders symbolized the arrogance of the times. The venture into war confirmed the sense of growing power but it also saddled the country with new responsibilities: the administration of foreign lands. Its hand would remain in Cuba and the Dominican Republic for two decades, in the Philippines for four decades.

The spirit of the time was expressed by Homer Lea[6]:

The continuation of this building [of the founding fathers], and the endless extension of the Republic, the maintenance of its ideals and the consummation, in a worldwide sense, of the aspirations of its founders, constitutes the only pure patriotism to which an American can lay claim or, in defense of, lay down his life.

44

A century of remarkable growth and progress stood as evidence of the American success story. The loose rein of government and the consequent decentralization of power had proven its worth in practical government. Americans were confident in the Constitution as the charter of their liberties. While the central government grew in size just to administer its assigned responsibilities, the limits of its jurisdiction were generally respected. No practical politician dared to challenge the constitutional order chartered by the founding fathers and cherished by the people. That challenge would come later.

Chapter 7

THE FABIAN ASCENDANCY

IN THE LATTER HALF of the nineteenth century, when the free-market economy and competitive capitalism were raising new standards of productivity in the United States, there was a parallel expansion of socialist political activity in Europe. There the battle against hereditary monarchy and a ruling nobility continued. Where, as in England, the monarch had been reduced to a symbol of nationhood, the monopoly capitalism of entrenched wealth remained a target. Except in England, where the oligarchy maintained a literature of personal freedom, socialism was the accepted mode of political thought and action.

The very imperfection of the human condition assures that all forms of government are open to criticism. There is not, nor can there be, a perfect society organized by people. Government, therefore, involves a question of relative values. Which form is more conducive to the development of individual talents and the realization of individual potential, taking these conditions as a measure of the "pursuit of happiness"?

Socialism argued that capitalism was structured to allocate excessive rewards to a small elite, the owners of industry, and to allow only niggardly benefits to the workers. It held that the state had a duty to correct this injustice and that the job could be done only by public ownership of industry, through which "profits" would accrue to society.

46

By the mid-nineteenth century, England had lived through a long and varied experience with parliamentary government. The people were proud of their liberties; but they also had painfully acquired knowledge of the performance of parliaments. The idea that parliament could take over and run industry simply was not credible. Therefore, in England, as in the United States, socialism was regarded as an alien and impractical kind of government, fit only for people who were not fit to govern themselves.

Still, the inequities of the capitalist economy were observed on every hand. Workers toiled long hours, six or seven days a week, for wages which barely enabled them to survive. The aristocracy was flaunting new forms of wealth as though to extend the disparity in living standards between owners and workers. And those unfortunate persons who through disability or inaptitude could not keep the worker's pace in industry, lived on the fringe of society as wards of private charity.

It was true, of course, that religious and other voluntary charitable institutions were substantially endowed to alleviate the sufferings of the least fortunate members of society. But to the political theorist this private alleviation of suffering seemed an inadequate compensation for the effects of bad government. He argued that if government were properly structured, all employable persons would be engaged at just and adequate wages and that society would provide adequate care for the unemployable.

The socialist was sure that justice was a simple problem of distributing the available wealth and that government could do the job. In place of the mediocre performance of democratic politics, he would substitute the rule of the elite, i.e., himself. But his utopia was not limited to national well-being. His dogma attributed war to the imperialism of capitalist societies, so he was confident that his politics would bring peace to the world.

With such zeal to reform the world and so simple a formula for doing the job, the socialist was conscious of his own rectitude and intolerant of the old order. He affected and enjoyed a sense of superiority derived from his possession of the true faith and of compassion for less fortunate countrymen.

The history of utopian schemes has little effect on the human learning process. A preference for dreaming lies deep in the human psyche. In 1824, Robert Owen of Scotland established a collectivist colony on 30,000 acres in New Harmony, Indiana. He said:[1]

> I am come to this country to introduce an entirely new state of society; to change it from an ignorant, selfish system to an enlightened system which shall gradually write all interests in one, and remove all causes for contest between individuals.

This is the spirit of ignorance and arrogance in which socialism still persists. But Robert Owen's venture failed in three years, and others like it have suffered a similar experience.

This kind of thinking found a fertile soil in England among intellectuals like H. G. Wells and George Bernard Shaw, who were so richly recompensed by the capitalist system. It found sympathy among other richly endowed persons who had inherited wealth and felt the injustice of holding such unearned power over others. It appealed also to lesser intellectuals whose rewards had been modest and who were sure that a planned society, directed by intellectual elites, could produce a more equitable social order.

In England, these advocates of socialism realized that the socialist cause could not be preached effectively to the people. The country had long since passed through the stage of revolutionary development that made socialism a viable political mode on the continent. Socialism, they decided, could be introduced into England only by a gradual insinuation into government of special measures enlarging governmental responsibility for the economic order.

In October 1883, a small group of Englishmen, bored with the existing order and reaching for new religious or political alternatives, met in London under the sponsorship of Edward R. Pease, a 26-year-old stockbroker who was to become Secretary of the Fabian Society.[2] In January 1884, the Society received its name and motto. In May 1884, George Bernard Shaw joined the organization, moved up to the Executive Committee, and made the Society a vehicle for his Marxist political convictions. In 1885, he introduced Sidney Webb and Sydney Olivier to the Fabian high command. In 1886, he brought Graham Wallas to the Fabian Society, completing his leadership cadre. By 1887, they could promulgate a frankly socialist credo to which all members were obliged to subscribe. The Society had its character and direction.

Outwardly, the Society would be conventional and prestigious, remaining aloof from the class warfare practiced by plebeian socialists. It would preach socialism on a higher plane, building influence in the leadership levels of government and society. It would eschew the socialist labels, enabling its converts in public life to maintain their connections with the Liberal and Labor Parties. It would achieve power through the established parties, advocating socialist measures as compassionate service to the people.

The policy of subversion embraced by the Fabians is an old tactic. Dean Inge described it well:[3]

> History seems to show that the powers of evil have won their greatest triumphs by capturing the organizations which were formed to defeat them, and that when the devil has thus changed the contents of the bottles, he never alters the labels. The fort may have been captured by the enemy, but it still flies the flag of the defenders.

The Society was by any measure a huge success. It destroyed the Liberal Party and converted the Labor Party into an instrument of socialism. The powers of government were steadily enlarged by taking from the people authority which the Fabian elites considered the people ill-equipped to exercise. By 1924, the Society achieved a brief summit of triumph in the ascendancy of J. Ramsay MacDonald to the Prime Ministership. Defeated in 1925 after the Zinoviev scandal, the Labor Party returned to office in 1929, to remain until 1931.

When it returned to power in 1946, at the close of World War II, the Labor government inaugurated a forthright socialist program of nationalizing industry and inaugurating far-reaching welfare programs. These programs were sustained by U.S. loans until 1951, when the Labor Party was defeated at the polls. The socialist programs had pushed the country to the verge of bankruptcy. It would be more than a decade before the people's memory of the fiasco dimmed enough to allow the return of the Labor Party to power. In 1963, upon the death of Hugh Gaitskell, Harold Wilson was elected to the Labor Party leadership. In 1964, Wilson became Prime Minister. Nineteen of the 23 members of his cabinet were members of the British Fabian Society.

The triumph of the Fabian Society was not limited to its domination of the Labor Party. Political successes of the welfare programs induced imitation by the Conservative Party. A new cast of thinking about the role of government infected the political scene and set all the British parties vying in promises of government services for the people.

These were triumphs of the Fabian elites but not of the British people. In a not uncommon paradox of human affairs, the rapid expansion of the political bureaucracy, advocated to help the working man, tended to improve the lot of the bureaucracy while worsening that of the working man. The huge bureaucracy of public servants became a charge against the earnings of the working man. Costs of British goods increased, reducing their competitive standing in world markets. Government employment set a lackadaisical standard of performance that tended to become a national work standard. As incentives for achievement diminished, the quality of production worsened. British society became a sick society, looking to American loans and devaluation of the pound to compensate for failure of its internal politics.

But these costs of socialist government were to become apparent only gradually and through decades of steady decline. No doubt they should have been predicted and opposed by the British Conservative Party, as indeed they were in the beginning. Unfortunately, the capacity to cast the real public interest in a favorable light has been a neglected talent of conservative politics. The conservative merit is not as self-evident as some who possess it conceive it to be.

CONNING THE SCHOLARS

At the turn of the century, the Fabian Society had achieved a prestige which attracted the attention and cooperation of like-minded elites in the United States. The movement offered a congenial haven for socialist intellectuals who were uncomfortable with the class struggle of factory workers and labor organizers. The concept of being a leader in the class struggle, living high above the sordid battle field but giving vital political direction to the cause, appealed especially to the pretensions and limitations of intellectuals.

The educational tradition in America had been one of openness to truth. A political system founded upon the best human judgment of the public interest could have no fear of truth. Public policy considered that any refinement of the truth could only benefit the public interest. Thus, it was logical for American universities to bring to their campuses outstanding socialist scholars from Europe. The university was regarded as a marketplace for sifting the competing claims of various systems to find the contribution which each could make to the public interest.

But the new socialist scholars did not accept the premises of the American educational system. They viewed themselves as the sole possessors of truth. They saw the U.S. Government as protector of the capitalist system, as a foe to overcome. When they rose in the academic system to become department heads, there was no toleration of competing political or economic concepts. An ancient intolerance possessed the university. Only instructors who embraced the socialist "truth" were considered qualified to teach. Students were to be indoctrinated with the socialist worldview and a zeal to correct the faults of the American system.

Whittaker Chambers has told us how the suave Fabian professors turned their students against the American political system:[4]

> Mark asked me into his office after class. He praised my editorial writing, but he wondered, with his infectious chuckle, whether the Russian Revolution was really as bad as I supposed, or whether Calvin Coolidge was as good. I perceived that in Mark Van Doren's world, which I was prepared to admire intensely because it was intellectually admirable, people thought that Coolidge was something much worse than bad. They thought he was funny. I presently learned that they thought Theodore Roosevelt was also funny, but with a difference: an element of venom entered in. I began to have that uneasy feeling, to which youth is especially susceptible, that my intellectual shirttails were showing.

In summarizing the effect of such education on his own career, Chambers wrote:[5]

> Columbia did not teach me communism. It taught me despair. I loved Columbia and still love it in the physical way with which most men ever after love the campus on which they passed formative years of their youth. In the last decades I have sometimes gone up to move alone—a foiled circuitous wanderer among the hordes of later alien undergraduates—among its remembered walls and walks (now greatly changed). But as a citadel of the mind, in the second decade of the twentieth century, I found its experience a trap.

Socialism had earlier come to America with the waves of European immigration. But that was a plebeian level of political conflict. Other Americans educated in Europe or traveling on business or pleasure brought back more sophisticated views of socialist utopianism.

In 1888, Edward Bellamy of Massachusetts, who had been educated in Germany and had retired from a newspaper career, published his novel of utopian American socialism, *Looking Backward.* Through the promotion of British Fabians, this novel was to become the best selling American book since *Uncle Tom's Cabin* and a vehicle for the spread of Fabian socialism among business and cultural leaders in the United States. When the Bellamy arrogance offended American patriotism, support of utopian socialism subsided. Not until 1905, with the organization of the Intercollegiate Socialist Society, did American socialists launch a concerted plan to build an American counterpart of British Fabianism. This was three years after the formation of the American Socialist Party.

In 1905 also, the Rand School of Social Science was founded in New York City to teach socialism, using a bequest of Elizabeth Rand. Through it, American Fabians created an educational advocate of socialism, just as Sidney Webb had done in establishing the London School of Economics and Political Science with a similar bequest a decade earlier.

In this first decade of the twentieth century, American Fabians made substantial progress in imitation of their British cousins. They had recruited a significant membership in higher education and in government and had assembled a snobbish elite of moneyed Americans to finance their programs.

SUBVERTING THE LAW

In 1909, Herbert Croly published *The Promise of American Life,* stating the Fabian criticism of American "capitalism" and setting forth the aims of American Fabians. Professor Clarence Carson has described this text as perhaps "the most thorough 'Fabian tract' ever written."[6]

Croly was a prestigious "liberal," a friend of President Theodore Roosevelt, a leader in "reform" movements. He was confident that the planned society of socialism would counteract the inequities of the capitalist order, though he did not openly advocate socialism.

The mask of progressive liberalism gave Croly and his associates a platform from which to tear down the American political system while professing to improve it. Croly thought the Constitution could be gradually amended by legal interpretation. Walter Weyl wrote in *The New Democracy,*[7] "Our newer Democracy demands, not that the people forever conform to a rigid, hard-changing Constitution, but that the Constitution change to conform to the people. . . . The Constitution of the United States is the political wisdom of a dead America." Weyl too thought it possible for the Supreme Court "by a few progressive judicial decisions to democratize the Constitution."

Thus, while our schools still taught the glories of the American system and the richness of our heritage, intellectual rot had infected the upper stratum of society. It was smart to display the "modern," "scientific reality" affected by socialism, to be alert to change and to scoff at the "eighteenth-century" political ideas of a rural America. In a few decades, the rot would extend to higher education and then to public education. A people conditioned to such "progressive" ideas would be eager to jettison their political heritage.

The Fabian program to rewrite the Constitution by judicial interpretation was revealing. It expressed the socialist view of power. The aim was to get power and then to achieve political goals. As in the Communist countries, the rule of law meant the use of law to serve the socialist cause. That the people might have created a Constitution which could restrain socialist political action was for them simply an unacceptable concept of law.

This demagogic view of law would in time be accepted by the American Bar, with a sophisticated rationalization of the dishonesty. But long before it became a vital force in politics, it was the gospel of American Fabians.

Our whole system of law is founded on the reality that words have meaning. Men are capable of expressing rules of behavior in language which has a common meaning. Were this not so, there could be no system of law.

We elect legislators, delegating to them the authority to make law binding on the community. Law can only mean what the legislators intend it to mean because we have not delegated the lawmaking power to any other element of government. If they did not intend it by their language, there is no such law.

No matter how carefully legislation is drafted, disputes about its meaning can arise when the law is applied to particular cases. That is why we have courts. Their function is to apply the law to cases.

The rules of judicial interpretation had been well established before the twentieth century. If the plain meaning of the law applied to the case, it settled the issue; because the plain meaning could reasonably be assumed to be both the intent of the legislators and the understanding of the litigants. If the impact of the law on the particular case was not clear from the statute, the court would examine the legislative history of the law to consider whether the legislative intent covered the case at issue. If it did not, the case was not covered because the courts had no power to give the law other meaning.

Thus, the assertion that the judiciary could make the Constitution mean what they wanted it to mean was a negation of our whole system of law. It proposed a subversion of the rule of law on which our whole system of representative government was based. Only a dictatorial subordination of law to the whims of the ruler could demand such use of law.

In Communist governments, the courts are no protection to any citizen against the oppression of government. The whole function of law is to sustain the ruling power. Courts and legislatures are committed to that purpose.

In "democratic socialism," however, there is a profession of loyalty to the rule of law. Government is presumed to remain responsive to the will of the people. This pretense is but one phase of the over-all deception of "democratic socialism."

The Leninist who forthrightly proclaims his purpose to seize power by force and impose his rule on the people must be credited with honesty. The Fabian who affects a devotion to the rule of law even as he plots to subvert the law is lower on the moral scale. It is this socialist, masquerading as a "liberal" and concealing his true identity and purpose, who has won undeserved trust in our political system. He has, with the aid of our news media, succeeded in imposing his imposture on the people.

POLITICAL SUCCESS

The honest socialist in the United States who openly worked in the socialist parties to advance the cause achieved no significant political success. Eugene Debs was jailed for antiwar activity in World War I. Norman Thomas won respect for his honesty and dedication, but he won few votes. The people rejected the principles and the cause of socialism.

As in Britain, so also in the United States, socialism was to succeed by capturing the political leadership. It would infiltrate society from the top down; not by converting the workers but by seducing their leaders. It would succeed by showing Republicans and Democrats how they could build party power by practicing socialism while they professed a nominal attachment to the constitutional order.

The British preceptors, while professing (clandestinely) a devotion to "democratic" socialism, showed scant concern for the judgments of the people. On the contrary, they readily embraced authoritarian measures when such authoritarian measures seemed essential to support their new utopia:[8]

> The British champions of socialization and bureaucratization are no less fully aware than the Bolsheviks and the Nazis of the fact that under freedom of speech and thought they will never achieve their ends. Professor Harold Laski is frank enough to declare that a restriction of Parliament's powers is necessary to safeguard the transition to socialism. Sir Stafford Cripps, the favorite candidate of the self-styled liberals for Prime Minister, has advised a "Planning and Enabling Act" which, once passed by Parliament, could not be discussed, still less repealed again. By virtue of this act, which should be very general and leave all "details" to the cabinet, the government would be endowed with irrevocable powers. Its orders and decrees should never be considered by Parliament; neither should there be a recourse to the courts of justice. All offices should be manned by "staunch party members," by "persons of known socialist views." The British "Council of Clergy and Ministers for Common Ownership" declares in a pamphlet to which the Bishop of Bradford wrote the foreword that the establishment of real and permanent socialism requires that all the fundamental opposition must be liquidated; i.e., rendered politically inactive by disfranchisement, and, if necessary by imprisonment.

For fifteen years the Intercollegiate Socialist Society worked diligently to advance the cause of socialism on campus and in the academic world. Morris Hillquit became its shepherd, the Amalgamated Clothing Workers of America its mainstay, Harry W. Laidler its Secretary and Walter Lippmann its most famous product. Lippmann served as President of the Harvard Socialist Society and later on the Executive Committee of the ISS. But after 1914, when he published *Drift and Mastery* and won Fabian acclaim, Lippmann avoided open socialist identification.

During World War I, when the Socialist Party embraced a pacifist opposition to the U. S. war effort, with demonstrations and jail in consequence, the ISS discreetly took no stand on the war. It could adapt policy to the needs of the hour, avoiding the rigid conformity of the Socialist Party.

In 1921 when the demolition activities of more radical socialists had made that association unpopular, the ISS changed its name to the "League for Industrial Democracy." "Industrial democracy" was one of the claimed goals of socialism and an innocent-seeming aim of political activity.

The League for Industrial Democracy provided leadership and direction for American Fabians, including in its membership an impressive array of American "liberals" of the past half-century. As one student of its record commented, "Like the young people whom it was schooling in duplicity, the parent LID cultivated a liberal look and an air of candid innocence."

When Roger Baldwin, a St. Louis social worker who had just served a prison sentence for draft-dodging, was called to serve as Executive Director of the new American Civil Liberties Union—recreated from the ashes of the Civil Liberties Bureau of the American Union against Militarism, which he had previously headed—he pleaded, "Do steer away from making it look like a Socialist Enterprise. We want also to look like patriots in everything we do. We want to get a good lot of flags, talk a good deal about the Constitution and what our forefathers wanted to make of the country, and to show that we are really the folks that really stand for the spirit of our institutions."[9] From the beginning of this new venture, Baldwin understood that the key to socialist success was Fabian deception.

American Fabians followed faithfully in the footsteps of their British preceptors. Franklin Roosevelt reached the presidential office twelve years after Ramsay MacDonald reached the Prime Ministership. American seemed to lag about two decades behind Britain in the march toward socialism. The different political systems responded differently, with decentralized U.S. political authority offering more resistance to socialist "reform" than the British parliamentary order did. American attachment to the constitutional tradition could be broken down only gradually, through socialist education and slow political encroachment over a period of years. As Roger Baldwin knew, the "liberals" had to persuade the electorate that their programs of government service to the people represented the authentic development of the American political tradition.

In 1947, when socialist influence in the Democratic Party was trending dangerously toward Soviet communism and alienation from the American people, a new presence was created to restore the expedient politics of Fabianism. Americans for Democratic Action turned away from the pro-Soviet stance of the Henry Wallace Progressives to maintain an appearance of U.S. loyalty acceptable to the Democratic Party. Only through the power of the Democratic Party could the socialists continue to extend their control of government.

The success of the Fabian elites in the United States is scarcely less impressive than that of their progenitors in Britain. American Fabians have not attempted measures so imprudent as the nationalization of basic industries but they have shrewdly achieved a virtual control of corporate power through other measures of law and intimidation. They have dominated national policymaking, foreign and domestic.

These socialist elites, hidden in and controlling the political parties, are the chief enemy of America today. Their purposes and methods are deeply hostile to our system of representative government. For forty years and more they have effectively controlled the direction of both domestic and foreign policy. They are sensitive to Communist influence, but they, not the Communists, are our chief enemy. As Whittaker Chambers observed:[10]

> I held that such elements, while dangerous, were not communism's chief power in the West. I held that power to be something else—the power of communism to manipulate responsive sections of the West to check, counteract, paralyze, or confuse the rest. Those responsive sections of the West were not Communist, and never had been. Most of the minds that composed them, thought of themselves as sincerely anti-Communist. Communism manipulated them, not in terms of communism, but in terms of the shared historical crisis—peace and social justice being two of the most workable terms. They were free to denounce communism and Communists (and also anti-Communists) after whatever flourishes their intellectual innocence or arrogance might choose. Communism asked no more. It cared nothing, at this point, about motives. It cared about results.

Thus did the Fabians advance the cause of barbarism. Father Murray has described how the cause is served:[11]

> This is perennially the work of the barbarian, to undermine rational standards of judgment, to corrupt the inherited intuitive wisdom by which the people have always lived, and to do this not by spreading new beliefs but by creating a climate of doubt and bewilderment in which clarity about the larger aims of life is dimmed and the self-confidence of the people is destroyed, so that finally what you have is the impotent nihilism of the "generation of the third eye" now presently appearing on our university campuses.

We should judge the barbarian not by his suave exterior but by his work:[12]

> The barbarian need not appear in bearskins with a club in hand. He may wear a Brooks Brothers suit and carry a ballpoint pen with which to write his advertising copy. In fact, even beneath the academic gown there may lurk a child of the wilderness, untutored in the high tradition of civility, who goes busily and happily about his work a domesticated and law-abiding

man, engaged in the construction of a philosophy to put an end to all philosophy, and thus put an end to the possibility of a vital consensus and to civility itself.

Because the international uses of American power and the continuing health of the home base of that power are so critical to the course of civilization in this century, the Fabian influence in American policy is of critical concern to all free people. This influence has been exercised by American Fabians in close association with brother Fabians in the British government. The connection has been an important factor in the subservience of U.S. foreign policy to British influence.

Chapter 8

THE TWO-PARTY SYSTEM

WE HAVE SEEN that in the early years of the nineteenth century, old political parties were rejected and new parties were formed to meet changing crises of national concern. Always the conflict was reduced to two-party struggle, except in periods of transition like the 1856 and 1860 national elections.

This was in part a heritage of British politics and the tradition of a loyal opposition but even more importantly the product of our governmental structure. The presidential office, with all the endowments of power and patronage it entailed, was the target of party ambition. Small parties that lacked a prospect of winning the office could not retain a political following. They had to supersede or coalesce with one of the major parties. When the Republicans gained power, the Whigs faded.

A notable character of politics since the Civil War has been the durability of the Democratic and Republican Parties. They have successfully fended off all third-party challenges. No doubt the Civil War itself was an influence for stability: building allegiances that were not easily changed. As the Civil War receded in memory and influence, the parties became something of a class symbol, a family tradition to be maintained. As time passed, the two parties could agree that the American system of government depended on party loyalty, that third parties were somehow radical and un-American. This was their propaganda for self-preservation.

As the two parties built power and structure, it became more difficult for any third party to create the organization required for successful challenge. Unless one of the major parties made a blunder which antagonized the electorate, the prospect of successful challenge was minimal.

In the beginning, the survival instinct operated to keep both parties close to the general inclinations of the people. It also influenced them to adhere to tradition and to avoid innovation. Because the Constitution had retained in the states and in the people the authority over local public policy, this conservatism of the national parties did not inhibit the rapid growth of the country and the development of industry. It was in fact a catalyst of national progress.

As victor in the Civil War and emancipator of the slaves, the Republican Party enjoyed a prestige and following that made it the dominant party well into the twentieth century. These national achievements tended to overshadow the role of the party as representative of Wall Street. Increasingly, however, the stench of corruption reached the people as the wheelers and dealers dominated politics; and the people turned occasionally to the Democratic Party in search of an honest man.

Theodore Roosevelt brought a new vigor to the presidential office. In his trust-fighting and conservation roles, he sought to arouse public concern about the general direction of national policy. His reform movement was not a usurpation of the power of the states but an assertion of the responsibility of the national government for national problems transcending the powers and interests of the states. Although he had friends and associates among the Fabians of his time, Theodore Roosevelt never subscribed to their policies. He had too great a devotion to the American system of free enterprise to regard socialism as an improvement of it.

In his trust-busting and other "progressive" activities, President Roosevelt had seemed to be stealing the programs of the Democrats. He had seemed to castigate his own party to win the approval of Democrats, though he could with justice claim that he was invigorating the Republican Party to keep it alive. In 1912, by heading a third-party ticket, Theodore Roosevelt split the Republican Party, assuring the election of the Democrat, Woodrow Wilson. That outcome was the apparent goal of wealthy backers who saw greater promise in a Democratic Administration.

The first important access of the Fabians to political power was achieved in the Administration of Woodrow Wilson, who had been a professor of government before becoming President of Princeton University and Governor of New Jersey. Colonel Edward M. House, the President's personal confidant and adviser, was closely attuned to Fabian influences both in the United States and in England. Colonel House was also closely attuned to Wall Street and to the banking interests, which had so great an influence on the Wilson Administration. It seemed as though the two influences had found common goals of national policy.

THE ONE-WORLD SYNDROME

The Wilson Administration is remembered chiefly for the President's plan for a League of Nations and for his failure to secure U.S. adherence to the pact. The Administration made other, more far-reaching decisions affecting the course of the country. Creation of the Federal Reserve Board, the popular election of Senators, and the capacity of British influence to impel American intervention in war on the continent of Europe were more important than U.S. allegiance to or repudiation of the League of Nations.

Illusions about "making the world safe for democracy" were fostered by war propaganda. It now seems incomprehensible that Americans of that day could have been so naive about the realities of world power as to believe the League of Nations propaganda.

The one-world syndrome has a powerful attraction even today for unsophisticated people of good will. It is alleged that wars are caused by national divisions and that the merging of sovereignty in one-world government would free humanity from the scourge of war. This thesis is a comprehensible tenet of religions seeking to remove the causes of strife among human beings. But as a political precept for ordering human affairs, it can hardly be given a respectable classification.

The United States and Canada live side by side, with no border fortifications and with closer harmony of political and social institutions than is to be found within the Soviet or Red Chinese political systems. Both nations respect the fact that political union could be of no benefit to either. Their separate sovereignties are no obstacle to the preservation of peace.

If such compatible nations reject the organization of a common government, how foolish it is to speak of creating world government over the United States and the Soviet Union! That obviously cannot be done until the differences which cause war are removed—and then there will be no need for world government.

World peace remains a rational goal for human endeavor. But it is ill-served by schemes for world government which waste energy and cultivate illusion. The suppression of barbarism will not be accomplished by such measures.

As President of Princeton and Governor of New Jersey, Woodrow Wilson had seemed to possess a keen perception of the merits of the American political order. But once in the office of President, his values seemed to change. He became obsessed with a purpose of establishing universal peace, not alone because of the experience of a bloody war but also because he had brought into his administration Fabian scholars long obsessed with the task.[1]

"The English," Wells had said, "are a people necessary to mankind," and, with a kind of abandonment to his ethnic origins that Lord Russell has managed to resist, he boasted that the great effort to establish a secure

59

peace in his time for all peoples—Wilson's League of Nations—was a "product of the English mind on both sides of the Atlantic, and could never have existed but for the faith of the English in reasonable dealing."

President Wilson stated his aims on January 8, 1918:[2]

What we demand in this war is nothing peculiar to ourselves. It is that the world be made fit and safe to live in: and particularly that it be made safe for every peace-loving nation which, like our own, wishes to live its own life, determine its own institutions, be assured of justice and fair dealing by the other peoples of the world as against force and selfish aggression. All peoples of the world are in effect partners in this interest, and for our own part we see very clearly that unless justice be done to others it will not be done to us.

The League of Nations and the United Nations are monuments to the unique aberration of American political leadership in the twentieth century. Presidents have led the people into futile attempts to escape from the reality of international relations through ineffectual panaceas for world problems. The effect has been to arrest U.S. influence for favorable international settlements by deferring to emotional utopianism about building peace. The Soviet Union uses the United Nations purposefully to advance its own interests, but the United States tolerates actions hostile to its interests in the foolish belief that some merit attaches to withholding its veto.

The League of Nations became a partisan issue. Although some prominent Republicans supported the Wilson initiative, the Republican Party, led by Senator Henry Cabot Lodge of Massachusetts, rejected the League. Republicans correctly assessed public skepticism about the Wilsonian plans to reform the world.

A generation later, Republican opposition had been dispelled. After a decade of socialist influence on the Franklin Roosevelt Administration, and a war in alliance with the Soviet Union, the United Nations could be created with support from both major parties. Public opinion had been conditioned for another sally into utopia.

After their defeat on the League of Nations issue, American Fabians started an educational campaign to prepare the people for the future. It was alleged that the ultimate failure of the League of Nations to be effective in preserving the peace was caused by U.S. refusal to adhere to this pact. If the United States had been a member, this thesis alleged, the League would have preserved the peace.

The claim was fanciful and unrealistic. In the Japanese invasion of Manchuria the United States sought strong counteraction. It was the League which reneged. Any presumption that the United States could have influenced British and French policy more effectively from inside the League was contrary to reality, as subsequent experience with the United Nations has shown. The effect of League membership after World War I would have been to dim U.S. perception of the real obstacles to peace.

FDR GATHERS POWER

During the depression of the thirties, Franklin Roosevelt changed the political balance in America. He captured for Democrats the majority position held since the Civil War by the Republicans. He was an acutely perceptive and practical politician with a capacity to understand realities hidden by political prejudice.

As an example of his daring, consider his feat of bringing Negroes into the Democratic Party while retaining the allegiance of Southern Democrats. American Negroes, associated with the Republican Party since their emancipation by Abraham Lincoln, had to be wooed with special attention and favor. Southern Democrats could be compensated with federal subsidies for agriculture and flood control. If any other Democratic leader had supposed that the party of Southern democracy could steal the Negroes away from the Republicans, he remained quiet about so absurd a proposition. But Franklin Roosevelt did it.

The operation was perfectly logical. When Roosevelt took office, both parties had conservative and liberal elements. In both parties, the conservative elements were immovable. A Southern Democrat would never vote for a Republican. An Old Guard Republican would never vote for a Democrat. Both conservative factions were unimportant politically: they were simply there.

The elements of leverage in the two parties were the liberals and the bloc voters. Liberals represented a mode of thought crossing party lines. Adherents would cross party lines to vote for any attractive candidate who espoused their cause.

The bloc voter had a very special sense of interest. He had one cause which measured his vote. He didn't care what other policies of the party or candidates might be. If you were for him, he was for you.

Roosevelt called the Fabians to his banner by creating his New Deal and offering leadership posts in government to prominent liberals. They became key figures in his attacks on the Depression. Their policy of increasing federal intervention in economic affairs became his policy. A rapidly growing federal bureaucracy would provide the sinews for a new majority party.

The idea that the credit of the central government could be used in lieu of taxation to finance vast new federal programs gave a virtually limitless perspective to Roosevelt's planning. He could provide subsidies from the federal treasury to all the political blocs he chose to court. He drew organized labor from the non-partisan stance of Gompers and Green with federal legislation favoring its organizing objectives. He drew the blacks away from their Republican ties by bringing black leaders into special roles in the party and in government and by opening government to increased employment of blacks. It was the elementary politics of local elections, but it had not been used in national elections for generations. By making the interests of bloc voters his interests, Roosevelt made their votes his votes.

Although his economic measures were ineffectual in reviving production, the Roosevelt policies were successful in building a political majority which would break the two-term tradition inaugurated by George Washington. And then, before the total failure of his economic policies could overtake him, he was swept into the tide of World War II, first through British orders for American weapons and then through his personal leadership in war. The country emerged from the conflict vastly in debt and gravely afflicted with illusions of grandeur. This spirit found expression in organizing the United Nations and offering nuclear weapons to international control.

In drawing the American people away from the sound principles of the American political economy and launching them into uncharted seas of political expediency, Franklin Roosevelt opened the Pandora's box of debt and corruption which was thereafter to plague the Republic. Adrift from their traditional moorings, the people could be swindled by any demagogue. Professor Walt Rostow has attributed to Winston Churchill a relevant statement:[3]

> Those who are possessed of a definite body of doctrine and of deeply rooted convictions upon it will be in a much better position to deal with the shifts and surprises of daily affairs than those who are merely taking short views, and indulging their natural impulses as they are evoked by what they read from day to day.

President Roosevelt's passion for peacemaking was at once the prejudice of Fabians and the dependable artifice of politics. The error was not in seeking peace but in harboring such nonsensical notions about how to achieve it. His elitism was singularly lacking in an intelligent awareness of the national interest in a predatory world. His personal illusion about "making a Christian" out of Stalin was typical.[4]

> The dangerous change wrought by Franklin Delano Roosevelt transformed not our lower classes but the minds and hearts of our intellectual elite, converting more and more of them into moral aristocrats. Condescendingly tolerant of the self-seeking of the less privileged, Roosevelt's liberal intelligentsia learned to abandon itself to the secret joys of moral superiority, refusing to cross picket lines, or blame the poor for their greed, criminals for their crimes, Negroes for their riots. Such an elite can never have enough of disadvantaged persons to help or commiserate with, and a leveling up of others to their level of self-righteousness becomes a political impossibility. They become, in their own eyes, the "unacknowledged legislators of the world." A political system of ordered freedom must either thrust them up into idleness, as ornaments of its best days, or suffer them to encourage the great levelers, East and West, to fight the last great war to end all wars, to upraise the lowly and crush the arrogant.

Because his personal leadership and the necessities of war preserved national unity in a time of crisis, the damaging effects of the Roosevelt tenure were not immediately apparent. But it was he who opened the gates to the barbarians. He was the demagogue par excellence who sundered the bonds of our constitutional order and substituted a blind attachment to his person. He turned the people away from local self-reliance, which he had praised as governor of New York, to inaugurate programs of federal intervention in local government. The Fabians had long been yearning for the power to turn the country toward socialism. Franklin Roosevelt provided that power, as well as the rhetoric about his personal concern for the working man that would make the change of policy acceptable to the people.

As we have noted, the Fabians are not open advocates of socialism but pretend to be seeking a middle way. Their thesis, adopted by the Roosevelt Administration, has been described by Professor von Mises:[5]

> There should be neither full capitalism nor full socialism, but something in between, a middle way. This third system, assert its supporters, would be capitalism regulated and regimented by government interference with business. But this government intervention should not amount to full government control of all economic activities; it should be limited to the elimination of some especially objectionable excrescences of capitalism without suppressing the activities of the entrepreneur altogether. Thus a social order will result which is allegedly as far from full capitalism as it is from pure socialism, and while retaining the advantages inherent in each of these two systems will avoid their disadvantages. Almost all those who do not unconditionally advocate full socialism support this system of interventionism today and all governments which are not outright and frankly pro-socialist have espoused a policy of economic interventionism. There are nowadays very few who oppose any kind of government interference with prices, wage rates, interest and profits and are not afraid to contend that they consider capitalism and free enterprise the only workable system, beneficial to the whole of society and to all its members.

Franklin Roosevelt seemed to revel in deviousness. Perhaps this was part of his political astuteness, but he would never do directly what could be done circuitously. Arther Krock wrote of Roosevelt's plans to seek a third term:[6]

> Vowing he was ready and anxious to terminate his Presidential tenure, at the end of a second term, Roosevelt all the while was deviously and successfully operating to eliminate all potential Democratic successors.

His unprecedented hold on power and the national unity enjoined by war tempted Franklin Roosevelt to overrate his own wisdom. In the end, that misjudgment made him an easy target for the wiles of a Stalin ably assisted by Soviet agents who had infiltrated the Roosevelt government. Once again the United States won the war and lost the peace.

The extended rule of Franklin Roosevelt marked a turning point in American government. Thenceforth politics seemed to acquire a power and purpose of its own, divorced from the interests of the people. Government would come to be regarded not as a service to the nation but as a power to be used by elites for elites, with all the dissimulation needed to preserve a fiction of responsiveness to the people.

The first Roosevelt term was a repudiation of the promises made to the people. The Democratic Party platform of 1932 was a sober document breathing traditional American politics, not a blueprint for socialism. Professor Paolucci has noted the tenor of that election:[7]

> In the depths of the Depression a majority of the common mass of Americans had voted for reduced government spending and for states rights, and the Socialist Party got less than 100,000 votes. Norman Thomas, the Socialist presidential candidate, was dumfounded by the results. "In such a revolutionary situation," he wrote, "it was not merely or chiefly the Socialist vote that was smaller than one would expect. The Communist vote increased little over that of 1928." What was behind this collapse of the minor left-wing parties? Did it mean that, as in 1896, "their ideas had captured one of the major parties"?
>
> The Socialist leader would not delude himself. "Never in a time of depression," he concluded, "did the principal candidate of the outs offer so little as Governor Roosevelt. He won."

Roosevelt acted shrewdly in building his coalition of dissidents by blaming the Republicans for the Depression. But in building his consensus, he showed himself a master of expediency and a victim of the siren promise of socialism. Elitism was congenial to his breeding and disposition. Still voicing occasionally the high principles of our political heritage, he turned the country away from them.

REPUBLICAN RESPONSE

The Roosevelt propaganda operation was so successful in projecting an image of dynamic concern and activity that despite his failure to revive the economy, he enjoyed overwhelming popular support in the 1936 election. Despite his talk about "malefactors of great wealth," the Roosevelt fiscal programs were eminently satisfying to Wall Street. The Republican Party bankers chose Governor Alfred Landon of Kansas to take the licking in 1936, in the expectation that they could then supply an Eastern liberal candidate for the 1940 election.[8]

Landon lost in a landslide. By 1936 the liberal Republicans felt that Roosevelt had created a new politics by bidding for bloc votes and that they could not afford to lag in devotion to the poor, the blacks, and the workingman, the sick, the underprivileged, the undernourished, the oppressed, the minorities. But lag they did. Republicans had a lingering sense of fiscal responsibility that Democrats had long ago shucked and that seemed to inhibit their political promises.

By 1940, when Franklin Roosevelt was facing the third-term obstacle, Senator Robert A. Taft of Ohio was the nationally recognized leader of the Republican Party and its logical candidate for the presidency. The Wall Street powers crushed that candidacy. They rushed forward with great fanfare to advance the cause of Wendell Willkie, a corporation lawyer and utility executive with minor political experience as a member of a socialist club in college and as a member of the New York Democratic Committee. Congressman Usher Burdick said of the Willkie blitz:[9]

> I believe I am serving the best interests of the Republican Party by protesting in advance and exposing the machinations and attempts of J. P. Morgan

and the other New York utility bankers in forcing Wendell Willkie on the Republican Party . . . There is nothing to the Willkie boom for President except the artificial public opinion being created by newspapers, magazines, and the radio. The reason back of all this is money. Money is being spent by someone and lots of it. This is a good time to find out whether the American people are to be let alone in the selection of a Republican candidate for the Presidency, or whether the "special interests" of this country are powerful enough to dictate to the American people.

Wall Street did dictate the convention choice, and it was Willkie. The Morgan and allied interests were content to lose with Willkie. Franklin Roosevelt was their man and they needed him for a third term. They used Willkie to protect Roosevelt from Taft.

Senator Robert A. Taft represented the last effective champion of responsible government in our political parties. In 1952 he was again denied the presidential nomination through the chicanery of liberals within the party. He then worked loyally for the election of Dwight Eisenhower, and died in 1953, early in the new administration.

The Eisenhower Administration represented less than a pause in the country's slide into socialism. Though the President was personally fond of the old rhetoric, he was keenly aware of the political climate and not disposed to change it. His creation of the new Department of Health, Education and Welfare enlarged the federal trickle in these fields into a new torrent of paternalism, statism and federal deficits.

President Eisenhower understood the realities of power and so was not intimidated by Soviet bluffing (as John Kennedy was to be). In his first five years in office, he was ably assisted by Secretary of State John Foster Dulles. Thereafter, he succumbed to the bad advice of Milton Eisenhower about Cuba policy and to the aspirations of Secretary of State Christian Herter for détente through summitry and the "Spirit of Camp David." That was when the Communists took Cuba and Laos.

It just didn't make any difference any more which party was in power. Though it was to be another decade before Governor George Wallace pointed out that reality to the American people, the truth had become apparent in the Republican rejection of Robert Taft. The party had to have a man who would continue Democratic policies. Eisenhower was pliable enough to serve, and he wore the halo of a war hero.

TWO PARTIES—ONE POLICY

The consequence of this identity of the parties was the effective denial of the citizen's franchise. The theory of two-party government is one of vigorous opposition between the parties. We grant that power corrupts. We hope that a vigorous opposition party will limit that decay by exposing the corruption and offering a worthy alternative. That is how representative government serves the people.

If you do not have an opposition party, you cannot have representative government. One-party government may be dictatorial or benevolent but inevitably it becomes corrupt. When two parties embrace a philosophy of paternalism, and identical foreign and domestic policies using a common propaganda, neither party is capable of rescuing the country from their commonly held error. We have in practice a one-party state with the stain of corruption which that condition fosters.

The effects of such party alignment are not immediately discernible. Custom and the resistance of the people to change exercise some restraint on the grab for power. The United States is a powerful country with highly productive industry. Its credit could be exploited by politicians for decades before demonetization of the currency would be forced and the dollar would become a second-rate medium in international trade. The approach of the day of reckoning was obscured by the assurances of both political parties that our national affairs were being well managed.

The cumulative weight of erroneous policy and indecisive leadership finally overtook the United States in the 1960s. President John Kennedy gave free rein to socialist folly in foreign policy in the sixties, just as Franklin Roosevelt had given free rein in domestic policies three decades earlier. The consequence was the Bay of Pigs debacle, a browbeating at Vienna, the sham neutralization of Laos, the loss of East Berlin, and a growing war in Vietnam culminating in the U.S.-planned overthrow of our faithful ally, President Ngo Dinh Diem. This was corruption with a vengeance.

Lyndon Johnson had long held high place among the liberal leaders of the Democratic Party. He fancied himself another Franklin Roosevelt. But a Senator from Texas has certain cultural obligations that must be respected if he is to remain in office, so the Johnson liberalism did not exclude some illiberal notions for the benefit of the home folks. These defections from the true cause were enough to disqualify him for the presidency in the eyes of the liberal elite. Despite his prestige as Majority Leader of the United States Senate, his candidacy was bitterly opposed by Democratic liberals in 1960. They were shocked into disbelief, if not revolt, when John Kennedy asked Lyndon Johnson to be his running-mate in the 1960 campaign. And when the Kennedy assassination raised Johnson to the presidency, shock was great in the liberal ranks. To lose Kennedy and gain Johnson in one tragic event seemed like a multiplication of evil.

President Johnson knew he was on trial. Could he win the confidence and support of the liberal intellectuals who had provided such devoted service to John Kennedy? He would show them that he was the true liberal. Making skillful use of the emotional distress caused by the assassination and summoning his own superb legislative leadership to guide the Congress, he had enacted in a remarkably docile session the Kennedy legislation so long stalled in Congress.

While President Johnson was performing with such distinction for the liberals, the persistent illusion of fellow Southerners that he was somehow conservative played to his advantage. As Arthur Krock noted:[10]

66

The fact that Harry F. Byrd of Virginia, the most conservative and influential Democrat in Congress, was in charge of the Johnson for President movement in the South attests to the firmness of what proved to be one of the most mistaken concepts in the history of American politics—that Johnson would campaign on the line of his Senate record and pursue it as national policy if elected to the presidency.

In 1964, conservatives in the Republican Party achieved notable unity when they nominated a conservative candidate and adopted a conservative platform. But the Goldwater campaign was signally mismanaged and President Johnson went on to win a sweeping election victory.

Johnson also won large majorities in both houses of Congress, enabling him to launch new legislation in proof of his liberalism. His voting rights bill setting five Southern states apart as targets of special legislation seemed to revive the lawless Congress of Reconstruction. Supreme Court approval of the legislation no longer bore any relationship to law nor to the Constitution. This was class legislation prohibited by the Constitution but appealing to the prejudices of the Court.

Perhaps it mystified Lyndon Johnson that this flood of liberal legislation did not solve the national ills. His measures of relief for civil rights, poverty and education seemed only to exacerbate tensions and conflict in the country.

WAR POLICY

The Vietnam War, in which Lyndon Johnson had received a chaotic South Vietnam mess and bad policy from the Kennedy Administration, steadily worsened. The assassination of President Diem had placed the leadership of South Vietnam in the hands of an incompetent junta headed by General Nguyen Van Minh, soon dispossessed by General Nguyen Khanh in a January 1964 coup. The Army of the Republic of Vietnam was divided and weakened. The enemy moved aggressively to expand his forces and territory. By 1965 President Johnson was faced with the choice of accepting defeat or of introducing U.S. combat forces to defend South Vietnam. Lyndon Johnson was not a complacent loser. He chose to fight.

That was his undoing. Lyndon Johnson could travel with the Kennedy liberals in domestic legislation but he could not stomach their readiness to deliver South Vietnam—a strong and secure bastion of freedom when the Kennedy entourage came to Washington—into the hands of Communist aggressors. He could not as the leader of the world's most powerful nation accept defeat at the hands of North Vietnam.

At first the dissent of Senators Gruening and Morse and Church seemed unimportant. In practice, their demands for withdrawal from the war served to rally Republican support to the Johnson war policy and thereby to protect the Administration from public pressure to defeat the enemy. Victory never became a political issue. Neither party favored it. The debate was between military restraint and surrender.

The two parties and the news media were in agreement that public dis-

cussion of achieving peace through victory might enkindle a public demand for such a policy and force the Administration to adopt it. The
policymakers had been induced by British warnings to fear that any invasion of North Vietnam or Laos would bring Red China into the war. Consequently, public debate was limited to the alternative of U.S. withdrawal
from the war.

Despite this control of the news media, polls showed in 1965 and 1966
that the American public believed the country should end the war by defeating the enemy. The people's judgment was superior to that of their
elected and appointed officials.

As the war dragged on with growing attrition of life and property, the
clamor for withdrawal mounted. The Administration policy of fighting
endless, indecisive war on the territory of an ally as long as the enemy
chose to continue aggression was indefensible both on moral and practical
grounds. It was only a question of time until the people, with the possibility of victory excluded by both political parties, would choose withdrawal.

Near the end of the Johnson tenure, the President had lost the support
of his own staff. A substantial element of his defense appointees were
persuaded that the war could not be won and that the U.S. should cut its
losses. The liberals whom Lyndon Johnson had chosen to associate with his
Administration showed themselves grossly ignorant and wholly incompetent
in the matter of war. Their minds were filled with trite socialist clichés.

THE NEW RACISM

The war was only part of Lyndon Johnson's mounting troubles. On the
home front the blatant alignment of the Administration with the civil-
rights radicals assured the activists that they could defy state law with
impunity. They were assured of the protection of the Attorney General
and federal courts.

The Selma-to-Montgomery march, in defiance of state law and with the
protection of federal troops, put Johnson to the test. He never faltered.
The Watts rioting in August 1965 was a triumph for radical revolutionaries over the addled liberals who thought they could pacify the terrorists
with negotiation. If Lyndon Johnson supposed that civil-rights leaders
could do no wrong, he had much to learn.

In July 1967, Newark, New Jersey and Detroit, Michigan were put to
the torch. In both cities, Democratic municipal authorities, addled by the
prevailing Democratic propaganda about oppressed minorities and subverted by the federal poverty program, ordered police not to restrain the
looting with which both riots opened. With this invitation to loot, many
citizens of the inner cities responded and large sectors of the communities
became involved before federal troops were summoned to restore order.
America was reaping the harvest of Johnsonian paternalism and political
expediency.

The Kennedy Administration had moved[11] to accommodate the press-backed militancy of the young black Marxists by providing foundation funds for voter-registration drives in the South and by using the office of the Attorney General to support private challenges to state police laws. The Johnson Administration carried the federal intervention much farther with stacked presidential commissions endorsing black militancy, condoning crime, and advocating vast federal subsidies to buy or to compel compliance with liberal notions of proper social behavior.

In February 1968, the Kerner Commission blamed "white racism" for the black riots of 1965 and 1967. The presidential commission had been packed with liberals sympathetic to the Johnson civil-rights policies. It had been staffed with radicals intent on indicting the United States as the oppressor of black citizens. The report was a scandalous misrepresentation of fact and history that showed the extremes to which liberals could be pressed in deference to the reigning folly.

The Kerner Report was a blueprint for the destruction of the United States. It embraced the Marxist thesis of class oppression, with blacks as the oppressed class and whites as the oppressors. It proposed a socialist solution: the empowering of the central government with vast appropriations to intrude into every facet of the lives of its citizens to right the wrongs which had presumably been inflicted on black citizens. The report was a brief for class warfare which indicted past lawlessness and justified any retribution black citizens might impose on white society in the future. It seemed consonant with President Johnson's pathetic attempt to cast his Administration on the side of the revolution when he told a joint session of Congress, "We shall overcome!"

When, after the assassination of Dr. Martin Luther King, Jr., rioting broke out in Washington, D.C., President Johnson gathered black civil-rights leaders at the White House for consultation. They asked him to restrain the police and let community leaders handle the conflict. The President agreed and orders were issued.

The President and his Attorney General had learned nothing from the experience in Watts, Newark and Detroit. When the small bands of rioters were not stopped, when looting was tolerated by posted police, when winds of human impulse and arson fanned the lawlessness into a major conflagration engulfing the business district of the nation's capital—then the Army had to be called to restore order.

Government seemed to be disintegrating, but the Johnson Administration continued blithely on its course. The liberal never doubts his own wisdom because all error is presumably external to him. When, in 1920, Edgar Ansel Mowrer asked the Premier of Italy why he did not use the police to restrain the contending Communist and Fascist gangs in Rome, that "statesman" replied that he was "letting steam out of the revolution."[12] The people lost faith in representative government and called on Mussolini to protect their liberties.

The persistent incapacity of weak democratic governments to preserve public order is the Achilles heel of representative government. Professor Paolucci has asked the appropriate question:[13]

> Why is it that, when the symptoms of anarchy come to the surface and touch leaders of our intelligentsia who have risen to administrative offices, such men try to talk them away by warning that if the responsible individuals causing the disorders don't stop, the end will be some form of fascism? Why do they not say that the end will be the proper use of sovereign police power by the duly constituted government? Is fascism, or a dictatorship of the revolutionary elite under the banner of Communism, the only form of coercive state power competent to prevent riots and total fragmentation of the social order?

REVOLT OF THE PEOPLE

In 1968 the defeat of the Tet offensive in Vietnam was turned into a great victory for South Vietnam. But superficially the enemy attack seemed to undermine President Johnson's promise of negotiating an end to the war. Liberals who had argued that the war could not be won rose up to scream "I told you so."

Senator Eugene McCarthy won an impressive vote against Johnson in the 1968 New Hampshire primary. Senator Robert Kennedy announced his opposition to the President in the election of 1968. Discouraged and disheartened by this response to his liberal administration, Lyndon Johnson withdrew from the presidential race.

The country at last seemed to realize the folly of the socialist binge that Lyndon Johnson had led. The liberal articulation of Marxist premises was undermining concepts of law and order and personal responsibility. It was fostering crime and revolution. Government was in default.

Candidates Richard Nixon and George Wallace, both keen students of the American scene, correctly diagnosed the temper of the people. In 1968 the Democratic landslide of 1964 was converted into a dramatic rejection of the Democratic presidential candidate, Hubert Humphrey. The Democratic presidential vote dropped from 61 percent of the total popular vote in 1964 to 43 percent in 1968. The people could hardly have given a more resounding dismissal to the Democratic performance.

And yet Richard Nixon did not respond to that popular mandate. In his campaign he condemned the inflation caused by the Democratic deficits, but in office he accumulated greater deficits for greater inflation. In his campaign he condemned the welfare mess, but in office he proposed to multiply the welfare rolls and welfare assistance through a plainly socialist "Family Assistance Plan." In the campaign he had hinted at a plan to end the war, but in office he merely continued the Johnson-Clifford plan to turn the fighting over to the South Vietnamese. The scale of fighting increased. In the campaign, be spoke of sustaining our alliances, but in office he betrayed the Republic of China by condoning its illegal expulsion from the United Nations and the transfer of its seat to Red China. In the campaign, he criticized Democratic neglect of strategic weapons security, but in office he allowed the United States to slide into an inferior and worsening position vis-à-vis the Soviet Union.

Why did Richard Nixon, elected on a platform reflecting the more traditional ethic of the Republican Party, in office embrace foreign and domestic programs espoused by the liberal wing of the party? The clear record is that Richard Nixon, rescued from oblivion after his defeat in the California gubernatorial race of 1962, ensconced in a Rockefeller law firm in New York City at a handsome salary and free to travel the world to consult with national leaders in foreign lands, knew his employer. When in 1968, the temper of the country required a public image of conservatism and devotion to law and order rather than a continuation of the liberal bent of prior years, Richard Nixon rather than Nelson Rockefeller was the man to carry the Republican banner. In office, President Nixon was hemmed in on the foreign policy front by Henry Kissinger, the Rockefeller adviser on foreign affairs, and on the domestic front by John Mitchell, Nixon law partner and Rockefeller bond attorney.

The captivity was not uncongenial to Richard Nixon. He was essentially a mercenary in politics. The 1968 conservative pose could be adopted because it was what the people wanted. It could be assumed again in 1972, after four years of playing the liberal role, because that again was what the people wanted. The words had no relevance to anything Richard Nixon believed nor to anything he had done or would do.

As we review the politics of recent decades we note a curious characteristic of representative government—the irrelevancy of politics. The course of government does not depend on who is elected. It is independent of the will of the people. Government, with the assistance of the news media, has the capacity to act against the better judgment of the people, and does so.

The people are restive, dissatisfied with the course of government. But what can they do? They are inured by long practice to the two-party system. They know it is not functioning properly. But what is wrong? What is the alternative?

71

Chapter 9

THE MONEY POWER

THE AMERICAN CITIZEN sees politics as an exercise of his franchise to elect officials who will perform stated duties for assigned periods. When the voter fulfills his responsibility, he turns back to his business and his golf until the next election.

This perception of the political process as simply the election of competent officials is a scandal of our time. The real political process is hidden from public view by a concert of our news media which conceals the true sources of political power.

It is not that the influence of money on politics is unknown. Perceptive writers in every generation have reported the truth. Those who have wielded power have boasted of their achievements. But this is a limited literature and must be searched out; it finds no reflection in the common news media of the day. Thus, a basic perception of the reality of politics, so vital to representative government, is lacking in our society.

Some citizens, through their special interest in a phase of government, e.g., public education, have learned that public officials need guidance while they are in office, if they are to perform in response to the citizen's interest. They and like-minded persons organize a club or association to monitor and guide official actions. In time, all of the powers of government become influenced by blocs having a special interest in particular activities.

Some of these bloc interests win legislative or executive favor and achieve special status as beneficiaries of subsidies from the public treasury. The people become burdened with protective tariffs to benefit industry, farm subsidies for farmers, bounties for urban renewal, funds for poverty programs, appropriations for health lobbies, education lobbies and welfare lobbies. The common ground of all the special interest blocs is money, either in direct subsidy or in legislative advantage. So, even though the ordinary voter is little aware of it, the game of politics is money.

Oswald Spengler pointed out that reality fifty years ago in his *Decline of the West.* "Democracy," he wrote, "is the rule of money." In an authoritarian state, the moneyed interests are subject to the power of king or dictator; but in a democracy, money buys everything. It buys the intellectuals of society to its service. When money has corrupted the whole society, the people rebel and call on Caesar to restore the rule of blood. As Spengler put it:[1]

> The private powers of the economy want free paths for their acquisition of great resources. No legislation must stand in their way. They want to make the laws themselves, in their interests, and to that end they make use of the tool they have made for themselves, democracy, the subsidized party. Law needs, in order to resist this onslaught, a high tradition that finds its satisfaction not in the heaping up of riches, but in the tasks of true rulership, above and beyond all money-advantage. A power can be overthrown only by another power, not by a principle, and only one power that can confront money is left. Money is overthrown and abolished by blood.

Money seeks the centralization of power. True competition is a condition of risk to be avoided. For money, monopoly is a condition of security to be sought. Thus, the drive of a moneyed society is to the building of monopoly, both economic and political. As one critic noted:[2]

> The first essential point is that the American industrial or business system is a power system. The power of which it is the vehicle is unprecedented in its magnitude. And this power is not diffused throughout the system but concentrated in a relatively few great corporations—more exactly in their managements, or concretely, in the hands of a few men, who in effect direct the activities of the economic-political system, determine its forms, create and distribute its profits and select the path of future growth. The second essential point is that the power of this immense economy and polity, or political economy, is an omnipresence in American society. No institution—certainly not government or the university, and not even the Church—is immune from the touch of it, nor is any family or individual.

Money is our measure of wealth. Wealth is a measure of status. It was in ancient times the king's gift to his retainers, the mark of special privilege of the ruling class. In removing royal authority through democracy, wealth established its own dominion over the people. Liberated from the royal sanction, the elites of wealth now rule the country. They manipulate politics to protect their wealth, else new powers might arise to dispossess them.

It must not be supposed that the simple possession of substantial wealth confers such political power. The oligarchs of power are a select group of private investment bankers who control governments in the democratic societies. Their operations are hidden from public view. They are not identified with the banker whom the ordinary citizen knows in his community as an intelligent, compassionate and honorable man.

The operation of the investment bankers have been reported by Professor Carroll Quigley of Georgetown University in *Tragedy and Hope,* a book ignored by political scientists.[3]

> These bankers came to be called "international bankers" and more particularly, were known as "merchant bankers" in England, "private bankers" in France, and "investment bankers" in the United States. . . . One of their less obvious characteristics was that they remained as private unincorporated firms, usually partnerships, until relatively recently, offering no shares, no reports, and usually no advertising to the public . . . This persistence as private firms continued because it ensured the maximum of anonymity and secrecy to persons of tremendous public power who dreaded public knowledge of their activities as an evil almost as great as inflation. As a consequence, ordinary people had no way of knowing the wealth or areas of operations of such firms, and often were somewhat hazy as to their membership. Thus, people of considerable political knowledge might not associate the names of Walter Burns, Clinton Dawkins, Edward Grenfell, Willard Straight, Thomas Lamont, Dwight Morrow, Nelson Perkins, Russel Leffingwell, Elihu Root, John W. Davis, John Foster Dulles and S. Parker Gilbert with the name "Morgan," yet all these and many others were parts of the system of influence which centered on the J. P. Morgan office at 23 Wall Street.

The operations of these bankers in the political sphere were screened from the public, but not from political leaders. Their role was known, especially in England:[4]

> In 1852 Gladstone, Chancellor of the Exchequer, declared, "The hinge of the whole situation was this: the government itself was not to be a substantive power in matters of finance, but was to leave the Money Power supreme and unquestioned." On September 26, 1921, *The Financial Times* wrote, "Half a dozen men at the top of the Big Five Banks could upset the whole fabric of government finance by refraining from renewing Treasury Bills." In 1924, Sir Drummond Fraser, vice-president of the Institute of Bankers, stated, "The Governor of the Bank of England must be the autocrat who dictates the terms upon which alone the government can obtain borrowed money.

In the United States, there was no national bank to manipulate, but the investment bankers had other fields to conquer:[5]

> The influence of these business leaders was so great that the Morgan and Rockefeller groups acting together, or even Morgan acting alone, could have wrecked the economic system of the country merely by throwing securities on the stock market for sale, and, having precipitated a stock market panic, could then have bought back the securities they had sold, but at a lower price. Naturally, they were not so foolish as to do this, although Morgan came very close to it in precipitating the "Panic of 1907," but they did not hesitate to wreck individual corporations, at the expense of the holders of common stocks, by driving them to bankruptcy. In this way, to take only two examples, Morgan wrecked the New York, New Haven and Hartford Rail-

road before 1914 by selling to it, at high prices, the largely valueless securities of myriad New England steamship and trolley lines; and William Rockefeller and his friends wrecked the Chicago, Milwaukee, St. Paul and Pacific Railroad before 1925 . . .

In Britain in the period 1908-1911, the ideological heirs of Cecil Rhodes used the Rhodes Trust to organize semisecret Round Table Groups to advance the federation of the English-speaking world.[6]

By 1915, Round Table Groups existed in seven countries, including England, South Africa, Canada, Australia, New Zealand, India and a rather loosely organized group in the United States (George Louis Beer, Walter Lippmann, Frank Aydelotte, Whitney Shepardson, Thomas W. Lamont, Jerome D. Greene, Erwin D. Canham of the *Christian Science Monitor,* and others). . . .

At the end of the war of 1914, it became clear that the organization of this system had to be greatly extended. Once again the task was entrusted to Lionel Curtis who established, in England and each dominion, a front organization to the existing Round Table Group. This front organization, called the Royal Institute of International Affairs, had as its nucleus in each area the existing submerged Round Table Group. In New York it was known as the Council on Foreign Relations, and was a front for J. P. Morgan and Company in association with the very small American Round Table Group. The American organizers were dominated by the large number of Morgan experts, including Lamont and Beer, who had gone to the Paris Peace Conference and there became close friends with the similar group of English "experts" which had been recruited by the Milner group. In fact, the original plans for the Royal Institute of International Affairs and the Council on Foreign Relations were drawn up at Paris.

Thus, it was this collaboration with British leaders which sparked the formation of our most prestigious and influential foreign policy organization in the United States, an organization whose members would move quietly between high posts in government and the leading law firms, banks and industrial corporations of New York City:[7]

The New York branch was dominated by the associates of the Morgan Bank. For example, in 1928 the Council on Foreign Relations had John W. Davis as President, Paul Cravath as vice-president, and a council of thirteen others, which included Owen D. Young, Russel C. Leffingwell, Norman Davis, Allen Dulles, George W. Wickersham, Frank L. Polk, Whitney Shepardson, Isaiah Bowman, Stephen P. Duggan, and Otto Kahn. Throughout its history the Council has been associated with the American Round Tablers, such as Beer, Lippmann, Shepardson and Jerome Greene.

The academic figures have been those linked to Morgan, such as James T. Shotwell, Charles Seymour, Joseph P. Chamberlain, Philip Jessup, Isaiah Bowman and, more recently, Philip Moseley, Grayson L. Kirk and Henry M. Wriston.

In the aftermath of World War I, Britain still appeared to the world as a great power. She was soon to concede naval parity to the United States. Nevertheless, the obsequious attitude of the U.S. bankers toward their titled British associates was in sharp contrast with the friendly but independent and self-respecting attitude of the American people:[8]

On this basis, which was originally financial and goes back to George Peabody, there grew up in the twentieth century a power structure between London and New York which penetrated deeply into university life, the press, and the practice of foreign policy . . . The American Branch of this "English Establishment" exerted much of its influence through five American newspapers (*The New York Times, New York Herald Tribune, Christian Science Monitor,* the *Washington Post,* and the lamented *Boston Evening Transcript*). In fact, the editor of the *Christian Science Monitor* was the chief American correspondent (anonymously) of the Round Table, and Lord Lothian, the original editor of the Round Table and later secretary of the Rhodes Trust (1925-1939) and ambassador to Washington, was a frequent writer in the *Monitor.*

WALL STREET

The power and influence of Wall Street had long been an issue in American politics. As industrial America grew in size and strength, as corporate power expanded, as government franchises for railroads or other ventures became prizes of politics, the role of the Republican Party as the agent of Wall Street became common knowledge. What the people did not know was that the bankers exercised effective control over both parties. Professor Quigley tells us:[9]

> When the business interests, led by William C. Whitney, pushed through the first installment of civil service reform in 1883, they expected that they would be able to control both political parties equally. Indeed some of them intended to contribute to both and to allow an alternation of the two parties ir public office in order to conceal their own influence, inhibit any exhibition of independence by politicians, and allow the electorate to believe that they were exercising their own free choice. Such an alternation of the parties on the federal scene occurred in the period 1880-1896, with business influence (or at least Morgan's influence) as great in Democratic as in Republican administrations . . . The inabilities of the investment bankers and their industrial allies to control the Democratic Convention of 1896 was a result of the agrarian discontent of 1868-1896. This discontent in turn was based, very largely, on the monetary tactics of the banking oligarchy.

The bankers controlled politics by controlling the nominating conventions of the parties. When they had selected the candidates, they could wait with confidence for the judgment of the people in November elections. Total control of the parties was not required; it sufficed to keep the presidency and the Congress in safe hands.

In the United States today, the people entertain a delusion that they elect the President of the United States. A pause for thought would make clear that their only role is to choose between the two candidates offered by the major parties. Those who control the nominating process really choose the President.

With occasional exceptions when some figure captures the public fancy, as Senator Barry Goldwater did in the Republican Party in 1964, winning the party nomination is essentially a question of money. Within limits, money can buy the nomination for you. It can command superior talent in managing and directing your campaign, in projecting a pleasing public image, in organizing the party system for your advantage. We saw this in 1972 when Senator Fred Harris dropped out of the Democratic race and Senator Edmund Muskie folded up his tent before the convention. Senator George McGovern had ample financial backing to win the Democratic nomination but a dearth of funds for his election campaign. Somebody wanted him to be the candidate whom President Nixon would defeat.

Political money is used not for bribery but in perfectly legal ways to reserve the presidency for men who are docile and subservient to the financial powers. It is used to hire competent political help, to support "right thinking" in the party ranks, to draw influential persons away from potentially hostile leaders. All the money power wants to do is to control the President of the United States and the Congress.

The same process prevails in other national and local elections through money control of both political parties. Only "right thinking" men and women receive the party favor. The few cases when men of exceptional talent and independence win public favor in opposition to party policy do not jeopardize Wall Street control of government.

The sums spent on elections in the United States in recent years have been scandalous. Candidates spend fantastic multiples of the salary value of a position to win public office. The money is not spent without purpose. The office has values other than its salary in bestowing federal appropriations of $300 billion annually on favored enterprises, in making new raids upon the workers' earnings, in protecting vested interests with a hand in the public pocket.

New York City is the financial heartland of the United States. Here are centered the great banking houses of the country through which the financing of corporate and public enterprises is managed and the sensitivity of the economy to political influences is most acutely felt. Among these seats of financial power in New York and the cabinet and sub-cabinet seats of political power in Washington, there are a constant flow of information and a steady flow of personnel to keep government in tune with the financial powers of the country. This vital flow of information and people continues, whichever party reigns in Washington. The changing of posts with a change of party makes no change. Democrat or Republican, cabinet officers represent the same law firms, industry, corporations, and banking houses.

This concurrence of financial and political interest really controls the policies of the country. Through control of the news media, the financial interests can commit the government to unpopular policies and sustain those policies against public opinion, as in the Korean and Vietnam wars. They can elect their own presidential candidates and defeat political opponents of their policies.

THE FEDERAL RESERVE SYSTEM

Although the Morgan interests exercised an effective control over politics, they still did not have the central bank control of currency issue enjoyed by their British associates. In 1832, President Andrew Jackson had vetoed renewal of the charter of the Bank of the United States. He then withdrew U.S. deposits from the bank, causing its collapse. For eight decades the United States had no central bank. The issuance of currency became a function of the national government, with each addition to the currency authorized by Congress. In this period, national policies affecting the coinage of silver and the issuance of greenbacks became critical political issues.

By 1911, after a long period of Republican rule, Wall Street concluded that the time was ripe for the re-establishment of a national bank on the model of the Bank of England, with powers over the issuance of currency dissociated from the legislative process. Under the leadership of Senator Nelson Aldrich, Chairman of the Senate Banking and Currency Committee and maternal grandfather of Nelson Aldrich Rockefeller, Congress passed a bill creating a national bank of the United States.

President Taft, aware of the Wall Street image of the Republican Party and fearing that the Aldrich bill was too blatant a steal to stand public scrutiny, opposed the bill. In the 1912 elections, the banking interests retaliated by supporting the Bull Moose flight of Theodore Roosevelt from his Republican ties and by simultaneously financing the Democratic contender, Woodrow Wilson. With Republicans divided, the Democratic victory was assured.

When Woodrow Wilson was elected and installed in office, a dutiful and grateful Democratic Party passed the Aldrich bill, now disguised as the Federal Reserve Bank bill. Thus was the power to create new money delivered into the hands of the private bankers who control the Federal Reserve System.

At the time the Federal Reserve law was passed, the requirement of a gold reserve, and other law affecting coinage, seemed to exercise some public restraint on the capability of private bankers to manipulate the money supply. But in time these restraints were reduced and finally eliminated. Today the country has a fiat currency manipulated by the Federal Reserve System. These bankers hold power over the wealth and incomes of citizens that no country should ever place in the hands of private citizens. The Federal Reserve Board can, by increasing or restraining additions to the money supply, change the entire value of U.S. industry as reflected in stock market values. It is asking too much of human nature to suppose that men will not guard their interests in such manipulation of the economy.

Traditional market economists have recorded the history of money in Western society, the reach of government to control the coinage in content and value, and eventually to substitute paper for gold. They have attributed the debasement of the currency to "government," generally without noting that in a democracy, "government" is managed by special interests. The Governors of the Federal Reserve Banks may nominally be employees of the government but they are more fundamentally private bankers who guide the monetary policy of the government. We must look for the sources of inflation not alone in the short-term political advantages of deficit spending, but also in the considered policies of our bankers. The development of banking in recent centuries has been a story of the use of government by private bankers to consolidate their power and to achieve their purposes.

In the period prior to 1931, which Professor Quigley dubbed the "Age of Financial Capitalism," the bankers were generally supporters of hard money against the persistent clamor for easy money. Since the Great Depression, their attitudes have changed. They have embraced the Keynesian policies of deliberate inflation as a means of stimulating the economy. They maintain a facade of opposition to inflation but the position is perfunctory. In reality they promote public debt in all echelons of government and policies of expanding government services which feed the inflationary spiral. Note, for example, the contradictory words of Dr. Arthur Burns, Chairman of the Federal Reserve Board, on December 29, 1972:[10]

> The only responsible course open to us, I believe, is to fight inflation tenaciously, and with all the weapons at our command. Let me note, however, that there is no way to turn back the clock and restore the environment of a bygone era. We can no longer cope with inflation by letting recessions run their course; or by accepting a higher average level of unemployment; or by neglecting programs whose aim is to halt the decay of our central cities, or to create larger opportunities for the poor.

Dr. Burns would fight inflation by renouncing the weapons essential to success. He makes it clear that the bankers have approved the vast spending programs launched by the federal government in building up a national debt of $450 billion. His opposition to inflation is ritual, not real. No doubt the bankers will be well-protected when the crash occurs.

Homer Lea, who wrote in an age of more prevalent honesty in government officials, saw the effects of avarice in his time:[11]

> Industrialism is only a means toward an end and not an end in itself. As the human body is nourished by food, so is a nation nourished by its industries. Man does not live to eat, but secures food that his body may be sustained while he struggles forward to the consummation of his desires. . . . When a man has no aspirations, no object to attain during life, but simply lives to eat, he excites our loathing and contempt. So when a nation makes industrialism the end, it becomes a glutton among nations, vulgar, swinish, arrogant, whose kingdom lasts proportionately no longer than life remains to the swine among men . . . the difference between national industry and commercialism is that while industry is the labor of a people to supply the needs of mankind, commercialism utilizes this industry for the gratification of individual avarice. It is this commercialism that, having seized hold of the American people, overshadows and tends to destroy not only the aspirations and worldwide career open to the nations, but the Republic.

FULL EMPLOYMENT—THE PLANNED INFLATION

After World War II, Congress adopted (in the U.S. Employment Act of 1946) a national goal of "full employment." The Act provided that "it is the continuing policy and responsibility of the federal government to use all practicable means . . . to promote maximum employment, production, and purchasing power."[12]

This Act was the final undoing of national fiscal responsibility. We have noted in the statement of the chairman of the Federal Reserve Board that full employment could be achieved only by manipulating the money supply to achieve a steady rise in the price structure. That option was rejected in the postwar German Republic, which is constitutionally required to balance its budget, but it has since been adopted by the great powers of the Atlantic world. Today, the great powers are practicing a currency inflation which methodically robs the working people of a substantial portion of their savings. "Full employment" has become a cover for the most flagrant and systematic robbery of the working man in the history of the world. It is practiced with the collaboration of organized labor, which takes credit for a rising wage structure.

In a systematic inflation of the money supply, the manipulators profit. They assess the predictable consequences of this fiscal policy and use the knowledge to their own advantage. Only the workingman, who depends upon the integrity of government to protect the value of his savings, suffers the full damage of inflation. The money he has saved for the education of his children, for his retirement, and for the protection of his family proves to be inadequate. He and his widow are thrown on public charity, to beg from government health and welfare benefits to replace what government has stolen from him.

The process of controlling the money supply is political. It derives from the constitutional responsibility of Congress "to coin money, regulate the value thereof, and of foreign coin." There is implicit in this responsibility an obligation *to preserve the value of the money* so created as a medium of exchange. In delivering to the Federal Reserve Board a now unrestricted authority to depreciate the value of money with only a nebulous goal of "full employment" to guide the exercise of those powers, Congress has effectively abandoned its constitutional responsibility and has delivered the people into the hands of the bankers.

How ironic that the Democratic Party, the party of the people, should have been the instrument of their delivery into such bondage! But that is the nature of party politics. Its object is obedience to the powerful while pacifying the people with a facade of popular controls. What the Republican Party could not do because of its known Wall Street ties, the Democratic Party could do by exploiting the public misconception that the party was not controlled by Wall Street.

How ironic that organized labor, commissioned to protect the worker's interest, should be conned into this despoilation of the worker! The compulsion of the labor leader was to win higher compensation for his workers. If these increased wages exceeded productivity gains, they would cause unemployment unless that consequence was aborted by increasing the money supply, and consequently the price structure. Instead of holding their bargaining within a framework of sound money, the labor leaders opted for bigger wage gains, with inflation. In that choice they lost everything, for inflation consumed not only the worker's wage gains but his savings too. Keynesian economics may be a boon to bankers but it is a cross for the working man.

The money power seems to bring all other forces in homage to its interests. Inflation is made to seem attractive to those who should and could stop it. As economist Murray Rothbard has put it:[13] "Clearly, the inflationists' ideal is some kind of world paper money, manipulated by a world goverment and Central Bank, inflating everywhere at a common rate."

That is where we are headed.

ROMANCING THE LEFT

A mysterious aspect of the political scene for many citizens is the long history of encouragement given to left-wing radicalism by wealthy Americans occupying powerful positions in business, industry and the professions. Foundations have financed radical attacks on our cultural institutions.

Financing the Left was part of the Morgan program to control the country. If his agents were in the Left, they could influence or control it to suit his purposes. That is what they did. Professor Quigley has given examples of the Morgan reach:[14]

> The associations between Wall Street and the Left, of which Mike Straight is a fair example, are really survivals of the associations between the Morgan Banks and the Left. To Morgan all political parties were simply organizations to be used, and the firm always was careful to keep a foot in all camps. Morgan himself, Dwight Morrow, and other partners were allied with Republicans; Russel C. Leffingwell was allied with the Democrats; Grayson Murphy was allied with the extreme Right; and Thomas W. Lamont was allied with the Left. Like the Morgan interest in libraries, museums, and art, its inability to distinguish between loyalty to the United States and loyalty to England, its recognition of the need for social work among the poor, the multi-partisan political views of the Morgan firm in domestic politics went back to the original founder of the firm, George Peabody (1795-1869).

The influencing of public opinion was a constant care of the Morgan interests, met not only through the Council on Foreign Relations but through a multitude of other activities as well:[15]

> *The New Republic* was founded by Willard and Dorothy Straight, using her money, in 1914, and continued to be supported by her contributions until March 23, 1953. The original purpose for establishing the paper was to provide an outlet for the progressive Left and to guide it quietly in an anglophile direction. This latter task was entrusted to . . . Walter Lippmann . . ."
> The first editor of *The New Republic*, the well-known liberal Herbert Croly . . . makes perfectly clear that [Willard] Straight was in no sense a liberal

or a progressive, but was, indeed, a typical international banker and that *The New Republic* was simply a medium for advancing certain designs of such international bankers, notably to blunt the isolationism and anti-British sentiments so prevalent among many American progressives, while providing them with a vehicle for expression of their progressive views in literature, art, music, social reform, and even domestic politics.

One of the best known Morgan partners, Thomas W. Lamont, had a continuing affiliation with left-wing causes:[16]

> . . . all the evidence would indicate that Tom Lamont was simply Morgan's apostle to the Left in succession to Straight, a change made necessary by the latter's premature death in 1918. Both were financial supporters of liberal publications, in Lamont's case, *The Saturday Review of Literature*, which he supported throughout the 1920s and 1930s, and *The New York Post*, which he owned from 1918 to 1924.

Other famous persons had Morgan connections which were obscure or unknown:[17]

> An important element of this nexus was *Asia* Magazine, which had been established by Morgan's associates as the journal of the American Asiatic Society in 1898, had been closely associated with Willard Straight during his lifetime, and was owned outright by him from January 1917. In the 1930s it was operated for the Whitneys by Richard T. Walsh and his wife, known to the world as Pearl Buck. Walsh, who acted as editor of *Asia*, was also president of the holding corporation of *The New Republic* for several years and president of the John Day Publishing Company. In 1942, after Nelson Rockefeller and Jock Whitney joined the government to take charge of American propaganda in Latin America in the Office of the Coordinator of Inter-American Affairs, *Asia* Magazine changed its name to *Asia and the Americas*. In 1947, when Mike Straight began a drive to sell the United Nations, it was completely reorganized into *United Nations World*.

The trick was to use the Left by financing it and controlling it:[18]

> All three—Straight, Wallace and the Communists joined in the attempt merely as a means of defeating Truman. Straight (Mike-Ed) was the chief force in getting the campaign started in 1947 and was largely instrumental in bringing some of the Communists into it, but when he had them all aboard the Wallace train, he jumped off himself, leaving both Wallace and the Communists gliding swiftly, without guidance or hope, on the downhill track to oblivion. It was a brilliantly done piece of work.

And they all lived happily ever after:[19]

> The significant influence of Wall Street (meaning Morgan) both in the Ivy League and in Washington, in the period of sixty or more years following 1880, explains the constant interchange between the Ivy League and the Federal Government, an interchange which undoubtedly aroused a good deal of resentment in less-favored circles, who were more than satiated with the accents, tweeds, and High Episcopal Anglophilia of these peoples.

Since the time of Morgan, the Fabian influence in financial circles has increased and is doubtless also a factor in the persistent foundation support of radical projects. The judgments of foundations go far beyond encouraging constructive change or maintaining contact with the Left. They raise a question whether these sheltered funds are being used for or against our country.

J. P. Morgan's program for controlling public opinion by controlling the news media was not futile. Money will buy newspapers and magazines. It will hire skilled writers who will write what you want written. History can be managed by repetitive use of the same propaganda and with assurance of achieving similar effect. Sheila K. Johnson noted the pattern in a commentary piece puncturing the new euphoria about Red China.[20] "At least in part," she wrote, "fellow-travelling reports about China appear to be identical in motive and message to those emanating from the Soviet Union during the 1930s. There is the same yearning to see—even if it takes rose-colored spectacles and some selective blind spots—the perfect society leading, in turn, to the perfection of man himself." Mrs. Johnson noted the predilection of the Left to defend its own dictatorships, citing John Fairbank: "If their (the people of China) highly organized and moralistic efforts at regeneration are to be stigmatized as regimentation, then we must ask whether our own unregimented efforts are equally adequate to our far different needs and circumstances." Apparently Professor Fairbank not only approved the Communist dictatorship in China but was prepared to consider similar "regeneration" here. Merchants can buy scholars for every cause.

THE LURE OF TRADE

The question of who directs national policy might indeed be unimportant if the direction were good, if the country were launched on a course of vigorous progress and growth. When, however, the country is caught in a precipitous decline of internal discipline and order, of national strength, of international respect, of national security, and even of national solvency the people must ask, Who is setting the course? The ship of state is heading for the rocks.

Since President Roosevelt's recognition of the Soviet Union in 1933, U.S. policy has been conditioned to cooperation with the Soviet Union. There was a temporary revulsion during the Hitler-Stalin Pact, soon terminated by Hitler's attack on the Soviet Union.

The goals of the Soviet socialist state were clearly defined by Lenin and have been faithfully pursued by his successors. They encompass the destruction of freedom in all the world through the installation in all countries of a "dictatorship of the proletariat." This dictatorship would destroy all who oppose the regime. The state would allow no competing ties of family, friendship, religion, or idealism in society. Never before in the history of the world has any dictator undertaken such total control over the lives of his subjects. The most barbarous tribes of history allowed more individual freedom.

Before Roosevelt, the United States had recognized the barbaric quality of Leninism and had denied recognition to the Soviet state. But then the ambitions of wealth intervened. Even before recognition, American entrepreneurs worked with the Soviet government under mining and trade concessions. The Chase National Bank served as U.S. fiscal agent of the Soviet government. The Soviet economy was in desperate need of the technical skills and tools of the United States to rebuild the economy wrecked by Bolshevist incompetence. It seemed to Wall Street that vast opportunities for trade and profit lay in improved relations with the Soviet Union. Such trade, bankers argued, would stimulate American industry and lift the country out of the Depression.

In reality, as Dr. Antony C. Sutton of Stanford University has demonstrated,[21] Western technology and resources were rushed into the gap to save the Soviet Union from collapse. Singer, General Electric, Westinghouse, DuPont, Ford and RCA supplied know-how and materials and built factories. They reaped some profits but no harvest of trade.

In this performance, the bourgeois democracies fulfilled the prediction of Lenin:[22]

> On the basis of observations gained during my years of exile, the "cultured" class of the capitalist countries of Western Europe and America, i.e., the ruling classes, the financial aristocracy, and bourgeoisie and the idealistic democrats should be regarded as deaf-mute and treated accordingly. . . .
> The deaf-mute capitalist hoarders, their governments, the Chambers of Commerce, the federations of industries, bank groups, steel kings, rubber kings, aluminum kings and others will close their eyes to the above mentioned truths and so become blind, deaf, and dumb. They will grant us credits, which will fill the coffers of the Communist organizations in their countries while they improve our armaments industry by supplying all kinds of wares, which we shall need for future and successful attacks against our suppliers.

Soviet leaders wanted only the know-how and tools of the capitalists while they developed their own industrial skills. Trade was controlled by the Soviet state and was minimal. Some American firms profited from the sale of skills and tools but the United States continued to languish in the Depression. The Soviet Union took the skills and tools it bought so cheaply and forged ahead toward its goal of becoming a world superpower.

Franklin Roosevelt's rapprochement with the Soviet Union could not be justified by trade alone. It had to be compounded with idealistic pretensions and noble sentiment to make the Bolshevik alliance palatable to the American people. Embers of the League of Nations endeavor were still smoldering in the Democratic Party. They were fanned to proclaim that the policy of ostracism had been a failure, that peace and good will could be furthered by friendly intercourse, that all regimes change under the influence of their environment and that we could by our example restore the Soviet Union to the comity of our Atlantic civilization.

This was, of course, the grand illusion. Dictators expand with success and contract only with defeat. The illusion that the lion would be deterred by the innocence of the lamb was touching but irrational. And yet this illusion has been assiduously fostered in the United States since 1933 as an essential prop of our foreign policy. Forty years of failure have not dispelled the illusion—because our policymakers, influenced by Wall Street, have not deviated from their purpose of reaping the mythical harvest of Soviet trade.

From that rapprochement to the present day, Wall Street has never restrained its appetite. The Chase National Bank has been an effective trustee of the Soviet interest. The Soviet Union, with all its industrial achievements, is still technologically backward. It cannot put astronauts on the moon because it cannot make the tools and products required for the task. It still looks like a great market for U.S. merchants.

How does a bourgeois merchant regard the accomplishments of the Communist regimes? We get some insight from David Rockefeller's report on the visit of the Chase Manhattan group to Red China in 1973.[23] "One is impressed immediately by the sense of national harmony," he said. "From the loud patriotic music at the border onward, there is a very real and pervasive dedication to Chairman Mao and Maoist principles. Whatever the price of the Chinese Revolution, it has obviously succeeded not only in producing more efficient and dedicated administration, but also in fostering high morale and community of purpose." This is the kind of reporting which naive Americans were sending back from Hitler's Germany in 1935 and from "Potemkin villages" of the Soviet Union in 1943. Surely our American merchants have a better grasp of the real nature of these regimes. Don't they ever see the protests of Aleksandr Solzhenitsyn and Andrei G. Sakharov and the other Soviet scholars who have courageously criticized the cruel Communist tyranny imposed on a long-suffering people? If David Rockefeller does not know what happens to any Chinese who lacks a "pervasive dedication" to Chairman Mao, the people do.

Mr. Rockefeller knew that he was on a conducted tour and was seeing what his hosts wanted him to see. Yet he offered as his conclusion that "the social experiment in China under Chairman Mao's leadership is one of the most important and successful in human history." This recalls an earlier American characterization of Stalin's similar slaughter of the Russian peasants as "an experiment, noble in purpose. . . . " How indeed can Americans pass off as "an experiment" such barbaric slaughter of millions of peasants!

We must assume that Mr. Rockefeller knows better. These are the conventions of cultivating trade, and merchants are easily persuaded that trade promotes peace, not war. Because assent of the American people is necessary for such deals, they must be soothed into acquiescence with flattery of an implacable enemy.

There have, of course, been interludes of political confrontation. The Hitler-Stalin pact was a blow to American propaganda about "the experiment, noble in purpose" of socialism in the Soviet Union. When the U.S.S.R. attacked Finland in 1939, President Franklin Roosevelt issued a ringing condemnation of the Stalin regime, but he never ceased to number American Communists among his best friends. Full cooperation was restored when Hitler attacked Stalin.

To rationalize its policy of trading with the enemy, the United States government claims that trade promotes peace. As Dr. Sutton has shown, peace promotes trade but trade does not promote peace. This fallacy about trade enjoys a renewed popularity in the Nixon administration as the Soviet Union and Red China once again exploit the privileges of detente and build up their industries to support a new assault on the United States.

TERMS OF TRADE

The new terms of trade have taken an ominous turn. In the 1920s and 1930s, the financing of U.S. private ventures in the Soviet Union was done by private capital, judging and taking its own risks. In the 1970s, however, Congress has removed the barriers to federal financing of exports to Communist countries. Thus, the question of risk is removed from private calculations because the seller is immediately reimbursed by the United States. The judgment of risk therefore passes to a government bureaucrat who is committing public funds and who is ill-qualified to judge the risk and is subject to great private and political pressure to disregard the risk.

It is ironic that in the Agriculture and Consumer Protection Act of 1973, Congress extended to Communist countries the right, previously denied, to buy U. S. agricultural products under Public Law 480 at subsidized credit as low as two percent—this after the ill-advised sales to the Soviet Union in 1972, which sent U.S. consumer costs skyrocketing. When Senator Jesse Helms of North Carolina sought to amend the bill to require for these sales a rate of interest equal to the cost of money to the U.S. Treasury, his proposal was defeated. But why indeed should the United States make its costs of money available to foreign buyers? Why shouldn't other nations pay their own costs of money on the international market, at least when we have a product in world demand? Is U.S. credit so loose that it can be extended to all world transactions?

When bankers risk their own funds in foreign ventures, we can be confident that prudent judgment will be given to the enterprise. When government assumes that risk, the only interest of the banker is to increase sales volume. It is bad public policy which interposes the government as guarantor of such enterprise.

Congressman Ben B. Blackburn of Georgia noted the irrationality of U.S. financing of sales to the Soviet Union:[24]

At the same time, its own policy with regard to its gold reserves is based on Lenin's formula: "We must save the gold in the U.S.S.R." This formula adequately explains a strange paradox being presented to the world and the American people. A country rich in gold reserves, the Soviet Union, is seeking loans from a country, the United States, whose currency is under sustained attack and whose gold reserves are woefully inadequate. The authoritative studies about the Soviet gold reserves state the latter at over 20 billion. Inasmuch as there are no rules outstanding which can be presented for conversion to gold, it is fair to say that the Soviet gold reserves are free and clear. It is estimated that approximately $88 billion—U.S. dollars—are floating in the Eurodollar and other financial markets. What possible rationale can be put forth to support the concept that a gold-rich nation should be financed and subsidized by the nation which is experiencing a currency crisis and serious problems arising out of its inequilibrium in the balance of payments?

We could multiply examples of national policies set by our oligarchy of wealth against the interests and better judgment of the people. There is eloquent testimony that government in harmony with the people is good government. This was the belief of the Founding Fathers, who proclaimed that the people are sovereign and government is their servant. We do not have such government today.

THE POLICIES OF AMERICAN BUSINESS

Rule by an oligarchy of wealth is inimical to that principle of American government. It would, however, be in harmony with socialist government wherein, even in its democratic form, the planned society requires rule by an elite. A socialist system, requiring centralized direction from the top, is congenial to Wall Street. The American system of rule by the people is not.

American industry prefers to do business with one government in Washington rather than contend with the laws of fifty states. It is at least sympathetic to every national usurpation of local authority and often the advocate of such change. As in the recreation of a central bank, it knows that its aims can be achieved only through political action. Industry therefore maintains influential lobbyists in Washington to monitor Congress, and it places its young executives in policymaking positions in government through its influence with the ruling political party.

American industry is internationalist-minded. For decades, the Rockefeller Foundation, the Ford Foundation and associated representatives of Wall Street thinking have worked diligently to create in the American public a belief that international action—through the League of Nations, the United Nations, the World Council of Churches and other international instruments—was the key to peace and to outlawing of war. That American industry had a concurrent purpose of opening the world to its trade, products and services was of course true. There remains the serious question whether minds so internationally oriented can prudently be entrusted with the custody of our national interest. The recent experience of the United States argues with Oswald Spengler that the rich are ill-qualified to exercise political power:[25]

But the genuine prince and statesman wants to rule, and the genuine merchant wants only to be wealthy, and here the acquisitive economy divides to pursue aim and means separately. One may aim at booty for the sake of power, or at power for the sake of booty . . . .

He who is out for purely economic advantages—as the Carthaginians were in Roman times and, in a far greater degree still, the Americans in ours—is correspondingly incapable of purely political thinking. In the decisions of high politics he is ever deceived and made a tool of, as the case of Wilson shows—especially when the absence of statesmanlike instinct leaves a chair vacant for moral sentiments.

The money power has destroyed the integrity which once resided in government. Through its manipulation of both political parties, it has made government a private fief, insensitive to the people and to the public interest. It has aborted the vision of an America, free and honest.

The consequence of elite rule is minority government. Though the forms of popular rule remain, they are empty. The people vote, but only for the candidates put before them. As in the authoritarian states, access of candidates to the ballot is carefully controlled—but here, in two political parties instead of one, and by financial manipulation instead of by party monopoly.

It may be argued that someone must exercise political power; and that the financial and legal elites represented in our great banks, foundations, law firms and universities are best qualified to direct the country. It can indeed be argued that in terms of intelligence and perfected skills, Wall Street should run the country.

That argument neglects the fundamental character of wealth and the severe restraint which it imposes on human intellect. Homer Lea, that perceptive student of history, wrote:[26]

Commercial acumen is necessary to accumulate wealth, but that capacity possesses not the slightest ability to prevent the destruction of its edifices or accumulations. Nay, more, wealth so benumbs man's ability to comprehend its limitations that, unless both combatants are simultaneously suffering from the same green sickness of this misconception, it is self-destructive and its riches only add to the splendor of its sarcophagus.

After surveying the ruins of the Roman Empire, Edward Gibbon concluded that the condition most conducive to the development of military genius is one of honorable poverty. It would be difficult to find any human talent for which the most favorable condition of development is the possession of wealth—unless that talent could be the amassing of more wealth. But even here, the search for excellence fails. When Byzantium was threatened by the Ottoman Turks in the middle of the fifteenth century, the wealthy Byzantine merchants refused to provide the Emperor Constantine with funds to pay for Hungarian allies to join in the defense. When Byzantium fell, the merchants were killed and their families were sold into slavery. Vision is not a characteristic of wealth.

Chapter 10

INDUSTRY—
THE RUNAWAY MACHINE

AMERICAN INDUSTRY is acclaimed as a miracle of organized human activity. In researching the secrets of nature and adapting new knowledge to human service, in the development of new compounds, artifacts and methods to serve social needs, U.S. industry has been pioneering, aggressive, resourceful and constructive. In adapting business organization to changing needs and opportunities, in distributing rewards to workers, in maintaining worker opportunity and morale, American business has been notably successful. But in understanding the political foundations of its phenomenal growth, industry has been backward.

Perhaps Peter Drucker was voicing the general illusion of industrialists when he wrote: "An industrial society is beyond capitalism and socialism. It is a new society transcending both."[1]

His vision of a superior society in which government and industry collaborate to achieve higher standards of efficiency and productivity is the same wishful thinking that inspires Fabians to promote the "mixed economy."

Drucker argues that the "industrial society requires a very strong and powerful central government." He rationalizes what is happening because he does not understand the real interplay of politics and industry. As

Spengler warned, the owners of industry seek new sources of wealth in controlling government, but they overreach themselves. Or, as Earl Browder contemporaneously described the Drucker scene:[2]

> State capitalism, in substance if not in formal aspects, has progressed farther in America than in Britain under the Labor Government. . . . The actual, substantial, concentration of the guiding reins of the national economy in governmental hands is probably on a higher level in the U.S.A.

It is true in a different sense that government must be powerful. It must be independent of and must stand above all the economic blocs of society. Its police powers must cover all groups in maintaining a sound rule of law for the whole society. But it must not become the tool or servant or partner of any of these groups. Government must stand above banking and industry and labor if it is to administer a rule of law fair to all and serving the common good. This, unhappily, is not the position government occupies today nor toward which it is tending. Drucker's machine has burst the bonds of common sense and reasoned decision-making which politics should represent, and is running wild.

At the close of World War II, I was serving on General Douglas MacArthur's GHQ staff in Manila. After atomic bombs had been dropped on Hiroshima and Nagasaki, a small group of colonels gathered in the Admiral Apartments on Dewey Boulevard for informal discussion about the shape of the coming peace. One of the conferees was Colonel R. C. Kramer, a New York banker and financial adviser to General MacArthur.

Colonel Kramer remarked that in the postwar world, the United States would have to give dollars away in order to enable the rest of the world to buy our products. "Why," I asked, "would the United States do anything like that? We would be producing goods just to give them away. It would be lifting ourselves by our own bootstraps." Kramer answered, "Because we have built up a great industry with vast productive power. If we don't keep it busy, we shall have widespread unemployment, and our political leaders cannot allow that to happen. Our allies are prostrate, devastated by war. We must extend credit to them to rebuild their industries; and, in order to avoid building up excessive debt as we did after World War I, we must give them the money."

I remained skeptical. But I lived to realize that Colonel Kramer had given us an early explanation of the aid programs that Secretary of State George C. Marshall would launch five years later.

The war was hardly over when Congress declared a new national goal of "full employment." Full employment had long been the hope of all politicians but it had never before been considered a responsibility of the national government. How does a nation achieve full employment? This new goal provided an excuse for manipulating the money supply and for subsidizing every venture that promised to increase employment. It opened new vistas of national intervention in the economy and industrial visions of subsidy from the national treasury.

90

Through two wars, the people had come to expect high rates of taxation. Special measures can always be justified for national survival. If these rates could be extended into the postwar period to pay for rebuilding the economies of our allies and former enemies, they could be further extended to develop underdeveloped nations, thereby providing a continuous, endless subsidy for American business. This was the kind of exploitation of the people's taxes on which industry and organized labor could collaborate. Thus, they supported foreign aid appropriations, not for charity but for selfishness.

"Full employment" served to define so admirably the concurrence of interest of American business, organized labor and the political parties that it has gone largely unchallenged as an American goal. Yet, it is a turning to socialism; it proclaims that government will provide for all the people's needs. It is a repudiation of American politics, which once proclaimed that the works and production of industry are no responsibility of the national government except for the regulation of interstate and foreign commerce.

The full employment goal is bleeding America to death. It is a grossly irrational concept, created to feed our industrial machine blindly instead of programming that machine to serve the people intelligently. The concept of full employment as a responsibility of the national government is indefensible. It is a cause of national decline and demoralization.

Consider that concept in its international significance. Adam Smith pointed out that the only purpose of exports is to pay for imports. Imports make a contribution to the comfort or well-being of the people or to the needs of industry. We must export products to pay for those imports.

But full employment advances a conflicting notion. It asserts that we must export simply to keep busy, that we must provide outlets for our industrial machine. Production for no other purpose than to keep busy exhausts our national resources and wastes the labor of our people. It is a form of self-enslavement. It contributes nothing to the national well-being because it takes from the people the wealth they have produced.

The aim of war was often to enslave the enemy and use its people to perform works for the conquerors. Full employment reverses that relationship, harnessing the victorious people to produce goods for the vanquished. Americans are the new slaves of a runaway industrial machine. They have been deceived with unctuous statements that their generosity has saved civilization or with threats that the increasing income gap between "have" and "have not" nations may engulf the world in new class warfare.

It is not without cause that the poverty lobbies decry our massive national subsidies of American industry and demand a national program to eliminate poverty. It is not without self-interest that American industry supports national poverty programs to placate its critics.

Since World War II, the United States Congress has engaged in a frenzy of dispensing dollars all over the world: to the United Nations and its subsidiary agencies, including the World Bank; to rebuild the countries of friend and enemy alike. With a Federal Reserve System to cover every deficit, with every dollar given away regarded as an order for the purchase of U.S. goods and services and therefore a contribution to full employment, Congress seemed smug in its virtue. Confiscation of workers' earnings through high taxes *and* inflation seemed to be necessary to keep the machine running.

The United States has traveled far down this road, which leads to bankruptcy. As Henry Hazlitt has noted:

> Our politicians, and most of our commentators, seem to be engaged in an open conspiracy not to pay the national debt—certainly not in dollars of the same purchasing power that were borrowed, and apparently not even in dollars of the present purchasing power. . . .
>
> If someone were to propose that the debt be paid off at an annual rate of $1 billion a year, he would have to face the fact that it would take 289 years, or nearly three centuries, to get rid of it.

This rich country can and should pay off the debt at a much higher rate, say $20 billion per year. As when our young Republic paid off the debts of the Continental Congress, the evidence of fiscal integrity would more than compensate for the decreased economic intervention of the government in the marketplace.

Unhappily, the government has not yet faced up to its fiscal responsibilities but continues on its inflationary course, like a drug addict.

The monetary adjustment of 1971, long forecast by our allies unless the United States put its house in order, was a measure to avoid collapse. Price and wage controls invoked by the Nixon Administration—for the first time in a period of peace and surplus, not of war and shortage—showed how badly our economic machine had been damaged by the operating policies of big government.

A Congress incapable of fiscal discipline seeks remedies not in correcting its error but in grasping for more power. Instead of ending its deficits, it tries to restrain the effects of its profligacy by enacting price and wage controls. "Keynesian economics" and "full employment" represent harmful governmental tinkering with our economy to provide special benefits for favored blocs of our society. The damage they cause compels other measures to ward off the popular wrath. Our two political parties march steadily down the road to state control of all economic activity, known popularly as socialism.

It is a measure of the sterile quality of our intellectual leadership that these prescriptions go largely unchallenged, even by Americans who realize that freedom is a political condition that citizens cannot enjoy in the omnipotent state. How can economists and political philosophers embrace the thesis that we should give away the products of industry in order to keep industry busy? Are they incapable of conceiving a more rational design for our political system?

The very concept of a central government with full control of the economy hamstrings the economy and causes unemployment. This has been the record in England and in other countries where the "planned economy" of socialism has been adopted. Government intervention is hostile to individual freedom and responsibility—the very heart of creativity and productivity.

GOVERNMENT BY SUBSIDY

Government subsidy of private production, whether in agriculture or in industry, interferes with private responsibility under law, rewards weakness and incompetence, encourages wasteful production, and corrupts both politics and business. In the early years of the Republic, the protective tariff was an issue. By increasing import duties on selected items, the national government could raise needed revenues and at the same time protect domestic industries from foreign competition. Today, international bankers and allied intellectuals regard the protective tariff as a barrier to trade, but they strongly endorse the direct subsidy of U.S. industry by giving dollars to potential customers. In their boldness, they now claim a percentage of the worker's pay—taxes—for this purpose.

The reckless export of U.S. dollars to foreign lands, even when foreign financial markets are glutted and the dollar is in decline, illustrates the gross irresponsibility of the national government in both the Congressional and Executive branches. Congressman H. R. Gross has reported the quality of our national policy:[3]

> With the American dollar plunging to new lows in value on the international money markets, and with deficit spending still feeding the cancer of inflation in this country, the mindless spenders in the White House and in Congress have spawned another new foreign handout program.
>
> Approved by the House of Representatives last week was a bill to launch an organization to be known as the United Nations Environment Fund with $40 million, or 40 percent of the total $100 million deemed necessary to get this outfit started, to be filched from the pockets of U.S. taxpayers.
>
> In opposing the bill and in debate on the House floor, I asked the sponsors who it was and on what basis it had been determined that the United States should put up $40 million of the total $100 million fund when there are 130 other members of the United Nations.
>
> The answer came back loud and clear. *President Nixon is the promoter of this latest world boondoggle and he (Nixon) thought a "fair share" for the U.S. should be 40 percent or $40 million!*
>
> Incidentally, headquarters of this new Nixon-United Nations creation will be in Nairobi, Kenya, which assures our $40 million will be shipped abroad and spent. There is no evidence that Kenya or any Communist country will put up a dime for this so-called environment fund.
>
> To the question of how many other foreign governments have initiated action as has the U.S. Congress to contribute to the fund, the sponsors of the bill could name not one. The bill also provided that the $40 million "may be used upon such terms and conditions as the President may specify"— another unholy delegation of power to the President by an irresponsible Congress which turns handsprings in its zeal to authorize spending and then bellyaches if he doesn't spend it as they think he should.

All amendments to cut the $40 million and eliminate the delegated power to the President were defeated and it was approved by a vote of 266 to 123. Thus it is that the American public continues to be raped in Washington.

Our industrial machine must be brought under control. Without subsidy of either foreign or domestic sales, industry must produce for our domestic market. The demand of our people would be the measure of production. Our entrepreneurs could compete in foreign markets, using and risking their own capital in such ventures.

Congress is the lawmaker. It sets the rules under which industry performs. Its proper role is establishing relationships with foreign countries, regulating the performance of international corporations in the United States and facilitating useful interstate and foreign commerce. Through law, it should create a framework congenial to private initiative and freedom of action.

The interventions of Congress, serving the money power, have started our industrial machine on a runaway course. It may seem that reversing the course will be difficult. It may indeed take time, but until a change of *direction* is made, the country is headed for the fiscal rocks. However painful a program of terminating subsidies, dismantling the federal welfare bureaucracy and replacing government regulation with law may be, that course is the only alternative to fiscal disaster.

Chapter 11

THE RULE OF LAW

IT IS A CHERISHED American aphorism that we are ruled by law, not men. That is not, of course, true. But it represents a concept of government that Americans once regarded as a cornerstone of their political system.

The rule of law means to Americans that they have inherited tested rules of behavior from the English common law and that their elected representatives have supplemented these rules with other legislation for the governance of our society. Laws should be made as clear and unambiguous as possible. Nevertheless, since all of the possible applications of law cannot be anticipated, disputes will arise and courts must be constituted to settle the disputes. To be ruled by law is to live under a system in which the law is objectively conceived and impartially administered for the benefit of all the people.

Alternatively, rule by men is a system in which the judgment of citizen action or inaction is made by political leaders or their servile judges according to the current political estimate of the interest of the society. Thus, in the Soviet Union as in other Communist societies, law is a tool for controlling the people and protecting the state. If it is in any degree lacking in application to a particular case, the prosecutor and the judge supply that deficiency by citing the interest of the state.

Because Americans have long lived by the rule of law, they have come to believe that all law has the objectivity and impartiality illustrated in their own history. They forget that the rule of men is also enforced through a system of law. The differences are often not discernible in specific law but become apparant only in the operation of the system.

The rule of law has certain basic requirements which must be fulfilled.

1. Laws must be enacted by the people's representatives. The people are not subject to any law not so enacted.

2. The courts must apply the laws to cases *in accordance with the intent of the legislators.* This rule follows from the basic premise that the people are not subject to any law not enacted by their chosen legislators. It applies also to constitutional law. The Constitution can mean only what its originators and amenders intended. No court, President or Congress can legally give it other meaning.

3. The Executive must administer the law impartially, without fear or favor for any person or interest.

These rules were understood and respected in the early years of the Republic. It was not always easy. Some Presidents thought that winning public office conferred a right to be partisan, to favor friends, and to harass the opposition. But in general, the rule of law was the respected rule of American government.

In the decision of the Supreme Court in the Dred Scott case, Chief Justice Taney wrote that the Constitution ". . . speaks not only in the same words, but with the same meaning and intent with which it spoke when it came from the hands of its framers, and was voted upon and adopted by the people of the United States. Any other rule of construction would abrogate the judicial character of this court, and make it the mere reflex of the popular opinion or passion of the day."

It is a common role of the self-righteous today to condemn the Dred Scott decision as a failure of the Court to recognize the humanity of Dred Scott. These critics argue tacitly that the Court should have usurped the legislative function in a good cause. The Court had a better understanding of its own role and of the demands of justice.

The humanity of Dred Scott was not in question. He was a slave and slavery was an institution that the states had the authority to continue or to terminate. The Constitution had not made slavery a federal question and the Court had no authority to do so.

Chief Justice Taney's reference to abrogating the judicial character of the Court and making it the mere reflex of the popular passion of the day aptly describes the degeneration of the Court in this century in its ambition to serve as a superior legislative chamber. The turmoil over civil rights and school busing in recent decades reflects the degree to which we are subjected to the rule of men. The conversion of our legal system from the rule of law to the rule of men has been made by the very Court constituted to preserve the rule of law.

In the course of the nineteenth century, the meaning of the Constitution, the proper relationship of the states and the central government and the functions of the branches of the federal government had been well established. The law was widely understood and respected.

> It has repeatedly been held that no provisions of the federal Constitution and none of the amendments added to that instrument were intended or designed to interfere with the police powers of the various states.[1]
>
> In 1833, Chief Justice Marshall made it clear that the Bill of Rights did not apply to the states but only to the national government.[2]

The Supreme Court interpreted the law according to the intent of the legislators and rejected appeals to give new meaning to the Constitution or to statutes:[3]

> We are convinced that no such results were intended by the Congress which proposed these amendments, nor by the legislatures of the states which ratified them.

There has been a trend of recent scholarship to represent *Plessy* v. *Ferguson* simply as an erroneous decision of the Supreme Court which was later corrected by *Brown* v. *Board of Education* in 1954. That view misrepresents the fact. As early as 1849, a Massachusetts court, speaking through its chief justice,[4] held that the state did not deprive complainants of any right in providing separate but equal school facilities for Negro children. After passage of the Fourteenth Amendment, litigants challenged separate schools in Ohio, Indiana, New York, California, Nevada, Kansas, North Carolina, Missouri and Arizona, and in all cases, the highest courts of these states held that segregation did not deprive any person of the equal protection of the law, within the meaning of the Amendment. In 1927, the Supreme Court of the United States reviewed the law and held unanimously that the segregation of white and colored children in public schools was within the discretion of the state and did not contravene the Fourteenth Amendment.

These decisions were based upon well-established and widely accepted definitions of the distinct and separate powers of the federal government and of the states. In particular, the police powers lay in the province of the states and were outside the purview of the federal government (including the Supreme Court), except in narrowly defined constitutional areas. As Chief Justice Waite wrote in 1874, "Our province is to decide what the law is, not to declare what it should be."[5] Dred Scott was indeed the established "law of the land" and slavery was ended by changing the law, not by interpreting it.

The judicial decisions of the Supreme Court during the first quarter of the twentieth century were so consistent and clear as to leave no doubt about the meaning of the law. It seems to be more than a coincidence that the beginnings of judicial usurpation coincided with the growth of American Fabianism and its accession to power in the Roosevelt administration. The development of activist programs to end the constitutional government and institute a centralized, socialist order had made great progress in intellectual, legal and elitist political circles before disciples of the new order were appointed to the Court.

It took a judicial revolution to overthrow the established law. The doctrine of *stare decisis* had to be jettisoned. That doctrine has been defined:

> Especially in case of doubt, the solemn, deliberate, well considered, and long-settled decisions of the judiciary, and the quiet assent of the people to an unbroken and unvarying practice, ought to conclude the action of the courts in favor of a principle so established, even when the individual opinion of the judge would be different were the question *res integra.*[6]

How could a Court that showed such disregard of prior decisions expect later Courts to have any regard for its decisions? As Justice Sutherland wrote:[7]

> The judicial function is that of interpretation; it does not include the power of amendment under the guise of interpretation. To miss the point of difference between the two is to miss all that the phrase "supreme law of the land" stands for and to convert what was intended as inescapable and enduring mandates into mere moral reflections.

No doubt the Fabians were confident that their changes would be irreversible.

The Supreme Court needed some rationale for its program of disestablishing state power and centralizing authority in Washington. It chose the Fourteenth Amendment as the vehicle, disregarding the settled adjudication of that law as a limitation on state action against the liberated slaves and giving the Amendment broad general significance never contemplated by those who passed and ratified it. Gradually at first, boldly in due time, the Court declared that the Fourteenth Amendment extended to the states the limitations placed on the federal government in the Bill of Rights. There was not a scintilla of legal evidence to support the Court; but that did not deter it.

STRETCHING THE FOURTEENTH AMENDMENT

The usurpation of the legislative role was subtle and gradual and filled with so-called high-mindedness. It had been settled constitutional law up to 1925 that the Fourteenth Amendment imposed no restrictions on the states regarding freedom of speech, as the First Amendment imposed on the Congress. In that year, in *Gitlow* v. *the People of the State of New York,* the Supreme Court, while upholding the conviction of Gitlow for criminal anarchy on other grounds, declared that the due-process clause of the Fourteenth Amendment protects the First Amendment rights of freedom of speech and press from impairment by the states. Without any citation of authority, the Court merely assumed that the settled law was now changed. The Court thought that a rule salutary for Congress would be salutary for the states. *The authors of the First Amendment had not thought so, and with good reason.*

This gratuitous statement of new policy, neither relevant to nor required by the case at issue, reflected the growing power of the press as an instrument of the ruling oligarchy. State censorship of pornographic films and publications was being challenged by the growing hedonism of the social elites. Protected by the Constitution against federal censorship, the publicists mounted propaganda campaigns to persuade the public that no government should hold power over a "free press." They claimed the protection of the Fourteenth Amendment.

In 1944, Justice Owen Roberts spoke bitterly in a dissenting opinion about the reversal of settled law to which a majority of his colleagues subscribed in *Smith* v. *Allwright:* "The reason for my concern is that the instant decision, overruling that announced about nine years ago, tends to bring adjudications of this tribunal into the same class as a restricted railway ticket, good for this train and day only. . . . It is regrettable that in an era marked by doubt and confusion . . . this court . . . should now itself become the breeder of fresh doubt and confusion in the public mind as to the stability of our institutions."[8] But Owen Roberts had himself been a champion of judicial revision of the law on previous occasions. He complained only when the Court disagreed with his judgment of expediency. This is the end to which all such judgments of the judicial role must come. The rule of law is dead. Only the question of expediency remains.

In preparing his farewell address, President George Washington surveyed the first eight years of governmental experience under the Constitution. The dangers to good government—twisting and distorting the law to serve special prejudice or interest—were already apparent. Thus he warned: ". . . let there be no change by usurpation: for though this, in one instance, may be the instrument of good, it is the customary weapon by which free governments are destroyed. The precedent must always greatly overbalance in permanent evil, any partial or transient benefit which the use can at any time yield." He was speaking to the Justices of the Supreme Court in the Gitlow case, but the Justices were not listening.

It is the misfortune of democracy that men of great vision and integrity have charted a secure course for the nation, but lesser men succeed to the leadership, abandon high principle, collaborate with error, and subvert the public interest. The usurpation of powers by the Supreme Court passed with little public comment or censure until the *Brown* decision of 1954. In that case, the Warren Court reversed the settled law on segregation defined in 1896 in *Plessy* v. *Ferguson.* As recently as 1950 the Vinson Court had refused in *Sweatt* v. *Painter et al.* to consider a challenge to *Plessy* v. *Ferguson* in requiring equal facilities for a black law student attending the University of Texas.

In the *Brown* case, attorneys for the appellants deliberately falsified evidence presented to the Court. The Solicitor General of the United States, whose function is to defend the law, joined the plaintiffs in asking the Court to change the law. The Attorney General of Kansas chose not to defend the law until the Court questioned his absence; and he then testified that a decree barring segregation would probably not be serious to Kansas. He conceded to Justice Burton that "within 75 years the social and economic conditions and the personal relations of the nation may have changed so that what may have been a valid interpretation . . . 75 years ago would not be a valid interpretation of them (*sic*) constitutionally today."[9] There seemed to be a conspiracy of the defense not to defend the law.

The Court acted not as a court but as a legislative body. Sociologists were summoned to testify about the need for a change in the law, as would be proper in a legislative hearing. The Court argued that times had changed so as to warrant a change of law by edict. The Court undertook not merely to announce a new ruling but to use the federal courts as administrators of the application of the new law to the schools of the country.

As Rexford Guy Tugwell noted:[10]

> . . . the ambiguity may often have been intended. A rule, comprehensive but vague, giving only general direction to public policy and requiring return whenever application was in question would serve to keep the Court in the thick of things. Thus the Court would continue to be an active essential force whenever new initiatives were indicated.

In the end, the Court made a legislative decision, not a judicial decision.[11]

> We come then to the question presented: Does segregation of children in public schools solely on the basis of race, even though the physical facilities and other "tangible" factors may be equal, deprive the children of the minority group of equal educational opportunities? *We believe that it does.*

But the question and answer of the Court were not relevant to the legal issue because the federal government had no constitutional mandate to bestow equal educational opportunity. The question of law raised by the case was this:[12]

> Does segregation of children in public schools solely on the basis of race, even though the physical facilities and other "tangible" factors may be equal, *deprive the children of either group of the equal protection of the laws?*

This question the Court neither asked nor answered.

The question of segregation has been a thorny problem for political parties. Since Franklin Roosevelt's courting of the black vote in the 1930s, both political parties have affected public concern for civil rights. But both parties had maintained an armistice about legal segregation. In the District of Columbia, in schools controlled by the Congress, segregation had been maintained. The sweeping Roosevelt congressional majorities made no attempt to end segregation in the one jurisdiction where they had unquestioned authority to do so.

In joining the appellants in *Brown*, President Eisenhower may have planned to gain some Negro good will by endorsing a cause which the

Court might by every precedent be expected to reject. Surely it was not seemly for the President to ask the Supreme Court to make a change of law which he had never recommended to the Congress. Surely he knew that the proper course for a President persuaded of the merits of desegregation was to send a message to Congress asking it to enact a constitutional amendment ending legal segregation.

The readiness of the President and the Congress to condone—even welcome—the usurpation of their responsibilities by the Supreme Court reflected the decline of representative government. Elected officials of both political parties were collaborating in revolutionary changes in government, made by judicial edict, against the will of the people and without due process of law.

United States politics was not facing up to critical issues festering in society. Both parties seemed concerned only to retain power with the least possible alteration of the status quo. The Democratic Party had courted the black vote with a series of executive favors and promotions for black Democrats, and the Republican Party had followed a similar course in office; but both parties feared to stir the debate which a constitutional amendment would provoke.

In *Brown,* the Court decided that the international prestige and standing of the United States required it to terminate legal segregation. This was another legislative consideration that might have moved the political parties but had failed to do so. Congress was content to have legislative power exercised by a Court insulated from the public displeasure. The Court was doing what American socialists had predicted it would do when their disciples sat on the bench.

Journalist Arthur Krock noted the transformation of our government:[13]

In the transformation of the American system toward a mass democracy and a neosocialist welfare state, new interpretations, especially of the Fourteenth Amendment, by the Supreme Court have made the largest and most essential contributions to these objectives. The decisions, often by a close division among the Justices, that are landmarks in the transformation began in 1954. In the so-called "public schools" decision, the Court assumed the function (which the Constitution delegates to the executive and legislative branches) of making public policy whenever in the judgment of the Court, the public interest requires new policies and the other two federal branches have not supplied them.

Rexford G. Tugwell noted the limitations on legislation by a judicial body:[14]

But the Court's aloof commands were quite differently made than those the Congress might have issued. The latter would have been statutes; they would have been deliberated about at some length; and the enforcement costs and difficulties would have been taken into account. The Court was above such considerations. That it was not an appropriate legislative body was evident.

Professor von Mises had earlier identified the new standard of law adopted by the Warren Court:[15]

Primacy of the law means that no judge or officeholder has the right to interfere with any individual's affairs or conditions unless a valid law requires or empowers him to do so. *Nulla poena sine lege,* no punishment unless ordered by a law. It is precisely the inability of the Nazis to understand the importance of this fundamental principle that qualifies them as anti-democratic. In the totalitarian system of Hitler Germany the judge has to come to his decision according to *das gesunde Volksempfinden,* i.e., in accordance with the sound feelings of the people. As the judge himself has to decide what the sound feelings of the people are, he is sovereign on his bench like the chieftain of a primitive tribe.

It is in fact an awkward thing if a scoundrel evades punishment because a law is defective. But it is the minor evil when compared with judicial arbitrariness.

The judicial activism of the Warren Court must in considerable measure be attributed to the executive experience and lack of judicial experience of the Chief Justice. The first made him amenable to political rather than judicial decision-making and the second made him a willing ally of the experienced justices Black, Douglas and Frankfurter.

As Tugwell wrote in that same article,[16] "In the opinion of legal scholars, Warren's appointment was an affront to the profession. He would not have been eligible, it was said, for a professorship in any respectable law school."

The Chief Justice brought administrative, not judicial, expertise to the Court. Black, Douglas and Frankfurter were already engaged in a program of changing our Constitution by interpretation. They needed only the support of the Chief Justice to accelerate their revolution.

The *Brown* decision, reversing settled law, was bitterly opposed by citizens who considered it a lawless usurpation of legislative authority. They were prepared to submit to laws enacted by their duly elected representatives but not to endure the arbitrary tyranny of appointed judges. But that decision was only the beginning of a course of social engineering upon which the Court had embarked.

To assert that every child has a right to attend the nearest public school, instead of being bused to some distant school to maintain segregated schooling, made sense to Americans living outside the segregated systems. The rule seemed fair, even though the method of adopting it was unlawful. However, that rule did not define the Court's ultimate aim.

As time passed and housing patterns left many schools of a system segregated in fact, the Court conceived a duty to force racial mixing by doing what it had declared in *Brown* to be unlawful—busing children away from their local schools to achieve a politically desirable standard of race relations. The Court professed to be removing the vestiges of de jure segregation—a bald-faced misrepresentation. It was readily demonstrable that, because de jure segregation had removed educational pressures on housing patterns, those patterns were more mixed in the South than in the North.

It became apparent that the Court was taking seriously its role as super-legislature. Presidential commissions had warned the country about the danger of building two societies, one white and one black. The Court conceived for itself a duty to prevent that development by forced integration of the public schools. Education would, the justices believed, bring the two races together in harmony.

The introduction of compulsion into race relations destroyed the essential basis of racial harmony. Schools became youthful battlegrounds. Discipline was undermined by racial conflict. Educational quality deteriorated sharply in the affected schools. To give every child a right to attend his local public school, or to attend another public school of his choice when that choice does not transgress the rights of other students, is a rational and enforceable rule of law. But to assert that the state or any individual has a right to compel the attendance of children at other public schools not of their choice because public officials, educators or judges consider some undefined degree of racial mixing essential to educational excellence is not a rule of law at all. It is sheer tyranny and an abuse of the disposition of our people to obey the law.

Our people have not rebelled against this decree of the Supreme Court only because it has not been enforced nationally. The federal courts, in cooperation with the federal executive, have applied the law not as a general rule but only sporadically outside the South. They have worked on a case-by-case basis, taking care to limit resentment to a school district, county or city so that a general political rebellion would not be provoked.

This is the lot to which the rule of law has been reduced in our country: The law applies not to all the people but only to those who may be selected by the Court for its attention.

DEFENDING THE CRIMINAL

From its venture into education, the Warren Court extended its invasion of the police power by asserting jurisdiction over the criminal law of the states. In a series of decisions crippling law enforcement in the states and radically altering the established rules in both state and federal courts, the Warren Court inaugurated new rules handicapping the prosecution of criminals which became a major factor in causing the ensuing crime wave. After the retirement of Chief Justice Warren, the Court climaxed its calamitous intervention in the state's police powers by curbing the death penalty. The logical consequence of its unprincipled course seemed to have been reached.

The Court was confirming the vision of William Penn: "If men are not ruled by God, they will be ruled-by tyrants." The fundamental question about law is whether God is the source of law, as the Founding Fathers believed, or the state is the sole source.

The Reverend Rousas John Rushdoony has pointed out that when God is the source of law, all legislators, administrators and judges act *minis-*

103

terially, enacting and enforcing laws to support the mandate of Divine Providence. But when the state, unlimited by divine guidance, is the source of the law, the state becomes the god of that society:[17]

> The difference is fundamental. Where law is ministerial, the premise is that a higher law exists, and that it is the duty of man and the state to know and apply that higher law. Man cannot create law, because he is under law, and in every area of his life, physical, biological, economic, moral, and political, moves under law that has its origin beyond man and the natural order. Law is thus transcendental in its source and immanent in its application. It requires study, application, and amendment so that the truth of God's law can be better approximated.

When, however, the state is the ultimate authority, this influence does not exist:[18]

> The state then, instead of passing laws to conform with ultimate, transcendental law, creates law. There is no possible appeal against the legislative state if its premise is true. Right is what the state does . . . It is for this reason that, in Marxist societies, no right of dissent from the state is allowed. Former prisoners of the Marxist states have reported that the premise of all questioning on arrest is to gain or force a confession of guilt, because the state cannot be questioned even as to the legitimacy of its use of the power to arrest. Where the state is the ultimate order, then the state not only acts as the umbrella, containing all things under itself, but also as the infallible word in all things.

It is clear that in the first 150 years of our constitutional existence the Congress, the Executive and the Supreme Court acted ministerially. The Court speaking through Justice David J. Brewer in 1892 *(The Church of the Holy Trinity* v. *United States)* explained at length the basis for its conclusion that "this is a religious people" and "this is a Christian nation."[19] The conduct of our public officials showed a respect for Divine Providence.

In the past 56 years, the idea of the omnipotent state which made such headway in Russia, Italy and Germany and was then extended to Mainland China and other countries, has made inroads in the United States. The action of the Warren Court in striking down the use of an invocation to open the school day in New York State public schools was symptomatic of the new mentality.

American citizens who cherish our long-established tradition of honesty and responsibility in personal behavior and of honesty and the rule of law in public affairs must come to realize that the Supreme Court is today the most deadly enemy of these cherished ideals. The Court is tearing down the tried and proven structure of our free and prosperous society. As Arthur Krock wrote:[20]

> By taking over unilateral power to fix or alter public policies, by thereby making plain to Congress and the state legislatures what social and political statutes it would approve and what it would invalidate, the Supreme Court, headed by Chief Justice Warren, has become the prime force in the transformation of the American system from a federal union to a mass democracy, from the careful decentralization of power in the Constitution to concentra-

tion in Washington, and from a tripartite federal government to a government in which the Court is the managing director.

It is indeed shocking that these revolutionary changes in government have been screened from public recognition by high-sounding phrases about compassion for the poor and lowly and claptrap about making the Constitution work. Propagandists for the omnipotent state have used our educational institutions to plead speciously for their cause. Consider these excerpts from a popular political science textbook which ignores the unlawful quality of the Court decisions and the serious damage to our political order while it offers students a superficial rationalization of the process:[21]

> A country with a population approaching the two hundred million mark and with problems so complex that they were hardly dreamed of a decade or so ago could not possibly handle its affairs on the basis of the Constitution of 1787 alone.
> Because the process of formal amendment is cumbersome and time-consuming, other methods of developing the Constitution have been heavily relied upon. It is through these less formal devices that the Constitution has been kept reasonably abreast of the times. And it is through these latter devices that the Constitution of the United States has been flexible rather than rigid.
> . . . the formal amendment process has been bypassed in many instances. Necessary changes have been brought about by judicial interpretation, by congressional statute, and by custom and usage when it appeared that an amendment to the Constitution would be difficult to accomplish. The Constitution is less rigid than many commentators have maintained, but it must in all fairness be admitted that the amending process is such that it can claim little credit for keeping the United States abreast of changing conditions.
> In the last century or so, the decisions and interpretations of the Supreme Court have been a major factor in keeping the Constitution reasonably abreast of the times, far exceeding formal amendments in their influence.
> At times the Supreme Court has been subject to severe criticism because it has relied on precedent, and it is perhaps fair to say that such a course has at times made progress difficult.
> The interpretation of the developing Constitution has permitted the shifting of responsibility in innumerable areas from the states to the national government.
> The implied power doctrine makes it possible for Congress to act on local matters if these affect national policies. It is a foolish fallacy for anyone to think that a unitary system would suddenly change the nature of the political problems in the United States. The same types of problems would remain, and success in the political process would still depend upon compromising group and regional interests.
> The formal constitutional amendment process has played a relatively minor role in the centralization trend.

Indeed formal amendments did not change the Constitution, for the people would never have approved the changes wrought by the Court.

This apologia by political science elites for increasing authoritarianism in government is a defense of their own bad judgment:[22]

The "socially desirable objectives" are no longer "received" from society itself (as in the theory they should be): rather they are conceived in committee and imposed on society. The humanism ceases to evolve from below, and is directed from above; it remains scientific and becomes inhuman. This is the psychological dynamism of the system: the state tends to lose its character of servant, and assume that of master.

The impatience of the elites with all obstacles to the sway of their beneficent rule was expressed by Robert M. Hutchins in his syndicated column:[23]

. . . the states are a principal cause of our difficulties in coping with education, political parties and cities . . . Their chief function today is to handicap efforts to establish national standards and policies . . . The legislature does not legislate in any real sense of the word. The legislative program is the President's. And the task of keeping the Constitution up to date has been turned over to the Supreme Court.

This changing view of law represents the most critical damage to American government. It is the fountainhead from which other deterioration of society flows. The claims that judges have an authority and duty to adapt the law to changing political, economic or cultural conditions undermine the very concept of law. It is a legislative responsibility to maintain a clear body of law for the governance of society and to modify that body of law as changing political, economic and cultural conditions may require. To assert that the law should be changed by judicial interpretation is to deny the rule of law.

Our very capacity to write law depends upon the reality that words have meaning, which can be conveyed to the people. The rule of law requires that the law have that meaning and no other. To hold that judges can change the meaning of words to embrace interests and purposes never conceived by the authors is to deny our capacity to have any law at all.

Moreover, the assertion that the Supreme Court has authority to change law makes that body a super-legislature. The advocates of new law that cannot command majority support of the people nor of their legislative representatives can impose that law on the people by persuading the Court that the change of law should be made by interpretation. This is in fact the way in which the most drastic revisions of our law have been wrought in the past five decades. *The process is illegal.*

THE JUDICIAL REVOLUTION

The changing interpretation of the Fourteenth Amendment, which began in 1925, giving that law a meaning that had been rejected by all courts in the previous fifty years, drastically revised our system of government, destroying the authority of the states and erecting a new judicial oligarchy.

The Constitution assigned to the national government certain powers and authorities related to such common interests of the states as foreign affairs, national defense, control of the currency, and interstate commerce. It reserved to the states powers of local government, including especially the police power through which the basic governmental responsibility for maintaining order in society is administered.

The Bill of Rights was enacted for the benefit of the states and the people *to make specific the exclusion of the national government* from the exercise of the vital police powers reserved to the states. The early judicial history of the United States demonstrates that the federal courts were meticulous in respecting the authority of the states to judge these local questions.

The assumption by the Supreme Court that the Bill of Rights restricts the states makes that court the self-appointed arbiter of every exercise of the police power in every corner of this country. It destroys the federal character of our government by making the Supreme Court the administrator of state as well as federal law. It destroys the right of each state to define pornography and limit the production and sale of filth according to the mores of the local society. It opens the country to a flood of smut eroding the fibers of society.

This intrusion of the Supreme Court into jurisdictions previously reserved to the states has swamped the federal judiciary with cases it is ill-qualified to litigate. Questions not the proper business of any government are now solemnly adjudicated by the Supreme Court, as when on March 20, 1973, the Supreme Court heard the appeal of the *Pittsburgh Press* from a ruling of the Pennsylvania Civil Rights Commission that the newspaper must not print separate classifications of "Help Wanted" advertisements for men and women.

This flooding of the federal courts with trivia, including detailed administration of the public schools, has caused delays that effectively deny justice in important cases. Criminal justice is paralyzed by constitutional claims and by the ability of defense attorneys to delay trial until the prosecution witnesses are dead, unavailable, or uncertain in their recollection of the crime. Claims of reformers that they were setting a higher standard of justice are answered by the increasing crimes which those illusions have nurtured.

Chief Justice Warren Burger has sought relief in the institution of a sub-Supreme Court to screen appeals and dispose of those not requiring Supreme Court attention. But that is folly. The sensible cure for the Court's distress is to separate again the federal and state jurisdictions as they were so admirably defined in the Constitution.

A century of success in building a decent and productive society must be attributed to the decentralized character of our government. The states were individual sovereigns engaged in a competition of excellence. When New York State adopted a law of incorporation to replace the unwieldy procedure of granting legislative franchises, and when the law worked well, other states adopted similar laws. This single change, facilitating the organization of productive enterprise, made a great contribution to rapid economic growth in America. This competition of the several states, inviting exchanges of ideas, encouraging innovative improvement, promoting comparison, and stimulating progress, created throughout the land a respect for excellence which no central authority could have imposed.

While the reform of error and the preservation of integrity in government must ever be concerns of a self-governing society, prudence cautions us to beware the zealous reformer, who often holds a myopic view of society. In our decentralized society, he sees not the excellence and progress of the whole body but the differences of culture and of law among the sovereign states. He sees in one state what he conceives to be a better rule of law and he decries the failure of other states to measure up to that standard. He wants the Supreme Court to impose that standard on all the states. He would destroy the competition of excellence to impose his own will on all. This is a real-life re-enactment of the fable of the goose that laid the golden eggs.

CONGRESS IN DEFAULT

In 1967, Senator Sam Ervin of North Carolina, a distinguished constitutional authority, said: "The Supreme Court can compel Congress and the President to observe the Constitution—the only restraint on unconstitutional behavior on the part of Supreme Court Justices is their own sense of self-restraint." This is, of course, a misrepresentation of our governmental powers.

According to Article III, Sec. 2 of the Constitution, "In all cases affecting ambassadors, other public ministers and consuls, and those in which a state shall be party, the Supreme Court shall have original jurisdiction. In all the other cases before mentioned, the Supreme Court shall have appellate jurisdiction, both as to law and fact, with such exceptions and under such regulations as the Congress shall make." Moreover, the federal judicial system, in its trial and other appellate courts, is a creation of Congress.

Senator Ervin was speaking not of the law but of a sentimental mythology about three coequal branches of government. There are three branches, but they are not coequal. The architects of the Constitution knew that government must be capable of decision, so they put the decisive power in the Congress, which is regularly reconstituted by the people. The Court is an administrative agency of the federal government, with duties, authorities and pay prescribed by Congress, except for the specific jurisdiction of the Supreme Court defined in the Constitution. Congress is responsible for the judicial system of the United States.

When the Supreme Court usurps legislative jurisdiction, the Congress can reclaim the power by simple legislation terminating Court jurisdiction in the disputed area. All of the powers assumed by the Court in its unlawful interpretation of the Fourteenth Amendment to apply the restraints of the Bill of Rights to the states can be restored to the states by congressional legislation depriving the Court of jurisdiction in the usurped function.

Congress could by such law deprive the Court of jurisdiction over state law affecting freedom of speech and press, over education, over the qualifications of electors and the apportionment of state legislatures. The country would then be restored to the condition at law that pertained before the Supreme Court usurped legislative authority. The constitutional balance would be restored.

But Congress is not exercising its powers. It is acting as though the Supreme Court were some kind of high priesthood whose edicts should not be questioned by mere legislators. It is betraying the Constitution by default of its critical responsibility for overseeing the whole range of government activity—judicial and executive as well as legislative.

The default of Congress must be attributed to the interests of congressional leaders. In particular, the Chairmen of the Judiciary Committees of the two houses, which should bear responsibility for keeping the courts in their proper fields of action, have resisted moves to curb the federal courts. They have seemed to be in collaboration with the Supreme Court purpose of stripping the states of sovereign powers and concentrating these powers in the central government.

RULE OF THE PARTY

Any rational explanation of this default brings us back to the influence of the political parties. The political party is a power-seeking organism. It is in its essence hostile to the separation of powers built into our Constitution. The political party works to bring all of government—legislative, executive and judicial—under its control. Through the President as "leader of the party," it imposes discipline on its members in Congress. Through him it appoints to the Supreme Court and to lesser federal courts, party members dedicated to the party's interest.

The sole aim of party politics is to win elections. Thus, the party becomes expedient and opportunist in practice, combining with any forces, good or evil, that will help it to win elections. The party adopts a pious demeanor to co-opt religious leaders even as it makes surreptitious alliance with powerful criminals who can sway elections. Pious and patriotic pronouncements of public officials have misled the people about the nature and aims of the political parties.

In earlier years of the Republic, when the Constitution was a cherished document of the people's liberties, political leaders regularly pledged their devotion to the constitutional order. The parties operated within the constitutional restraints and the country prospered. Since the administration of Franklin Roosevelt, however, party politics has taken a new line. The socialist denigration of the Constitution as an outdated document designed for an agricultural economy, the assertion that Congress must not be deterred by the Constitution in its duty to help the people, the condemnation of appeals to constitutional law as living in the eighteenth century, all have become common talk of party campaigns. The parties now hold themselves above the Constitution, responsible to nothing but their own interest.

It is this kind of thinking about public affairs that leads men to believe the law should be administered for the benefit of friends and for the discomfiture of political opponents. Those who claim that the law is not an objective, impartial rule binding on all citizens but must be applied in a way to achieve desirable aims are merely serving the party. In respect to law, the party attitude in the United States is similar to that of the party in the Soviet Union, though the aims are different. The law is to be used for political advantage. We have a government of men, not of law.

This is the course, unhappily, which politics has taken in the United States. The sources of excellence in our society are being destroyed. We are caught up in a zeal for uniformity and standardization in a paternalistic utopianism. This is the process by which societies become paralyzed, static.

We are being delivered into bondage by judges who cannot comprehend and respect the excellence of the American constitutional order. Congress has the power and the duty to set aside the usurpations of the Court and to restore the constitutional order. It cannot do so because Congress is the prisoner of the political parties which in turn are dominated by our oligarchy of wealth.

Chapter 12

BLACK AND MARXIST

"Black Revolution" is too loose a designation of the racial strife which has persisted with varying intensity since the sit-in at a Woolworth lunch counter in Greensboro, North Carolina in 1960. That defiance of segregation in privately owned facilities offering a public service marked a movement of the black struggle for "equality" from the courts to the streets. The federal courts remained a crucial force in the ensuing strife, with new rulings denying police protection to private facilities offering segregated public service. But the thrust of the movement was the mass assault on segregated facilities operating under established state and federal law. The law violators acted as on a stage, with the emotional support of national news media and with the assured support of the Warren Court as fast as it could be brought to bear on the issue. They whipped up in the North a passion to change the South, a passion that would subside only when the North's de facto segregation came under fire.

The general movement embraced a broad spectrum of motivations, from sincere white sympathy for the Negro and honest Negro striving for the elimination of racial distinctions to the ritual liberal attack on our decentralized government and Marxist incitement to class warfare. It has had a devastating effect on American society and especially on our political institutions, an effect which in its ultimate reach today remains unpredictable.

The Eisenhower years were preoccupied with court administration of school desegregation, with a major conflict of federal and state power at Little Rock in 1957. The new sit-ins were contained without serious trouble. The law took its course. Breaches of the law were handled by responsible authorities, though now under the glare of national publicity.

In the fall of 1960, John F. Kennedy was elected President by a narrow margin of the popular vote and a tide of black votes released by his telephone call to Mrs. Martin Luther King about the imprisonment of her husband in a Georgia jail. In the new administration, militant black leaders were quick to claim the spoils of office, aware that the solid black vote had carried the election for the Democrats. For eight years, the Democratic Party became the vehicle of the movement. Massive rioting broke out in our big cities. Extensive urban areas were destroyed by vandalism and fire. America indeed looked like a sick society.

THE ORIGINS OF STRIFE

From its beginnings the United States was a tolerant society. Early settlers had in many instances been refugees from religious and political persecution. Though the persecuted are often not themselves free of prejudice, the shared risks of pioneer living built bonds of common understanding. The long ordeal of the Revolution gave common purpose to the diverse communities of the Atlantic seaboard, and the Constitution cemented their union in liberty.

Thus, the very diversity of the origins, experiences and cherished beliefs of the several colonies required that the Constitution be a very loose rein, respecting their differences of culture and allowing to each his own preference. This was the liberty which attracted immigrants from all over the world. Every group could maintain its own culture. If children born in the United States moved from their inherited culture to a more general culture, that was a matter of personal choice and interest. If they preferred to maintain a separate culture, as the Amish did, that was part of their freedom.

In the United States, the ancient political loyalty related to nationality and culture had been superseded by loyalty to a principle of personal freedom and responsibility embodied in the Constitution. Dutch immigrants could settle in Holland, Michigan and continue there the cherished culture they had brought from Europe. Irish immigrants could settle in Boston in cultural neighborhoods (now wrongly called ghettos) alive with the spirit of their own past history and experiences. On the Eastern seaboard, the cultural neighborhood provided a reception depot for the new immigrant where he could be comfortable with his own clan while he learned from earlier arrivals how to get along in the New World.

The United States was an open society. The new immigrant was not under any compulsive discipline of the state. So long as he obeyed the law and earned his own living, he was accepted as a member of society, eligible in due course for citizenship. This was a far cry from the socialist conception of the state as a father figure bearing a responsibility for every member of society.

This open nature of our society was a critical factor in determining the course of our history. The "loose rein" of government allowed latitude for the development of the entire potential talent of the whole society, not restricting enterprise to any class or group. The politics of living tended to be comprised within the state law. Combinations of self-interest competed with other combinations of self-interest.

Tolerance is a willingness to allow the existence of a different proposition. It did not require Englishmen to think that Irish culture was as good as their own, nor did it require Irishmen to think that English culture was as good as theirs. In fact, the feeling of pride which each felt in the superiority of his own heritage was an important element of the American landscape. That kind of pride is an essential element of morale and even self-respect. It is not hostile to the general welfare of the community. It is entirely consistent with loyalty to the United States to have such diversity of ethnic and cultural outlook within society.

This is the society into which the freed slaves were thrust after the Civil War. They were free men, compelled only to obey the law and to earn their own living. They had the strong backing of the Reconstruction Congress and the protection of the victorious Union Army. They were exploited by carpetbaggers seeking profit in a new power structure. But they were incapable of managing the regional economy and necessarily had to fall into slots they could fill in a viable economic order. Their skills had to be fitted into the pay scales and jobs of the community.

The North finished the war with a sense of responsibility for the freed slaves. Congress strove to protect them, but the administration of local government by Washington could only be an emergency and temporary measure. In due course, the responsibility for state administration had to be restored to the states.

In the North, a sense of concern for the freed slaves dimmed only as the Civil War receded from memory. Howard University in Washington, D.C. and Tuskegee Institute in Alabama were established by Congress for the education of freedmen. Private philanthropy sponsored other educational institutions to prepare the freed youth for higher responsibility in society. Booker T. Washington, as the President of Tuskegee Institute, became a leader of national action for the improvement of Negro skills and income in society. George Washington Carver became an honored example of skills that earnest black citizens could contibute to society. With the cooperation of Republican Presidents and a long tenure of the

Republican Party, the cause of Negro improvement had a sympathetic hearing in the national capital. Negro leaders were inspired by the belief of Booker T. Washington that in a free society, the advancement of black citizens was limited only by the knowledge and skills they could assimilate and use.

In the years of liberation, Negroes were no more insulated from the diverse currents of our open society than other sectors of the American public. As Marxism and finally Bolshevism made inroads into American society, converts were recruited from the black leadership—especially, as in the white community, among those with higher education, such as W. E. B. Dubois. But until the middle of the twentieth century, these repudiations of the American political order were as isolated and unimportant in the black community as in the nation at large.

When the country was tormented by the Great Depression of the Thirties and socialists were extolling the Soviet capacity to maintain full employment, it seemed to American Communists that the occasion for recruiting the black proletariat had at last arrived. But their advances were spurned. Black leaders rejected the Marxist propaganda of class warfare. Only the Communist youth movement was successful in recruiting potential leaders who might in another day and time provide leadership for a black revolution.

Twenty years later this investment in black youth had matured. Young men schooled in the doctrines of socialism, angry at the "oppression" of their race, skilled in the arts and in politics, were ready to crash the fading facade of the old political parties.

The pretenses of Marxism and Leninism are based upon the perversion of history. They depict a continuous class struggle in which the wealthy class has striven throughout history to hold the working class in bondage. This is a myth to stir revolutionary fervor but it has no basis in history. It may be useful in stimulating class hatred to support the Communist Party's reach for power, but that would seem to be its only utility.

In fact, the history of mankind is the history of the family. Brothers and cousins may indeed fight over consequential or inconsequential matters, but they hold a sense of kinship. Society is created by the common interests of families and by the quality of the leadership they can provide. Enemies captured in war might be enslaved but the tribe or nation was an association of warriors in which the rewards of leadership had the approval of the assembly.

The Marxist perversion of history has in recent decades had an impact on some Negroes in the United States because it seemed to give them a plausible explanation of their condition. In the Marxist lexicon, all workers are slaves of the owning class; so the Emancipation Proclamation merely changed the lot of blacks from legal to economic slavery. The thesis offers a convenient rationalization of poverty, but it disregards history and the true cause of the human condition.

114

The racial strife of the Sixties did raise anew a basic question white Americans had considered long settled: Could the principles of the American union supply those bonds of unity so essential to nationhood, which have in history been supplied by ties of blood? For if principle could not surmount differences of race, the American state had a shaky foundation.

Bagehot wrote, "Unless you can make a strong cooperative bond, your society will be conquered and killed out by some other society which has such a bond."[1] That had indeed been the experience of history. Jacques Maritain spoke of the same bond:[2]

> Nothing matters more in the order of material causality, to the life and preservation of the body politic than the accumulated energy and historical continuity of that national community it has itself caused to exist. This means chiefly a heritage of accepted and unquestionable structures, fixed customs and deep-rooted common feelings which bring into social life itself something of the determined physical data of nature, and of the vital unconscious strength proper to vegetative organisms. It is, further, common inherited experience and the moral and intellectual instincts which constitute a kind of empirical practical wisdom, much deeper and denser and much nearer the hidden complex dynamism of human life than any artificial construction of reason.

White Americans supposed that in 180 years of growth, that bond had been solidly established. Though the country still reflected cultural diversity, the performance of all cultural groups under the stress of war seemed to reflect a true national unity.

Although interracial contacts were limited, the prominence of black athletes and musicians in the front ranks of national performance seemed to promise a growing acceptance of black talent in all public activities. Except for reporting the successful litigation of the National Association for the Advancement of Colored People, which generally enjoyed white approval in the North, and recounting efforts of the Urban League to increase black employment in predominantly white occupations, the press gave scant sign of discontent in the black community. In consequence, the rebellion of the Sixties took most white Americans by surprise.

Franklin Roosevelt had held black loyalty in the Democratic Party with jobs, favors and flattery, without ever alienating his white Southern constituency. But that kind of politics would not do in the Sixties. In 1961, John and Robert Kennedy were told in no uncertain terms that the black vote, consolidated by black militancy in the closing years of the Eisenhower Administration, had decided the 1960 election. A payoff was demanded, not in crumbs and social prestige but in forthright action by the federal government to remove the vestiges of racial discrimination from American society. Black leaders dèmanded massive support of the campaigns they had inaugurated.

It should be noted that the black militants demanded not merely their legal rights long denied in some states but new "rights" never expressed in any law, and actually prohibited by our Constitution. They wanted government to enter into the mind of the private employer to judge whether his hiring was motivated by the competence or the race of the applicant. They would force private clubs to admit and serve Negroes. In short, they demanded a new government control of private association and contracting which would fix Negro quotas in employment, a radical departure from the settled American concepts of law. The President, Congress and the Supreme Court acquiesced. As Arthur Krock was to write:[3]

> . . . the Department of Justice under Presidents Kennedy and Johnson has spinelessly established the fact of being a Negro as a grant of immunity for most notorious flagrant violators of both the civil and criminal laws.

In a memorable but then unreported meeting in the White House with black leaders early in 1961, Attorney General Robert Kennedy promised to support the campaigns for black voter registration in the South and to furnish money for the program from the Taconic Foundation.

There could be no public criticism of federal measures to protect black citizens in the South against racial discrimination, which denied the vote to qualified Negroes. It was the clear duty of the Attorney General under the Constitution and supporting statutes to put an end to that discrimination. Although the qualification of electors was a state responsibility, the abuse of that authority in some jurisdictions through double standards for black and white citizens was such transparent violation of the Fourteenth Amendment that any federal court could have quickly defined and outlawed the practice. Such a forthright defense of black citizens would have done credit to the Kennedy Administration, but the initiative might have alienated white political leaders in the Southern states.

However, for the Attorney General of the United States to conspire with black militants to violate the police laws of the Southern states, thereby to create a climate of conflict in which Northern anger at Southern segregation could be aroused to support federal intervention and new legislation, is in itself an ugly violation of law. It cannot be condoned by considerations of political expediency. Both political parties had long neglected their constitutional duty to protect the full rights of black citizenship in the South. But new violations of law by the federal government and an accommodation of the Marxist rhetoric of oppression were not the way to remedy the injury done to blacks. It was a way for the political party to avoid the blame which was its due.

We have noted the difference between the federal and the state powers as defined by the Constitution and the deference which the Supreme Court had in earlier years paid to the judgment of the states in administering state police powers. This was the rationale of *Plessy* v. *Ferguson* authorizing segregated transportation, provided equal facilities were provided for both races. The Court respected state judgment that separate facilities were necessary for good order and racial harmony, provided that no discrimination in facilities could be countenanced.

Whether the Court judgment of the requirements of public order in the aftermath of the Civil War was reasonable could be argued. The Court was not unanimous. But there could be no countenancing under any color of law of the blatant discrimination against black citizens which subsequently developed in some sectors of the South. The country urgently needed a strong federal intervention to outlaw discriminatory state and local practice and to protect the rights of black citizens.

Although the Supreme Court historically had been deferential to reasonable state judgment in the exercise of police powers, it had not been hesitant to outlaw abuses of that power which infringed the basic rights of citizens. The neglect of Negro rights in the South had been purely a default of executive government, an accommodation of the political parties to discrimination which was politically tolerable.

CO-OPTING THE MARXIST RHETORIC

Challenged by militant blacks armed with the slogans of Marxist rhetoric, the parties moved for a new accommodation. They embraced the Marxist rhetoric of revolution and sought to lead the movement. Instead of acting within the bounds of law and prudence, they joined in the emotional attacks on American history and institutions, thinking by such tactics to convert the conflict to political profit.

The unanimity and eagerness with which Northern politicians in both parties embraced the cause of revolution was a scandal. Having failed to render justice to black citizens, they then scrambled to absolve themselves of blame. They condemned the system or the people but not the party or the politicans.

The response of the liberal politicans of both parties has been described by Willmoore Kendall:[4]

When the civil rights movement did come into existence, when it first began to describe itself as a revolution and first began to proclaim that it would not take "No" for an answer, there was nothing for the white liberals to do except go along with it, and go along with it on a "the sky's the limit" basis. A civil rights demonstration violates a local ordinance in, say, Birmingham? Well, you can't make an omelet without breaking some eggs, now can you? In general we in America don't approve minorities that won't take "No" for an answer—that is, minorities that seek to dictate policy. Well the grievances of the Negroes are intolerable, aren't they? One gets the impression, as one rethinks the early history of the civil rights movement, that no white liberal spokesman or leader took the trouble to ask himself—certainly none asked himself out loud—"Might this business go too far? Might there come a point where I'd have to get off the train? If I say C, I must say D, but how if I say J? Must I also say K?" Most particularly—I think—for somewhere along the line I should be entitled to do a little needling—no white liberal spokesman seems to have asked himself, "How strongly can the civil rights leaders count on me once, if I may put it so, the movement gets out of the South—once, if I may put it so, support of the civil rights movement isn't one and the same thing with striking at those white Southerners, whose senators and representatives block the whole liberal program in Congress?

President Lyndon Johnson appointed the National Advisory Commission on Civil Disorders, chaired by Governor Otto Kerner of Illinois and including prominent politicians of both parties, to investigate and report upon the public disorders of 1966-1968. The Commission was staffed with radical personnel, who incorporated into the Commission Report the language of white oppression and white racism which was the stock in trade of the Marxist revolution. Members of the Commission meekly accepted the staff findings.

The charge of white racism levied in the Kerner Report was a typical Marxist attack on the free society. It presupposed an omnipotent government of the white majority holding a black minority in subjugation and enforced poverty. This is the calibre of Marxist perception, but it is not reality.

In the American society which allegedly suppressed blacks, some Negroes had become millionaires and the proprietors of prosperous businesses or professions. Individuals ranged from poor to prosperous to wealthy, as in the whole society. Education of a once enslaved class had advanced so far that the percentage of the total black population in college in the United States was higher than the percentage of the total white population in college in England. There are no facts to sustain the thesis of racial oppression in the United States.

These statistics were not of course summoned by the Kerner Commission. The aim of that Commission was to sustain the revolutionary attack on America and ask greater federal appropriations to meet the revolutionary demands.

The charge of white racism, except in application to small and remote pockets of the country, was a blatant lie. In reality, the history of the United States since the Civil War is replete with evidence of white concern about and sympathy for black citizens. In the Civil War itself, the American people demonstrated by enormous sacrifice a concern for its black people that no other nation had shown. The default of political parties should not be identified with the sentiment of the people.

"White racism" has become the battle cry of black racism. The Kerner Report, signed by maudlin and scared white politicians, was a triumph of Marxist class warfare. This dicussion requires a definition of racism, though that courtesy was not extended by the Kerner report. In its vague generalizations, the Kerner report treated pride of race as racism.

The preference of men for their own family, tribe or nation is a natural phenomenon, at once healthy and socially useful. Even a sense of the superiority of his race or culture is both normal and healthy. Racism is that perversion of legitimate pride which conceives a right to oppress and exploit other citizens because of their race. This attitude has persisted in some pockets of the South; but in the South generally it was long ago rejected. In the rest of the United States, it has never existed in any strength.

Within a free society, the mutual assistance of members of a group or

118

racial enclave for the betterment of all is perfectly legal and moral. It is no more reprehensible for Mormons or Jews to collaborate in economic endeavors than it is for Black Muslims to do so. If there is no hostility to other citizens nor purpose of defrauding them of their rights or interests, there is no racism.

The Marxist philosophy seeks to destroy every sentiment of family, tribal or racial solidarity or of religious attachment because these claims on personal loyalty obstruct that total submission to the state which the Communist Party demands. But in a free society, these are the cherished and most vital ties which give significance to living. They are entirely compatible with the security of the state, are in fact the cornerstone of its structure. Thus, the attack on legitimate pride of race or national origin was aimed at the binding cement of a free society—the morale of free men.

The false Marxist concept of life as a banquet of benefits which needs only to be divided equitably by government is the foundation of error. The basic reality of existence is that man must work for his food and shelter. In times past, he worked from dawn to dusk to produce the food and fiber for his sustenance. Civilization involves the work of organizing man's knowledge and labor to increase his productivity and his leisure.

The Marxist is a man whose only talent is the exercise of political power. Wherever he rules, civilization crumbles. He is incapable of evoking the human inspiration and cooperation required for the development of civilization. He is in essence the slave-driver, enforcing submission to his will. He perceives the free society as an exercise of power by others— exercise of a power which he could use more effectively for the common good.

His attack on the diversities of a free society is designed to make those differences a source of conflict. He uses them to destroy the society, creating chaos from which he hopes to rise like Prometheus to rule a new order.

When public officials elected or appointed to preserve and extend our civilization sacrifice the essential values of society to placate the militant Marxists, they betray the decay into which our political system has fallen. Kendall has described the theory of diminishing returns which induces politicians to placate militant movements:[5]

> The civil rights movement has lost steam because of its very victories under the Johnson Administration, especially the Civil Rights Act of 1964, and the Voting Rights Act of 1965. Political movements, to be sure, usually thrive on successes, whether electoral or legislative—as, at the first blush, we should expect them to. Such a movement, having shown its muscle by gaining first this objective (the opening of public accommodations to Negroes) and that objective (a Voting Rights Act whose intended purpose is to get hitherto disfranchised Negroes on the voting Polls)—what more natural than it should proceed, propelled now by forward inertia, to use that same muscle for gaining still further objectives and do so successfully? At some point, however, a movement's forward inertia becomes a matter of diminishing

119

returns: as the number of its objectives it has already gained increases, the number of objectives still to be gained decreases, and it has, in consequence, less and less to offer to its followers; it thus loses, little by little, its capacity to mobilize them, to appeal to their hopes and expectations, to spur them into action and thus, ultimately, its capacity to wring from its opponents the further concessions it demands.

But the Marxist revolution is not just one movement. It is a series of planned movements, each pushing the politician farther away from the sound ground of principle until he has lost the public confidence.

BLACK PROGRESS IN THE UNITED STATES

The simple truth is that Negroes in America have prospered far beyond the lot of black men elsewhere in the world. Starting at the bottom of the economic ladder a century ago, American Negroes have developed substantial status in art, service and the professions. Where else but in the United States could any class so placed and identified a century ago have risen to the national prominence in sports, music, the professions and government that American Negroes hold today?

To say that Negroes are poor is to misrepresent their condition in American society. Some Negroes are poor. We say the same of a sector of the white community, more numerous than the black poor, who have no claim of racial prejudice to explain their condition. The critical factor is that we have a ladder of excellence in which citizens of all colors and creeds can climb to levels commensurate with their developed talents.

SEPARATE SOCIETIES

It is true that the racial culture is more persistent than the ethnic culture. White immigrants from Europe tended in a generation or two to adopt the speech, dress, manners and business outlook of the general society—in all appearances to become part of it. Racial differences—black, red and yellow—were more distinctive and easily identified in a predominantly white society. Here too it was possible to adopt the speech, dress, manners and outlook of the general society and to win personal acceptance in it as many citizens of these races demonstrated. Chinese and Japanese immigrants seemed to make the transition easily. Negroes and Indians, greater in numbers and bound by cultural heritage, changed more slowly.

This is not to gainsay the dominance of white America. The United States is a branch of white European culture. It has been built by that culture and essentially by the intelligence, energy and drive of the white race. But it *is* to deny that Negroes have been oppressed and exploited by white America since the Civil War.

In a free society, those who are not tuned to the going work ethic are not exploited—they are ignored. They form as separate enclaves, as some American Indians have done, maintaining their own culture, undisturbed by the world about them. Other Indians have moved into the mainstream of American life to hold high office and responsible positions. But if they don't succeed in the competitive world, they can go back to the sanctuary of the tribe. Because America respects diversity of culture, the right of Indians to maintain a different culture is never challenged. Change must come from within.

So it has been with the Negro in America. In the transition from tribal Africa to slavery in America, Negroes had adapted their culture to a new way of life and to the Christian religion. As with all peoples, they had a cherished folklore and music and perception of life's values. It was different from the outlook of other Americans in some respects, just as the outlook of our tribal Indians was different. That this special culture of the American Negro was passed from generation to generation and that it was respected by other Americans requires no apology by anyone. Perhaps a socialist government would have destroyed that culture and dragooned blacks and Indians into conformity with Marxist materialism; but there was no reason for a free society to do so. We simply don't accord that kind of power to government.

Building on the false premise of racial conflict, adopted from the false premise of class conflict, American socialists have embraced the revolutionary ethic and used it to build federal power. New demands are placed on the central government to enforce "fair" employment standards, to enforce "fair" housing practices in selling and renting homes, to "improve" education, to provide medical care for all, to control the care and training of children from pre-school years. To enumerate these programs is to reveal the inroads of authoritarianism in our society.

The Black Revolution has been used effectively to accelerate the destruction of the American political system. It has been used not by Communists and subversives but by Republicans and Democrats indifferent to the rule of law, concerned only to accommodate the latest Marxist insurgency.

Political leaders of both parties have moved to dismantle standards of performance in both public and private service. Under pressure to increase black employment in activities where blacks have had little presence and no adequate development of qualifications, they claimed virtue in setting quotas, compassion in exempting blacks from college entrance standards, tolerance in hiring unqualified black faculty, justice in promoting blacks over better qualified whites. But in lowering standards for black workers and scholars, they were really asserting black inferiority. They were assuming that Negroes could not meet the standards of the general society. As Professor Paolucci has put it:[6]

Perhaps one day an American Negro dramatist may give us a tragic representation of the agony of freedom through which we are now living. If it is to be worthy of the Greek tradition, it will show us that when the white community in America assumes the blame for Negro riots, it is proving by

121

its arrogance that it is free in the profoundest sense; but it will show also that, in encouraging the Negro community to persist in its belief that it is somehow free and intrinsically equal, yet not responsible, the Riots Commission is obstructing the way to genuine equality in freedom at the last threshold.

It would have taken time for black men to qualify for the positions to which they aspired. But the firm and patient practice of justice required our country to do just that. The way should be open to blacks who can compete but they should fail as others fail when they cannot meet standards. The conversion of our society from one of merit to one of politics is but the latest blow dealt by our two political parties to America.

This abandonment of excellence as the measure of work value has a devastating effect upon our society. When political advantage becomes the measure of employment the worker has no compulsion to perform satisfactorily. If his work is sloppy and inefficient, he cannot be discharged because he would cry "white racism." In business, in hospitals, in all levels of public service, performance has seriously deteriorated. This is not a temporary condition. It is a permanent condition of political bureaucracy which has now been extended to much of industry. It is the inescapable price of political paternalism.

The myth of white racism has provided an excuse for government to intrude its deadening hand into citizen activity previously excluded from the jurisdiction of the state. Bureaucracy has mushroomed in service to the new system of thought control. But the bureaucrats cannot really control thought, nor judge it. They can only resort to quotas and other arbitrary judgments that propagate injustice instead of restraining it. In thus going beyond the sensible limits of law, judges and lawmakers have earned the contempt they now suffer.

In the ordinary course of human relations, judgment must be made about the quality of work performance. Where no consideration of race, nationality or religion enters, it is difficult for the man denied promotion to believe that the person promoted had superior qualifications. That judgment must be made by the boss, for the good of the business. Where race becomes a factor, it provides the disappointed worker with a rationalization of his loss of promotion. It is human to look for explanations outside one's personal shortcomings. Action of the federal and state governments in creating Human Relations Commissions has fostered these subjective misjudgments and exacerbated the consequent futile conflict in society. The Commissions are by their nature tending to create the racial conflict they profess to alleviate. They are an example of bad public policy.

In an all-white employment situation, workers denied promotion seek alibis in differences of religion, nationality or other possible influences on the boss's judgment. No doubt, in a free society and in private employment, these have in the past occasionally been decisive influences. But in a free and competitive market, the skill and the production of the worker must be the critical consideration.

In government, extraneous influences unrelated to merit can be minimized only by firm adherence to merit as the sole acceptable standard of judgment. It is no more rational to have quotas for blacks in government than to have quotas for Catholics or Jews. The federal civil service had achieved high prestige for its recognition of merit before it was converted to racial preference in the Sixties by a Democratic Administration allied with black radicals.

American Negroes—or at least the more vocal ones on the news fronts—seem to be searching for a new culture. Some of them have obviously embraced the Marxist philosophy and are trying to apply it to their situation in America. But the great bulk of the black population is working loyally within the American system to qualify for employment and to earn a comfortable living for itself. There is foolishness in much of the new African vogue. The American Negro's culture is American. It was forged in the history of slavery, of emancipation and of freedom. He is a full-fledged citizen of the greatest country in the world—a country in which he can develop his talents and make his own way in life unhampered by a dictatorial regime.

To have a fondness for the land of one's ancestors is natural, but to try to create an African culture in the United States is retrogressive. The American Negro has passed so far beyond the progress achieved by his African brothers that to talk of adopting their culture is sentimental nonsense. Few Americans of foreign ancestry have any desire to return to the homes of their ancestors to live, though they may maintain a sentimental and respectful regard for those lands. The responsibility of American Negroes is to help to bring their African brothers up to the standard of living which has been achieved in America, not to turn back to a primitive and sometimes barbaric culture.

Even if American Negroes were to turn back, seeking some lost dignity in pre-slavery times, they could find no common heritage:[7]

All that American Negroes have in common that is of genuine national significance is their Americanism. In their racial, ethnic make-up they are as varied—indeed, far more varied—than the mass of blacks of the African continent. Their national unification would be infinitely more difficult than the national unification of all Europe or all Asia. The American Negro, like the American WASP, is thoroughly American. And he will come to think and feel himself to be an integral part of the national "we," once the internationalist stranglehold on our civil society is broken.

In short, the home of the American Negro is here. Like all citizens he is expected to obey the law and to earn his own living. He is free to live in his cultural neighborhood and maintain traditional customs or to move into the mainstream of American life. If he is to be a useful member of society, he must be a loyal member of society, not an ally of the enemies of America.

If our black citizens have, in some degree, been alienated in recent years, their confusion has been caused by the alliance of our political parties with black radicals. The political leaders of America seemed to be saying about American society all that the Marxist critics were saying about it. The two-party system had become a vehicle for advancing the revolution, for burning the cities, for stirring racial strife. It gave both credibility and money to the revolution.

The poverty program advanced by President Johnson gave power to the black radicals. Traditional controls on the expenditure of federal funds were waived. Standards of federal employment were eliminated. The Johnson Administration could put on the federal payrolls, in high-sounding positions with excessive pay and little work, cadres of militant reformers, black and white, who would then become the paid henchmen of the Democratic Party. And this scandalous waste of the public funds, not to help the poor but to placate the black revolutionaries, advanced a remarkable new social theory. Administrator Sargent Shriver concluded that the criminals of society were distinguished from the honest poor by their display of leadership qualities. The poverty program therefore recruited criminals to provide the leadership which would lift the ghetto poor out of their apathy. No doubt Mr. Shriver knew that the revolution had already recruited the criminals and that this grant of positions and power would satisfy the revolutionary demands. What it would do to America became apparent in the urban riots of 1966, 1967 and 1968.

This savage denigration of America would not have been possible without the enthusiastic cooperation of the "liberal" news media. From start to finish of the black rioting, the news media were like a bellows blowing on the flames, intensifying and spreading the conflagration. As politicians live by their public images, they were in large measure constrained to take positions sanctified by the news media.

No doubt many reporters were inspired by a desire to help the black poor achieve better living standards. Their liberal views of limited government as lacking in concern for the underprivileged gave scant basis for questioning the revolutionary propaganda. But behind the reporters, in the news and editorial rooms of America and in the board rooms of the corporate executives, there must have been deeper reasons for this assault on the American political system. The revolutionaries were in time restrained by the electorate's rejection of the Democratic Party; but the sharp increase in federal power, the vast increase in the federal bureaucracy, the intrusion of federal law into every phase of American life must have pleased those who sought advantage in building socialism.

The racial strife of the Sixties raised questions in American minds about the future of the country. Some saw the conflict as an incurable malady which would undermine our political system. One observer wrote:[8]

> The melting pot no longer melts. This is not a new manifestation, but its effects were dramatized only in the 1950s and 1960s. U.S. society now consists of many ethnic—and particularly many racial—minorities, too small for any single one to dominate, too large to assimilate in any foreseeable future. The result is a fractionalized society with all the problems of differing value systems and clashing social and economic aims.

This is the view of many who regard an amalgam of blood as the basis of unity and who therefore fail to understand the essence of the American melting pot as the catalyst of political unity rather than as the forge of cultural unity. It had never been the aim of the American political system to create cultural unity. On the contrary, the system was designed to tolerate the cultural diversity which existed in the thirteen colonies.

Action of the federal government, notably through the Supreme Court, to concentrate all political power in Washington, may augur the abandonment of that political ideal. There is some reason to believe that the virtual panic with which the federal courts have handled racial conflict betrays a conclusion of the "establishment" that racial integration is essential to political order. That would be an erroneous conclusion drawn logically by our ruling intelligentsia, who are so alienated from the American political order that they are incapable of understanding it.

There is no reason whatsoever to believe that our system of cultural diversity has failed to produce political unity. It is not the diverse ethnic minorities who have jeopardized our unity: it is the white leadership of our society, led astray by Fabian theories.

With a people as solidly grounded as our own in the principles of liberty, the threat of Marxist militants, black or white, has never been a serious challenge to public order. The ordinary, prudent responses of public officials would be enough to contain any trouble. In the Great Depression, there was no serious class conflict.

By the Sixties, the essential perspectives of the American people had not greatly changed. They were sympathetic to the underprivileged and intolerant of injustice but they were also intolerant of official malfeasance which excused and encouraged breaches of law. The great change had occurred in our national leadership. In the courts, in the Congress, in the Executive, among our intellectuals but not among our ethnic minorities, strange new ideas of political policy bearing a startling resemblance to the foibles of socialism had taken root. Relativism and existentialism and positivism had taken root, rendering our leaders incapable of confronting reality.

The challenges of Martin Luther King and Stokeley Carmichael and Rap Brown should have been no problem for competent political leaders. The laws should have been enforced. The primacy of public order should have been sustained. Breaches of the law should have been prosecuted and punished, whether they were made by white officials or black militants. Needed legislative changes should have been advanced. If we had had a leadership willing to do and capable of doing what it was sworn to do, there would have been no serious racial strife in the Sixties. But if our officials had done their duty, there would not have been the great increase in federal powers engineered through the Sixties by the President, the Congress and the Supreme Court. It is only in such times of stress that so radical an increase in the powers of government can be imposed on the people.

It was the failure of government to act which gave the radicals a free hand in fomenting riot and rebellion. When the big riots started, the police were ordered by public officials to stand aside from the looting, thus encouraging the amazed populace to join in the theft and vandalism. Government made the riots.

It is a loose and inaccurate reading of these events to hold that racial strife is a serious threat to public order. The real default lies in the political leadership of our society—in the political parties, and in the powers which direct political policy. The Negroes of America are as loyal to our political system as any other element of society. We have simply been through a period in which the alliance of government with black Marxists has silenced the voices of responsible members of the black community. When black lawlessness is politically rewarded, how can black people be expected to criticize it?

But some did criticize the militants, and their voices were virtually excluded from the news media. When in 1964 the Reverend Joseph Harrison Jackson was re-elected to a twelfth year of leadership of the five-million-member National Baptist Convention, he criticized the fomenters of discord and concluded:[9] "We cannot be saved as a people unless America is saved as a Nation." When has anyone ever seen the Reverend Jackson on a national television program examining racial relations in the United States? His was a voice to be silenced.

The evidence may not support a conclusion that the racial strife of the Sixties was contrived to expand the federal powers and curb the powers of the states. We know there are people in high office who welcome the result, but we cannot show that they planned it. It is possible to show, however, that national leaders who can generally be identified with the Americans for Democratic Action as an agency of Fabian socialism have an ideological sympathy for the black Marxists that disposes them to satisfy the black demands. The remark of Senator Hubert Humphrey, an ADA founding member—"I have enough spark left in me to lead a mighty good revolt under those conditions"[10]—was symptomatic of the disposition of the national leadership.

Our cities really weren't burned by black rebels. Blacks only used the Molotov cocktails. The cities were burned by our public officials who used the strife to increase their power. The race issue should have been settled when it was raised and national unity should long ago have been restored. Unhappily, the measures taken at that time, instead of resolving the question, have embedded it in our political system as a continuing source of strife. Some black leaders have been led to believe that government owes them continuing special advantage and largesse from the federal treasury. We have institutionalized discrimination and black racism in civil-rights bureaucracies, which have a vested interest in conflict. We have injected race, monitored by federal bureaucracies, into housing, employment, voting and other activities.

Until all these bureaucracies are dismantled and their enacting laws rescinded, our political system will continue to be the chief cause of racial strife in America. These institutions make discrimination the basic thesis of law, and that is wrong for America. We need no law giving special favor to any class or group. We need one law for all—one law binding on all citizens, a law of national unity in cultural diversity.

There is ample power in all minorities today to protect their rights in law. None of them need special protection of the federal government. What the country desperately needs is to get the federal bureaucracy out of the business of administering race relations. That is a task for law and the courts.

Chapter 13

FREEDOM OF THE PRESS

It seems to be a goal of the American news media to persuade the American people that a free press is the cornerstone of their liberties. Professional newsmen make the assertion as an article of faith. A people jealous of their freedom cannot be ruled by such shibboleths. "Freedom of the press," like patriotism, can be a refuge of scoundrels.

A truly free press is indeed one of the signs of a free society. In fact, freedom of the press and freedom of the people are so closely related that the condition of a national press is one of the critical signs of society's condition. Is the political order preserving the people's freedom? You will find the answer in their press.

In the United States in recent decades we have experienced great development in the power and presence of our news media in American life. The money spent for television advertising in political campaigns is one acknowledgment of this new power in the public life of the nation.

A free press is not an independent good; it is a relative good. It has a special importance in our political system. Our commitment to the sovereignty of the people requires that the people have access to all information and opinion bearing on public policy. Only when they have such untrammeled access to relevant information can the people exercise their sovereign responsibility with vision and wisdom.

In this light, we must measure the qualities of our press not alone by its independence from government but by its independence from every other pressure or bias. In a society such as ours, a press free of every governmental restraint but consumed by a passion to shape public policy to its own view of the public interest could be the greatest enemy of our freedom. It would deny public access to information and opinion contradictory of its own judgment. Jacques Maritain told us what a free press must be: "A free people needs a free press, I mean free from the state, and free also from economic bondage and the power of money."[1]

We have had in the United States in the past dozen years a tragic example of media disservice to our country. Throughout the long course of the war in Vietnam, our news media, and especially the national television networks, have exercised a positive censorship over war news conveyed to the American people. As early as 1961, reports from South Vietnam consciously disparaged the courage, skill and fortitude of our ally while extolling the integrity and commitment of the Viet Cong. As the scale of military operations increased and North Vietnamese army units entered the battle, the favorable treatment was extended to Ho Chi Minh and his troops in the South. Even when U.S. Army and Marine units entered the battle, the brazen partiality of news reporting to the enemy continued. To the very end, the campaign of slander of our war effort continued. In July 1972, *Air Force* magazine reported:[2]

> It is true that, on May 23, NBC News showed a film of South Vietnamese marines in a village called Phon Bieng. The village obviously was aflame, and NBC told its listeners the marines themselves were to blame. "Instead of defending it, they ripped it apart," said the script, recited by a reporter named Phil Brady.
> The truth of the matter was that the fire had been started by North Vietnamese mortar shells and the marines had tried, futilely, to put it out. To its credit, NBC broadcast a correction twenty-four hours later. What they did not tell their listeners in the correction is that their Phil Brady was nowhere near Phon Bieng. When he recorded his narration he was in Hong Kong, putting inaccurate words on a film sent from Vietnam.

On the home front, a similar policy prevailed. Programs about the war offered government officials adequate opportunity to present their views of sound policy. But in these programs there was no concealment of network preference for the persons and views of persons opposing the war effort.

As between the governmental view that the United States should help its ally in South Vietnam and the socialist view that the United States should abandon South Vietnam to Ho Chi Minh's rule, there was disparity of treatment but not exclusion. The critical censorship occurred in the rigid and virtually total exclusion from a public hearing of the traditional alternative available to the United States: ending the war by defeating the enemy. You can search in vain through the national television discussion programs of these dozen years for more than a fleeting statement of the view that the United States or its ally should or could defeat the enemy.

Why was the option of military victory excluded from information made available to the American people? One factor was the decision of the press, made apparent in the campaign to overthrow President Ngo Dinh Diem, that U.S. policy should accommodate the conquest of South Vietnam by Ho Chi Minh. In 1962, Americans for Democratic Action had called on the U.S. Government to cease giving support "to such dictatorial governments as that of President Diem of South Vietnam." American Fabians had no heart for opposing the extension of socialism to South Vietnam, and Fabian thinking dominated the powerful Eastern newspapers.

Arthur Krock had noted the growing control of news reporting by the editorial offices of the *New York Times*:[3]

> . . . with the growth in scope, size and capability of the extraordinary news-collecting medium—and in the huge gross revenues that have accrued from the patronage of its community—certain disquieting changes seem to me to have been the consequences. Among these are over-organization; the second-guessing treatment applied to highly qualified reporters by a growing horde of editors in the New York office. . . .

There can be no doubt that the contrived reporting of the period represented management policy.

Television perception of the war was at one with the views of the *New York Times*, the *Washington Post* and the *Los Angeles Times*. Moreover, exclusion of the option of victory was the policy embraced by government, by the administration and by the Republican opposition. There was in this matter an almost total concurrence of government and news media judgments of the public interest.

This default of our press was not caused by any lack of freedom from government controls. Rather, available evidence suggests that the news media may have been influential in shaping the government judgment. From his interview with President Kennedy on May 5, 1961, Arthur Krock informs us of the President's concern about *New York Times* reporting of the Vietnam scene:[4]

> . . . the President did express the view that, if the *New York Times* would not print (certain) stories by David Halberstam (from Southeast Asia), most other news editors wouldn't either: "They follow your selection of what is fit to print in matters of national security."

The *Times*, whatever its motivation, had embarked on a program to discredit our ally in South Vietnam, and this campaign had a potential for redirecting U.S. policy. It seemed that the New York-London Fabian axis was working diligently, with New York in the subservient role, as usual. In due course the Kennedy Administration adopted the same Fabian view of the war which shaped British policy.

This exclusion of the alternative of victory from U.S. policy was the crucial error of the war. This was the American decision, made first by President Kennedy, which encouraged North Vietnam to wage war against the South. The misjudgment was compounded of ignorance about war, idle fears of Soviet or Red Chinese response, and British influence.

We need not here demonstrate the folly of that judgment. What is here of concern is that a "free press" was free to keep from the public information which it considered hostile to its own view of sound policy. That kind of "freedom of the press" should be anathema to the people.

The clamor of the national news media about freedom of the press is merely a claim of their own right to manage the news. Public policy must reject the claim. It remains to be demonstrated that management by government is worse than management by selfish private interests, susceptible to foreign control. Public officials are at least sworn to serve the public interest.

Our history of press freedom is related to an era when the costs of publication were moderate and means were widely available to the public. Under these circumstances, the capacity of citizens to publish their own public journals excluded any interest or bloc from achieving a monopoly position. In these circumstances, the competition of the marketplace assured that the public interest in comprehensive news coverage would be served. "Freedom of the press" did then state the imperative of our political order.

MONOPOLY OF THE PRESS

This condition no longer obtains. The news media are now organized in great corporations commanding extensive resources. They are essentially monopolistic in character. And if there is one area of our society in which monopoly should be intolerable, it is in the news media.

Costs of publishing have so increased in recent decades that only a few of our largest cities now have competing newspapers. In many of our largest cities, where only two newspapers are published, they are under common ownership. Thus, monopoly is the rule. Moreover, our newspapers are dependent upon wire services which are also monopolies. This vulnerability of our press to control by private monopoly hostile to the public interest constitutes a critical flaw in our political organization.

The Associated Press and United Press International were organized in a time when newspaper practice separated the opinion of the editorial pages from the "objective" reporting of the news pages. It then seemed that a national or international organization devoted to gathering "factual" news would be no threat to the political process. Times have changed. The practice of excluding opinion from the news pages has been discarded. Under the guise of "interpretive reporting," the wire services, and local reporters too, tell the public not what happened but the significance of what happened. They color or suppress the facts to create images deemed desirable by the news service. Through these changes, the news pages of our national press have become a powerful instrument for shaping the people's views of public questions. The instrument is doubly effective because of the lingering public

131

illusion that the news pages are factual in their context. Moreover, the wire services now offer what they call "news analysis," special editorial judgments about current issues which should be carried on editorial pages, but are not.

A monopoly news service with such far-reaching power to shape public opinion cannot be ignored by powers concerned about politics. Such an enterprise operates in the interest of those who own it.

The reality is that "freedom of the press" has long since been destroyed in the United States. Our press has remained free from government control but it has been captured and used by private monopolies, which conceive a right to judge what information the public should receive. These owners have increased their powers in recent decades as independent and competing newspapers have been eliminated, absorbed or purchased.

Reporters soon learn which attitudes and styles win approval of management and bylines for the writer. In time the correct attitudes become the uniform view of the press. One reporter wrote:[5]

> New York journalism was a chamber of mirrors and echoes, and the "mood" we called America's was ultimately our own mood, distilled mainly from talking to each other.

This bias of the newsman colors his reporting. Edgar Ansel Mowrer, whose experience is unsurpassed, wrote that "nothing is less welcome to a newsman than to have to report without bias the doings of a government he dislikes."[6]

Today reporters are not expected to curb their bias. They are part of a system for controlling public attitudes.

Oswald Spengler wrote in 1922:[7]

> What is truth? For the multitude, that which it continually reads and hears. A forlorn little drop may settle somewhere and collect grounds on which to determine "the truth"—but what it obtains is just its truth. The other, the public truth of the moment, which alone matters for effects and successes in the fact-world, is today a product of the Press. What the Press wills, is true. Its commanders evoke, transform, interchange truths. Three weeks of press-work, and the "truth" is acknowledged by everybody.

A decade later, Adolf Hitler wrote in *Mein Kampf:* "By clever and sustained propaganda, an entire people can be made to believe that heaven is hell and the most miserable existence is a paradise."[8]

When the power of the press to shape the public mind is so widely recognized by scholars and practitioners, it is a strange delusion of our people that they are getting the truth from our news media. Elementary knowledge of human nature should alert them to the reality that they are being brainwashed in the interest of those who control the media. Perhaps the delusion is a hangover from the days of a more competitive press. Perhaps it is a contrivance of the press itself, to conceal its real role. And maybe there is an ingredient of misplaced faith, as Willmoore Kendall explained public complacency:[9]

> People are now too accustomed, in area after area of their lives, to having experts do their thinking for them to be disposed to kick up a fuss against

132

any particular set of experts. Experts tell them how to care for their bodies, and they obey. Experts tell them what books to read, and they obey again. Experts make the decisions about foreign policy that get them into wars they fight, and the decisions about tax policy that determine how much of their incomes they can selfishly spend on themselves; and they no longer even know the words they would have to use in order to argue back. They are out of the habit of bringing to bear their own cherished convictions, their own preferences and prejudices. The experts tell them, indeed, that they shouldn't have prejudices—their own value—judgments, as they are now fashionably called. People are, I say, out of the habit of bringing these things to bear on any matters more grand than choosing their personal friends or deciding whether to paint the garage door.

There is evidence of growing skepticism among our people as the arrogance and false reporting of the media reach flagrant dimensions. But this is not an area where individual action can be effective. The maintenance of a free press requires the force of law and the support of the body politic.

This monopoly condition of the press in the United States is a product of government neglect. The monopoly press has assumed the role of guardian of press freedom and has proclaimed the danger of governmental censorship. Politicians in the Congress and in the White House flinch at the thought of challenging these pretensions. It is clearly a responsibility of government to maintain freedom of the press from private monopoly, but government has failed in this duty to the people.

The question of a free press obviously cannot be left to the economics of production, so that only persons commanding great wealth can control newspapers. We have laws that outlaw such concentrations of power, but they are not being enforced by the Attorney General. Congress must now enact more explicit laws to dismantle corporate concentrations of newspaper ownership. It must break up chains and cartels and require local ownership of local newspapers. There is no requirement or place for government censorship, but there is desperate need for a new charter of press freedom to outlaw monopolies in the dissemination of public information.

Special legal restraint must be placed also on the size and reach of wire services or syndicates that undertake to provide press services to the newspapers, to the end that monopoly be precluded in this field.

These constructive measures to protect our political system are precluded by the mythology that a "free press" will protect the people's freedom if only the press is protected from government controls. Citizens concerned with the health and survival of our freedom must realize that the critical issue is the people's right to know; and that this right is today forfeit not to government but to private monopoly in our press. Congress must act to restore press freedom as a vital service to the people.

THE FRANCHISED MEDIA

In radio and television, we have a related but different problem. In this field, where limited channels and power are available for use, Congress has established a governmental regulatory function. It has prescribed in law that monopoly shall not be permitted and has charged the Federal Communications Commission with administration of the law.

The Federal Communications Commission has issued a "fairness doctrine," which requires licensed stations to give balanced treatment to controversial issues of public interest and concern. This rule is a dead letter because the Commission has never created method or means for its enforcement.

There has been much self-serving propaganda from the networks, and tacitly from the Commission, to the effect that the fairness doctrine is not a practical and enforceable rule because it would require government censorship of station performance. That is false. The fairness doctrine is a statement of the people's right to know. It states that every franchise holder has a duty to treat controversial public questions in balance, that he may not use his position to favor his own prejudice. That is a requirement that every person or corporation holding a due respect for freedom of the press should embrace willingly. This is what freedom of the press is all about.

. On controversial public questions, it is a matter of simple administration and not censorship to determine what the chief differences are and then to give protagonists of these positions an opportunity to present them to the public. That is all the fairness doctrine requires.

What public policy now requires is enforcement of the doctrine. The Federal Communications Commission should establish a monitoring element to assure compliance. With a modest staff it could very soon collect evidence to substantiate the present arrogant disregard of the rule and force franchise holders into compliance with it. The practice of waiting for public complaints (which are then ignored) is no proper way for the Commission to administer its responsibility for so vital a matter of public policy.

The Commission long ago issued rules limiting the ownership of television and/or radio outlets to six stations. This nominal compliance with congressional antimonopoly policy has been neutralized by Commission toleration and even favor for the network monopolies. The three major networks have, by exclusive contracting, created monopolies of television and radio time and programming. It matters little to public policy who owns the stations when private monopolies committed to the shaping of public opinion control the programs.

The network system of exclusive contracting has made a mockery of Commission regulation and of the public interest. Commission jurisdiction extends only to the stations, not to the networks. With stations holding exclusive network contracts, it is impracticable for the stations to comply with fairness standards. In practice, the stations become captives of the unregulated networks and the Commission becomes a defender of the network monopolies which it was called by law to prohibit. Congress has acquiesced in this subversion of the public interest.

These defaults of the Federal Communications Commission and of the Congress have enabled the networks to play a dominant role in shaping national policy. By grossly slanted reporting of the news, they promoted and made possible the Kennedy betrayal of President Diem in 1963. In this event, the network bias was in general concert with that of the *New York Times* and the *Washington Post*.

The congressional antimonopoly policy can be made effective, with corresponding protection of the public interest, when stations have full control of their own programming. The Commission can outlaw exclusive contracting of station time to networks for unknown future programming. It can require each station to purchase and be responsible for the specific programs shown on its broadcasts. It can also require stations to deal only with program producers who offer their shows on an open basis to all stations wishing to purchase them. The network grip on national programs would be broken. Stations would be liberated. Such regulations as these, which are well within the authority of the Commission and are responsive to congressional policy, would enable the Commission to hold stations to compliance with the fairness doctrine.

The immediate effect of such regulations might be small. Because the networks are the chief producers of programs, they would doubtless continue to be the chief suppliers. It is probable that most stations would continue to buy the programs previously scheduled. But the regulations would allow new producers to compete on an equal footing with the networks. As station managers learned to survey the entire market before buying, networks would compete with one another as well as with independent producers in ways which are not now possible. The cost of such competitition might indeed be painful for poor producers but it should develop better programs for the public.

The effect should be especially salutary in television news programs. When local stations can cancel biased network programs which offend the popular judgment and contract for better replacement programs, the variety of popular interests in various sections of the country will compel a diversity of reporting. Station managers familiar with the local scene can best judge the needs of the community. They will choose from program offerings those most suitable to their needs. In sum, when the network monopoly of programming is broken and competition is restored in this field, that act alone will in large measure provide the balanced news treatment which the public interest requires.

We have considered the problems of monopoly ownership or program control in the major news media. It remains to note the problem of local monopoly of the several media. In many communities, newspapers and radio and television stations are under common ownership. The economics of media service have tended to foster such concentrations of ownership for the capital and operating savings realized. Nevertheless, the monopoly of local news service is against the public interest. Regardless of the cost of service, the Federal Communications Commission should outlaw the ownership of radio and television franchises by newspapers or other printed news services. Local ownerships should be separate and independent with any cross-servicing arranged by arms-length contracting.

NEW POLICY NEEDED

The American news media in the past forty years have rendered signal disservice to the nation. They have been a pliable instrument of Soviet and British foreign policy in misinforming our people about our national interest in a free China. They misrepresented the significance of Fidel Castro's attack on the Batista government in Cuba. They undermined President Diem in Vietnam and contributed to the chaos and bloodshed which followed.

It is indeed a remarkable phenomenon that the news media of a country can so consistently be opposed to the true national interest. How can one rationalize such a parade of error? Why does the press attack our government when it is right and applaud it when it is wrong?

Some Americans attribute the error to Soviet influence on policy-making. Moscow does have some influence through American industry, and it doubtless still has agents in our government; but the evidence does not suggest that Moscow has so much influence on policy-making. The correlation of U.S. policy is with British policy. U.S. decisions so hostile to our national interest have generally been consonant with the British interest. As Professor Quigley has informed us, the Council on Foreign Relations was formed in collaboration with Britain. And the powerful American interests that embarked on that venture were of the press as well as the financial and diplomatic fraternities.

We have noted that the press in large measure controls politics. But money controls both. Whittaker Chambers wrote of these elites:[10]

> The forces of revolution in the West are an intellectual proletariat, disinherited, not in this world's goods with which they are often incongruously replete, but disinherited in the spirit. The revolt of the intellectuals of the West almost without exception begins (no matter how it ends) as the frantic threshing of those drowning in the materialism of the West, a convulsive struggle against the death of the spirit. This is the answer to the fatuous, reiterated question why men like Arthur Koestler or Whittaker Chambers became Communists.

No doubt these Fabian socialists, working in concert with British policy, have a design for the world. But it is not the American design. It is rather the restoration of omnipotent government with the elites in power. It is a very old story in human history.

When Vice President Agnew in 1969 opened his attack on media bias, he struck a responsive chord in the public consciousness. The people had resented the brainwashing though they had been unable to prevent it. They thought they had found a new champion in the Vice President. In 1973, Mr. Clay T. Whitehead, the White House Staff Assistant for Communications Policy, aroused some concern by calling upon the franchised stations to be more critical of network programs, more responsible for the programs transmitted.

Whatever the motivations of the former Vice President and Mr. Whitehead, it seems clear at this point that President Nixon has no intention of taking effective action against the monopolies. He used the Vice President and Mr. Whitehead to convey to the public a false impression of administration concern. Actually, he has had in the office of his Attorney General the capacity to move against the press monopolies. His appointees to the Federal Communications Commission had opportunity to improve administration of the fairness rule, but did not do so. We must conclude that President Nixon's actions are in support of continuing the monopolies in press and television. Like President Johnson and other predecessors, he is administering public policy for the benefit of the financial powers which nominated and elected him.

Who can doubt that this continuing disservice to the public interest is an achievement of the two political parties? They have written the law, they have appointed the administrators, they have been paid by the beneficiaries. They have closed their eyes to the public interest in their pursuit of the spoils of public office.

During the past half-century we have experienced in the United States a dynamic expansion of the broadcast media and a growing concentration of power in the newspaper industry. In both broadcast and print media, highly profitable monopoly positions exercising great influence on public policy formation have been established with the collusion or acquiescence of the Congress, the Presidents, the Federal Communications Commission and the two political parties. The consequent manipulation of public opinion to tolerate bad public policy has been a major factor in the decline of the United States. The very survival of our form of government requires that these monopolies be dismantled and that a strictly limited and widely dispersed ownership and control of news media be adopted as a cornerstone of the people's liberty.

137

Chapter 14

LAW ENFORCEMENT

THE GROWING CRIMINALITY of American society must be a serious concern of every citizen. As the fundamental duty of government is to preserve public order, failure in this responsibility challenges the worth of the political system. Citizens *in extremis* will turn to another system that can preserve public order.

In the early years of the Republic, our pioneer society, with its emphasis on personal liberty and limited police forces, saw substantial levels of violence. A chief restraint was the strong moral and religious foundations of society. This was the spirit which tamed the wilderness. By this century, the homicide rate was still high, compared with European countries. This led Homer Lea to conclude that "All law presupposes the exercise of force in its execution; hence we find that crime increases proportionately at this power deteriorates."[1]

That description of the role of force is only part of the equation of public order. The basic factor is the self-discipline of the people. If they are conditioned by their tradition to high standards of public order, a minimum of force will be required to contain aberrant behavior. When a people lose their tradition of high moral behavior, increasing force must be used to restrain criminality.

138

Thus, the problem of order is first a problem of social discipline. According to Aristotle, as man

> . . . is the best of animals when perfected, so is he the worst of all when severed from the bonds of law and justice. For the disposition to injure others is most pernicious when it is equipped, as it is in man, with the strength of intelligence, which ought to be used for good purposes but can very well be used for bad. That is why, if he is without habitual discipline or virtue, man is the most unscrupulous and savage being alive, worse than all others in his indulgence of carnal appetites.[2]

As George Washington recognized, the foundation of social discipline is moral training and the foundation of moral training is religious training. The capacity of any state to maintain public order in the absence of religious training is in question; but of this we can be certain: no state can have both order and freedom without religious training.

A perceptive critic of the American scene has warned us:[3]

> Political freedom is endangered in its foundations as soon as the universal moral values, upon whose shared possession the self-discipline of a free society depends, are no longer vigorous enough to restrain the passions and shatter the selfish inertia of men. The American ideal of freedom as ordered freedom and therefore an ethical ideal, has traditionally reckoned with these truths, these truisms.

It is the experience of history that deterioration of the social fabric begins at the top, among the elites which enjoy the economic benefits of society, and not among the working class. Decay begins with religion, with a new cynicism and sophistication among the self-styled intellectuals who conceive that they can get along very well without God. Thus:[4]

> When they are not toppling governments but are busy at their books, serious students can learn from the pages of an Aristotle or a Polybius or an Alexis de Tocqueville or even a Crane Brinton of Harvard that in times of crisis there has regularly occurred a "transfer of the allegiance," or in Crane Brinton's words, a "desertion of the intellectuals to the ranks of the unruly." Crane Brinton also reminds students of the history of revolutions that the first phase of that desertion of the intellectuals to the ranks of the unruly consists of their encouraging the government—if it will listen—to respond eagerly to "revolutionary demands on the part of the organized discontented, demands which if granted would mean the virtual abdication of those governing."

Civilization and order seem in some degree to be self-destructive. Men raised in a disciplined social order often have no comprehension of the bonds which hold it together. They conclude that force is not really necessary to restrain criminality, that compassion and preaching will reform the criminal. So, as they tolerate criminality, they encourage its spread in the community, releasing the savage and unscrupulous appetites described by Aristotle. In the United States, this kind of sentimentality has played a substantial role in the deterioration of law enforcement.

In our society, a perversion of the Christian ethic has contributed to decay of social bonds. The pioneer Christians in this land were hardy characters who knew the difference between right and wrong and had no doubt about the responsibility of each individual for his personal behavior. They believed and practiced that justice required the punishment of lawbreakers. But in this century, the Christian ethic has deteriorated into a weak and spineless caricature of the biblical teaching. Church authorities have embraced foolish notions about changing the nature of man by humoring his passions, about eliminating war by disarmament, about reforming criminals by kindness. This kind of errant utopianism propagated by organized religion has fostered the spread of crime and immorality.

It was a nominally Christian state governor who first suspended and then commuted the death penalty for inmates of the state penitentiary, saying that he could not in conscience allow the executions. But he did not explain how he could in conscience take the oath of office as Governor to faithfully execute the laws, if he could not in conscience execute the laws. This is the kind of mixed-up morality which seems to attend the deterioration of law enforcement in the United States. It is powerfully propagated by sectors of society affecting high ethical principle as they tear down the social order.

This softening of the Christian ethic, this excursion into maudlin sentimentality, is not without powerful succor. It is unconsciously allied with revolutionary forces which reject not only the whole Christian ethic but the very foundations of all civilization—Greek, Roman, Judeo-Christian, Hindu or Chinese. Our modern Jacobins represent the reincarnation of barbarism. Their first object is to destroy the present social order. They have no improvement to offer, but are confident that when they have power they will find something. Their agents, witting or unwittingly, have been described by one of the most perceptive observers of the American scene:[5]

> There are those who assert that revolution had swept the United States. That is not true. But there are some who are trying to bring it about. At least, they are following the vocal technique which has led elsewhere to the tragedy of liberty. Their slogans; their promise of Utopia; their denunciation of individual wickednesses as if these were the wards of liberty; their misrepresentation of deep-seated causes; their will to destruction of confidence and consequent disorganization in order to justify action; their stirring of class feeling and hatred; their will to clip and atrophy the legislative arm; their resentment of criticism, their chatter of boycott, of threat and of force— all are typical enough of the methods of more violent action.

The first target of the revolutionary forces is the system of law enforcement. In the United States, under cover of racial strife and with the cooperation of the news media, they have gone far to persuade citizens that the police are enemies of the people. This is of course the dogma of class warfare, but older Americans must be concerned to see it so blatantly proclaimed by radicals and tacitly approved by the news media. Police are the cornerstone of public order. As the Reverend John Courtney Murray wrote:[6]

We can start from a fact of political history, that every government has always claimed what is called police power, as an attribute of government. This power in itself is simply the principle of self-preservation and self-protection transferred to the body politic. It extends to the requirements of public morals, public health, public order, and the general comfort of society. The only question is: how far and in what circumstances does it extend to all these social values?

Father Murray has spotlighted another point of attack. What role does government have in upholding public morals? Isn't morality something that should be left to religious preference and individual choice? Should consenting adults be allowed to indulge any behavior that does not injure other parties?

It is shocking indeed that such infantile notions of liberty are gaining acceptance among mature intellectuals. Of course the state, representing the community, has a vital interest in the moral quality of the community. Just as the individual has a legitimate care for his health, the community has a legitimate care for its health. The health of the society as well as its hope of survival depends on its moral quality. The state's interest in the moral quality of society may even conflict with and take precedence over religious standards of morality.

Thus, the early commitment of the Mormon Church to polygamy for religious reasons could not be countenanced because it was in conflict with our law on marriage and the family. The preference of a couple to live together out of wedlock also challenges the institutions of marriage and family, which are the bedrock of our civilization. It must be treated as a disease of the community. To assert that individuals should be allowed to indulge the vilest perversions of nature with the cooperation of consenting adults is to abandon the discipline so necessary to human excellence and to encourage reversion to barbarism.

The sum of these assaults on law enforcement is augmented by changes made in law and government. The original constitutional structure was admirably suited to meeting the needs of a rapidly growing society. But today instead of having the police power firmly lodged in the state, where it could meet the real needs of the local communities, the Supreme Court has lifted it to the national level and to rules of administration grossly ineffective in coping with the threat to public order.

The Supreme Court, in its attempts to define insanity and pornography, so confused the law that the justices themselves could not agree in later cases what the law was. They established a precedent of freeing known criminals, unquestionably guilty, because of alleged procedural defects in the trial. The State of California at one time had in its constitution a more rational and just rule of review:[7]

No judgment shall be set aside . . . in any case, on the ground . . . the improper admission . . . of evidence . . . or for any error as to any matter of procedure, unless, after an examination of the entire case, including the

141

evidence, the court shall be of the opinion that the error complained of has resulted in a miscarriage of justice.

The settled rules of criminal law administration have been suspended by the ill-considered decrees of justices narrowly concerned with only one immediate passion. The arrogance and confusion of the Supreme Court seemed to reach a peak of irrelevancy in the capital punishment cases when the majority ignored the law to vent their personal judgments of what the law should be, and their judgments of what the law should be revealed how ill-qualified they were to sit in judgment of their fellow men.

In our unique system of government, with concurrent state and federal sovereignties existing over the same people and in the same area, each citizen was subject to two sets of law and two sets of lawmakers. The Constitution defined a separation of powers which in the past enabled the two sets of law to coexist amicably. In recent decades, however, the trespass of the Supreme Court and Congress upon state responsibilities caused increasing confusion and delay in law enforcement as the jurisdiction of the states was compromised.

We have noted that the chief authority for this expansion of federal powers was judicial interpretation of the Fourteenth Amendment; and that the change, initiated to protect "freedom of speech" from state restraint, received its chief impetus in Supreme Court definition of the civil rights of citizens. In this course of action, the Supreme Court burst into the field of criminal law enforcement, which theretofore had been the province of the states. In consequence, the federal courts have been flooded with constitutional appeals from state law enforcement or judicial action and the whole process of law enforcement has bogged down. The federal courts are not constituted and should not be constituted for the judicial responsibilities they have assumed.

The enforcement of federal law is the responsibility of the Department of Justice and the Attorney General of the United States. For this work, the Department of Justice maintains an office of the Federal District Attorney for each district court jurisdiction in the country. Federal prosecutions and other legal actions are normally processed through these District Courts. Special cases may on the initiative of the Attorney General be taken to other courts.

The outstanding work of the Federal Bureau of Investigation under its late Director, J. Edgar Hoover, gave the people an impression of integrity and competence in federal law enforcement which the record does not sustain. Bureau authority was limited to the investigation of crimes and the gathering of evidence to support prosecution. But the decision to prosecute or not to prosecute rested with the Attorney General. Thus it was possible that a criminal against whom convincing evidence had been assembled might be exempted from prosecution if political interest warranted such action.

142

Before the inauguration of President John F. Kennedy, tradition and public opinion had sustained a high level of integrity in the Department of Justice. The federal government was not without its scandals, as the trial of Secretary of Interior Albert B. Fall in the Harding Administration demonstrated; but that trial was a sign that such conduct would not be countenanced in the President's Cabinet. In those years, the Attorney General of the United States was usually a respected national figure who would not sell his soul for the office he held.

Prior to 1960, it had been a general rule that the campaign manager of the successful presidential candidate would serve as Postmaster General in the new Cabinet. Postmasterships blanketing the country were the lawful spoils of office for rewarding faithful political followers in the cities, towns and villages of the land. Through this political network, the Postmaster General prepared for the next campaign.

POLITICS IN JUSTICE

When John F. Kennedy was elected President, his father, Joseph P. Kennedy, insisted that Robert F. Kennedy, the successful campaign manager, be appointed Attorney General. The sons remonstrated but the father insisted.

Joseph P. Kennedy knew American government as well as any man. And few men in industry knew American business enterprise as well as he did. The father realized that the transfer of postmasterships to civil service protection had in recent decades divested the Postmaster General's position of its former power and influence. He knew also that the growing concentrations of power in American industry and questions of federal law relating to mergers made the Attorney General's office a powerful fulcrum from which to compel industry support of Administration policy. Thus, it was from this office that Robert F. Kennedy exercised his concern for the reelection of his brother.

We have noted how the Attorney General committed his office to a secret agreement with black leaders in 1961 to defy state law in the South. So too, when the steel companies in 1962 raised prices in disregard of a presidential stabilization policy that had no legal foundation, the Attorney General's use of the Federal Bureau of Investigation to interrogate informed newsmen and steel company officials caused public scandal. President Kennedy used the contracting powers of the federal government to discipline the steel companies. They bowed to his demand and rescinded the price increases.

The event marked the great increase in the power of the President, a power now independent of law. It contrasted with a similar event sixteen years earlier when the leaders of American industry had more backbone. When in 1946 President Truman decided that a steel strike was injuring the national welfare, he had the federal government seize and operate the steel industry. Ben Fairless, who was then the President of the U.S. Steel Corporation, took the government into court to demonstrate that the President of the United States had no legal authority for the powers he had assumed. The federal court sustained the complaint and ordered the federal government to return the steel properties to their owners and to pay damages for trespass.

In 1946, American industry understood that it existed under a government of law. It was prepared to fight to defend its legal rights against encroachment by government. But by 1961 industry management had been transferred from the strong hands of builders to the weak hands of lawyers and bankers. With no concern beyond the immediate crisis, they would bow to the extralegal demands of a President. To avoid conflict with a major customer, they would compromise the independence of American business.

At the time of the racial conflict in Oxford, Mississippi in 1962, Maj. Gen. Edwin A. Walker, who had resigned from the United States Army after the Kennedy Administration removed him from command in Germany (*before* investigating newspaper allegations against him), went to the scene as an observer. Newspaper reports depicting him as a leader of violence were false; his efforts were to calm the students and avoid violence. Nevertheless, on the basis of diagnosis by a federal prison psychiatrist who had never seen General Walker, and the authority of a federal judge who accepted such contrived evidence, the Federal Bureau of Investigation arrested General Walker and committed him to a federal mental institution in Springfield, Missouri. General Walker had to submit to testing procedures for mental illness before a writ of habeas corpus could secure his release from federal custody.

What this event revealed was the degree in which an utter disregard of law and due process had possessed the Kennedy Administration. Law had become a tool to sustain the edicts of the President and to smash all opposition to his authority. In this time, the mind of Washington was not far removed from the mind of Moscow. The zealot convinced of his own righteousness is the enemy of law and of justice.

In the Johnson administration the corruption of federal law continued, often accomplished by the Attorney General and the federal courts under the cover of "civil rights" programs. The critical factor was the desperate necessity for the Democratic Party to retain the Negro vote as an element of its coalition. Radical and ambitious young Negroes were threatening to leave the party. They demanded that the federal government accept responsibility for the welfare of black citizens, even where problems were purely local and not subject to federal jurisdiction. The propaganda about constitutional civil rights conferred by the Fourteenth Amendment provided an apology for federal usurpation of state police powers. Congress set up federal poverty programs in local communities, controlling or ignoring

144

local jurisdictions in management of the programs. In years of steady expansion of federal powers, the groundwork had been prepared for this great leap into socialism. Officials and judges who had been persuaded that justice could be achieved only through socialism found in the mere claim of racial crisis and discrimination, without supporting evidence, reason enough to brush aside the Constitution and due process. The Supreme Court and President Johnson were of one mind.

When in the Nixon Cabinet the President's campaign manager became his Attorney General, the pattern of power was obviously being continued. When the Attorney General withdrew objections to International Telephone and Telegraph Company's merger with the Hartford Insurance Company, after ITT representatives pledged a $100,000 contribution to support the 1972 Republican Presidential Convention in San Diego, California, the Attorney General's continuing role as campaign manager became apparent. When in 1972, after Attorney General Mitchell had resigned that office to become Chairman of the Committee To Re-elect the President, agents of the Committee were apprehended with detection equipment in the national office of the Democratic Party, Mr. Mitchell hurriedly resigned from the Committee and retired to New York.

The Nixon administration was as reluctant as the Johnson administration to prosecute Marxist law violators. Trials were delayed until public interest had subsided sufficiently to make a lenient verdict or acquittal politically tolerable. After the scandalous conduct of both attorneys and defendants in the trial of the Chicago seven, the federal appeals court released the convicted law violators on bail, to roam the country and even to leave it, while the judges dallied for years before finding defects to nullify the trial.

The evidence of these years reveals a growing brazenness in the use of federal power for party advantage. Both political parties have rejected the idea that the President is the representative of all the people and that all citizens must stand equal before the law. The new ethic is that the power of government must be used to build the power of the party—to help the friends of the party and to harass its foes. It requires no clairvoyance to see that this corruption of the Department of Justice constitutes a serious deterioration in the quality of government. Law enforcement is the key to public order. When exemption from the law can be purchased from the ruling political party, virtue is for sale.

The example of the Nixon administration found a counterpart in the general deterioration of the federal judiciary. The judges seemed to consider that their duty was not to apply the law but to grant pardon for the offenses against society. They had lost the wisdom of a noted British jurist who warned: "To acquit a criminal is to commit by his hands all the offenses of which he is afterwards guilty."[8]

Federal judges had not been schooled in the criminal law and were ill-

145

qualified to administer it. Many of them were gullible dupes for every pretense of constitutional privilege. The Supreme Court assumption of jurisdiction over the police power has been a disaster.

TO RESTORE INTEGRITY

As in so many other aspects of public life, the idea that law must be administered fairly and equitably was implicit in the moral and religious ethics of our forefathers. There was no law that a prosecutor or judge could not use his discretion unfairly. It just wasn't done by honest men.

The cure for such deterioration of public morality must be a return to the ethical and religious foundations of our society. As Arthur Krock wrote:[9]

> . . . it is neither futile nor silly to seek to revert to the more practical and effective approaches to these problems that were in use before the current socialist-liberal philosophy and the new economics weakened this nation and others in the non-Communist world. For the twentieth-century liberals have made a titanic failure of their own approaches, among the most grievous being the breakdown of law enforcement and the rise of mob rule in the United States.

Pending that return to the fundamentals of our political order, there are measures which can be taken to adapt government to the actual mores of our time. The public confidence in federal law enforcement could be restored by making the Department of Justice, like the Federal Bureau of Investigation, a non-partisan administrator of the law. The President and his cabinet officers now have their own counsel, separate from the Department of Justice, in their own offices. An independent office of federal law enforcement created by Congress and with powers defined by Congress could remove federal law enforcement from the political arena and restore standards of impartiality once taken for granted in our society.

A salutary and less drastic change might be made by a requirement in law that the Attorney General's office be filled by a person of different political party from the President's. This requirement might be so stated that confirmation would require the concurrence of a majority of the members of the Senate not of the President's party. The presence in this office of a person of other political loyalty would reduce the present inclination of Presidents to use law enforcement for political advantage.

The sign of political corruption is the complacency with which both political parties regard the deterioration of law enforcement. Does the government refuse to prosecute or does it prosecute indifferently breaches of law by organized groups exercising political influence? Is the slackness of law enforcement the direct consequence of its political sensitivity? A political party cannot be expected to decree any reduction of its own corrupt influence over law enforcement. Only the people can do that; but they are blocked by the political parties.

Chapter 15

THE MORAL CLIMATE

THE QUALITY OF a civilization is determined by its moral climate. National leaders aware of their responsibility must give first attention to the preservation of the ethical standards of the nation. History tells us that in all lands and times, religion has been the chief support of morality. As President Washington said in his Farewell Address:

> Of all the dispositions and habits which lead to political prosperity, religion and morality are indispensable supports. . . . And let us with caution indulge the supposition that morality can be maintained without religion. Whatever may be conceded to the influence of refined education on minds of peculiar structure, reason and experience both forbid us to expect that national morality can prevail in exclusion of religious principle.

The statement of President Washington was not at the time considered unique or memorable. He was merely speaking the conventional wisdom of the time. The truth of his statement was understood by all citizens. "We hold these truths to be self-evident . . ." was still the cornerstone of the American political philosophy.

In 1799, President John Adams stated in his proclamation of March 6:[1]

> It is also most reasonable in itself that men who are capable of social arts and relations, who owe their improvements to the social state, and who

147

derive their enjoyments from it, should as a society, make acknowledgements of dependence and obligation to Him who hath endowed them with these capacities and elevated them in the scale of existence by these distinctions . . .

In a similar way, President Lincoln on May 30, 1863, summoned the people to prayer:[2]

Whereas the Senate of the United States, devoutly recognizing the supreme authority and just government of Almighty God in all the affairs of men and nations, has by a resolution requested the President to designate and set apart a day for national prayer and humiliation; and whereas it is the duty of nations as well as of men to own their dependence upon the overruling power of God, to confess their sins and trespasses in humble sorrow, yet with the assured hope that genuine repentance will lead to mercy and pardon . . .

These samples from the words of our Presidents could be multiplied a hundredfold. They reflect the expression in public life and policy of the deep religious and moral sentiment of the people. It is only in the twentieth century that similar expressions have become a pious fraud when they are uttered by unbelievers in deference to public sentiment.

This intimate union of government and religion reflected the reality of both in the lives of the people. It reflected also the public conviction that the powers of government were subordinate to Divine Providence and especially to the sacredness of man. As John Courtney Murray stated it:[3]

The whole consensus has its ultimate root in the ideal of the sacredness of man, *res sacra homo.* Man has a sacredness of personal dignity which commands the respect of society in all its laws and institutions. His sacredness guarantees him certain immunities and it also endows him with certain empowerments. He may make certain demands upon society and the state which require action in their support, and he may also utter certain prohibitions in the face of society and state. He may validly claim assistance, and with equal validity he may claim to be let alone.

Our founding Americans were chiefly people of biblical Protestant morality. Their lives were ruled by the presence and guidance of God.

THE UNBELIEVERS

In every society in every age, there are skeptics and iconoclasts who reject the prevailing morality and assert rights in opposition to it. When the convictions of a society are strong, the voices of cynicism are weak. But if the faith of the society in its ideals weakens, the dissenters will tear it to fragments.

Father Murray noted that:[4]

Unbelief in America has been rather easy-going, the product more of a naive materialism than of any conscious conviction. The American unbeliever is usually content to say, "I am not personally a religious man" and let the subject drop there. American unbelief is usually respectful of belief, or at least respectful of the freedom to believe. And this fact has been important in influencing the general climate in which our institutions work.

148

But that statement is true only of an earlier America. The intolerance of the atheist in the twentieth century is as virulent as that of the religious partisan of the sixteenth century. While prudence restrains the expression of that intolerance in any free society, the animus exhibits itself in many ways, notably in the behavior of outwardly tolerant public officials. We have today a subtle campaign of officials in high office, notably on the Supreme Court, to impress their secularist convictions on public policy:[5]

> The secularist has always fought his battles under a banner on which is emblazoned his special device "the integrity of the political order." In the name of this thundering principle he would banish from the political order (and from education as an affair of the city) all the "divisive forces" of religion. At least in America he has traditionally had no quarrel with religion as a "purely private matter" as a sort of essence or idea or ambient aura that may help to warm the hidden heart of solitary man. He may even concede a place to religion-in-general, whatever that is. What alarms him is religion as a thing, visible, corporate, organized, a community of thought that presumes to sit superior to, and in judgment on, the "community of democratic thought" and that is furnished somehow with an armature of power to make its thought and judgment publicly prevail. Under this threat he marshals his military vocabulary and speaks in terms of aggression, encroachment, maneuvers, strategy, tactics. He rallies to the defense of the city; he sets about the strengthening of the wall that separates the city from its enemy.

The secularist drive to separate government from God has had a large measure of success, insomuch as to lead another philosopher to declare:[6]

> The modern age is not a sacral, but a secular age. The order of terrestrial civilization and of temporal society has gained complete differentiation and full autonomy, which is something normal in itself, required by the Gospel's very distinction between God's and Caesar's domains. But that normal process was accompanied—and spoiled—by a most aggressive and stupid process of insulation from, and finally rejection of, God and the Gospel in the sphere of social and political life. The fruit of this we can contemplate today in the theocratic atheism of the Communist state.

The danger to the nation is not from the Communist but from the nominally loyal citizen within the walls who is working for "democratic socialism," and who propounds a series of plausible errors to subvert the moral order. Whittaker Chambers described his confrontation with this force, before he turned to communism:[7]

> It was liberalism that I was now about to encounter, often without knowing the nature of the force that worked on me, and it was to perform on me its historic task in our times. It was liberalism (both in the honest meaning of that word and in its current sense as a cover-name for socialism) that, in the form of the higher intellectualism, was about to work on my immature and patchwork beliefs. In its bland, emollient, persuasive climate, all the more effective because I could not even identify it, the bond of my frail ideas was gently to leach and melt away until they crumbled in absurd ruins. My religious gropings first hesitated, then ceased, embarrassed by their own callowness in that warm light of reason, smiles, and tolerant irony. My instinctive sense of practical purpose in life and in politics was to yield to a glorifica-

149

tion of the purposeless play of ideas for their own sake in the mind untrammelled by convictions. Any sense that some things are true and some things are false was to yield to the moral relativity summed up by Hamlet and quoted by one of my instructors: "There is nothing good or bad but thinking makes it so." At last, where there had been something, though uncouth, there was nothing. Into this vacuum, there sprang something which was waiting just around the corner—something which at first I had no way of identifying, but which I presently learned was Marxism. And as I watched the havoc of the liberal influence, first appraisingly, then bitterly and condemned it at last as negative, aimless, and mischievous, I welcomed the positive and radical force the more eagerly.

But this force, which in the 1920s was so powerful in some universities, is not limited to the campus. Its disciples have aged, and they have moved into positions of high trust in government, in industry, in the professions. It is from these elites that the passion to desacralize America now flows. It is revealed in actions: in the suppression of simple prayer in public schools, in denigration of the police, in the relativism which extenuates crime as a failure of society, in the fallacy that poverty is the cause of crime, in permissiveness which condones perversion, in the national legalization of abortion against the culture and expressed wishes of the people. In a gradual but relentless march toward their goal, the secularists have used the power of government to serve their intolerance.

The story is new in America only in its recent emergence. The drama had been enacted in other lands long ago. Even as our American Revolution was being fought, a ferment of atheism and materialism was spreading on the continent of Europe, preparing the way for the French Revolution. The division of Christendom through the Reformation had provided fertile ground for atheist allegations that both sides in the religious wars were telling the truth about each other. The vogue of Voltaire and Rousseau had developed schools of thought which treated religion as a primitive superstition unworthy of modern man. No doubt some seers found exhilaration in the illusion that they were now free of divine constraints.

That history is of interest now only to show that our civilization has a long history of dissent from the prevailing morality. The dissent received some acceleration in the nineteenth century from the expansion of science, the development of man's material resources and the delusion that ultimate knowledge had been reached. In the twentieth century, it received the reinforcement of national political power through Lenin's conquest of Russia. In this century also, the introduction of a pseudo-scientific rejection of religious belief into institutions of higher learning has paralleled a decline of religious practice and belief in the upper strata of society.

This turning away from traditional morality has been accommodated by changing church standards of morality. It has been most damaging among the ruling elites of our society—among intellectual leaders, industrial leaders, political leaders, education leaders and judges. Scholars may differ about the decline of the churches in America, whether their lessening influence as a moral force is due to the weakness of the churches or the growing power of secularism. There is no gainsaying the fact that Tocqueville's description of the churches in America would have no application today to any but a few fundamentalist Christian and Jewish sects. The great churches of the nineteenth century have become social welfare organizations, preoccupied with the "social gospel" which some roughly equate with Marxism, inexpert and indifferent about man's relationship with the Creator. In many of the churches, men who wear the cloth openly preach immorality and hedonism as from a new gospel.

In religion as in politics, the default is in leadership. A generation has been bureaucratized into predictable response to a liberal stimulus. Thus, the defense of morality falls to the people. But they find that the means of preparing youth in the disciplines of civilization have been captured by the enemies of their culture.

The traditional morality of our society has been under attack from two directions. It is attacked by agents of an external enemy who recognizes it as a cornerstone of national strength and a target of his subversion. It is attacked also by loyal citizens who reject that morality for reasons of conviction, expediency or profit. It is not defended by a politics of accommodation to every hostile pressure.

The external enemy cannot engage in overt attacks on public morality. His agents must act through elements and from positions in our society that can win public sympathy or command public support. His task is to espouse every divisive or degenerate cause which can be used to weaken the United States. His monetary and legal assistance can be crucial in launching or sustaining organizations and movements that serve his purpose. We see some of his activities in movements which are overtly Communist or Communist-related; but we know from his organization and method that he has planted in other positions of influence agents who show no overt evidence of his control.

Fyodor Dostoevsky, who knew the tactic well, described it in *The Possessed*, speaking in the character of Verhovensky:[8]

"Listen," said Verhovensky, "We'll make an upheaval. Our party does not consist only of those who commit murder and arson. No, we have plenty of members. I've reckoned them all up . . . The teacher who laughs with children at their God—the lawyer who defends an educated murderer because he is more cultured than his victims—schoolboys who commit crimes for the sake of the sensation—juries who acquit every criminal—school masters, bitter and bilious—vanity puffed up—brutal and monstrous appetites—the Russian God has already been vanquished by cheap vodka.

"Subversion—overthrow from the foundation—this begins with the transvaluation of values, whereby what has hitherto been thought evil is rationalized to appear good, and good made to seem evil. It begins—and ends—in the field of ethics . . . Crime, it argues, is not really crime. If one only understood all motives, who would blame the criminal? Heroes are not really heroes.

151

"Subversion thus begins as a sort of universal tolerance, motivated not by compassion but by cynicism. Its effect is to blur all standards by awakening skepticism regarding purity of motive—or the possibility of there being any purity. . . . When the process has gone far enough, when the masses of the people are able to justify anything by rationalizing that all men are the creatures of economic circumstances or their infantile conditionings, and that religion, the state, and society are altogether but reflections of the dominant interest, then conditions are ripe for the most ruthless gangsters to seize power."

If the Communist youth of America espouse a hedonism that would never be tolerated in a Communist state, this is part of their attack on the United States. Their task is to corrupt the youth of America under the pretense of warning against capitalist imperialism. They regard bourgeois youth as stupid. If Communist attorneys press in the courts for removal of every restraint on their right to conspire against the United States, this is part of their war on America. If they attack the very legal processes of our courts with contemptuous behavior, torrents of abuse and claims of mythical rights, they are demonstrating to their followers the cowardly quality of bourgeois justice. But they are also demonstrating a shrewd assessment of the vulnerabilities of our political institutions.

We have seen in this century a conscious drive to rid public life of its religious constraints. Our news media have by precept and example pushed the thesis that in our society, religious constraints on personal behavior are out of place. Thus, state laws against abortion are attacked as being of religious origin, though they were in fact derived from the common law of England. Persons might dispute whether capital punishment is of religious or secular origin, since such sanction antedated the law-giving of Moses.

THE PRIMACY OF MORALITY

The attack on religion is but a veiled attack on morality, which is the strength of the state. The pernicious notion that individual immorality is not a proper concern of the state is a patent absurdity. Its own strength, which depends upon the morality of its citizens, must be a vital concern of any state which expects to survive. In fact, the argument can and must be made by prudent rulers that the interest of the state requires the maintenance of moral standards basic to the health and vitality of the community. Religion normally supports those moral requirements. It may not subvert them. If religion acts to subvert the state, religion must be disciplined by the state. As Maritain said:[9]

. . . assuming the formation of some religious sect aimed at the destruction of the bases of common life, say, prescribing collective suicide or racial annihilation, it would be up to the state to dissolve such a religious sect, as well as any other association either criminal or destructive of national security. All this deals with the administration of justice, and implies the equality of rights of all citizens, whatever their race, their social standing, or their religious denomination may be.

152

In the U.S. constitutional order as it was originally constituted, we had an admirable structure for fostering morality in a democratic society. Our decentralized system of government, with each state having jurisdiction over its own culture, allowed a diversity consistent with the needs of local traditions.

As in matters of material progress, so also in matters of morality, there was a competition of excellence among the states. The decline of lynching in the South was a response to the moral censure of sister states and public opinion in the country. Federal authority intervened only after public opinion had virtually ended the practice.

As we have previously noted of politics, our American Fabian socialists had a strong distaste also for the cultural diversity of our system. If one state had enacted "modern" legislation to change ancient mores, why couldn't all states do it? In the Fabian view, the power of the federal government should be asserted to achieve uniformity.

We have noted the zeal of the Warren Court to impose the Bill of Rights restrictions on the states. That move was a not so subtle action of the Court to establish its own authority over a whole range of governmental powers previously excluded from its jurisdiction. The Court, an element of the federal government excluded from power over speech, press and religion, became by its own action the supreme authority in these fields. How drastically our government could be changed by the unchallenged pretensions of a few judges.

The assault on public morality is made on many fronts and with great power. It is aided with both private and public funds. We can examine a few of these actions to illustrate their quality.

ABOLISHING SCHOOL PRAYER

In accord with the culture of our society, it had long been practice to read a verse of the Bible in public school classes and to ask God's blessing on the day's work. In seeking to reconcile Catholic, Protestant and Jewish views of an appropriate invocation for starting the school day, a New York State Committee recommended and the school system adopted a simple prayer.

When use of the school prayer was challenged in the courts, the school board was sustained until the appeal reached the Supreme Court. There, in the case of *Engel* v. *Vitale*, the Court outlawed the prayer by finding that the use of the prayer constituted "an establishment of religion." The real issue, the removal of every vestige of religious culture from the public institutions and activities of the state, was mandated not by law but by the Court.

This arrogant Court could thus overthrow a rule of law and practice of our society which had flourished since the foundation of the Republic. Under the Constitution, the views of various religious groups had been accommodated within the local communities in a spirit of toleration and

153

cooperation. That spirit of toleration and community, that respect for our national culture, was alien to a Court composed of men who had become divorced from the culture. Their zealous concern to create a state stripped of all religious influence overshadowed their legal judgment.

For groups of diverse religious and political composition meeting in some public cause to open their session with an invocation was and had long been a practice in America. What could be more appropriate in a public school than to teach children to practice the culture of their parents? This is the spirit in which responsible officials meeting with parents devised the New York State school prayer. The finding of the Court that the use of such an invocation constituted "an establishment of religion" is as ridiculous a judgment as any judicial body has ever offered in defense of its action. Unfortunately, there is no requirement that action of the Supreme Court must be based on competent interpretation of the law. Mediocre and irrational reference to the evidence will serve zealots just as well.

The Supreme Court had asserted years earlier in an opinion of Justice Brewer that "we are a religious people." The Warren Court undertook without reference to that opinion to repudiate it and to assert a new rule of law excluding all influence of religion in public education. The Court was striking at the very foundations of the civilizing process.

SOCIALIST ATHEISM

The socialist theory of government constructs an authoritarian state which provides for the needs of the people, assuring justice and prosperity for all. Democratic socialists believe that this political society can be built while preserving individual rights and freedoms. They therefore press increasingly for new exercises of governmental power, always of course to achieve some "good" cause reflecting the readiness of liberals to use public money to enlarge state power.

One of their first ventures and greatest prides is the public school system, inaugurated to provide free schooling for the poor and quickly expanded to provide "free" schooling for all. Citizens perfectly able financially to pay for the education of their children could wax enthusiastic about the merits of free public schools. They could not foresee that in paying taxes in lieu of tuition, they were creating a politically managed bureaucracy which would in time inevitably lead to the degradation of education.

State control of education has from the beginning been a central plank of socialist theory. Education was to be the tool with which the state (or the ruling elites) would shape the perfect socialist society. A public monopoly of schooling was the logical first step in building this phase of the socialist order.

Public schooling was started by the states at a time when all Americans agreed that education was an activity excluded from the constitutional grant of powers to the national government. Nowhere, by any remote connection, is education a constitutional responsibility of the federal government. Yet, under the guise of protecting undefined "rights," the Supreme Court has asserted a constitutional mandate to regulate the public schools of the country.

Do the states have a constitutional right to terminate the public school systems they created, and establish some other system of universal education more conducive to excellence? Certainly not! A Supreme Court zealous to protect this cornerstone of socialist orthodoxy has ruled that the support of public education is now an obligation of the state. Authority which the body politic had reserved to itself is now claimed by the Court. When was the Constitution so amended?

The chief relic of an earlier day of private religious education is now the parochial school system of the Catholic Church. Such are the vagaries of history that this parochial school system, created to resist the Protestant evangelism of the public school system, is today a cultural defense against the atheism of the public school system.

In the first conversion to a public school system in Massachusetts, the state legislature simply incorporated the existing schools of the Congregational Church into the state system. With universal, compulsory school attendance, the Catholic Church became alarmed that the atmosphere and practices of the system would influence impressionable young Catholics to join the Congregational or other Protestant churches.

In recent decades, the Supreme Court, raising a new constitutional thesis about separation of church and state, in violence to the First and Fourteenth Amendments, has outlawed the simple, voluntary recital of a nondenominational invocation at the opening of the school day as an "establishment of religion." There is no constitutional objection to reading the vilest pornography to children, but it is constitutionally forbidden to read to them from the Bible.

These measures mark the growing power of *socialist atheism* in our society.

If atheism is simply a disbelief in the existence of God or a belief in cosmic determinism, a tolerant society would make no collective objection to the private entertainment of such beliefs nor to private proselytizing for them. The essential requirement is that advocacy must be held within the bounds of respect for other beliefs in a pluralistic society. There are doubtless many atheists in America who live within such a framework.

Socialist atheism is another breed. It is a political creed highly intolerant of all religious practice, regarding religion as a superstitious practice used by the capitalist state to impose conformity on the working man. It rejects the convention of governmental toleration of religious diversity without favor to any sect. Its purpose is to use state power to destroy religious culture and thereby to "liberate" the people from superstition. God is a power center in conflict with the socialist state.

Socialist atheism finds its full development in the Soviet Union and

Red China. In the West, its intentions are fully elaborated in Marxist-Leninist literature but are subdued and obscured in political propaganda. Power must first be acquired by other means.

The differences of religious groups, including atheists, are easily agitated by those who would create social conflict. Being in some degree uninformed about the beliefs and purposes of other groups, each group is vulnerable to misrepresentation about the others. Toleration is ruptured by charging others with intolerance.

The religious conflicts of the seventeenth century were in the eighteenth supplanted by the wave of militant atheism. In the French Revolution, *socialistic atheism* ran riot in a blood bath of terror which evoked a world-wide revulsion. In the nineteenth century, the excesses of the French Revolution pale into minor tragedy beside the mass slaughter of peoples wrought by Lenin, Stalin and Mao. This endemic barbarism of *socialistic atheism* is rarely mentioned in our news media. The pervasive voice of democratic socialism will, when pressed, regret the excesses of communism, without associating the excesses with the very fundamentals of socialism. Silence excuses the barbarity.

Thus, in our society, the democratic socialist who is also an atheist believes that religion is an anachronism which handicaps progress. He would not support the oppression which is practiced in the Communist empires but he is sympathetic to measures which dismantle without excessive conflict the religious culture of the people. This is the mentality which is today so vocal and powerful in Western politics. Its influence is evident especially in the cultural edicts of the United States Supreme Court. The public school is a special object of its concern.

Let us assume that the state has a valid interest in providing universal basic education. How should a free society fulfill such an assumed obligation? By issuing a purchase order for the services required.

Because parents who are financially able to provide for the education of their children will do so, the responsibility of the state is only to provide education for those families unable to do so. The state defines the scope of education which the public interest requires and issues purchase orders to qualified suppliers.

In providing education, the state must not become the destroyer of the people's culture. Therefore, its order provides for teaching of basic knowledge and skills in mathematics, literature, history and geography, leaving it to the supplier to render these services in a cultural climate suitable for the citizens served. When the state undertakes to use education to achieve cultural uniformity, it has trespassed on freedom and embraced a fundamental tenet of socialism.

The intrusion of socialist precepts into the thinking and decision-making of the Supreme Court has been elaborately illustrated in the opinions of the Supreme Court. This perspective was basic to its decisions on school

156

prayer, forced busing, pornography and control of state electoral districts—all of which asserted new national authority in spheres of government theretofore reserved to the states or to the people.

In the area of pornography, there has been some judicial retreat from the licentiousness promoted by the rulings of the Warren Court. But in the protection of a public school monopoly of the public purse, there has been no retreat.

Public education has serious basic handicaps which condemn it to corruption and decay. It is political, it is monopolistic, it is bureaucratic, it is inflexible, and it is stripped by politics of the high purpose and devotion to truth which is essential to a healthy educational climate. A prudent society would be looking for a different structure for its universal education. Nevertheless, if there is to be public education, it should as a governmental responsibility be administered equitably for all citizens. It should be offered as a service for those who wish to use it. It should not become the tool for political control of the people.

As the public schools became the educational resource not of the poor alone but of all citizens, their role in society was expanded to provide a wide variety of courses and activities which increased the costs of education. In some communities the schools became the youth country clubs of a prosperous society. State accreditation raised standards by prescribing degree standards of teachers and defining acceptable physical facilities.

In communities where children of the well-to-do were going to public schools and the poorer working people were sending children to parochial schools, the original premises of public education were turned topsy-turvy. Public funds were being used to subsidize education of the well-to-do and were being denied to the poor.

State legislatures in states with large Catholic school populations became increasingly concerned and sought ways to aid the parochial systems. At every turn, they found their measures vetoed by the Supreme Court. Although higher religious schools had received federal payments for the education of veterans, it was held that primary and secondary schools could not be similarly compensated for basic education. Credits could not be allowed against state income taxes for private educational expenses at the primary and secondary school levels because such credits provided no benefit to the users of public schools (who had no such expense). The state could not make even a token payment—say 20 percent of cost—for secular education meeting state standards given in private schools because the funds so paid would benefit religion.

The Court was foundering in its own disregard of law and logic. Words no longer had meaning. If a church was fully subsidizing secular education, which had been defined by the state as a public necessity, a partial payment of the secular value of the educational service did not subsidize religion—it merely reduced the church's subsidy of a public function.

157

This simple question of public policy has been so distorted by socialist zealotry, humanist intolerance and the political influence of the public school bureaucracy that rational discussion of the issue is virtually excluded from the public purview. Public schools are so great a sacred cow that even in plain view of their deterioration, constructive adjustment of public policy cannot be considered.

A recent editorial expressed the attitude.[10] It approved the denial of aid to private schools which are not church-related because the primary purpose (imputed) of the law was to help parochial schools. The clear purpose of the law was to recognize the public service rendered by all private schools and thereby to maintain some diversity in basic education. When the Court and the editor could think of no cogent reason to deny such recognition to non-sectarian private schools, they chose this weak pretext for invalidating a perfectly legal statute which would terminate the public school monopoly of public funds for basic education.

In its desperate reach to outlaw public support of private basic education, the Court declared that such legislation would be "divisive." The claim is a straw man. In Britain, where a state church does not dispute the public payments to church-related schools of other denominations, equity does not exacerbate tensions—it ends them. Only socialist atheism is so intolerant of other cultural values that it seeks to exterminate them. This force, infiltrated into public education in America through John Dewey and his associates in the first half of this century, has espoused a public monopoly of basic education without religion as the formula for its success. A Court of the same mind dutifully serves the concept.

LICENSING PORNOGRAPHY

For a century and a half, the authority of the states to restrict the publication and distribution of pornographic materials within their jurisdiction had been unquestioned. The federal government had been involved in the question chiefly in the authority of the Post Office Department to deny the use of the mails to such materials.

With the assertion of federal court authority over state action affecting free speech, the question of pornography assumed a new importance. The Warren Court undertook to set national standards but qualified its opinion with a show of respect for "community standards" of propriety. In the end, the Supreme Court became confounded in its own confusion and virtually removed all legal restraint on the distribution of pornographic publications. It opened this land to a flood of filth which unquestionably has seduced youth and fostered criminality in our society.

The idea that in any rational society political policy questions such as this should be determined by a bench of judges isolated from the people is preposterous. But that is the way such vital questions are treated by American government today.

There is not a word in the Constitution nor in any other duly enacted legislation which denies the states a legitimate interest in—nay, a duty to protect, preserve and enhance—the public morality. That the First Amendment prohibits state control of pornographic materials is solely a construction of the Supreme Court imposed on the country by judicial fiat in response to the protests of individuals, insignificant in number, who entertain a determination to enrich themselves by debauching our society.

The Presidential Commission on Obscenity and Pornography appointed by President Johnson and chaired by William B. Lockhart made its report to President Nixon on September 30, 1970. The Commission was staffed with personnel long known as advocates of unlimited license for pornographic publications. Predictably, the Commission found no evidence that pornographic materials contributed to social delinquency and criminal behavior. It recommended unrestrained publication of pornography in the United States with some modest effort to keep materials out of the hands of children. Because presidential commissions are usually appointed from the ruling elites of our society, this expression of opinion on public policy is indicative of the trend of national leadership.

In five cases decided on June 21, 1973 (*Slaton, Miller, Orito, Paladini* and *Kaplan*), Chief Justice Warren Burger, speaking for the Court, restored in large measure the authority of the states to define obscene materials and behavior and to punish prohibited conduct. This drawing back from prior attempts of the Court to set federal standards, under an interpretation of the First Amendment which tolerated increasing licentiousness, seemed to augur a new deference of the Court majority to the reserved powers of the states. The tangled web of the Court's foundering prior attempts to establish a national rule was persuasive that some matters are better left to local authorities.

CONTROLLING POPULATION

On March 27, 1972, the Presidential Commission on Population Growth and America's Future appointed by President Nixon and chaired by John D. Rockefeller III made its report to the President. This Commission stressed the urgency of population control, proposing the widespread dissemination of birth-control information, aids and services. It proposed the distribution of birth-control information and artifacts to minors without the knowledge and consent of their parents. It recommended the repeal of state anti-abortion laws, leaving the decision to the woman and her doctor. Here we are offered again a plan and program for America.

President Nixon rejected the recommendations of the Rockefeller Report. But why did he appoint to the Commission members who he knew would submit such a report? Was his rejection political expediency—while the Report stands as a guide for future legislation to build the kind of society to which the Rockefellers are committed? It seems improbable that

159

the President could have been so ignorant of the qualifications of the Commission members that he could not anticipate their conclusions or that he was so ignorant of governmental processes that he could not have found members to give him a different report, if he had wanted it.

The Rockefeller Report culminated a drive over recent decades to commit governmental policy to the spread of birth-control practices in the United States. Advocates of planned parenthood, anxious to justify their craft, have conceived a prospect of overpopulation, poverty and starvation on earth. To this end, they have manipulated statistics to picture impending disaster.

We know that famines were common even in ancient times when the world was underpopulated. This was because food supplies were perishable and were harvested only for immediate consumption. In times of crop failures, food was scarce. This condition was not changed with population growth. With more hands to clear the land and to plant and harvest the crops, more food was produced. But production was still subject to the vagaries of weather and blight. Only in this century has famine been virtually eliminated as a phenomenon of human existence. With the capacity to save food surpluses and to transport them to points of need, crop failures in the Soviet Union and Red China in 1972 could be met with supplies from the United States.

Throughout millennia, doom-sayers have fretted about the prospect of human disaster from overpopulation. Always they figured the increase of population without figuring the corresponding increase in food production. Today, when food supplies are more adequate than ever before in history, they have not ceased their dire prediction.

In the past half-century, human control of disease has sharply increased the life expectancy of peoples. With births continuing and deaths partially suspended in the period of transition, we experienced a surge of population. The remarkable thing about this phenomenon is that the world made the transition without mass starvation anywhere. Human resourcefulness met the challenge.

Some population authorities have been taking this period of population expansion as a sign of impending catastrophe. They have panicked. They have sought desperately for means to avoid disaster. They have decided that a new morality is required to save civilization. Traditional Christian morality must be changed. Atheism claims a new cause.

The population enthusiasts conceive a society in which the enjoyment of sex will be separated from procreation. Through fertility control, sex can become an ordinary pastime unrelated to childbirth. Then the state can, by setting procreation patterns, control population—and conceivably even the selection of parents for maximum eugenic advantage to the race. This is the concept of future society visualized by the Rockefeller Report

160

and implicit in every appropriation of federal funds for planned parenthood, birth-control clinics, and population control.

This conception of human society is derived from a materialistic view of creation that rejects all notion of divine influence in world affairs. It is entirely irreconcilable with Christian ethics, which must, therefore, be modified to accommodate the thesis of class conflict and elite management. The attack on traditional morality proceeds on many fronts, orchestrated by the news media.

LEGALIZING ABORTION

Abortion, the taking of innocent human life in the womb, has throughout our Judeo-Christian history been regarded as a criminal act. In early centuries of the Christian era, when biological knowledge was relatively primitive, it was supposed that life was imparted to the fetus at the time of "ensoulment," presumed to be at the time the child first stirred in the womb, about the sixth month of gestation. The law therefore protected the child from that time, according to rights of personhood. The law was in principle sound, according to existing knowledge of the biological process of human development.

Modern medicine has now established that human life begins in the zygote at the time of conception. The zygote has within itself all the potential of its future development, needing only food and protection according to its state, just as the human child after birth must have food and protection to survive. The logic of established law requires the state to protect the human life from its beginning, which we now know to be at conception.

Running counter to this enlightened view of nature and morality, we have in recent decades suffered a national slackening of sexual disciplines and a consequent increase of illegitimate births. As religious and moral restraints have decreased, families have turned increasingly to abortion to avoid the social consequences of illegitimate conception. As abortion promised to become a lucrative medical practice, strong measures to legitimize abortion were initiated in the states, using the thesis that abortion was a matter between a woman and her physician, not a matter of public concern. In the initial thrust of the advocates, several states liberalized their anti-abortion statutes. Some federal courts undertook to declare the old statutes unconstitutional. However, the great majority of the states adhered to the established morality and maintained the old statutes. Wherever referenda were held, proposals to liberalize abortion were defeated. Some states repealed their recently adopted liberal statutes, and in New York State, Governor Rockefeller vetoed the repeal.

It was in this climate that the Supreme Court intervened in what had been a state jurisdiction. With its decisions of January 22, 1973 on the

161

Texas and Georgia cases, it legalized abortion in 46 states where state law had defined abortion as criminal. It made abortion in the first three months legal without any restraints of government, it authorized some state regulation of abortions in the second three months, and it authorized full state regulation of abortions in the final three months.

This intervention of the Supreme Court in a matter outside both its jurisdiction and its competence, in disregard of medical knowledge about development of the human person in the womb and of the reasonable implications of the common law, and in disregard of the culture of the people expressed overwhelmingly in state law, marks a new peak of judicial tyranny. There can be no explanation of this decision in law or in the will of the people. This is apparently the sociological decision of men who consider abortion a necessary tool in population control, as the Rockefeller Commission had concluded, and who were determined to impose it on the people "for their own good."

ABOLISHING CAPITAL PUNISHMENT

The decision of the Supreme Court issued on June 29, 1972, in the appeals from Texas and Georgia convictions, was a display case of Court confusion and irresolution. There was no majority opinion; each of the five justices concurring in the result gave his own reasons for doing so. If ever there was a demonstration that Supreme Court edicts are not based on the law, this was it.

The Supreme Court had, before these decisions, virtually suspended executions in the states by agreeing to accept challenges claiming state capital punishment to be "cruel and unusual punishment" prohibited by the U.S. Constitution. Thus, without any regard for the merits of the cases, all executions had been suspended since. Having so acted on its own account, the Court—or some members of it—accused the states of capricious action on criminal cases, not related to the merits. It found that, statistically, the poor and the black suffer a disproportionate percentage of capital punishment. It seemed to think this was somehow unjust, as though punishment should be correlated with race and economic conditions instead of with criminality. Justice Thurgood Marshall considered capital punishment essentially "cruel and unusual" punishment, but he did not dispute the fact that the people who wrote the Constitution did not think so. He would substitute his opinion for the judgment of our lawmakers.

We may grant the sincerity of the justices, but nothing more. We cannot find any trace of integrity in their interpretation of the law. Nor do we find in such judicial pronouncements the quality of wisdom and understanding which the people have a right to expect from the High Court. The majority in this case acted not as judges but as political activists.

Special arguments had been raised against capital punishment; but it should not have been beyond the competence of the Court to sift through them. Statistics were juggled to indicate that capital punishment does not deter criminals—alleging a condition contrary to nature. Criminals are highly sensitive to their own personal interest and quickly adapt their behavior to the law. The misrepresented reality was that failure of some states to enforce capital punishment laws had reduced the protective effect of those laws for society.

How can the country maintain standards of morality and decency in public life when the highest court, which should be a model of probity and wisdom, sets such an example of dishonesty? The action on capital punishment seemed to cap a long program of fostering criminality in the United States.

THE PIED PIPERS

The drama of the generation gap, so effectively projected by the new educational movement and the news media, was a contrivance to estrange youth from traditional morality by indoctrinating them with a revulsion against "old-fashioned" and "unsympathetic" parents. This was the rationale for seducing youth from the ancient wisdom and leading them into the quagmire of licentiousness and revolution. The new breed of zealous sociologists who professed to find in socialism and materialism the keys to a bright new world could impose their phony nostrums on college youth divorced from both history and philosophy, clay in the hands of would-be seers.

Herbert Hoover had foreseen and correctly evaluated the thrust of these attacks on religion and morality:[11]

> . . . what I am interested in in this inquiry is something that transcends the transitory actions, as important as they are, something far more pregnant with disaster to all that America has been to its people and to the world. No nation can introduce a new social concept, philosophy or a new culture alien to its growth without moral and spiritual chaos. I am anxious for the future of freedom and liberty of men. That America has stood for, that has created her greatness; that is all the future holds that is worth while. The unit of American life is the family and the home. Through it vibrates every hope of the future. It is the economic unit as well as the moral and spiritual unit. But it is more than this. It is the beginning of self-government. It is the throne of our highest ideals. It is the center of the spiritual energy of our people.

Fortunate were the youths and families who adhered to the ancient wisdom about God and man, who embraced the cherished disciplines with pride and assurance and respect for a great heritage. For them, drugs and war and generation gaps were no problem at all. But woe to those who marched with the pied piper into alienation, despair and death. Their wasted spirits languished in prison or in exile. Their corpses find an early surcease from a life made agonizing by drugs or madness.

The wages of sin is death. Maybe the truth is trite, but it is better remembered than learned anew in each generation at what cost to youth, at what default of the elders! In our generation, we have wandered far in public policy from the wisdom of President George Washington.

THE PEOPLE DISSENT

There is an aura of unreality about these prescriptions for a new America. It seems improbable that a majority of the Congress, or of either political party, or of government employees, or of any other representative cross-section of the American people would subscribe to such plans for our country. So why does the Congress support and finance such programs? Are its members so uninformed that they don't know what is happening?

If we try to find and identify the people who share this vision of America's future, we come upon a clique of intellectuals identified broadly as "liberals," many of them ensconced in and using powerful foundations and identified with the Fabian plan for America. We encounter the Rockefeller brothers and their legion of public servants. We find bankers like W. R. Draper, who heads the Population Council of America, a voice for the population panic and the new morality. We find a few political leaders in Congress and in the Executive who are avant-garde. And we find a nest of professionals in the Department of Health, Education and Welfare busily engaged in building larger appropriations for the programs.

How is it that this handful of our elites can lead this nation along a path so hostile to the inclinations and interests of the people? The short answer is that representative government is not functioning in the United States. An oligarchy of wealth determines policy. The political parties are scarecrows concealing from the people the real leadership of the country.

It is a moot question whether any democratic society is capable of sustaining a moral position on any question. The generally passive quality of a free people exposes their institutions to manipulation for the self-interest of special blocs of activists within the society. Government of the people deteriorates into factionalism.

If a business group can reap handsome profits by showing pornographic films to the youth of the country, what force in society can contend with the legal skills of an Abe Fortas in the service of the group? If doctors can enrich themselves by performing a million abortions annually for an average fee of $400, what force can keep them from disregarding their ancient oath of Hippocrates?

In an authoritarian society, the leader can simply outlaw groups and practices hostile to the community health and safety. A democratic society can do so only if it has leadership which can command public support of the common good against the self-interest of special groups within the society. That requirement places a demand on democratic leadership which is seldom met.

164

Our political institutions are failing the test. In describing the Johnson presidency, Ayn Rand evaluated the kind of leadership which our political parties are supplying:[12]

> President Johnson was the climax of the policy of rule by consensus—and he fell as a martyr to the principle that principles are unnecessary. It took only four years to carry him from a popular landslide to so great an unpopularity that he could not venture to face the voters again. Rule by consensus is the practice of the belief that a country splintered into pressure groups can be run indefinitely by an expert contortionist-juggler, who would encourage the pressure groups, multiply them, and play them against one another, in the name of balancing their demands and reaching a consensus of compromises, by means of distributing favors and burdens at whim, on the expediency of the moment.

We cannot consider Lyndon Johnson an exception to the politics of the day. He was a master of the art which all American politicians now strive to perfect.

At root, the moral corruption of society is a failure of politics. It is a failure to preserve a political process responsive to the people. Immorality springs not from the people but from the elites, who, through money, have taken the reins of political power. Only a restoration of popular government can cure the malaise.

Chapter 16

THE EDUCATION EMPIRE

THE FUNCTION OF EDUCATION in any nation is to preserve and transmit the accumulated wisdom of the society. In ancient times, this was done by a corps of scholars and scientists attached to the Court. They trained the princes and counselled kings, even as Aristotle taught Alexander. They selected and trained their own successors. In China, where they achieved high standards of scholarship and service, these were the Mandarins. In those times, the organization of labor required the presence of most of the people in the work force to provide the food, fiber and shelter for all, or in the army to defend the nation. Only a selected few could be spared for the administration of government. In China, a truly democratic process of selection originating in the villages determined by examination who would be selected for special education and training.

As the productivity of social organization increased, more hands could be spared from the work force to serve in government. The bureaucracy grew. In times of collapse and retrogression, in "dark ages," the superstructure collapsed and populations were forced back to the basic work of keeping alive.

The advent and development of an industrial organization made radical changes in the organization of society. Increased efficiency of production and distribution reduced the requirement for farm labor. Industrial production fostered new concentrations of urban labor. And as the rewards of efficiency were shared by all, it became possible to reduce work hours per week and allow more leisure for the work force. It became possible to withhold children from the work force and therefore to provide formal education for them. As the efficiency of production increased, it became possible to hold young men and women out of the work force for longer periods and to extend the years of education.

Universal public education was pioneered in the United States because this was the economy which by its productivity first made universal education possible. We should understand that universal education is not some inherent "right" of citizenship but is the product of our economic system. If that system retrogresses, education will necessarily suffer.

In the early years of the Republic, education was in large measure a function of the churches. Teaching the Bible and teaching other human knowledge—numbers, writing, history—just went together. Young men studied law by apprenticeship to practicing lawyers. The first colleges were organized by the churches. When education was thus highly selective, was sought and esteemed by all, was respected for reputed knowledge and wisdom, it was not surprising that some persons saw in its extension to all the people a means of achieving utopia here and now. By the middle of the nineteenth century, economic progress in the United States had made such extension of education feasible.

The public school emerged as an institution fathered by Horace Mann in Massachusetts. In the late nineteenth century the public school emerged as a force in New York politics. Thereafter, the public school became a fixture of American society. It remained a state institution until the mid-twentieth century, when Congress began to provide aid to education as "assistance without control." That slogan deferred to the public belief that education should remain responsive to local control. But gradually the limitation of federal authority has been converted into outright federal control of public education. The small federal office of education has expanded into the Office of the Commissioner of Education in the Department of Health, Education and Welfare.

Education for improvement of the person and society has an irresistible appeal for Americans. Education seemed to offer that equal start for all citizens which would make this really the land of opportunity. The idea was so attractive that no one stopped to question the prudence of associating education with politics.

At first, the whole ethic and technique of public education were taken from private education. After all, the purposes of education and methods of teaching were well established. The teacher and the student had well defined niches in society. The purpose of the state was merely to make education available to all citizens.

From its beginning as a service to the poor, public education quickly expanded to provide a general public service to all who wished to use it—the wealthy as well as the indigent. As it provided a "free" service to all families, it quickly won general approval. Of course it was financed by the taxes of the people.

Public funds were lavished upon the public schools. In more prosperous communities, the public school became a center of social activity with a country-club atmosphere. Sports, arts, music, drama, were added to the curriculum. Parents could get it all free through the public school. Soon the public school had a virtual monopoly of education.

An institution so amenable to control by central authority had political potential which could not be neglected by rulers committed to shaping a new society. If they could shape textbooks, teacher training and educational philosophy to their ends, the Fabian planners could create a new Republic in the image of their socialist utopia.

To see how far they have progressed, we need only look at the present scene. Schools are closed while teachers are out on strike. Children are promoted regardless of accomplishment, so that, advanced beyond their capacity to comprehend, they are beyond help and totally alienated from society. Against the wishes of parents and the interests of children, pupils are bused out of their neighborhoods to distant schools. In this abomination of democratic government, politicians, courts and educators conspire to arrogate to themselves an authority over the people the Constitution never conferred on any public official. In some communities, schools are closed because voters have defeated bond issues or school taxes, expressing their disillusionment with public education.

The key difference between socialism and the traditional American view of society is this: Socialism advocates that the money earned by citizens should be taken from them and used by the government for the benefit of the people. The American political view holds that the people should use the money they earn for their own benefit and that the taxes of the government should be taken only for certain community services which the individual cannot provide or buy for himself: the national defense, foreign affairs, interstate commerce, and so forth.

While the American system contemplates that citizens should help one another through charitable and educational institutions and services, it does not preclude public personal services when public policy is well served. Thus, if the cost of general education exceeds the capacity of marginal income families to pay the price, public funds could provide the education. The difference is that whereas the American political system would provide public education for those who need it, socialism would provide public education for all citizens. Thus, socialism takes the control of education away from the citizen to place it in government while the American system leaves education in control of the people.

We can see this transition in American education. At first, public education was locally controlled and financed because that was the heritage of private education. Even state interference with local policy was minimal. Today public education has created an enormous bureaucracy with a vested interest in public funding. In many communities, the school budget consumes half or more of all government costs. Unionization of teachers and their participation in strikes have abrogated the professional character of teaching and reduced it to a craft. The inspiration is gone in some communities.

Government controls have been steadily extended, first in state bureaus and more recently at the federal level. Years ago, the parents and local school boards really controlled school policy, but today they are more window-dressing for the dicta coming from educational bureaucrats in Washington. Federal bureaucrats have the money and the zeal, so what can local authorities do? This domination of public education by "professional" educators with a vested interest in expanding their own empire has been fostered not alone by money and by the disposition of parents to provide every benefit for children but by a pretentious expertise professed by the educator. As one critical educator noted:[1]

> The professional educators do control our public schools; but I hold that the people—yes, the ordinary people—in our numberless local communities should recapture from the professional educators the control over the schools that they have usurped. I hold that the claims of the professional educators to special knowledge, based on special training, that entitles them to name the goals, determine the content, establish the standards, and call the turns on the political philosophy that is to prevail in our public schools—I hold that those claims are false claims, false claims, moreover, that ordinary people are plenty capable of detecting and exposing once they have set their minds to it. I hold that the major effect of the professional education movement has been to complicate what is essentially a simple matter. Let us remember that there were teachers, good teachers, moreover, long before there were professional educators, and not only good teachers but well educated men and women who had been taught by them.

In education as in government, our people are surrendering the responsibility of citizenship to bureaucratic elites who profess to know what is best for the people. Our political system is not reserving to the people the control of policy and leaving to the specialist questions of detail; it is delivering the control of policy to the bureaucracy and telling the people to be still.

It is the nature of socialism to be authoritarian. The bureaucrats say they know best. They are intolerant of criticism and impervious to improvement. Because their judgment is "best," policy can allow no deviation from its prescriptions. This is the factor that is reducing American public education to a shambles. That is how the bureaucratic mind of socialism functions. It is incapable of entertaining the discriminating judgments of merit on which a free society functions and grows. It is limited to bludgeoning judgments which obliterate that refinement of discernment on which justice depends.

If local government, instead of setting up public schools, had simply paid the tuition of all students needing public assistance, a system of private schools—independently owned and managed, and competing for the people's patronage through performance—would be in operation today. In paying for the education of their children, parents would exercise a close scrutiny of the schools, as parents paying for private education do today. By their choice of schools, they would reward excellence and reprove mediocrity.

In such a system, great diversity would be possible. Parents who in the present system are highly critical of public education could, simply by allocating their tuition money, create schools responsive to the parents' demand for excellence. Instead of the strikes and riots which now plague public education as a direct product of the political nature of the system, we would have a system of great energy and initiative, sparked by competition and offering excellence far beyond the highest reach of public education.

HIGHER EDUCATION

The early claims for free and universal public education were made in behalf of citizenship. It was claimed that a literate electorate was essential to self-government, though the contrary thesis had been demonstrated in the American Revolution. In earlier centuries, the selection of more intelligent youth for advanced education had perhaps cultivated an illusion that education improved intelligence.

When public education at the primary and secondary level was well established, it was to be expected that the growing educational establishment would urge the value of college education. By this time, support for education was a sure-fire recourse of politicians. With the aid of the federal land-grant programs and strong local support, state colleges and universities developed rapidly. Some institutions specialized in the agricultural and mechanical education of chief interest to their people. But soon the colleges expanded to universities with full courses in the arts and sciences.

At that level too, the expansion for higher education, free or for nominal fees, is crushing by competition the fabric of private higher education except in heavily endowed institutions. Important questions of public policy are raised. As higher education is generalized not for the benefit of citizenship but to enhance the status and earning power of the individual, why should it become a charge against the community? Why indeed should the young man who is apprenticed to learn a trade after finishing high school pay for the education of his neighbor who goes to college? Moreover, the college education is a financial asset. The young man ambitious for such self-improvement can borrow the cost of his education and repay the loan from his later earnings. Many of our youth have done so.

Would it not preserve a more responsible attitude on the campus and therefore be better public policy to require all governmental institutions of higher learning to charge full tuition and other costs to all students? We have had ample evidence in recent years that the generosity of the tax-payers in providing free higher education is wasted on some of our student bodies. There are of course other reasons for the campus disquiet—notably in the weakness of faculties and administrators who have tolerated barbarians and barbaric behavior, first among the faculty and then among the students.

In higher education, too, the federal bureaucracy has tended not to improve education, but to worsen it. Federal control and federal money are imposing a dictatorship on higher education. In a notable address to the American Association of Presidents of Independent Colleges and Universities on December 4, 1972, Dr. George C. Roche III of Hillsdale College warned of the reach of federal bureaucrats into private education through the medium of federal financing of university programs. Under the guise of "equal opportunity" and "non-discrimination," federal officials are imposing racial quotas on faculties and on students. They have brushed aside standards of excellence to assert the primacy of political expediency, on threat of depriving institutions of planned funding.

The remarkable aspect of this denigration of higher education is that it is programmed by educators ensconced in the federal bureaucracy, carefully selected from the Fabian vanguard to extend the federal control of educational policy. Socialism has no respect for the traditional standards of higher education; it is interested only in the use of education to achieve social and political effects.

There is a colossal conceit in the whole operation which reminds us of Spengler's comment about Plato: "When Plato, Aristotle and their contemporaries defined and blended the various kinds of classical constitution so as to obtain a wise and beautiful resultant, all the world listened, and Plato himself tried to transform Syracuse in accordance with an ideological recipe—and sent the city downhill to its ruin."[2] That is what our politicians and educators are doing to this country today.

There have been protests against the reign of secular humanism in our universities, but they go unheeded. They are not relevant to the concerns of institutions no longer concerned about excellence and justice but fully subordinated to political policy. Father Murray wrote:[3]

Psychologically, it is not without significance that evolutionary scientific humanism should be the favorite creed of our contemporary social engineers, with their instrumental theories of education, law, and government. And it seems that their inevitable temptation is to hasten the process of evolution by use of the resources of government just as it is to advance the cause of scientific humanism by a somewhat less than human application of science.

In protest, Father Murray defined some of the limits of university authority which professors should respect:[4]

The assertion I chiefly wish to venture, however, is that the university is committed to its students and to their freedom to learn. Its students are not abstractions, and whatever may be the university's duty (or right, or privilege or sin) of noncommittalism, the fact is that many of its students are religiously committed. To put it concretely, they believe in God. Or to put it more concretely, they are Protestants, Catholics, Jews. The university as such has no right to judge the validity of any of these commitments. Similarly, it has no right to ignore the fact of these commitments, much less to require that for the space of four years its students should be committed to being scientific naturalists within the university, whatever else they may choose, somewhat schizophrenically, to commit themselves to be outside its walls.

Jacques Maritain has said:[5]

Those who teach the democratic charter must believe in it with their whole hearts, and stake on it their personal convictions, their consciences, and the depth of their moral life. They must therefore explain and justify its articles in the light of the philosophical or religious faith to which they cling and which quickens their belief in the common charter.

Surely this must be the heart of education in America. If education is to preserve and transmit our heritage, the work can be done only by those who are deeply dedicated to the task.

The thesis advanced in some educational circles that higher education has some purpose above or beyond national aims, which requires it to harbor for the sake of completeness or for a pseudo tolerance the avowed or covert enemies of our society, is a pernicious and destructive threat to both education and society. Men and women loyal to our political and social institutions are quite capable of learning all that is to be known about the hostile ideological pretensions of other systems and only they are qualified to tell the truth about such systems.

These false pretensions of open-mindedness in higher education have fostered attitudes of indifference to or hostility toward our own political and social values. Some sectors of our universities have become cradles not of liberty but of atheism and treason, as history attests. It is time to clean out these nests of disloyalty and man the ramparts of education with loyal citizens.

We can begin by taking government out of education. There is no future for American education in the embrace of the federal bureaucracy. It is a suffocating envelopment, like the coils of a boa constrictor. Freedom lies in the opposite direction.

In order to liberate education, parents must begin to pay for it directly, not through taxes. The citizens of a community must reject additional school taxes and place a tuition charge on public education, with suitable exemptions for families too poor to pay. At first the charge would be small, but as Congress continues to depreciate the dollar and additional costs are met from tuition charges, tuition would in time become the chief support of the system. In time, full tuition could be charged to parents able to pay. Parents who pay tuition to the schools would surely reassert their control of the schools. The process might well begin with higher education.

It is difficult for people accustomed to the paternalism of kings and socialist governments to imagine the joy and exhilaration of being free. Today, in America, a reverse process is in high gear. The people are rejecting freedom to accept the yoke of government. They are being wheedled by demagogues who assert that government services are free. But no government service is free. It is all paid for by taxes extracting the cost from the worker's pay. Instead of paying the direct cost of a service, which he might have done with his own money, the worker pays in addition for a vast governmental bureaucracy to administer the service. In one corporate survey of a service to be rendered by government for the people, it was found that 60 percent of the cost would go to the supervising government bureaucracy and only 40 percent would reach the target people.

We see this trend in all areas of government. In personal health care, which should be no concern of the federal government, the question is not whether those in need should receive free care but whether all citizens should receive free care. The spectacle of sick millionaires receiving free medical services under Medicare is part of the folly of socialism which disables all public policy.

It is not credible that the workers of America would support the fraud of these "free" public services if they understood what was happening. It is the worker, not the millionaire, who pays for the services. The worker would be far better off to use his taxes to pay for his own services.

On this issue, the legislative policy of organized labor has been counterproductive. There is a strong strain of socialism in American organized labor. While the dominant elements reject theories of government ownership of industry and consciously prefer the capitalist system, they hold a heritage of socialist sentiment that all kinds of health, welfare and education services should be furnished "free" by the state. Even when the ineptitude of government service is widely demonstrated and the excessive cost of such service to the worker is documented, organized labor persists in supporting government programs which extend the folly. It ill serves the working man by such policy.

In education as in other fields of public activity, our political system is fostering decline and corruption. The directing voices, reflecting the Fabian purpose, recommend more money and more federal intervention. Socialism knows no other answer.

We can search in vain through the history of the past century for any evidence that either of our two major parties has made a single constructive contribution to American education. On the contrary, the parties have vied with each other in breaking down our sound system of education, multiplying an oppressive bureaucracy and undermining the morale of teachers and students. Their only capacity is to drift with the pressures of the hour, moving steadily toward disaster. Political expediency offers no other end.

Chapter 17

THE POLITICS OF POVERTY

LEONARD E. READ, that perceptive analyst of the foibles of our time, has called social justice ". . . man's greatest injustice to man, antisocial in every respect; not the cement of society, but the lust for power and privilege and the seed of man's corruption and downfall." Of claims that "social justice" is an expression of mercy and pity, he writes: "These virtues are strictly personal attributes and are expressed only in the voluntary giving of one's own, never in the seizure and redistribution of someone else's possessions."[1]

The impulse to help the poor, which leads a person to contribute from his own means for that purpose, is an impulse of charity; but the impulse which impels a person to take means from others to help the poor, in disregard of the individual merits of the taking and the giving, is an impulse of politics that affronts justice. It is another example of the intellectual confusion of the times that the churches, formerly agencies for mobilizing the charity of individuals in service to distressed humanity, now complacently assign the responsibility for charity to government and are content to lobby for greater welfare appropriations.

Frederic Bastiat stated the case in 1848:[2]

Exact justice is something so definite that legislation which had only justice in view would be virtually immutable. It could vary only as to the means of

174

approaching ever more closely to this single end: the protection of men's persons and their rights . . . the forces of government would attain this goal all the better because they would all be applied to preventing and repressing misrepresentation, fraud, delinquency, crime, and acts of violence, instead of being dissipated, as at present, among a host of matters alien to their essential function. . . .

Every time we deem an action to be good and beautiful, we should like, quite naturally, to see it made the general practice. Now, when we see in society a force to which all gives way, our first impulse is to enlist its aid by decreeing the action and imposing it on everyone. But the question is whether one does not thereby degrade both the nature of this force and the nature of the action, rendering legally obligatory what was essentially spontaneous and voluntary. As far as I am concerned, I cannot get it into my head that the law, which is force, can be usefully applied to any purpose other than repressing wrongs and maintaining rights.

It is of course a function of the state to define and maintain a just social order through the promulgation of law which encourages and rewards virtue, which reproves and outlaws anti-social action. This duty is not limited to the repression of common crimes and delinquency but extends also to the organization of industry in ways which assure the subordination of agglomerations of private power to the common good. In a proper political order, it does not embrace the public administration of charity; but we find in history that this assumption of responsibility for the distribution of charity is the lodestone of politics in prosperous societies and the corrupter of governments. It happened in Rome:[3]

Under Greek influence, one of the finest young statesmen of Rome came up with the suggestion—altogether unprecedented for the realistic Romans—that "justice" be made the internal unifying principle. Now that we have no enemy to force us to compromise our conflicting interests, said Tiberius Gracchus, let us put conflicting interest aside and agree to give everyone his due. It was to be a "square deal" for everyone, taking from those who had too much and giving to those who had too little. But the young man found that while he quickly built up a following among those who stood to gain by his proposal, he built up the hostility of those who stood to lose by it. The result was bloody rioting and eventually slaughters on both sides, ending first with the beating to death of Tiberius Gracchus, followed ten years later by the killing of his younger brother Caius. Discussion wouldn't suffice, evidently, to keep the peace keepers of the Mediterranean world united.

Professor Paolucci found in Polybius a warning to the Romans of the impending dissolution of the Republic:[4]

A time comes, he had predicted, when millionaires take to the hustings to excite the wildest appetites of the multitude; the meanings of freedom and equality are soon confounded, and the situation becomes daily more riotous until, in desperation, all are disposed to welcome the despot.

The parallel with the United States now is striking.

There was a voice against the fallacies of the day but it went unheeded by those who wielded the political power:[5]

175

In the fifth century A.D., after events had proved their incapacity to keep lawless barbarians from looting and burning vast neighborhoods of their principal cities, the Roman secularist-humanitarians continued to congratulate themselves for their strict adherence to the ideal of universal peace sustained by world government. Their chief critic in those twilight days, St. Augustine, acknowledged that it was a formidable task to show what is essentially wrong with that fine-sounding ideal.

Whittaker Chambers commented upon this softening of the comfortable societies in their pursuit of abundance:[6]

> For it seems to be a law of life and of history that societies in which the pursuit of abundance and comfort has displaced all other pursuits in importance soon cease to be societies. They become prey. They fall to whatever power can rally the starving spirit of man even though the rallying faith is demonstrably worse than the soft complacency that would suffocate the spirit in abundance. The fall is more certain because a failure of spirit leads invariably by some inward influence to a failure of intelligence.

In the early years of our history, the corrupting power of money was a constant concern of our statesmen. The attempt of promoters to gain favor or franchise from government was commonplace. As the powers of government increased:[7]

> John C. Calhoun, who had turned nationalist in the great days of Southern presidential leadership, turned states rightist again to warn against a social division of the nation into a taxpaying minority and a tax-consuming majority, governed by a partisan faction kept in office through public bribery.

In this century, first in Britain and then in the United States, the Fabian socialists urged extensive state welfare as a means of serving justice and diminishing the disparity of incomes in a capitalist society. These sophisticated power-seekers were of course aware that professing compassion for the underprivileged and inaugurating "bread and circuses" were means of building political power. They adopted a pose of righteousness and set out to enlist the Christian churches in the cause. At a conference on World Cooperation for Development held in Lebanon in April 1968, Lady Barbara Ward Jacobson, in a report on Christian conviction and motivation, said:[8]

> There can be nonviolent revolutions. All our efforts must be directed to change without violence if it will be possible. But if injustice is embedded in the status quo and its supporters refuse to permit change, then, as a last resort, Men's Consciences may lead them in full and clearsighted responsibility to engage in violent revolution. A heavy burden then rests on those who have resisted change.

In a land of general prosperity and growing leisure, not unlike the Rome of Tiberius Gracchus, the pursuit of physical comfort, the avoidance of pain and suffering, have become the obsession of prosperous citizens. Whittaker Chambers noted that[9]

> Nothing is more characteristic of this age than its obsession with an avoidance of suffering. Nothing dooms it more certainly to that condition which is not childlike but an infantilism which is an incapacity for growth that im-

176

plies an end. The mind which has rejected the soul, and marched alone, has brought the age to the brink of disaster.

Woodrow Wilson and the Democrats, "the party of the people," opened the door to the centralization of political power by amending the Constitution to authorize a national income tax and to provide for the popular election of Senators; and by passing the Federal Reserve Act. The next Democratic President, Franklin Roosevelt, used the depression emergency to inaugurate federal work and welfare programs to build up his political machine. His disciples expressed indignation at the lack of compassion in the Congress, a view surviving today. A generation later, the Warren Court would intervene to remove any constitutional obstacles to the federal compassion:[10]

> The Warren Court found even the Congress unresponsive to the anguish of the poor. The Court set about establishing equal representation, equal justice, and equal rights. It required that educational facilities for the children of the poor be comparable to those for the more fortunate. To make matters more difficult, the Court insisted that the schools should not be racially separate. Not only were the poor to be served, but old tensions were to be eliminated in the serving.

It is the perennial illusion of politicians, whether governor or judge, that with sufficient money and power they can make all things right. This conceit divides politicians from the statesmen. They end by building empires, ill-designed, mal-administered and ridden with strife. Their reach for power exceeds their grasp, so their city collapses. Convinced of their own wisdom, estranged from the people, they rush on to destruction:[11]

> . . . the modern state has as a matter of empirical fact, proved impotent to do all the things it has undertaken to do. Crime and civic virtue, education, the stimulus and control of economic processes, public morality, justice in the order and processes of law—over all these things the modern state assumed an unshared competence. But it has proved itself incompetent in a fundamental sense. The reason is that "the state depends for its vitality upon a motivation which it cannot by itself command." As long as motivation can be assumed to be existent in the body politic, the order of politics (in the broadest sense) moves with some security to its proper ends. But if the motivation fails, there is no power in the state itself to evoke it.

It is indeed unfortunate that the common literature of formal education has become the handmaiden of these corrupting political processes. The literature of the Fabians has become the literature of the university. The subversion of our American political system is condoned as the course of history:[12]

> No matter what may be the political or economic organization of the state, there is a trend throughout the world for governments to use the collective resources of the community to enhance the economic and social well-being of its citizens.

The bursting of the constitutional restraint by judicial activism, precisely because the people would not have approved the action, is misrepresented as a response to the popular will:[13]

177

The United States government has engaged in various welfare activities, not because of outside pressure, but because considerably more people in the United States favor these particular programs than oppose them.

And again, the implied necessity of the times and the assumed will of the people are summoned to defend the federal intrusion into local affairs:[14]

Many persons believe that a modern industrial nation must furnish expanding social services, that the states were slow to move in this direction, and that the grant-in-aid device permits desirable and necessary programs to be developed within the framework of the federal system.

Thus did the intellectuals, the news media, the bankers and the politicians all agree that poverty must indeed be the concern of government.

A POLITICAL TOOL

Poverty is today a chief prop of politics. Hand-wringing about the spectacle of illness and want in America is the stock-in-trade of election campaigns, especially with Democratic politicians, as new promises to remedy the conditions are made every two years. This talk is the touchstone of success in politics.

Politics has an overwhelming capacity to live in the present. Voters never ask what happened to the promises of the last campaign. They seem unaware that the Democratic Party has plied this line for forty years and that the problem is more acute now than when the federal government first entered the lists. Somehow, mysteriously, politicians can still be credible as they repeat the old promises.

The basic elements of this drama are the continuing presence of poverty in our society and the deep sympathy of the American people for all who are in want. No matter that politicians have promised and promised, failed and failed; if poverty exists today, the people want something done about it.

Some citizens fear that the welfare lobbies are fastening an irresistible grip on American politics and that no reform is possible. This is a misreading of the political scene. Although the political power of the welfare interests is formidable—especially in the bureaucracy with a stake in programs—the decisive political power in the United States rests with the working people. It is their assent to welfare programs which sustains welfare. Only when the working man comes to realize the fraud which has exploited his pay and his compassion will there be welfare reform.

There are some basic aspects of poverty which today are lost in the welter of sentiment and politics. A Christian society has lost its bearings. Throughout history, the poor have been the ammunition of politics. Demagogues have commanded mobs to overthrow established authority and seize power. Once established, the concern of the demagogue is to make himself secure against the mob which raised him to power.

The religions of the world have from time immemorial enjoined com-

178

passion for the poor. In Judaism, a special concern for widows and orphans was commanded of the faithful. The simple poor were pitied, and helped when possible. Their shortcomings were extenuated as a consequence of poverty. Society expected little of them.

THE GLORIFICATION OF POVERTY

Jesus changed all that. He told the poor that in their poverty, they were closer to heaven. It was the rich man whose chance of getting to heaven was like the chance of a camel passing through the eye of a needle. Poverty, instead of being a pitied condition of misfortune, was to become the estate of the wisest men and women in the world. In response to the Gospel of Jesus, wealthy young men and women of the Mediterranean world gave up fortune and family to live lives of prayer and sacrifice. They found a heavenly joy and fulfillment in serving God and their fellow man. But the greatest impact of the Gospel was on the poor. Jesus did not extenuate their transgressions. He taught that they were responsible to God for their behavior. Other religions had preached personal responsibility to the rich, but Jesus preached personal responsibility to the poor.

That is how Christianity converted the Roman world. It came up from the bottom, from the poor and lowly who were honored and respected by the Gospel.

Throughout the Christian world, the peasant, the worker, has been a man of character and dignity. He knows his duty to God and man. He fears God and no man. He is not ashamed of his poverty, nor envious of wealth. Whether he deals with king or bishop or fellow worker, he respects the man who performs his duty well. There is no cringing in his demeanor. As a son of God, he knows that his eternal reward will be measured not by his station in the world but by how well he used the talents which God bestowed on him.

This view of poverty is all but lost in America today. It persists among some youth who hear the call of Jesus and devote their lives to His service. But even among the Christian clergy in the United States, the Gospel is no longer preached to the poor. Their sins of envy, their crimes of theft, assault and robbery are excused as a response to the society which allows poverty to exist. The churches seem to think they can cure poverty by promoting federal appropriations for the poor. But that is not the way Jesus saved the poor.

Jesus taught that poverty is the most honorable estate man can achieve. The poor hold moral excellence within easy reach. To teach that wealth and comfort are a prerequisite to morality is to repudiate Christian teaching. That is the error on which America is embarked today. It is the gospel not of Christianity but of materialism.

Poverty is not the cause of immorality. But immorality is often the cause of poverty. The person who in self-pity wars against society is not likely to become a useful member of it. Only when he has achieved a sound relationship with God and his fellow man will his mind be capable of directing a socially useful employment of his talents. We see also that poverty is not the cause of crime in society. Immorality is the cause of crime. To offer the poor bread without the Gospel is to offer them stones for their hunger. Only the Gospel can lift them out of their poverty.

This is the tragedy of our prisons. They may keep a prisoner in comfort for a few years, they may intimidate him with the power of the state, but they have no cure for his immorality. Our society no longer understands the power and place of religion in public affairs.

WELFARE WITHOUT CHARITY

With typical secular blindness, our government supposed that poverty was simply a lack of money. Somehow the system didn't put enough money into the hands of those who needed it. So the government started programs to give money to the poor. That was an inexhaustible pit. The poor were a sieve. No matter how much money you gave them, the poor spent it and remained poor. So government started programs to help the poor in other ways. It hired social workers to help them change their lifestyles, to teach them how to use money prudently. It built special housing to provide the poor with decent living conditions. But the poor took the money and kept their lifestyles. They wrecked the buildings provided for their housing.

The poor proved to be smarter than the social workers. They learned how to beat the system. They broke up families (nominally) to qualify for additional income from Aid to Families with Dependent Children. They learned to draw multiple checks by registering in different offices under different names. Even with an army of bureaucrats consuming much of the welfare money, government could not keep up with the fraud in the welfare system. Government is incapable of teaching morality. But government is capable of teaching immorality, and that is what U.S. welfare programs have been doing. The subsidy of illegitimacy in the guise of helping children illustrates the moral degeneracy of American politics.

President Johnson's poverty program was not a program to help the poor. It was a program to save the Democratic Party. It was his response to the demands of black political leaders for more abundant patronage from the public treasury. President Nixon proposed a new welfare program. He would double welfare rolls and costs, adding payments to the working poor, making welfare a federal responsibility with direct payment from the federal treasury, requiring states to supplement the federal payments with state payments to maintain income levels. His proposal was rejected by the Congress as an imprudent adventure which would worsen the welfare mess.

THE ROLE OF GOVERNMENT

It should be obvious from our experience that U.S. welfare programs are grievously misdirected. In concept, they show no comprehension of the nature of poverty. Their only achievement seems to be the distribution of money to a growing political bureaucracy living on the taxes of the workers.

Honest government at the local level might be capable of distributing public money to the needy families of the community. Honest government at the state level is probably too remote from the need to make an equitable distribution of funds to needy citizens. The federal government is so remote from the individual needs of citizens across this land that to involve it in a war on poverty is, as a simple matter of organization, *preposterous*.

Government at the local level cannot do what it might do because it is strangled in regulations promulgated by remote bureaucrats in state and national capitals. Waste and fraud are legalized by the politically-inspired regulations. The simple reality our people must face is that government is incapable of administering welfare. But happily, the companion reality is that there is no need for federal involvement in this field.

We have seen a Senate committee holding hearings on poverty in rural North Carolina, with suitable television broadcasting to persuade the nation that greater federal programs of care for the poor were needed. No one asked whether that county was rich enough to take care of its own poor, and if it was, why the rest of the nation should be called to help. And if the county was too poor to care for its needy poor, surely the state of North Carolina was not too poor to do so. How then had the care of these citizens in rural North Carolina become a national problem of concern to the United States Senate?

It seems obvious that the United States Congress and our national news media are engaged in a program to enlarge the powers of the federal government, at tremendous cost to the people and without cause. It is simply impossible to make a rational case for federal involvement in welfare assistance. The motivation must lie in a general plan for building national powers and degrading state powers in our federal system. This is the avowed purpose of Fabian socialists.

The argument against state involvement in welfare is of a different order. While every state is clearly capable of caring for its own poor, every county, city or other local subdivision may not be capable of doing so. At this level, the question is whether the state should be involved on any regular basis. If the state assumes a responsibility for welfare, it institutionalizes the service with a bureaucracy interested in its own expansion. That decision dries up sources of private charity because the people assume the state is taking care of the poor. While the growth of fraud will vary with the quality of state administration, the incentive to fraud is built into such a relationship between politicians and voters.

Let the state refuse to set up welfare benefits. The responsibility then falls to private charitable institutions. Religious institutions and private secular foundations care for the poor. The community cares for itself. In time of economic recession, if the burden exceeds the resources of existing institutions, the local government may supplement private contribution with special payments to the private service agencies. But government should not establish competing services. It should contract for the expansion of existing private services while the emergency lasts. In dire emergency, the state legislature may appropriate funds for welfare services, reinforcing those communities whose resources have been exhausted.

With such organization, the responsibility for helping neighbors would rest directly with the people, not in government. Assistance would be rendered directly by individuals and institutions highly motivated for such service. The example of the Mormon Church, which cared for its own members through the Great Depression, is an illustration of the capability of the American people to take care of their own.

But this is not the kind of rational social organization toward which we are headed. It is the structure from which we have come. As we reject a basic wisdom related to man and his institutions, we are enveloped in mounting confusion, in chaotic and ineffectual programs. Our measures to combat poverty are in their essential nature destined to fail.

If we are to wage an effective war on poverty, the campaign must be soundly conceived and directed. The first requirement is to understand the nature of poverty. Every worker has a social obligation to assure that all in his community have access to the essential food, clothing and shelter to support existence. This is a duty of his humanity. Because he cannot personally search out the needy, he gives money to his church or to other institutions engaged in this work.

When these needs are met, poverty must be regarded as an honorable estate. Many citizens will embrace it in service to God or their fellow man. Others will embrace it as a spiritual discipline fostering the growth of wisdom. All who live in that estate in honest and faithful service, whether from choice, misfortune or quality of talent, are to be respected by the community. Society must recognize that persons have different talents, and that the greatest of these is not the talent for acquiring wealth.

POVERTY IN PERSPECTIVE

Our present view of poverty as a blight or scourge to be corrected is a product of the age of materialism and of socialist politics. The overwhelming concern of our politics about wealth has destroyed our philosophic perception of true values.

The concern of the people as sovereigns, beyond assuring the essentials of life for all, must be to create a system in which just rewards are rendered for service to the community. This is best achieved by mutual agreement between those who render and those who use a service. But even such individual contracts require a system of law and justice to sustain them. Our whole economic order depends on the laws of our society. It is through laws enacted that the community influences the economic order. The community must constantly examine its economic order to assure that the structure of law rewards constructive initiatives which serve the community and outlaws non-productive manipulation of wealth for personal advantage.

For example, we have noted that the creation of corporate organization gave great impetus to business enterprise. In that respect, the state acted wisely. But there is evidence that existing law allows the manipulation of corporate resources and organization by individuals to amass personal fortunes without any constructive purpose and even against the community interest. These events suggest that our system of corporate organization has not kept pace with the needs of the community. Government, which has a responsibility to keep law in service to the people, is neglecting its duty.

This condition is noted to illustrate that government does play a critical role in the economic life of the community. To maintain the framework of law within which economic activity is conducted, government must monitor that law to assure that it continuously fosters equity and justice in society.

The failure of government to maintain a system of law which encourages industry and discourages financial manipulation of equities is undermining the confidence of the American citizen in his government. For example, in an earlier age when child labor was exploited, the government passed compulsory school attendance laws and minimum wage laws. But in our time when child labor is no longer a social problem, there is evidence of character damage to students required to continue schooling beyond their capacity to learn, and of marginal earners, including untrained youth, excluded from employment by minimum wage laws. We need not here explore the changes in law urgently needed to sustain the health of our economic system, but let us note that government is neglecting its responsibility.

Government also affects our economic system, and the problem of poverty, by a policy of inflation which robs the people of their savings. As we · have noted, this unconscionable dishonesty is destructive of responsible citizenship. Citizens who have earned economic security are deprived of it and thrown upon public charity through the deliberate policy of government.

This behavior of government is the product of our political system. With both political parties committed to the replacement of the American political order by a centralized system of state planning, prudent measures are no longer feasible. There is no opposition party to show that the "welfare mess" is entirely a creation of the federal government, without warrant in need or reason. Who will show that "poverty" is a political ploy for building a supporting bureaucracy? There is nothing in the political order to restrain party aggrandizement.

Our political and information structures are not informing the people about the true effects of our poverty programs.

Chapter 18

BUILDING THE WELFARE STATE

IT SEEMS ASTONISHING in retrospect that the Fabian socialists could so easily have subverted the American political ethic of proven excellence, saturating it in a few short years with the ancient error of socialism. Success may indicate the preference of the people for paternalism and their tiring of the responsibility of liberty. But this choice was never clearly the issue. The political tactic was to offer the people "free" services from government—to render governmental assistance not only to the ill and needy but to all voters.

It was a clever plan, basically corrupt, and it worked. It worked because there was no effective voice to show the people the fraud of these pretensions. The American political ethic had been taken for granted. No special defense of it had ever been required, and none had been prepared. When Franklin Roosevelt launched his assault on traditional political morality, there was no effective defense of traditional values, except in the rejection of his scheme for packing the Supreme Court. Congress hadn't the wit to make sound policy.

But there was protest. Some seers warned of the error and prophesied the consequence to which such folly must lead. Alfred E. Smith, who preceded Franklin Roosevelt as Governor of New York and as Democratic candidate for the presidency, defined with admirable precision what was being done to government and to the country.[1] Other leaders spoke up. But President Roosevelt had the firm support of our bankers and industrialists and the new medium of radio for projecting his promises to the people. The protests of concerned citizens were overwhelmed by the skillful news management of Charles Michaelson, the presidential press secretary.

The success of the new welfare politics in electing and re-electing Franklin Roosevelt virtually silenced political opposition to his programs. The Republican Party decided that welfare politics was the only viable politics, so it adopted the Roosevelt initiative, always trailing behind the Democrats.

The dominance of the new political mythology, even over the minds of "conservative" practitioners, was illustrated in an interview with Congressman Howard E. Smith, Chairman of the House Rules Committee and one of the reputedly staunch conservatives of the Congress. In response to a question about the place of the Constitution in modern government, Congressman Smith said that the Constitution, made for a rural society, had to be adapted to modern needs.

This was, of course, the kind of sophistry by which the liberal Democrats held their conservative colleagues in support of party programs. Perhaps it was inevitable that in twenty-five years of repetition, these false statements would acquire an aura of truth. They served to rationalize the Democratic centralization of power, if Congressman Smith considered that to be a necessary course of modern government.

In the Senate, Robert Taft waged a losing battle against the socialist trend. He held the full confidence of the people of Ohio. His honesty and integrity were respected by his colleagues and by the country. He could rally support against the most blatant power grabs but he could not change the direction of government.

Despite the Roosevelt successes, a current of dissent persisted among some Southern Democrats and some Northern Republicans. After Roosevelt's passing, these forces combined to offer an opposition to the more radical directions of Democratic policy. For a while, a bipartisan coalition restrained the more extreme schemes of the liberal activists. This was a period of discouragement for zealous liberals whose vast programs of federal welfare were curtailed. As one liberal writer expressed his disappointment:[2]

> The last four Eisenhower years were wasted. They were a time of economic stagnation, of lost opportunities for starts on the problems of the cities and the schools and on the reinvigoration of the federal system, problems which all but overwhelmed us in the 1960s. What seemed to many almost a halcyon period, the longest period of peace we have known as a nation in the last thirty years, and an era of muted strife and partisanship at home, was, so far as our domestic needs were concerned, an expensive holiday from responsibility.

EXPLOITING THE WAR POWERS

War seemed to provide a useful tool for the enlargement of federal powers. It made acceptable the increase in taxes which would otherwise have been resisted. It required an acceptance of authoritarian government foreign to peacetime rule. After war, there was a legacy of high taxes and government authority as war powers were only partially relinquished. Although war powers were only partially invoked in the Korean and Vietnam wars, the excessive duration of those conflicts had serious effect in developing a higher tolerance of government controls.

After World War I, as in prior national wars, the enemy was defeated and we could return to our peaceful pursuits. In 1933, our military forces were down to a strength of 136,500 in the Army, 91,200 in the Navy, and 16,000 in the Marine Corps.

The aftermath of World War II provided a different experience. We had been allied with one enemy to defeat another enemy. In defeating the Nazi and fascist enemies in Central Europe, we had destroyed the European balance of power and opened the door to Soviet expansion. As the Soviet Union moved to impose its rule on Eastern Europe, it became clear that the United States had demobilized too fast. The Soviet coup in Czechoslovakia, the awakening of Western Europe to its danger and the call for U.S. assistance brought the United States to an unaccustomed posture of armed readiness in time of peace.

Weapons had to be modernized and produced. New plants had to be built. Building construction, housing, jobs, land booms—all lay in bringing defense industry into a congressman's district. Members of Congress were plied by developers and Chambers of Commerce to bring new defense industry into the community. This was the alliance between Congress and defense industry which President Eisenhower referred to as the "military industrial complex" in his message to Congress. Because it was new, expansive and the beneficiary of a liberal tax policy, defense industry was the boom business of the Fifties. It carried great weight in politics as it bore rewards to the powerful members of Congress. The big corporations won lucrative contracts.

Traditionally, after war, American industry returns to its commercial production. But the Cold War brought a new and continuing relationship with government. It changed government in more ways than President Eisenhower realized. Commercial industry was no concern of government, but defense industry was government industry. Would government, through its dominance of defense industry, find in it an opening to the control of all industry? The extralegal action of President Kennedy and Secretary of Defense McNamara against the steel and aluminum industries in 1962 argued that the Chief Executive was developing a sense of responsibility not alone for defense industry but for all American industry.

The fact that the U.S. had a government of limited powers defined in the Constitution was barely mentioned. Washington bureaucrats now needed only to assert a national interest in order to intervene in any activity, private or public. This concept of federal authority aroused scant concern

186

in the news media. The omnipotence of federal officials seemed to be accepted as part of the current reality.

THE GOLDWATER REVOLT

In the course of politics, there was special significance in the Goldwater campaign of 1964. This was the first time in thirty-two years that either party had nominated an avowed conservative for the presidency. That achievement was the work not of the party leaders but of a grassroots revolt of the people against three decades of liberal politics. Senator Barry Goldwater, a colorful and popular spokesman for conservative politics, became the rallying point of a national aspiration for honesty in government.

The movement failed. The assassination of President Kennedy had so identified the Democratic Party with him that no Republican could have been elected. The overwhelming support of the news media as well as the defection of many liberal party leaders split the party and assured a Goldwater defeat.

Although ineptitude in management of the campaign contributed to the resounding defeat of Senator Goldwater, still the basic lesson of American politics was not obscured. Politicians in league with the banking-industry elites, commanding the resources of the news media, were all committed to a liberal policy from which no deviation would be tolerated. The parties were merely a facade to anesthetize the public while the oligarchy exercised power.

A similar result was achieved in 1972 with the defeat of Senator McGovern. He represented a challenge to the liberal orthodoxy from the radical Left. Leaders of the Democratic Party turned against the candidate just as Republican liberals had done in 1964.

PRESS SUPPORT

As long as national policy had the concurrence of the news media, there was no way for any opposition view to reach the public. President Kennedy realized this in 1963 when he decided to adjust national policy to the view of the *New York Times.* He could retain media support by replacing South Vietnam's President Ngo Dinh Diem with a leader amenable to the concept of a coalition government in South Vietnam. This was the British prescription for solution of the strife in Vietnam, an extension of the formula which Kennedy had accepted for Laos in 1961. The difficulty with this solution was to make it acceptable to the American people. Kennedy could do that with the cooperation of the media. If the plan succeeded, all U.S. forces could "honorably" be withdrawn from South Vietnam in 1964.

President Kennedy succeeded at home but failed in South Vietnam. The foolishness lay in supposing that a nation so deeply embattled against Communist aggression could so easily be reconciled to surrender. General "Big" Minh couldn't do it.

At home, a massive media campaign to denigrate President Diem and his

187

government was launched. It had the full cooperation of Communist elements in South Vietnam. The media campaign aroused American hostility to the reported "oppression" of the Diem government and prepared acceptance of the November coup. What is of special significance to this study was the capacity of a handful of newsmen representing the *New York Times* and the two wire services to brainwash the professional press with false reporting. I recall the editor who said to me, "You know that when people commit suicide to protest oppression, they must be suffering terrible persecution." I explained that there was no religious repression in South Vietnam and that self-immolation for political protest or to win excellence in the next life was a part of Asian culture—but my words had no effect. Wire service reports "from the scene" were persuasive.

Across this country, editors and newsmen who should have known from their experience that the reports from Saigon grossly misrepresented events in that city, accepted the stories uncritically. No doubt they were influenced by the credence which the *New York Times,* the *Washington Post* and the *Los Angeles Times* gave to the reports. How easily it was done: The people were led to accept an unconscionable policy of government when that policy was supported by the media. Nor was this the first instance of such power in the press.

When the *New York Times* idealized Fidel Castro as a freedom fighter and denigrated President Fulgencio Batista of Cuba, the broad acceptance of these caricatures must have influenced President Eisenhower to withdraw military and moral support from the Cuban government, leading directly to its fall. Elements of press and government which had correct information contradicting the *Times'* fairy tale suppressed that information. Newsmen who should have known better joined in the *Times'* propaganda campaign. The American people, the Cuban people and public policy were ill-served.

These events demonstrate the degree to which our news media are subject to manipulation by a handful of men in controlling positions. This is done not by ordering newsmen to sustain a given policy but by using on special missions—in Cuba, in Vietnam, or elsewhere—newsmen who are minded to report in the desired vein. Directing editors at home use the reports to whip up public support for the desired policy or program.

President Johnson must have known that he would lose press support when he failed to install a coalition government in Saigon. But that course was now impracticable. Having overthrown President Diem, the United States was stuck with what remained. When the generals who acquiesced to American insistence on the removal of President Diem "to improve the war effort" learned that the real purpose was to form a coalition government with the Communists, they would have none of it. They overthrew the Minh government. If the United States now abandoned South Vietnam to the Communists, its duplicity would be revealed.

Feasibility was no restraint on the news media. The policy of discrediting

188

our war effort and praising the enemy continued. When in the 1964 presidential campaign, Senator Barry Goldwater seemed disposed to win the war with air and sea power, the media mocked and scoffed and misrepresented his position. He was pictured as the kind of leader who might use the nuclear bomb irresponsibly. And, *mirabile dictu,* Lyndon Johnson was for the moment treated as the great peacemaker. After the Goldwater defeat, the disintegration of South Vietnamese fighting forces under the impact of U.S. limitations on war policy forced President Johnson to send U.S. combat troops to join the battle. The alternative was to accept defeat at the hands of North Vietnam, and Lyndon Johnson was not prepared to submit the United States to such disgrace—not even to court the *New York Times.* In consequence, he fell from grace.

The news media continued to undermine popular support of the war. "Peace" marches were glorified. Communist barbarity against the South Vietnamese was ignored. Communist military actions were cast in heroic dimensions. The fighting qualities of the South Vietnamese soldiers were belittled. Newsmen sought out disgruntled or pot-smoking American soldiers for interviews to convey to the home folks the impression that war was degrading our youth.

By 1968, Senator Robert F. Kennedy captured the media banner with a promise of coalition government in South Vietnam. But by that time the peace movement was getting out of hand. Its alliance with the Communist Party and with all the Communist fronts in the United States had given it a treasonous aspect which repelled the American people. The moderate language of Richard Nixon was more in keeping with the mood of the country.

The people were weary but unconquered. The persistent refusal of our leaders to defeat the enemy allowed no honorable exit from the war. The people accepted withdrawal of U.S. forces conjoined with a build-up of South Vietnam for its own defense. By this formula, President Nixon reduced U.S. casualties in the war and detached the American people from the increasing anguish of this ally, South Vietnam. The news media cooperated in de-emphasis of the radical peace movements which then disintegrated, ignored as irrelevant. There was significant interference with the Republican Convention at Miami in 1972.

These events might be taken to indicate merely that the American people favored a centrist position rejecting both extremes. That is the impression which politicians and the news media strive to convey. No doubt the people do favor a centrist position, but it is a position very different from that to which the country is committed. The people disapprove the policy of weakness before Communist aggression, of financing Soviet and Red Chinese industry, of tolerating contempt for law at home, of financing foreign aid, except military aid to allies. These positions are "centrist" not by the judgment of the people but by dictate of the elites. The oligarchy sees them

189

as essential to the welfare of American industry and to the avoidance of nuclear war. It is the capacity of these elites to enforce policies against the will of the people, through the control of public information, which demonstrates the failure of our political system and constitutes a danger to our national well-being.

DECLINING ROLE OF CONGRESS

The transformation of our political system from a decentralized republic to a centralized authority with subordinate state governments could be accomplished only through the powers of government. While the industrial elites might urge and the news media might denigrate or praise, the government had to act to change the constitutional balance. We have noted the Supreme Court's contributions to the process. It remains to note the willing concurrence of the Congress in building the welfare state.

Congress plays the central role in the national government. It holds an ultimate power over the Executive and the courts, though that power is restrained by the specific constitutional powers vested in those branches. Congress was limited also by exclusion of the central government from the powers and authorities reserved to the states.

The efficacy of this structure of law and government had been demonstrated in the nineteenth century. Immigrants from foreign lands had rushed to the United States to share in the freedom, opportunity and prosperity which the new system offered. It might have been expected that the Congress, presiding over the Republic as its chief instrument of government, would be keenly aware of the merits of the system and alert to defend its own role. That impression might have been conveyed by Fourth of July oratory at the turn of the century.

As the country grew, the political parties grew. The rewards of political activity increased. Pressures from industry and from reformers for party action increased. Party organization was perpetuated. When Speaker of the House "Uncle Joe" Cannon appointed committee chairmen, the House of Representatives had a strong leadership to direct its programs. The House became the dominant force in the national government. A President could get only the legislation that the Speaker approved. This organization provided the Congress with a keen sense of its own character and role. Congress acted as a body aware of its constitutional responsibilities and dedicated to their fulfillment.

The reformers attacked Speaker Cannon as a tyrant and demanded more "democracy" in the House organization. The President, they said, should be recognized as the party leader. In response to these pressures, the power to appoint committee chairmen was taken from the Speaker and these offices were filled by vote of the party caucus, according to seniority. No doubt the reformers foresaw and sought the far-reaching consequences of this change, but it seems unlikely that many other members of Congress did. With an array of senior House members holding chairmanships by right of seniority, the Speaker was divested of most of his power. Though he was nominally the party leader in the House, he had to negotiate policies and programs with the committee chairmen. He was leader not by his office but, if at all, by his personal capacity to rally committee chairmen to support his policies. In recent decades, the House has had no effective leader, except perhaps Speaker Sam Rayburn of Texas. (The same was true in the Senate where the Majority Leader could get effective action only by cooperation with Committee Chairmen.)

This change fragmented the House organization, staff as well as leadership. With the committee staffs looking to committee chairmen for guidance, there was no correlation of staff work to serve any central purpose or policy. This weakening of Congress occurred at a time when the power of the presidency was expanding. Zealous advocates of centralized authority urged presidential activism.[3]

> In our era a strenuous effort has been made to reverse the priorities. Champions of "presidential leadership" urge that the constitutional checks and balances on the powers to perfect the Union be abandoned at the same time that they advocate surrender of the prerogative powers to preserve it. The words of Professor James MacGregor Burns on the subject read like a parody of Lincoln's. Jefferson and his fellow Republicans were wrong, he says, in their fears that a strong presidential office would endanger the individual rights of the people. "What has happened is precisely the opposite—The powerful modern presidency has in fact become the most effective single protector of individual liberty in our governmental system." Yet, so much more could be done, he urges, if we could break out of the old checks and balances. "In glorifying the Madisonian model," he writes, "we have thwarted and fragmentized leadership instead of allowing it free play—Even the strongest and ablest presidents have been in the end more the victims of the Madisonian system than the masters of it. Our need is not to win an election or a leader, we must win a government."

After President Franklin Roosevelt sharply increased federal spending, his capacity to deal directly with committee chairmen in terms of the programs they desired for home districts or states brought these legislative leaders into direct relationship with the President. Though the President of course worked through the Speaker, there was full understanding that the power lay with the President. Federal taxes, federal programs and federal patronage increased.

These changes in congressional organization accelerated the trend to executive government. As head of the party, the President drew on the party loyalty of the congressional leaders. This soon became total dependence on the President. Perhaps the apogee of this trend was the statement of Speaker John McCormack after the Johnson election victory of 1964 that the duty of the Democratic Congress was to fulfill the promises which the President had made during the campaign.

The consequence of these changes was a critical weakening of Congress,

191

because it no longer constituted an independent legislative body aware of its own responsibilities for national policy. It now looked to the President and his growing bureaucracy to make the studies, recommend the legislation, and justify funding. Congress moved from its role as the dominant, directing, legislative organ of government to a semi-judicial role as the reviewer of recommendations made by the executive. The real control of government was surrendered to the Executive from whom the initiative for change had to come.

EVADING LEGISLATIVE PROCESS

There are of course some normal delays in legislative process. Before Congress can act to make or change law or to appropriate funds, it goes through a public hearing procedure in which advocates and opponents of the legislation have an opportunity to speak for the public record. The lawmaking process is necessarily and properly deliberate, cautious, thorough.

These deliberate processes are frustrating to zealous reformers who would like immediate action. Delay can also be frustrating to a political party, which may want to make or change law in ways that are opposed by the people.

The legislative process can be avoided by delegating powers to the President. For example, Congress has the basic duty to create by law the structure of government. It has sought in recent decades to avoid that responsibility by delegating to the President the power to make changes in the executive establishment, subject to disapproval of the Congress within a specified period. This law gives authority to change government organization to the Executive and reserves the power of the veto to the legislature. The constitutional assignment of responsibility has been changed without constitutional amendment. Is the action legal? Indeed it is not, although it has not been challenged in the courts.

The President is not bound by any rules of legislative process when he does the work of the legislature. He simply announces the changes in an Executive Order and lays the order before the Congress with such explanation as he chooses to give. Congress goes through no legislative process to make the change. It may simply ignore the Executive Order. Law is made without due legislative process.

Congress has also delegated legislative power to certain independent and semi-judicial rule-making bodies, but these delegations generally specify that legislative hearing procedures will be followed. The wisdom of these delegations is open to challenge but they at least appear to be made to bodies supplemental o the legislature. It is the delegation of legislative power to the President that is most pernicious.

An especially flagrant example of the corruption of legislative process is embodied in the pay-setting procedures proposed by President Johnson in the closing months of his administration and approved by Congress. It is of course embarrassing for members to propose and hold hearings upon increases in their own pay. The Johnson bill avoided this embarrassment by providing that the President should appoint a Commission on senior executive pay scales to make periodic recommendations to the President for changes in these scales to maintain comparability with scales in private industry. When the President approved the recommendations and forwarded them to Congress, they would become effective unless disapproved or modified by the Congress.

The first change under this new law became effective under President Nixon in 1969 and pay scales were astronomically increased. These increases were made under a President who had expressed concern about inflation. It would have been impossible for Congress to have put such increases through legislative hearings at a time when Congress was giving much smaller increases to lower-grade federal employees. By eliminating legislative process the deed was done. This is the kind of thing Congress has resorted to in its zeal to avoid the embarrassment of its own public responsibilities.

CHANGING SENATE ROLE

The Senate was designed to be the body to represent the states, while the House through popular election was to represent the people. The election of Senators by state legislatures was compatible with the constitutional role of the Senate. While that method of election prevailed, the Senate was a veritable assembly of statesmen honored for culture and talent.

In the Wilson Administration, Congress proposed a constitutional amendment for the popular election of U.S. Senators. This change to popular election of Senators was a serious undercutting of the states' role in the federal structure. The Senate became a body, like the House, severed from the state government and therefore looking only to national responsibilities. This change accelerated the trend toward centralization of power in Washington. That was its purpose. The Wilson Administration was committed to the centralization of government at the national level. What is most surprising is that leaders of the period had so little understanding of our decentralized government and so little attachment to it that they could be swept by cries of "democracy" into making the change.

With Congress acting so hastily to divest itself of its constitutional responsibilities and the President reaching out for ever-expanding power, it was inevitable that the federal courts would also seek a share of the legislative power. In *Brown* v. *Board of Education* the Supreme Court asserted that it acted because Congress had failed to act, and because it felt the prevailing law was an embarrassment to our international relationships. But the failure of one branch of government to exercise its constitutional powers in a manner deemed adequate by the other branches does not give the other branches authority to assume the neglected powers—though that thesis has been asserted by the political parties as well as by the Court.

There is a connection between the move for the popular election of Senators and the Court initiatives to apply the Bill of Rights restrictions to the states. Though the Court acted more than a decade after Congress, there was behind both measures a Fabian belief that increasing centralization of political control was the order of the time.

POWER OF THE PURSE

Although the delegation of legislative powers, the popular election of senators and the judicial usurpation of legislative power contributed to the decline of Congress, the crucial default was probably surrender of the money power. Delegation of monetary powers to the Federal Reserve Board, with authority for automatic increase in the money supply to cover congressional deficits, has demoralized the Congress. It has become incapable of keeping its own house in order.

The early Works Progress Administration programs of the Roosevelt Administration were emergency measures in a time of distress but they served to inculcate a public acceptance of federal intervention in local affairs. They were a failure, but not the last to be undertaken:[4]

> My own idea is that it does not matter how many mistakes one makes in politics, so long as one keeps on making them. It is like throwing babies to the wolves: once you stop, the pack overtakes the sleigh. This explains why it is that the present [A. J. Balfour] administration prospers.

From that modest beginning the federal government ventured into steadily mounting waste of the people's savings. It undertook to rebuild the inner cities with urban renewal programs, but only retarded the normal cycle of private renewal. It inaugurated Model Cities programs, to expand the concept of urban needs, but there was more spending than achieving. It built public housing projects, which soon became a shambles, instead of furthering the normal economic upgrading of the poor to older housing as the more affluent residents moved to the suburbs. Congress seemed conditioned to ever higher spending in reckless disregard of prudent administration.

When President Nixon proposed revenue sharing through additional appropriations to states and local communities, Congress was ready. But congressional leaders resisted the call for earmarked grants to take the place of existing aid programs. They felt that Congress should control the expenditure of monies it collected in taxes. In that cavil, Congress was right. The way to decentralize was to have the states collect in taxes the money required for local programs.

This could be done by an equitable sharing of the income-tax revenues. The virtual federal monopoly of the income-tax source is not an equitable sharing. Sharing could be equalized by allowing a credit of up to 50 percent of income taxes due the federal government for income taxes paid to a state. Then, because the 50 percent would be taken by the federal government if not by the states, all states would be encouraged to increase state taxes to 50 percent of the total federal tax obligation.

194

Fifty percent of the federal income tax would roughly equal the federal grant-in-aid programs which could concurrently be terminated. The states would then collect the monies they spend, overcoming the objection to uncontrolled spending of federal grants. The federal bureaucracy would be demobilized. Revenues and responsibilities would be in harmony for the first time in half a century. The efficiency of public service would be improved. This adjustment of income tax revenues offers a means of decentralizing the present bloated federal welfare ventures to the states, where they belong if they are to be continued at all. It will also achieve substantial savings in overhead.

The whole question of taxes and spending requires drastic revision of policy and control. Our once-healthy economy seems on the verge of foundering because of national fiscal policies. History warns us that democratic governments should never be vested with unlimited taxing and spending powers. Taxing, borrowing and spending powers of all governments— national, state and local—should be strictly defined and limited by law which can be changed only by recourse to all the electors. It is otherwise impossible for public officials to resist the demands of special interests for public subsidy.

An example of great statesmanship in this American tradition has been given by the Byrd family of Virginia. In 1910, when the proposed amendment to authorize the federal government to lay and collect income taxes came before the Virginia House of Delegates for consideration, Richard E. Byrd, father of the late Senator Harry F. Byrd and Speaker of the House, spoke eloquently in opposition.[5] Under his leadership, Virginia rejected the amendment.

But Speaker Byrd's wisdom was not limited to the federal sphere. He led in a constitutional revision which set strict limits on the powers of state legislators to tax and spend, with such effect that in 1965, when Senator Harry F. Byrd died, the state of Virginia had a surplus in its Treasury.

Senator Byrd was hardly cold in his grave when educational, medical and banking lobbies, with the concurrence of Governor Mills E. Goodwin, moved to revise the Virginia Constitution. The severe limits on the taxing and bonding powers of public authorities were moderated and new plans were made for increased spending to use the state credit for public subsidies. Virginia was abandoning its great tradition. The new political leadership could not sustain the standard of political integrity set by Richard and Harry Byrd.

The U.S. public debt[6] of about $450 billion is supplemented by U.S. guarantees of about $1.5 trillion on various insurance, pension and guaranteed loan liabilities to produce an enormous exploitation of the national credit. That is why the national credit is in bad standing internationally.

When in 1972 President Nixon asked for legislation authorizing him to limit federal spending to $250 billion, Congress properly refused though it knew the limitation was needed. The scandal was that the Congress was incapable of limiting its own appropriations. The federal budget was so vast and uncontrolled that literally no one knew what was in it.

Apologists for Congress will say that it has merely followed the popular mood and that its decline reflects the will of the people. There is too much contrary evidence to make that thesis tenable. Where there is a large group of prestigious and influential citizens who identify their personal ideology with the centralization of government power and who work zealously to accomplish that goal, we should not attribute their success to the will of the people. There was no popular mandate for the creation of a Federal Reserve Board nor for the delegation of legislative powers to the Executive. These were the programs of an elite remote from the people and exercising political power dissociated from the popular will.

The reality today is that Congress is a kept institution. It really makes no pretense of fulfilling its constitutional responsibilities. It has certain residual powers of law-making and appropriating that it performs perfunctorily in accordance with the pressures to which it is subject. Congress doesn't know and doesn't seem to care what the will of the people is. It cares only about the demands of powerful pressure groups, which, in concert with the news media, launch their campaigns for legislation and for federal funds. David S. Broder wrote: "As costs have risen, candidates have been forced to turn increasingly to rich men and affluent interest groups for their funds."[7]

The one element of government that was designed to reflect the will of the people no longer does so. The problem of government is in large measure to restore the Congress to its primacy as the law-maker of our society.

THE WAR POWERS

The anguish of liberal politicians incapable of comprehending the realities of war has led in recent years to congressional criticism, especially in the Senate, of the President's war-making powers. A Democratic Congress which obediently followed the lead of a Democratic President into the morass of endless war has recoiled from giving such *carte blanche* to a Republican President. Its leaders have joined the mindless peace advocates in seeking to restrain the President with legislative resolutions and fund cut-offs. Their behavior underscores how heavily the Congress has been dominated by the party interest rather than the national interest in its adherence to catastrophic policy. But this failure goes also to the organization of Congress to perform its basic function.

In our country of divided powers, the legislative power is the policy-making power. The executive power and the judicial power are administrative powers. Law-making is policy-making. It is clearly the responsibility of the Congress—not of the President—to decide when and where to wage war. It is the duty of the President to conduct the war, *bringing it to the earliest possible, successful conclusion.*

In Vietnam, the great default was the failure of Congress to make a clear policy decision about the war for guidance of the President. It left all the policy decisions to the President while individual members of Congress then carped about how the war was being conducted.

The relevant reality is that Congress is not properly organized either to make policy or to make law. It is dabbling in details of war, poverty, drugs, juvenile delinquency and federal contracts but is totally incapable of making policy. It looks to the President to say what laws are needed. This deference of the Congress to the President raises a serious question about our constitutional structure. The Founding Fathers were keenly aware of the evil of legislative tyranny and sought to avoid it by providing a Chief Executive elected by the people. While the deterioration of legislative process may be inevitable, there is reason to believe that in our system it has been accelerated by use of the presidential office.

The parliamentary system properly subordinates the executive branch to the legislative branch while the American system creates a contradiction between the constitutional supremacy of the Congress and the practical supremacy of the President as party leader. The party leader should be in the House of Representatives, not in the Senate or the Executive Office. Serious attention must be given to the wisdom of modifying the Constitution to assure continuing legislative leadership. Otherwise the country seems headed for a dictatorship decreed by party interest.

The course of the United States in the years of change from its traditional organization and morality has been well summarized by newsman and philosopher Arthur Krock:[8]

> But as an eyewitness of governmental and other public action throughout these years, I formed the opinion that the United States merits the dubious distinction of having discarded its past and its meaning in one of the briefest spans of modern history.
>
> Among these changes are a federal union almost replaced by a mass federal democracy controlled by an alliance of politicians and special interest groups; fiscal solvency and confidence in a stable dollar driven from the national and foreign marketplace by continuous deficit spending, easy credit, and growing unfavorable balance of payments in the international ledger of the United States; the free enterprise system shackled by organized labor and a government-managed economy; the Republic transmuted into a welfare state subsidized from Washington; a self-reliant people widely seduced by federal handouts; spoiled generations—young and old—led to expect the government to provide for all their wants free of any requirement of responsible citizenship; a Supreme Court assuming overlordship of the government and all the people to fit the political philosophy of the current majority; and a Congress reflecting the people's apathy toward this assumption and forgoing the use of its constitutional powers to curb the Court's seizure of jurisdiction in areas for which it has no warrant in the Constitution or the statutes. Yet despite the apparent general acceptance in this country of a judicial autocracy, composed of citizens whose offices were obtained without benefit of suffrage, and whose qualifications the popular branch of Congress—the House of Representatives—is barred from appraising, it is also the federal judiciary that is constantly defied by the population groups that make a career of violating the

law. Most ironically, the commands of federal lower-court judges in the name of the law frequently terminate as mere scraps of paper.

THE MISES RULE

The central tenet of socialism is that the State must own the means of production. Its thesis is that private ownership of productive resources leads to the exploitation of man by man and to the creation of social classes. Socialism undertakes to prevent that development by holding title to productive plants and equipment in the state.

There is a disjunction of reason in this claim of socialism. All progress in human knowledge and skill is made by individuals. The progress is encouraged when the rewards of success accrue to the individual talent. Ownership of the product of one's labor is the chief and most important reward because it accords with the human sense of justice. What the individual has created of his own talents and resources is his.

Socialism jumps to the conclusion that what is socially useful must belong to the state. But virtually all the products of individual talent and ingenuity are socially useful. Thus socialism places ownership or control of virtually all production in the state. The link between the individual and his creation is broken. We see the consequence in the depressed and degraded workers of the socialist state. As economist Percy L. Greaves, Jr., said in his funeral eulogy of the late, great Professor Ludwig von Mises, "strengthened by the vision and understanding that Mises has passed on to us, let us resolve to use our God-given reason to promote the immutable, irrefutable Mises message: political interference produces results contrary to its purposes. It makes matters worse, not better, from the viewpoint of its sponsors. If this immutable, irrefutable Mises message can be learned, his contributions may yet save our civilization and we may have peace among nations and prosperity among people."

We need look no farther than the recent history of the United States for proof of the Mises economic rule. The increasing intervention of the United States government in the economic processes of American society, so sharply accelerated since the depression of the thirties with endless declarations of high purpose, have instead deeply worsened economic conditions and brought a once-healthy economic order to the verge of collapse— to the devaluation of its currency, the disavowal of its obligations and the abandonment of its moral leadership.

What Ludwig von Mises so clearly foresaw should have been transparent to all Americans. This country—once a beacon of freedom and prosperity for all the world to see—had not been built upon the tenets of socialism. It had flourished under a rule of law which secured private property to its owners and the rewards of industry to the industrious. How, in the face of all the world's experience, and of a history in America of flight from the socialist systems of the Old World, could American intellectuals be wheedled by the promises of socialism? Alas, *le trahison des clercs* is not new to human history.

There is indeed a great challenge to the best minds of the age to preserve, under changing conditions of life in modern society, the sound principles of private ownership and a free-market economy. The task requires an alertness and adaptability in modifying the legal system to accommodate the new conditions and to outlaw those abuses of private wealth associated with excessive political power, economic monopoly and public subsidy. It is not served by government intervention in the economic process, for government is necessarily incompetent in this order. Government can function in this order only as the tool of vested interests which use the governmental powers to serve their private ends.

Chapter 19

WAR

THE SUPREME TEST of politics is war. Since the first purpose of government is to provide security for the nation, war reveals how well government is performing its most essential function. It is trial by fire.

This reality has been realized historically in the training of princes. To prepare for future responsibility as leaders of the nation, they were trained in the art of war as well as in the skills of statecraft. Totalitarian regimes can follow the ancient rule by training political leaders for war. Lenin incorporated the principles of war into the basic training of Bolshevik political leaders.

Democratic states maintain no similar training program for national leadership. After a war, they may elect a Washington, a Taylor, a Grant or an Eisenhower to the presidency, but in the ordinary course of events, the politician who wins election has had no significant training in the art of war. Democratic political process simply does not value that talent.

The conditions of existence in a free society foster a false sense of universality. Citizens gain an impression that their world is the world. When they maintain decent relations with their neighbors, it seems perfectly reasonable that all the world should do so. If their communities can exist without war, depending upon law and reason, why shouldn't all the world do so?

By its very nature, a free society is open to diverse and conflicting forces.

An enemy who wishes to subvert it can with the simplest deception send his agents into it to foment strife, manufacture discord, and fragment the very consensus on which survival depends. Because the society is by practice a forum for continuing debate, it becomes difficult to define limits on the range of allowable conflict. It is comforting but fallacious to assume that democracy has some inherent strength which will expose and defeat all attempts to subvert it.

Within a democratic society, there will always be a corps of pacifists who refuse to fight. These people claim all the benefits of the society but refuse to defend it. Because a democratic society tends to be tolerant of such aberration, the sentiment can spread, undermining the will of the nation to defend its interests. Pacifists are not found in totalitarian societies, except in prison, so the influence there is small. Then too, the ordinary factionalism of a free society means that there will often be a substantial element opposed to the decision to fight. A prudent enemy will use all his resources to make this dissenting faction as large and contentious as possible.

The people sense the distinction between their internal differences and their differences with other countries. They realize that in time of war they must put aside internal differences and unite against the external enemy. But when the cause is poorly defined and the political leadership is weak and divided, the country may fail to unite for war. Then its power is blunted and the prospect of failure is great. It is by such divisions that free societies are destroyed.

Furthermore, it is the disposition of free societies to pursue wealth and comfort rather than excellence, so they become especially vulnerable to illusions about peace and security which render them easy victims of conquest. The art of war in time becomes a lost art; so that when the state faces a mortal threat, it has neither knowledge nor means to defend itself.

Democratic societies are normally a product of wars fought for freedom. In their beginnings, they have a martial tradition and a martial spirit. In time, however, military talent and interest are lost in the pursuit of wealth and ease. As Homer Lea wrote: "The first and most difficult task of statesmen is the preservation of the national or militant instinct intact in the virtue of the people."[1]

As the United States moved to assist South Vietnam with a program of counterinsurgency, General Lansdale had reason to note the difficulties created by leaders ill-trained for war:[2]

> The arrival of this team caused me to reflect wryly on the different values placed by our side and by the Communists on the unconventional aspects of revolutionary conflict. Staff officers who were steeped in the conventions of Western life had picked these individuals for me, evidently in ignorance of the actuality of a Communist "people's war" such as the Vietminh urged. On the other side, the best Vietminh teams were composed of personnel trained for political-military action in an isolated school, where final examination was conducted personally, individual by individual, by Ho Chi Minh himself—similar to what Mao Tse-tung had done in China. This personal involvement in

turning out cold war professionals would be an alien concept to any of the Western leaders I know, none of whom had any real familiarity with the daily actions on cold war battlegrounds. After all, the presidents and premiers on our side had arrived on top by a different route from Communist leaders, who had clawed their way up through the harsh realities of revolutions.

Democratic political systems have developed some outstanding military leaders, notably Robert E. Lee and Douglas MacArthur in the United States. But the use to which a country puts such leaders depends upon the quality of the ruling political leadership. The general rule is that the military leadership deteriorates with the civilian leadership, but with a lag.

In Pakistan after independence, the parliamentary government deteriorated and corruption became so scandalous that the national leaders asked General Ayub Khan to assume the presidency. Only the army could offer a national leader of integrity in time of crisis.

The story of the soldier overthrowing the civil power, whether Caesar at the Rubicon or Napoleon before the Paris mob, is a story of weak civil government. The structure of civil government becomes filled with time-servers incapable of giving leadership which the occasion requires. The soldier rules by general consent because no one else can do the job. Lenin, Mussolini and Hitler came to power under similar circumstances.

In the light of history, it must be recognized that the United States, like every other democracy, faces this critical problem of leadership in war. All the strength and power of a nation can avail nothing if its resources are not developed and wisely used in war. The country has come through some agonizing experiences, first in Korea and then in Vietnam. The most powerful nation in the world has not known how to respond to the challenge of puny but militant hostile powers. It has wasted its youth and its wealth in futile and unnecessary warfare. No country in the world would have dared to war against the United States if the confusion and incompetence of its leadership had not made it an inviting target.

The recurring destruction of democratic governments is shaped by illusions that they can survive without making war. The wish to possess wealth in security is father to the thought. Wealth and power create a false sense of security. The attack of a small power seems no threat to the great power, so its leaders trifle with the conflict. They think they can conduct the war without curtailing the selfish pursuits of the population. Only a few men will be called to die. In that mood, they temporize indecisively with military measures, encouraging the enemy to enlarge the conflict.

These considerations have a timeliness for the United States because our country has twice been defeated in war in recent decades. The experience raises urgently the question whether our political leadership is incapable of waging war intelligently; for if this condition has been reached, it will not be long before our Republic dies. When a rich nation reaches this state, there is always a more vigorous and prudent power prepared to wage war.

THE AGONY OF LOSING

We can discern in our war experience the critical weakness of our political system and make some estimate of future requirements.

We had never been defeated in the history of the Republic. We had fought two victorious wars on the continent of Europe. We had defeated a Kaiser opposed to Britain and we had defeated a national socialist dictator opposed to Britain. We had defeated an Imperial Japan which attacked us.

In our two losing wars, our nominal opponents were the socialist governments of North Korea and of North Vietnam; but in reality, both wars were planned and waged on the other side by the Soviet Union. The refusal or inability of our leaders to recognize the true nature of these wars was a critical error. Clausewitz wrote, "The first and most important of all strategic questions is to decide the kind of war you are in."

Our basic disability was a misjudgment of the threat posed by the Soviet Union and how to meet it. As World War II came to a close, President Truman recognized that the aggressive behavior of the Soviet Union in Eastern Europe raised serious questions of policy for the United States. He directed Clark Clifford, then serving as counsel to the President, to make a survey of our interests and to propose an appropriate policy for our relations with the USSR. Mr. Clifford made the survey, consulting the cabinet officers concerned and, in September 1946, recommended a policy representing the consensus.

Mr. Clifford's report reflected a general awareness of U.S. leaders about Soviet intentions:[3]

> The language of military power is the only language which disciples of power politics understand. The United States must use that language in order that Soviet leaders will realize that our government is determined to uphold the interests of its citizens and the rights of small nations. Compromise and concessions are considered, by the Soviets, to be evidences of weakness and they are encouraged by our "retreats" to make new and greater demands.
>
> The key to an understanding of current Soviet foreign policy, in summary, is the realization that Soviet leaders adhere to the Marxian theory of ultimate destruction of capitalist states by Communist states, while at the same time they strive to postpone the inevitable conflict in order to strengthen and prepare the Soviet Union for its clash with the western democracies.
>
> This government should be prepared, while scrupulously avoiding any act which would be an excuse for the Soviets to begin a war, to resist vigorously and successfully any efforts of the USSR to expand into areas vital to American security.
>
> The United States, with a military potential composed primarily of highly effective technical weapons, should entertain no proposal for disarmament or limitation of armament as long as the possibility of Soviet aggression exists.
>
> The United States should realize that Soviet propaganda is dangerous (especially when American imperialism is emphasized) and should avoid any actions which give an appearance of truth to the Soviet charges. A determined effort should be made to expose the fallacies of such propaganda.

But then the report proposed action seemingly in conflict with its understanding of Soviet purpose:[4]

> Our best chances of influencing Soviet leaders consist in making it unmistakably clear that action contrary to our conception of a decent world order will redound to the disadvantage of the Soviet regime whereas friendly and cooperative action will pay dividends. If this position can be maintained firmly enough and long enough the logic of it must permeate eventually into the Soviet system.
> Even though Soviet leaders profess to believe that the conflict between capitalism and communism is irreconcilable and must eventually be resolved by the triumph of the latter, it is our hope that they will change their minds and work out with us a fair and equitable settlement when they realize that we are too strong to be beaten and too determined to be frightened.

The Soviet Union had been functioning for almost thirty years with singular adherence to the doctrines of Lenin. President Roosevelt had extended recognition in 1933 in hope that friendly association would moderate Soviet aims, but Stalin had worked with Hitler to loose the Nazi attack on the democratic powers. The United States had extended vast material assistance to the Soviet war effort and had undertaken a cooperative assault on the western front at great cost to itself, but these measures had not in any degree moderated Soviet purpose.

There was simply no basis for an intelligence conclusion that our concept of a cooperative world order was in any degree reconcilable with Soviet purposes and ambitions. Mr. Clifford's intelligence estimate should have said so. Then he would have had to face the question, "How do we deal with such irreconcilable conflict?" Perhaps our leaders could have solved the problem if they had faced the question squarely.

One astute observer of the conflict has recently stated its irreconcilable character:[5]

> There is simply no substratum on which a structure of peace can be built among the Big Three nuclear powers except transient expediency covered by the rhetorical formula of coexistence. There is instead a manifestly irreconcilable ideological conflict between the free and totalitarian worlds. And there is another irreconcilable conflict, of an imperialist-territorial character, within the totalitarian camp itself. The latter, a cold war that has been burning for a dozen years, the United States did not ignite, and it will never be smothered by mere prayers for peace.

United States policy was so lacking in coherent purpose that the Military Operations Subcommittee of the House Committee on Government Operations could report in 1958: "Under present methods of operation, we do not know what we are trying to accomplish through military aid. . . . Our military aid programs are not clearly related to a strategy of defense, nor are they based on a realistic assessment of country capabilities to contribute to that defense."[6] Indeed, how could they be so related when our basic strategic assumption was that the Soviet Union would cooperate in the interest of world peace?

If the United States had recognized the nature of these wars in the beginning, it could have commanded the Soviet Union to stop them, and the Soviet Union would have had no alternative but to do so. The Soviet leaders were not prepared to wage war against the United States over any issue in Korea or Vietnam. They wanted only to weaken the United States through satellite war without becoming directly involved.

The situation was illustrated by Secretary of State Dulles in 1957 when the North Vietnamese were moving against the Plaines des Jarres Airfield in Laos. Secretary Dulles called in the Soviet ambassador and addressed him in these terms. "Mr. Ambassador, please tell Premier Khrushchev that if he doesn't stop that aggression in Laos, we shall cause more trouble for him in Eastern Europe than he can handle. Thank you. Good day." This was the action of a diplomat who understood both war and Soviet policy. There was no further aggression in Laos while Dulles was Secretary of State.

This was, unfortunately, a solitary and isolated example of such competence in recent U.S. diplomacy. There was no similar understanding in the U.S. government when North Korea attacked in 1950 nor when North Vietnam attacked in 1961. Ever since World War II, the United States has been engaged in a mission of ordering a peaceful world through cooperation with the Soviet Union. Secretary Dulles was engaged in that mission too; but when the Soviet Union sought to initiate satellite war in Laos, Secretary Dulles knew that peace could not be served by pretending not to see the move. He put responsibility where it belonged.

In Korea, the Truman Administration accepted the fiction that it was fighting North Korea. Instead of demanding that Stalin stop the attack or suffer our response in Eastern Europe, the United States fought a costly war of attrition against North Korea and Red China while begging the Soviet Union to intervene in behalf of peace. In battle losses, in resources expended, in loss of reputation, and in the prestige conferred on an inferior enemy, the war must be counted a defeat for the United States.

So too in Vietnam, the Kennedy Administration could have ended the North Vietnamese aggression just as Secretary Dulles had done in Laos. Instead, it pretended that the Soviet Union was not a belligerent and that the issue could be settled in South Vietnam. It was so deeply committed to the negotiation of peace with the Soviet Union that it felt compelled to pretend the Soviet Union was not the aggressor in Vietnam.

This shrinking from the risk of war renders leaders incapable of dealing with an enemy. When the enemy has tested and confirmed the attitude, he can extend his aggression with impunity. It should be entirely clear that in 1950 and in 1961, the Soviet Union was in no position to enter war with the United States. If our leaders had insisted, the aggressions in Korea and Southeast Asia would have been stopped promptly, without public fanfare.

Instead, Mr. Clifford fudged his intelligence estimate with an assumption that our differences were reconcilable and that the Soviet Union could be brought around to our view of a world order with firmness and kindness. Apparently the leaders consulted by Mr. Clifford could not bring themselves to face reality. They preferred to cherish a false hope, just as they had been doing for thirteen years.

If détente is possible, it becomes a rational goal, to be pursued prudently. But if détente is impossible, seeking détente is suicidal because it merely builds up the strength of the enemy. The suicidal quality of the U.S. quest for détente is apparent in all American policy since World War II. We have been strengthening the enemy and wasting our own strength. This is the real significance of the wars in Korea and Vietnam. While the United States was committed to a basic policy of courting the good will of the Soviet Union, how could it act decisively against Soviet satellites? It could only assume the ridiculous posture of begging the Soviet Union to mediate the attacks it had launched and was supporting.

Throughout this period of bleeding the United States, the Soviet Union was weak and vulnerable. It could not have launched these attacks against a resolute and responsible U.S. policy. The Soviet Union was probing to see how much bleeding the United States would tolerate. Even though they knew our illusions, Soviet strategists must have been astonished by the puerile quality of our reaction.

The other errors of these wars flowed from this basic refusal of our leaders to deal with the situation confronting them. A sequel to the pretense of Soviet non-involvement was the decision to allow sanctuary to Red China in Manchuria and to North Vietnam in Laos, Cambodia and North Vietnam. That decision in Korea made it impossible for our forces to hold the Yalu River line and invited the Chinese re-conquest of North Korea. In Southeast Asia, it made the defense of South Vietnam impossible and enabled the enemy to persist in his aggression.

The folly of our policy in Vietnam is fully recorded. Advocates of the policy have made the record, demonstrating how human reasoning can be attenuated by false hopes when war is the issue. It is clear that these conceptions of policy, motivated by unwarranted fears of Red Chinese intervention in Vietnam and by the pressures of British diplomacy, represent pathetic misconceptions of the prudent use of military power in war. Our forces were dissipated and rendered ineffectual by these irrational appraisals in the highest levels of policy-making. The crucial error was allowing the enemy sanctuary in Laos, Cambodia and North Vietnam from which to wage his "War of Liberation" against the South. Why should an aggressor cease his attack when you have guaranteed the security of his operational base? The continuing refusal of American leaders to recognize the Soviet Union (and later Red China) as the true enemy in Vietnam caused the train of disasters in that conflict.

The American commitment to the Truman Doctrine was made at a time when the country possessed overwhelming military power. Although its conventional forces had been drastically reduced, U.S. possession of the atomic bomb and of strategic air forces was a decisive barrier to Soviet expansion—

if and when America chose to draw the line. The Eisenhower-Dulles extension of the Truman Doctrine through regional agreements to other danger points on the Soviet periphery was made in that same confident spirit.

However, when Stalin tested the American will, the will was wanting. When he blockaded Berlin, the United States did not remove the blockade but flew over it. When he launched a satellite aggression in Korea, President Truman at first responded with interposed military forces; but after the Chinese intervention, his will disintegrated as he accepted stalemate and sued for peace.

A decade later, with the restoration of a Democratic administration in Washington, the years had taken their toll. The politics of peace had drawn the party leaders farther away from the reality of war. The will to defend freedom had all but disappeared.

There is a cringing quality in the American intellectual faced with the reality of war. His instinct is to escape by flight. He cannot comprehend the soldierly thesis that safety lies forward. Thus, as the North Vietnamese assault on South Vietnam was launched, the desire of Kennedy intellectuals was to force a coalition with the Viet Cong in South Vietnam as a step toward American withdrawal. They were not outraged by Ho Chi Minh's breach of the 1954 Geneva accords. They did not consider the unification of Vietnam by invasion of the North from the South. They extenuated the North Vietnamese invasion as part of a civil war, but they believed an invasion of the North from the South in this "civil war" would provoke Red Chinese or Soviet intervention. They had no conception of the U.S. obligation to maintain peace in the world—none of that thinking which led President Truman to pick up the Soviet gauntlet in Korea. Apparently the high costs of appeasement in Korea had persuaded them that the outposts of freedom should not be defended.

Here was a country at peace, under the protection of the United States. It was assaulted by North Vietnam in a thinly-veiled invasion. Surely the rational response should have been to repel the invasion summarily and to punish the aggression. Instead, the exclusive concern of the Kennedy intellectuals was how to escape from our commitment to protect South Vietnam from Communist aggression.

In the face of war, the intellectual had lost his capacity to think coherently. Although the United States had overwhelming military strength which neither Red China nor the Soviet Union would dare to challenge for any gain in Vietnam, these policymakers accepted the thesis that a Soviet satellite could attack an American ally with impunity, but a counterattack on the Soviet satellite would provoke world war! We must indeed marvel that the ministers of a greater power would accept such a proposition, but they did.

Soviet propaganda had encased American minds in fear of nuclear war and the escapist proposition that peace could be achieved only by negotiation. Thus, the reality that peace can be preserved only by fighting for it was banished from the American policy. War, not peace, ensued.

The decline of a nation is measured by just such changes in the intellectual responses of its leadership. Who can doubt that in the long twilight of the Roman Empire, political leaders gave continual reassurance that their policies were in the public interest, even as they had lost the capacity to deal with reality.

The significance of these experiences is that American leaders have preferred defeat in war to the abandonment of their illusions about negotiating peace with the Soviet Union. They have preferred a wasting of the nation to the alternative of confronting reality. When wealth and power are great, politicians tend to believe that some loss of both will not be conclusive. But the decision to accept defeat is conclusive for a great power. It marks the back of the slope, the beginning of the descent. Defeat in war is not something which even the strongest nation can accept lightly. It is so compelling an indication of incompetent leadership that the integrity of the society is compromised.

During the Korean War the ordinary citizen knew that the United States should win the war, if war there was to be, quickly and decisively. When. instead the war dragged on with heavy casualties and protracted negotiations at Panmunjom, no amount of propaganda about peacemaking could obscure the default of American leadership. The people called a military leader to the Presidency.

So also in Vietnam. The public expectation that the United States would win the war quickly was realistic and instinctive. When, instead, we became involved in a long and futile war of attrition, the people may not have appreciated the niceties of strategy and diplomacy but they knew that their leadership had failed the test of war. They turned to the other political party for a new President.

A SOFTNESS TOWARD MOSCOW

By this time the leadership disability had extended to the other party. It was also committed to the illusion that it could bring Soviet leaders to act in the cause of peace, and pretended that the Soviet Union was not the author and strategist of this war against the United States.

President Nixon, with a popular mandate to reverse the Johnson policies, chose instead to continue them. He proclaimed his intention of resolving the war by negotiation. He suffered without reprisal the shooting down of our reconnaissance aircraft over international waters off the coast of Korea. He sent Henry Kissinger into three years of fruitless negotiations in Paris, all the while intimating that progress was imminent. He engaged in protracted talks on strategic arms limitations, again without progress, only to surrender to Soviet demands in 1972 to achieve agreement. The totalitarians are always ready to accept surrender.

President Nixon did break the sanctuary barrier by raiding the North Vietnamese bases in Cambodia. He supported a South Vietnamese raid against the North Vietnamese bases in southeastern Laos, at Tchepone. But that was the end. A Red Chinese invitation to our ping-pong team looked so much like détente that the President rushed forward in quest of peace by negotiation. But these moves were designed to impose on the United States a paralysis which could not be achieved by military operations. They were the cover for a massive build-up of North Vietnamese forces equipped with Soviet tanks for a decisive invasion of the South. Although he had full warning of the North Vietnamese concentrations, which violated the conditions of our suspension of bombing the North, President Nixon would not allow our air forces to attack the assembly areas. North Vietnam launched twelve of its fourteen divisions in the greatest assault of the war, wreaking great damage and heavy casualties in the South. That was the way the enemy played ping-pong.

In reprisal, President Nixon resumed bombing Hanoi, mined the access to Haiphong Harbor and proclaimed a blockade. Then he went back to talking.

In October, a month before the presidential election, Hanoi offered a "peace plan" which provided virtually for the surrender of South Vietnam. President Nixon could not reject it, because it was evident that Senator McGovern would accept it. He entered negotiations, but the North Vietnamese exposed the plan with a claim that it had Kissinger's approval. President Nixon affected concern about some details which could be easily corrected, and thereby stalled past election day.

When in late December, the talks continued to be fruitless, the U.S. resumed and intensified the bombing of Hanoi. The responses of the news media and of certain politicians to this bombing repeated the long wartime pattern of criticizing every U.S. initiative:

". . . . why *should* bombing a people make them want to deal in good faith?" —Tom Wicker, December 26, 1972

"This (the bombing) is war by tantrum, and it is worse than the Cambodian and Laotian invasions . . ."—James Reston, December 27, 1972

"The American bombs falling on . . . North Vietnam . . . have dimmed prospects not only for peace in Indochina but for the wider détente for which all mankind has prayed."—*New York Times* editorial, December 30, 1972

". . . the elected leader of the greatest democracy acts like a maddened tyrant . . ."—Anthony Lewis, December 30, 1972

"Even with sympathy for the men who fly American planes, and for their families, one has to recognize the greater courage of the North Vietnamese people. . . ."—Anthony Lewis, January 6, 1973

". . . they [the enemy] are a people of extraordinary determination and bravery."—Anthony Lewis, January 8, 1973

". . . Mr. Nixon called on the bombers—an action, in my judgment, of senseless terror which stains the good name of America."—Joseph Kraft, December 24, 1972

"He has conducted a bombing policy . . . so ruthless and so difficult to fathom politically as to cause millions of Americans to cringe in shame and to wonder at their President's very sanity."—*Washington Post* editorial, January 7, 1973

"Over and over again Mr. Nixon has tried to bomb Hanoi into submission.

It has not worked before and it will not work today."—*St. Louis Post-Dispatch* editorial, December 19, 1972

"The best settlement would be to get out, . . . the American people long ago decided the war was a mistake, . . . the American people are mature enough to accept a bad settlement . . . it is hard to see any good reason for delaying the American withdrawal from Vietnam."—David Brinkley, December 19, 1972

"The news . . . about the Vietnam negotiations breaking down was very scary and depressing . . . Dr. Kissinger's boss has broken Dr. Kissinger's word. It's very hard to swallow . . . backing off from a ceasefire is a weight and comes very close to a breaking of faith, with Hanoi maybe, with Americans more certainly."—Harry Reasoner, December 19, 1972

". . . events suggest a return to the same old war.
". . . we cannot read about the heavy bombing . . . without a deep and despairing sense that peace is not at hand.
". . . Congress must and will act on the people's mandate for peace."—Senator Edward Kennedy, *New York Times*, December 27, 1972

No doubt the previous policies of the Johnson and Nixon administrations, attempting to hurt the enemy just enough to bring him to the conference table, but not seriously, had provided a basis for these pessimistic views about the effective use of force on the eve of a long-sought armistice. Administration policies had badly split the country on the question of our war purposes.

The armistice was a negotiated surrender. President Nixon agreed to withdraw U.S. forces from South Vietnam, provided our prisoners were released, even as the enemy held major portions of South Vietnam in force. With an armistice, there was no way for South Vietnam to recover control over the areas of its territory held by North Vietnam. Unless South Vietnam renounced the armistice after U.S. withdrawal and resumed the offensive to drive out the North Vietnam Army, the territory would in due course be annexed to North Vietnam. A new base for subversion of the South would be established.

This was not peace with honor. It was precisely the kind of defeat which a great power cannot accept without confessing impotence. The conditions for the occupation of South Vietnam had been established by North Vietnam with its spring invasion of 1972. That is when President Nixon was defeated.

This appraisal of the Nixon war policy reveals that it embraces the errors recited by General Taylor in defending the Johnson policy. President Nixon regarded military power not as a decisive force but as a means of forcing negotiation. He was more realistic in judging the prospect of Red Chinese intervention, willing to strike a little harder to get results, but still making reluctant and inadequate responses to the enemy initiatives. A qualified surrender was the only possible outcome of such war policy.

The Soviet Union has demonstrated, as in the March 1972 invasion of South Vietnam, that it has the capacity to stay prudent military action by the United States through the action of Soviet diplomacy. In a decade of negotiation about Vietnam, U.S. diplomacy has never shown any capacity to stay a Soviet action beneficial to its cause. This kind of inequality is the inevitable consequence of the false premises from which U.S. policy is projected.

Why then does the United States cling to these erroneous premises? What forces of mind or influence compel these attitudes? There are answers in the quality of American politics. The wartime perceptions of Lyndon Johnson and Richard Nixon, though colored by their own experience in World War II, were essentially those advanced by the Council on Foreign Relations, and more extravagantly by Americans for Democratic Action. They are the persistent misjudgments of the elites who have erroneously concluded that communism will mellow if we are kind to it. Such minds can be aroused to self-defense when hostile action is imminent but they are incapable of recognizing the true character of the enemy and acting prudently against him. Our train of disasters is the logical consequence of such a mind-set.

This abiding error of judgment has caused a serious decline of leadership. No President since Franklin Roosevelt has shown a sense of world leadership worthy of his office. Harry Truman at first seemed destined to fulfill the requirements; but then, under pressures of allies and of his own advisers, he faltered and failed in Korea. Dwight Eisenhower conducted a holding action on the world scene until he was induced by the Khrushchev peace offensive to withhold support from Cuba and to tolerate aggression in Laos. John Kennedy achieved world acclaim and sympathy but not world respect; his administration was a series of disasters. Lyndon Johnson was the captive of his advisers, a victim of the fears they inspired. Richard Nixon, who on his own testimony knew better, felt compelled in office to follow the false premise that our differences with the Soviet and Red Chinese leaders were reconcilable.

PROFESSIONAL DECLINE

On the military side, too, we have not had leaders of the stature of Admirals William D. Leahy and Ernest J. King and Generals George C. Marshall and Henry H. Arnold to advise our Presidents. It was not unusual during discussions of strategy and policy for Admiral King or General Marshall to point out most respectfully to Franklin Roosevelt the error of his way when the President advanced some militarily impractical proposal. These leaders had a sense of responsibility for the course of military policy which required them to protect the President and the country from commitment to palpable error.

After President Kennedy, at the behest of Secretary Robert S. McNamara, declined to appoint Admiral George W. Anderson to a second two-year term as Chief of Naval Operations and to extend the appointment of General Curtis E. Lemay as Chief of Staff of the Air Force for more than a year, it became apparent that the political leadership did not want to hear advice in conflict with its own preconceptions. Unless some military leader could break through that barrier and re-establish contact with the President, our military policy would be conditioned by the ignorance of politicians.

After the Bay of Pigs debacle, President Kennedy brought General Maxwell D. Taylor, a retired Chief of Staff of the Army, into the White House as a trusted adviser. It appeared that General Taylor might establish a relationship similar to that which Admiral Leahy maintained with President Franklin Roosevelt. In that service and in later duty as Chairman of the Joint Chiefs of Staff, General Taylor seemed to enjoy the confidence of the President. But General Taylor himself lacked an essential grasp of the military realities. He had in his rise to high rank become so subservient to the prevailing illusions about war that he could not escape from them. Instead of recommending forthright military action to end the conflict and accepting full responsibility for such a course, he compromised with the prevailing political fears and became the defender of catastrophic military policy.

In a review of General Taylor's book, *Swords and Plowshares,* Hanson Baldwin wrote:[7]

> Nor can this writer forget a conversation in the Pentagon when Taylor was Chairman of the Joint Chiefs, which dealt, prior to the event, with Vietnam. I had suggested that the situation appeared to be deteriorating so rapidly that U.S. ground combat troops might be needed. Taylor's reply was emphatic, definite and almost completely negative. "It would require perhaps twelve divisions," he said, "and the Army is not trained or equipped to fight a guerrilla war in jungles." This decisive judgment, expressed before any U.S. ground combat troops were sent to Vietnam is not fully reflected in this book. Indeed somewhere along the line either Taylor's opinion changed, at least in degree, or the President failed to get the word or some of the interim and compromise measures Taylor (and others) suggested (*viz,* his recommendation of 1961 to send U.S. helicopters and troops to Vietnam under the guise of flood relief) were a partial genesis, an unintended first step, in the pernicious policy of gradualism, later adopted by President Johnson.

What Mr. Baldwin really encountered was General Taylor's complete subservience to the prevailing political judgments. While that posture was appropriate in discussing policy with Mr. Baldwin or other outsiders, it was within the policy-making apparatus of the administration a terrible disservice to the country. As Homer Lea had written decades earlier:[8]

> The efficiency of every army is determined by the efficiency of its corps of officers. Though self-evident, it is not fully understood that in great wars the genius and knowledge, the ability and experience of general officers determine more than any other factor the success or failure of campaigns.

The Taylor mind-set, even after the disaster of the Vietnam war, is revealed in his book, *Swords and Plowshares.* Unable to distinguish between forthright honesty and disloyalty, he considers any independence of military judgment a breach of loyalty, as in his reference to[9] "such disgruntled generals as MacArthur and Van Fleet."

212

He showed scant comprehension of MacArthur's removal from command by President Truman: "The General's political maneuvers in opposition to the President, while serving as his field commander, were thoroughly obnoxious to most officers reared in the service tradition of complete abstention from partisan politics."[10]

This was the political cant of the hour, the allegation of British officials pressing for MacArthur's removal. In fact, MacArthur's opposition to the Truman war policy was based on military considerations and was expressed in strong representations to the Joint Chiefs of Staff; and because he was right, they were embarrassed to defend or explain their policy. His sole public expression of opposition was in a requested message to the Veterans of Foreign Wars that the Defense Department had ample time to censor but failed to intercept. His letter to the Minority Leader of the House of Representatives was a frank and nonpolitical military judgment requested by that official.

The Taylor "tradition" is a new tradition, and one which our military leaders must repudiate. The tradition of MacArthur and Van Fleet is an older tradition based on the bond between the officer and his men. As Homer Lea wrote:[11]

> The most promiscuous murderer in the world is an ignorant military officer. He slaughters his men by bullets, by disease, by neglect; he starves them, he makes cowards of them and deserters and criminals. The dead are hecatombs of his ignorance; the survivors, melancholy specters of his incompetence.

Homer Lea had learned from history, but the Vietnam War stands as additional testimony to his wisdom. That was the war which should never have been. The United States held such overwhelming military superiority that it had only to command the enemy to desist in order to bring the insurgency to an end.

Our President is not an omnipotent and all-wise emperor chosen by God to head our national family. He is a citizen elected from our ranks to serve us, a man charged with great responsibility and desperately in need of help. It is a perverted sense of loyalty which in war would leave him exposed to the ignorant counsel of diplomats and politicians and to the self-serving pressures of allies, without responsible professional strength and support in discharging his gravest responsibility. Yet that is the "tradition" which has prevailed in this country since World War II and to which General Taylor adhered.

As Hanson Baldwin wrote in his book, *Strategy for Tomorrow:*[12]

> The Joint Chiefs, in fact the uniformed officers of all services, owe loyalty and obedience to the commander-in-chief but they also have an obligation to the Congress, as well as to the President, to provide frank appraisals of all military matters. The fundamental fidelity is to the nation, not to any single administration, and the founding fathers undoubtedly intended to emphasize the dual loyalties involved.

In his review of *Swords and Plowshares*, Mr. Baldwin wrote:[13]

The obverse side of the coin is clear: more of our high-ranking military leaders, if faced with the dilemma of supporting military policies which they believe to be dangerous to the nation's future, should resign their posts not as a mutinous gesture but as conscientious indication that they cannot carry out the policies of the administration without fatally compromising their duty to the country and their loyalty to the men they command. Resignation, particularly by high-ranking military men, should never be a casual gesture but it can represent the only honorable alternative.

Our military leaders at the highest levels cannot dismiss their responsibilities for the safety of this country by saying that they obeyed the President.

The evidence of recent history suggests that the mistaken Taylor concept of military responsibility as an accommodation of political preferences is derived from the influence of General George C. Marshall. The training of Marshall and Eisenhower and the self-confidence of President Roosevelt had moderated the effects of that concept in World War II, so that it came to full flower only in Korea. There the abandonment of the old tradition of military victory was fathered by a Secretary of Defense who held the full confidence of the President. The changing attitude was made evident in a growing preoccupation with "civilian control," which grew to mean not loyalty to the President and the Congress but the transfer to civilian subordinates in the Defense Department and on congressional committees of responsibility for professional judgments these employees were ill-qualified to make. In time, the example of the high command evoked a similar deference to civilian inexpertise at lower levels. The reality of war was hidden as all pretended and many believed that our military policy in Vietnam was defensible under the circumstances. The private in ranks knew better. Soldiers in Vietnam knew that only the constraints of politics prevented them from defeating the enemy and ending the war.

ILLUSIONS OF PEACE

A dominant influence on this deterioration of leadership was the peace syndrome. National news media had raised peace to the status of a popular fetish. All considerations of honor, duty, prudence or self-interest were overwhelmed by opposition to any use of force in national policy. A spirit of pacifism was promoted. As Hanson Baldwin observed:

. . . what distinguished Vietnam during the formative years (until 1968) was the almost consistent anti-administration outlook of a large segment of the press, and the irrelevant, emotional, oversimplified or erroneous judgments of many of the reporters.[14]

What Mr. Baldwin did not stress was that the reporters were serving the pleasure of their editors, else they would have been replaced promptly. The same philosophy which conditioned the administration against victory directed the news media in pursuit of defeat. The news media were simply reflecting the panic long exhibited by some members of the intellectual community. They were persuaded that conflict must be avoided at any cost:[15]

From the time of the decision to develop the hydrogen bomb to this very hour, the government of the United States has had to provide for the common defense under a cloud of moral reproof, emanating from the community of internationalist-minded atomic physicists who continue to argue, as Einstein and his original group argued, that nations have no right to provide for their defense at the risk of war, especially not in this nuclear age. When it is suggested that their moralizing be directed toward the Communist leaders of Russia and China, the reply comes back that it is too late for that: the United States used atomic bombs against Japan, and the only way the Communist powers can be relieved of their fears, sufficiently to get them to put down their guard, is for the United States to take "whatever initiative has to be taken."

The avoidance of war, they believed, required an end to national sovereignty and the institution of world government:[16]

Norman Cousins of the *Saturday Review* is tireless in hammering out the call for a severing of the bonds of our sovereign political union. "At a time when the fingertip of a desperate man can activate a whole switchboard of annihilation," he wrote recently, "and when defense is represented by retaliatory holocaust, the historical social contract between man and the state has ceased to exist."

This blind passion for peace is a sole possession of western intellectuals. It is not shared by Soviet counterparts:[17]

What humanitarian love has thus far failed to accomplish may yet be accomplished by humanitarian fear. Adlai Stevenson, one of the high priests of the new creed, proclaimed the categorical imperative before the United Nations in these fervent words: "We must abolish war to save our collective skins. For as long as this nuclear death-dance continues, tens of million—perhaps hundreds of millions—are living on borrowed time." But while it seemed to him, and to many who shared his feelings, that fear of nuclear destruction should suffice to draw all mankind into a new consensus it somehow has not. Fear, evidently, can divide as well as unite; people are not all equally afraid. "We in the Soviet Union," Chairman Khrushchev thundered in the UN, "are not afraid of war! . . . If war is imposed on us, we shall fight for our country and we shall triumph, cost what it may. We are Communists; we have strong nerves; we have passed through a school of struggle. We fought against the white guards for four years; we brushed aside, smashed the enemies of the working class, and you want to frighten us with disputes! Well, gentlemen, bear in mind that you have not the guts for it, if I may use the expression."

It is not strange that men so swayed by passion become the unwitting instruments of war. They invite what they strive to avoid:[18]

The point is this: When great nations raise their desire for peace to the level of an absolute value, and declare themselves—through such men as Adlai Stevenson and Senator Fulbright—disposed to sacrifice everything, even their national identity, to establish it; when nations make peace their sovereign value, to which all things else must be sacrificed, they inevitably plunge themselves into the arena of war, for it is in that arena and not in halls of diplomacy that supreme national sacrifices are made.

215

Such misguided passion can indeed persuade men that they serve a higher purpose in opposing their homelands:[19]

It is an ancient malaise of intellectuals and accounts for their propensity to go into political opposition, out of love of country, when the economic and military power of the nation that bred them has reached its apex. H. G. Wells has been precisely that kind of anti-nationalist Englishman. Like Lord Russell he hated war and economic imperialism and protectionism that, from the Fabian socialist point of view, lead to war. Wells was inclined to blame his own England, especially, because she had the character and intelligence to lead mankind out of the present sorry arrangements of balance of power and nationalist hostility but was not using them.

The propaganda of the opinion makers had a decisive influence on politics. Politicians bowed to media sentiment and made public disavowal of resort to force. They busied themselves with promises of keeping the peace.

There were interludes which showed the latent readiness of the American people to support a righteous cause. When it was reported that enemy torpedo boats had attacked our naval units in the Gulf of Tonkin, during the 1964 presidential election campaign, the people overwhelmingly endorsed our reprisals. But the martial spirit was something the political leaders did not want to stir, for fear they could not control it, so the administration quickly returned to its peace themes.

The peace syndrome nurtured illusions about disarmament which in turn nourished the peace syndrome. It seems incredible that diplomacy could be so naive, but our diplomats seemed to think they could persuade aggressive, conquest-oriented powers like the Soviet Union and Red China to disarm. They could negotiate for a decade without ever facing up to the reality of Soviet purpose.

To imagine that the Soviet Union did not want peace but wanted instead to build a superior power for waging war was simply inadmissible. Disarmament negotiations presume equal devotion to peace on both sides. So the United States negotiated itself into unilateral disarmament. SALT I was a great victory for Party Secretary Brezhnev. He arrested and dismantled the strategic missile defenses of the United States without making any concession whatsoever from Soviet armament programs.

BRITISH INFLUENCE

Allied with the peace syndrome as a critical restraint on U.S. policy has been our alliance with Britain. For historic and cultural reasons, the United States has maintained a special relationship with Britain which it accords to no other power. The spectacle of Kim Philby telling the Central Intelligence Agency how to organize its work, even as he revealed to Soviet intelligence the identity of our covert agents in Europe, is symptomatic of the relationship. So also is the admission of Dr. Alan Nunn May, the Soviet agent in British science, to the secrets of our atomic bomb development.

American leaders have supposed that they had a community of interest with Britain which required full faith and credit relationships. British leaders have had no such illusions since the Fabian ascendancy in government. They regard the United States as a capitalist opponent of the socialism they endorse. They regard the Soviet Union as a socialist power which can be brought around from its Bolshevik extremism. They see themselves as mediators commissioned to bring the United States and the Soviet Union to the middle ground of "democratic socialism." The British are not therefore an ally in our confrontation with the Soviet Union but a balancing power working between us. Because Britain has no leverage on Soviet power, it can act only to restrain the United States. That was its role in Korea and in Vietnam, where British influence was apparently decisive in persuading the United States to accept the Soviet terms of satellite war, with sanctuary. British influence was effective because American leaders in government and in the news media bear a strange, colonial-like, deference to British judgment in culture and politics. This is the source of our illusion about alliance relationships.

The obsequious posture of American policy in deferring to British influence is rarely mentioned and never chronicled in American publications. There is an unspoken conspiracy in the news media against criticism of Britain. But the British are quite frank in reporting their own skillful service to British interests.

Commenting on Chinese intervention in the Korean War, Mr. J. A. Williams wrote:[20]

The advance to the Yalu River by the armies of the United Nations brought China into the war, and further escalation seemed possible as voices were raised in the United States in favor of bombing Chinese bases and lines of communication in Manchuria. . . an act which could activate the Sino-Soviet security pact. The prospect of a wider and more dangerous war in Asia was viewed with grave concern in London. It was appreciated that apart from the serious logistical problems that would result, a war with China would imperil most of Britain's interests in Asia: the unity of the Commonwealth would be undermined, the security of Hong Kong would certainly be jeopardized; the Chinese in Malaya and Singapore might be encouraged to give more assistance to the guerrillas, and the stability, which was essential for British commercial intersts in Asia, could be put at risk. An even greater fear was that the growing preoccupation with East Asia could weaken the defenses of the Western alliance in Europe. . . .

British anxieties were translated into diplomatic activity. In Washington, Peking and Lake Success during December 1950 and January 1951, British representatives, often in cooperation with their Indian counterparts, sought to restrict the fighting to the geographical boundaries of Korea and to get negotiations started between the major contestants. These efforts were not immediately crowned with success. Nevertheless, the United States government showed that it was prepared to exercise the restraint necessary to fight a limited war in Korea by relieving General MacArthur of all his posts on 11th April 1951. His return to the United States must have been a matter of great satisfaction to the British government, and its fears of a wider conflagration on the mainland of Asia further receded with the opening of cease-fire talks between the Chinese and American commanders on 10th July 1951.

217

Mr. Williams was of course mistaken in ascribing the Chinese invasion of Korea to the American advance to the Yalu. As Lin Piao explained after his successful attack,[21] he could undertake this operation because he was assured that his base in Manchuria would not be attacked by American aircraft. Prime Minister Attlee had persuaded President Truman that the war should not under any circumstances be extended to Manchuria.

We do indeed have important common interests with Britain but we also have vital differences. It may serve British policy to have the United States fight a wasting war in Asia or to maintain excessive forces in Europe, but it clearly is not in the interest of the United States to do so. In these matters, British leaders will of course serve their own interests. It is tragic that U.S. leaders have not had the wit to follow a different policy, one responsive to American interests.

Although this British influence on policy is also a socialist influence, socialism has its own direct influence on our policy-making. The foibles of democratic socialism include misconceptions about war as the product of capitalist imperialism. Thus, the socialist is conditioned to think that war will be unnecessary when he rules. As socialist thinking increasingly affects U.S. leadership, our capacity to face the reality of war diminishes. This reluctance to wage war is especially potent when we face the aggression of a socialist power, as in Korea and Vietnam.

In the fiftieth anniversary issue of *Foreign Affairs*,[22] the late Hamilton Fish Armstrong, who had been managing editor or editor for fifty years, took for his farewell message the subject, "Isolated America." He expressed in this essay the basic errors of Fabian judgment which had so greatly influenced American foreign policy in the period. Mr. Armstrong scoffed at "the alacrity with which the American people accepted the idea that they had come into World War I altruistically, in order to make the world safe for democracy (American democracy)." He resented "their readiness to suppose that President Wilson and his advisers at Paris had been bamboozled by wily European statesmen." Mr. Armstrong deplored U.S. rejection of the League of Nations. He thought that "something was gone from the picture that the world had formed in wartime of Americans, their adventurousness, their willingness to take risks had disappeared. There were Americans, too, who felt that the American dream had paled and who had twinges of conscience that their country was taking no part in the endeavor to make a new war less likely."

That is a good description of the Fabian illusion. It fed on a missionary spirit that the United States would carry peace to the benighted peoples of Europe, a spirit exploited by worldly and cynical allies who saw in Uncle Sugar billions of dollars of largesse for their economies.

Mr. Armstrong was part of that coterie of young Americans whom Colonel House had assembled to assist at the Paris Peace Conference. They worked with British Fabians to devise a structure which would prevent war. If they did not realize how grossly they had been misled and misused by Lloyd George and Georges Clemenceau, it is fortunate that the American people did understand. It is highly improbable that the twenties and thirties would have been so peaceful for America if it had been embroiled in the League of Nations. World War II came out of the cockpit of Europe, a product of the policies of our European allies, contrived without an American contribution. Only the innocent would suppose that the United States could have altered through League membership the policies of Britain and France in this period.

What was the Fabian view of the war in Vietnam? After fifty years, Mr. Armstrong was still sensitive to world opinion (translate British opinion). He wrote: "Our methods of fighting the Vietnam War are what have chiefly formed world opinion against us." After noting the complexity of modern diplomacy, Mr. Armstrong continued: "It does not make us feel a need, however, to be lenient in our judgment where they disguised disasters in cliches or cloaked the miseries of millions of refugees, harried hither and yon under a rain of bombs, under comfortable terms like 'resettlement' and 'reeducation.'

"It must be made less likely—for it can never be made impossible—for American leaders again to take the country into war unawares."

Thus, in the Fabian socialist view, it was not the North Vietnamese "socialist" invasion and aggressive war which caused South Vietnamese peasants to flee their homes but the "rain" of American bombs. American and South Vietnamese bombs were of course launched against the North Vietnamese Army which had driven the peasants from their homes, not against the peasants who had been resettled in more secure areas. How indeed could an American editor advance so gross a misrepresentation of the simple realities of warfare? Are American Fabians incapable of evaluating rationally the conditioning propaganda of the world socialist movement which passes for "world opinion"? History records that they are—and that they have imposed their own paralysis on American foreign policy.

We see the legacy of this attitude in the color given to events by *The New York Times*. In his impatience that Congress had agreed to a mid-August termination of U.S. bombing in defense of Cambodia against North Vietnamese aggression, Anthony Lewis wrote:[23] "For it is the villagers of Cambodia who will pay in death and destruction over the next five weeks for the settlement of the dispute between President and Congress. But whatever one's moral qualms at any more ravaging of that once innocent and beautiful country. . ."

It was quite beyond admission by such minds that the North Vietnamese "socialists" were waging aggressive war against the Cambodians and that the United States was aiding in the defense of the "once innocent and beautiful" people. If North Vietnam is not waging war, the United States must be doing it.

The sum of these influences is defeat in war, even when you hold the power to prevent war or to win it quickly. Soviet strategy has succeeded in bleeding the United States through satellite war in Korea and Vietnam. These defeats have undermined the confidence of the United States in itself. They have weakened the country physically and morally and have intensified the desire to achieve peace by negotiation. Soviet strategy could hardly have expected more than it has accomplished.

The experience of war has led in the United States not to recognition of error and a re-direction of policy but to continuation of the old policy. The United States remains committed to that retreat from responsibility which accommodation with the Communist powers compels. When so experienced an observer of the military scene as Hanson Baldwin can draw erroneous conclusions from the Vietnam disaster, we should be concerned about the extent of intellectual confusion:[24]

> Nor can the United States continue indefinitely in the role of "world policeman"; the costs are too high. This is the service that Vietnam has done; it has exposed the high cost of universally applied containment to keep the peace; it has forced a reappraisal of our overseas commitments and our vital interests. It should be obvious, without argument, that the demand on the U.S. economy, the U.S. taxpayer and U.S. patience in the decades ahead are too great to support a global policy of intervention.

That conclusion is riddled with the fallacies which Mr. Baldwin has in other analyses sought to expose. It assumes that the high cost of the Vietnam venture was in some measure a necessary cost of defending South Vietnam. Of course it was not. As Mr. Baldwin pointed out, it was the high cost of bad leadership. We cannot defend ourselves with that kind of leadership, so we must change the leadership, not the policy of supporting our allies.

The term "world policeman" is used by others in derogation of our alliance relationships. We are not policemen, unless we interfere in the internal affairs of our allies, as we did so disastrously in Vietnam under the bad leadership of the Kennedy Administration. As responsible allies we must share in the defense of all free countries which are prepared to fight for their freedom. To suggest that we should not is to surrender to the Communist enemy the lands and people we refuse to defend.

We are back to the Truman Doctrine, face to face with the reality that no free nation on the periphery of the Communist empire can maintain its freedom without a commitment of the United States to its defense. The Truman Doctrine is as sustainable now as when it served so admirably to protect Greece and Turkey. The United States has twice the industrial capacity of the Soviet Union. With the economic development of Europe and Japan, the free world has increased its margin of resource advantage. Only in military strength is the free world losing its advantage, and that loss is a function of will—of leadership.

In truth, the necessary costs of defending all free nations from Communist aggression are minimal. It would be tragic if the United States were to lead the retreat from this vital responsibility. We should not draw erroneous conclusions from the mismanagement of the Vietnam war.

The prevailing confusion of purpose reminds us of a warning given decades ago: "Whenever preparation for war is regarded only as an expedient applicable to abnormal conditions, and is postponed to the beginning of hostilities, then the nation, in modern times, is plunged into a struggle that shall terminate only in destruction."[25]

But American capacity to confront the reality of war and to act prudently in addressing it must be drastically revised if this country is to survive. There is no sign in either part of the required change. Leaders of Congress are addicted to the errors which have reduced the United States from pre-eminence in military power after World War II to a second-best position today. What the two-party system has wrought, the two-party system is incapable of changing. Its course is charted for disaster.

Chapter 20

AN AMERICAN FOREIGN POLICY

UNITED STATES FOREIGN POLICY comprises the sum of our relations with other countries, friendly or hostile. It should command the highest wisdom and prudence we can bring to the task of government. The nation may have time and opportunity to resolve its internal difficulties provided our freedom to act on them is not restrained by external forces.

Indeed, the first task of foreign policy is to preserve the national security. Americans tend to think of national security as a responsibility of the Defense Department, but it is in an earlier stage the chief function of the State Department. With security assured, the function of diplomacy in the United States is to promote good will and productive cooperation with all nations. When genuine friendship is established, commercial and cultural relations benefiting both sides should naturally follow. Because so much of the world has not yet learned how to organize work for higher productivity, we have a special opportunity to help other nations develop talents and resources. Cooperation to this end with nations so disposed is a logical extension of foreign policy.

These aims are simply stated, but in administering them with a wide range of friendly and hostile countries, we encounter a great diversity of issues. Should we placate a hostile power and seek to soften its animosity? And if that is our aim, what policies will be effective? If our friendly offices are rebuffed and the hostility persists, what can we do? What should we do?

What should our relationships with friendly powers be? Does mutual respect and confidence require two friendly powers to adopt an arm's length address with each looking realistically to its own as well as the common interest; or is friendship a family affair in which we indulge our generosity without regard to cost?

Obviously the sovereignty of friendly powers limits our capacity to help them. They may have economic and cultural traditions which do not adapt readily to modern productive systems. Do we then subsidize their uneconomic systems or do we insist on change?

If a friendly power has a traditional authoritarian government broadly acceptable to the people, should we pressure it to adopt democratic forms and organization? If it is attacked by a Communist neighbor in a "war of liberation," should we help to defend the friendly government? Should we make alliances with authoritarian governments that are hostile to Communist expansion, giving military equipment and training to defensive forces? What kind of equipment should we give, and how much?

These are problems of national existence in a world of conflict where an enemy is openly dedicated to the destruction of our free government and others like it.

We were fortunate in the early history of the United States to be born in a new world where we, though weak, were the major power. No local power could threaten us. We were protected from the European powers by the broad Atlantic; and besides, the European powers were too busy with their own quarrels to be interested in distant colonial lands.

We were in those times a very independent people, despite our weakness. We made war against Britain, a great power, and had our capital burned. We declared a Monroe Doctrine to put an end to European wars of conquest in this hemisphere. We thought we knew our rights and interests and we were ready to fight for them. The people were free and they meant to be free:[1]

> The best things in life are the things men value more than life and that is of course what it means to be free, for freedom is synonymous with willingness to die rather than accept subjugation. It is no less true today than it was in the days of Plato and Aristotle that the life of freedom is made secure only when a sufficient number of persons who are willing to die rather than not be free combine their willingness politically.

We were in the nineteenth century the beneficiaries of British power and policy. Because Britain for her own security maintained a balance of power policy which prevented unification of Europe, there was no power great enough to cross the ocean and challenge us.

The emergence of Bolshevism in Russia, just as the colonial empires were falling, transformed our security position. Our government recognized that the Bolshevist dogma proclaimed perpetual warfare against our culture and institutions. That is why the United States refused to recognize the Lenin and Stalin regimes until 1933. There was no sensible reason for entering diplomatic relations with a power that asserted it would use those relations to destroy you.

It is an interesting note on the psychology of nations that we changed our policy and recognized the Soviet Union just as the Age of Tyrants was nearings its peak. Mussolini with his fascist variety of socialism was the first to mobilize a national response to Communist tyranny. In the Far East, the Japanese militarists were setting out on the conquest of China. In Germany, Hitler had led the Nazi form of authoritarian socialism to power.

No doubt Franklin Roosevelt saw diplomatic relations with the Soviet Union as a restraint on Japanese ambitions in East Asia. But he was also pressured by visions of trade entertained by our bankers and industrialists as they strove to overcome the business depression. Also, he was not immune to ambitions of organizing peace in the world.

The premises of recognition were of course disregarded by the Soviet Union. It continued to infiltrate and subvert our society, accelerating these activities through the new opportunities offered by diplomacy. Strangely, the U.S. reaction was to conceal the subversion. Franklin Roosevelt pretended it did not exist. Although attempts to warn him and his cabinet were made, exposure of the extent of subversion came only after his death.

By that time we were on the verge of winning the Great War, exploding the atomic bomb and launching our new venture in world peace—the United Nations. We were to repeat the utopian gambit for world peace which raised so many hopes in the United States after World War I and such cynicism among European political leaders. Our political leaders betrayed the enslaved peoples of Eastern Europe for a hope that Stalin would cooperate to maintain world peace. Stalin was no less cynical than Clemenceau had been at Versailles. Americans seem incapable of keeping an eye on the ball.

What did the U.S. really do in helping to build a United Nations with Soviet and other Communist membership? Hearken to the eloquent testimony of Aleksandr Solzhenitsyn in his acceptance of the 1970 Nobel Prize for literature:[2]

A quarter of a century ago, in the great hopes of mankind, the United Nations organization was born. Alas, in an immoral world, this too grew up to be immoral. It is not a United Nations organization where all governments stand equal; those which are freely elected, those imposed forcibly, and those which have seized power with weapons.

Relying on the mercenary partiality of the majority, the UN jealously guards the freedom of some nations and neglects the freedom of others. As a result of an obedient vote it declined to undertake the investigation of private appeals—the groans, screams and beseechings of humble individual plain people—not large enough a catch for such a great organization.

The UN made no effort to make the Declaration of Human Rights, its best document in 25 years, into an obligatory condition of membership confronting the governments. Thus it betrayed those humble people into the will of the governments which they had not chosen.

The spirit of Munich was to become the spirit of the free nations in the twentieth century.[3]

> The spirit of Munich has by no means retreated into the past: It was not merely a brief episode. I even venture to say that the spirit of Munich prevails in the twentieth century. The timid civilized world has found nothing with which to oppose the onslaught of a sudden revival of barefaced barbarity, other than concessions and smiles.
>
> The spirit of Munich is a sickness of the will of successful people; it is the daily condition of those who have given themselves up to the thirst after prosperity at any price, to material well-being as the chief goal of earthly existence. Such people—and there are many in today's world—elect passivity and retreat, just so as their accustomed life might drag on a bit longer, just so as not to step over the threshold of hardship today—and tomorrow, you'll see, it will be all right. (But it will never be all right. The price of cowardice will only be evil: We shall reap courage and victory only when we dare to make sacrifices.)

And again, in that memorable message to those who suffered no scourge of tyranny, as to those who suffered greatly, Solzhenitsyn spoke:[4]

> . . . the simple step of a simple, courageous man is not to partake in falsehood. Not to support false actions. Let that enter the world, let it even reign in the world—but not with my help. But writers and artists can achieve more: They can conquer falsehood. In the struggle with falsehood art always did win and it always does win: openly, irrefutably, for everyone. Falsehood can hold out against much in this world, but not against art.

The cry of Aleksandr Solzhenitsyn against the United Nations is in truth a reproach to the United States, for only the United States had the capability to set a different course. We have noted the quality of policy analysis which led the U.S. Government after World War II to side with the Communist tyrants against the enslaved peoples to establish "peace" in the world. A policy so deeply in error gathers to itself a host of supporting errors. It requires assiduous brainwashing to exclude reality from the reach of reason.

THE ONE WORLD SYNDROME

The socialist view of war as a product of capitalism promises the world peace under socialism. How will that universal peace be achieved? By establishing world government and the rule of law, just as order is today preserved within the nation state. And how will world government be established? By voluntary association of world powers, as in the United Nations.

But the United Nations has not healed the world divisions. It has rather been a cockpit of conflict, exacerbating tensions and undermining the commitment of the free nations to principles underlying their very existence, as

Solzhenitsyn has noted. The whole thesis of world government is based on a ridiculous fallacy that the most important values in life are worthless and that a slightly prolonged existence in slavery is preferable to death for a cause. Patriots in all lands, and especially in the lands of the tyrants, have rejected so ignominious a role for the human spirit.

It must be a sign of decadence that such arrant nonsense has possessed intellectuals of the free world. The human brain has a capacity to reject all experience not compatible with possessed error.

When the first atomic bomb was exploded, Chancellor Robert Hutchins of the University of Chicago proclaimed, "The atomic bomb calls for world government."[5] He assembled a committee of scholars to write a constitution for the world.

Albert Einstein was among the scientists caught up in the intellectual fervor for world government:[6]

Making use of the "cumbersome method" of open letters which was for the time being his only means of communication with his Russian colleagues, Einstein hastened to assure them that he shared their view of the superiority of the socialist economic system, and of the inability of the capitalist system to maintain a healthy balance between production and the purchasing power of the people. He acknowledged also that its economic system forced the United States to pursue a dangerous imperialist course, granting loans to foreign countries to enable them to buy American goods, and making use of their economic dependence as weapons in the arena of power politics. But he was convinced, he said, that all such dangers would end if the capitalist countries ceased to be sovereign states, and that as long as the USSR delayed the process of internationalization under a world government, she was preventing what was really in her own best interest. "We all know," he emphasized, "that power politics sooner or later, necessarily leads to war, and that war under present circumstances, would mean a mass destruction of human beings and material goods the dimensions of which are much, much greater than anything that has ever before happened in history." After reasserting his conviction that the "concept and practice of unlimited sovereignty of nations" was the source of all our troubles, and that "as long as we still retain a tiny bit of calm reasoning and human feelings," we must not tolerate its continuance, he concluded: "This alone is on my mind in supporting the idea of world government without any regard to what other people may have in mind when working for the same objective. I advocate world government because I am convinced that there is no other possible way of eliminating the most terrible danger in which man has ever found himself. The objective of avoiding total destruction must have priority over any other objective."

But what precisely was it, in effect, that Einstein, Oppenheimer, and those who shared their views were asking the United States to do to relieve the Soviet Union's distrust? Einstein was unambiguous. Americans must never regard the Russians as a threat, even if their government declares itself to be an enemy of the United States. The important consideration was that the Soviet leaders want to establish a world regime in which there will be no class distinctions and no states. The American people should not object to that ambition. In fact the United States should cooperate to help realize the goal.

226

Perhaps it was logical for Einstein to expect the United States to surrender its sovereignty when so many of his academic associates were so minded:[7]

America is destined to lead the way, Professor Dewey insisted; and our first step must be to abandon our traditional reliance on "the principle of national sovereignty," daring, instead, to submit to an international legislature "affairs which limited imagination and sense have led us to consider strictly national."

Professor Walt Rostow worked out a rationale for a mellowing state softened by luxury:[8]

"Buddenbrook's dynamic," Rostow explains, is an expression derived from a novel by Thomas Mann and his intention in using it is to suggest that if we Americans will avoid provoking them, the Russians are bound to undergo a transformation that will make them, in time, just like us. For, according to Buddenbrook's dynamics, the first generation seeks material wealth, the second wants position, and the third turns to music and poetry and things of that sort that dispose human hearts for the life of peace. The Russians may act tough and strong now—and we must encourage them in it, to make them feel secure; but before long they will be as ready as we are for "acceptance of the age of the mass automobile, the suburban one-family house, and free mutual inspection."

Bertrand Russell preferred to achieve world government by forcing the Soviet Union to adopt the liberal politics of the West:[9]

If the Soviet Union refuses to cooperate, he asserted, then it would be better to force her now and get it over with while America has a monopoly. Like a modern-day Cato, he came forward with a recommendation that the United States force the issue. "In the near future," he wrote in October 1946, "a world war, however terrible, would probably end in American victory without destruction of civilization in the Western hemisphere and American victory would no doubt lead to world government and the hegemony of the United States—a result which for my part I should welcome with enthusiasm." Russell did not have in mind an unannounced devastating attack to drag the Soviet Union into the world regime. Every conceivable other means would have to be tried, as Einstein argued, to persuade the Russian leadership. Yet Russia would not let herself be persuaded, Russell believed, by any agency other than the government of the United States.

"Nor do I think (he concluded) that the necessary persuasion can be effected by arguments of principle. The only possible way, in my opinion, is by a mixture of cajolery and threat, making it plain to the Soviet authorities that refusal will entail disaster while acceptance will not." Against this "only possible way," Einstein thundered with the passionate moral indignation of a Biblical Prophet. To threaten or cajole the Soviet Union in that way, he declared, would be utterly intolerable.

Professor Paolucci made a telling commentary on this madness of the intellectuals:[10]

It took the bloodiest war in American history to secure an enforceable unity for the United States. It took the bloodiest wars in Roman history to secure an enforceable unity for the Mediterranean world. Who can doubt that it will take the bloodiest war in all human history to secure an enforceable unity of the Communist and free nations of our time? And yet it is alleged that we must long for such forced unity, and teach our children to long for it as the only hope of preventing war!

One nation which gave short shrift to the nonsense about surrendering sovereignty to a world organization was Israel. Its Foreign Minister, Abba Eban, wrote:[11]

Just as it would be reactionary to abolish those distinctions of language, literature, and art, which give to the human mind its infinite variety, so it would be retrograde to abolish the political sovereignties of peoples. A people's political outlook and social organization are just as integral a part of its culture as are its language, its arts, and its music. Therefore, while the international society is far from approaching the millennium of world peace, that failure does not reside in errors of organization. The idea of a collection of sovereign states confronting each other within the framework of equal obligations is the most progressive that the human mind can conceive. The importance of the individual sovereignty within the international community is derided too often by those who aspire to the domination of the international scene.

Abba Eban spoke at Yeshiva University about what he termed the "Toynbee Heresy":[12]

If there is any consolation, it is in the knowledge that we are being castigated in the name of all nation states. For Professor Toynbee regards national sovereignty as obsolete, and hankers after the more perfect system in which national identities were suppressed. The eclipse of nationalism by some supranational federalism has been predicted so often that it is one of the platitudes of twentieth century writing. But in fact, this century is the triumphant epoch of the nation state, and the burial ground of broader associations and groupings. Perhaps it is because we disprove the great sweeping thesis about the "institutional future" not belonging "to the western institution of the national state" that we are called upon to bear these unfaithful wounds (Toynbee's criticism), inflicted without love.

WORLD DISARMAMENT

The companion aberration of world government is world disarmament. In order to pursue it, advocates must make assumptions about Soviet intentions which are directly contradictory of declared Soviet doctrine and of observed Soviet practice. The United States and the Soviet Union are both assumed to desire world peace and continuation of the status quo. Only on such false premises can the unrealistic negotiations be continued.

Jerome Wiesner, former scientific adviser to President Kennedy and now President of the Massachusetts Institute of Technology, wrote in 1967:[13]

If in the face of the clear-cut mutual advantage of avoiding a strategic weapons race, the leaders of the world's two dominant nations cannot resist the pressures on them to deploy an ABM, the others will have to conclude that eliminating the arms race is not a serious agenda item in either country.

The Soviet advantage in a strategic weapons race could be achieved only by having the United States withdraw from the race. Professor Wiesner served that Soviet purpose by implying that a "mutual" advantage in avoiding an arms race would induce the Soviet Union to join in an arms limitation program. Events proved him wrong. Soviet leaders did not accept the Wiesner thinking. The United States stopped its strategic weapons building program, but it did so alone.

A Professor of Psychiatry told the United States what it should do:[14]

Tension-reducing moves should be undertaken unilaterally without insisting on prior agreements by the Russians to reciprocate. In a situation of mutual distrust it may be impossible to reach formal agreements which presuppose some mutual trust; but certain unilateral acts may put more pressure on an opponent to follow suit than an agreement. An example was Russia's unilateral cessation of testing nuclear weapons, which forced us to do the same, as did their unilateral resumption of testing.

An historian could take a more objective view of Soviet disarmament policy:[15]

The constant elements in Soviet disarmament policy since 1945 have been the defense of the sovereignty and territorial integrity of the Soviet state and its allies against any form of international control and supervision; the neutralization or abolition of the military advantages enjoyed by the Western powers, particularly their original lead in atomic weapons and their diplomatic alliances; and psychological and emotional appeals to the uncommitted peoples and nations designed to help in the attainment of the two primary goals.

The United States stopped building Minutemen missiles in 1965, reducing its planned program from 2,000 to 1,000. It refused to build an antiballistic missile defense system, because such action would "start an arms race." Even when it learned that the Soviet Union was deploying antiballistic missiles around Moscow, the Johnson Administration arrested the U.S. program, hoping that negotiations might induce Soviet leaders to forgo the destabilizing action.

When Richard Nixon took office, he too held the U.S. strategic weapons program in abeyance while the Soviet Union, with one-half U.S. industrial capacity, attained a superior weapons position. And then, to obtain an election year agreement, President Nixon, with the approval of a Democratic Senate, negotiated an agreement that conceded to the Soviet Union the superior position it demanded in the controlled strategic weapons systems.

If it seemed that the U.S. government was working to serve Soviet policy, that was only the logical consequence of the erroneous premise of U.S. foreign policy. When world peace depends on "softening" Soviet attitudes, politicians will sacrifice a lot to achieve very little softening— or only a hope of softening. Roosevelt did at Yalta.

THE NIXON DÉTENTE

President Nixon has carried the policy of appeasement to extreme lengths, outdoing his Democratic predecessors in concessions for peace.

His search for détente with the Soviet Union and Red China has undermined our alliances against communism around the world because all the lesser free world powers must accommodate the U.S. initiative. Communist subversion in the free world has been sharply intensified, forcing leaders in the Philippines and South Korea to suspend some democratic freedoms and processes. While U.S. leaders foolishly soften up their own people with false expectations of peaceful cooperation, Communist leaders use the opportunity to extend their wars of subversion. Sweet talk is for them only a better façade for war. The Brandt Ostpolitik in the German Federal Republic, the euphoria in Europe, the disintegrating bonds of alliance are all products of an American domestic necessity to wheedle the electorate with promises of peace.

But that is only the appearance of things. The American people could easily be aroused to an awareness of reality and to the necessity for opposing the Communist tyrannies. The decision against that course is made by merchants who think they can do business with the Communist powers. Just as Professor Wiesner thought the Soviet leaders should be sensible enough to put their capital into better living for their peoples instead of into armaments, our merchants think that Soviet leaders will prefer the economic development they can get from trade and will abandon their ambitions of world conquest. These estimates suppose that Communist leaders have the same outlook as Western professors and merchants. They don't, so the estimates are worthless—or worse.

Yet, President Nixon is acting on this false premise. When he grants credits to the Communist powers for food, he compensates for and thereby makes possible the Communist investment in armaments. The United States is truly financing the rope for its own hanging.

President Nixon is doing much worse than that. He is so bemused by negotiations with the tyrants that he is betraying their peoples. As free men, our true interest lies with the peoples of the Communist states, not with their masters.[16]

Each advance enables communism to expedite conversion by political control since, for those whom it controls, Communism has become the one reality. The West (whatever value the captive may give that word) becomes at most a hope, but a hope that has been defeated (that is why the captives are captive); and it is a hope continuously deferred. Hope deferred not only maketh the heart sick; it stirreth profound suspicions that there is something radically wrong with it. In this case, it stirs a suspicion that exactly to the degree that communism is felt to be evil and monstrous in its effects, there must be something organically wrong with the West that is unequal to prevailing against a power so conspicuously condign.

The oppressed peoples can fight the Communist overlords only covertly: by industrial slowdown, by awkward and inept performance, by doing just enough to avoid punishment, and occasionally—when opportunity offers—by practicing sabotage. The mediocre performance of the Soviet economy over half a century argues that this resistance of the workers is highly effective.

But then the United States comes to the rescue of the tyrants. It is helping to perpetuate a tyranny which would otherwise be forced to meet the people's demands for greater freedom. The United States claims for its policy an influence in such movements as that of Dubcek in Czechoslovakia; but it is in reality responsible for the failure of such movements, which the Communist governments would otherwise be forced to accommodate. And why does the United States follow such policy? Because the judgment of merchants prevails.

ADMITTING RED CHINA TO THE UN

In the United Nations, Albania had for years claimed that the question of ousting the Republic of China was merely a matter of credentials, not subject to veto. The United States had insisted that there are two independent states, the Republic of China and the People's Democratic Republic of Peking, and that the issue was one of expulsion and admission.

President Nixon undercut the U.S. position by proposing that the United Nations adopt a two-China policy, admitting Red China to the Council and assigning a seat in the General Assembly to the Republic of China. His *illegal proposal*, reflecting the U.S. decision to admit Red China to the United Nations, was the signal to other powers for adoption of the Albanian resolution. The United Nations decided that the Red Chinese delegates really represented the Republic of China, a charter member. This was the action of a world body theoretically dedicated to the rule of law. U.S. protests at the action which it had engineered seemed especially hypocritical. Its behavior drew the just contempt of some delegations.

In consequence of this change of policy, Red China has established embassies in all the major countries of the free world. Its capacity for espionage and sabotage is multiplied manyfold. It has a base in the United Nations for subverting every effort of free nations to promote international cooperation. It has received U.S. credits and food shipments.

And what has the U.S. received? A few bows and smiles; certainly not peace—another major invasion of South Vietnam. A worldwide increase in subversive activity. A steady worsening of its monetary position. An increase of domestic prices due to shortages created by shipments of grains to the Communist countries.

To support this policy of appeasement, the administration and its concurring press have projected a cloud of propaganda to obscure the issue. For example, a State Department bulletin of August 1971 on "Current Foreign Policy," treating the United States and the People's Republic of China, asserted: "It has become increasingly clear that no international order can be secure if one of the largest powers remains largely outside it and hostile toward it." That statement belies all evidence bearing on the

231

question. The Soviet Union was never so small a threat to its European neighbors as when it was *outside* the League of Nations. Since the creation of the United Nations, the Soviet Union inside the United Nations and not Red China on the outside has been the chief disrupter of international order.

This official statement represents the propaganda for world order which blindly pursues an aim of bringing all nations into one body—the United Nations, at this stage. This mentality excludes the much more promising option of creating a concert of free nations which Communist states could join only when their governments become subject to the will of their peoples.

ALLIANCE POLICY

The Atlantic Alliance has been sabotaged by two decades of American neglect. Vested interests content with the status quo simply abandoned the original aims of the compact. Pressures of the Fifties for European self-sufficiency through union were actually reversed, to support British sabotage of union. The alliance fragmented in futility on the question of an early German peace treaty.

In 1973, alliance supporters were clinging to the status quo. General Andre Beaufre, an eminent French exponent of alliance security, wrote:[17] "I think the American interest is primarily to help and protect the building up of Western Europe, and then—and only then—to withdraw substantially its military establishment in Europe." That had indeed been American purpose in 1950 when its troops were committed to Europe. But that aim had been achieved in 1957 when the Soviet threat was not serious. Because the American presence has since that time fostered European illusions of security and deterred European measures to match the Soviet military build-up, that presence has been counter-productive.

The basic faults of the European alliance have been duplicated in Japan, where reluctance of the United States to withdraw from wartime positions dispensed Japan from assuming a share of defense costs as its economy was restored. An American umbrella had not fostered a sense of alliance responsibility in Japan. When American officials began to speak frankly about the necessity for Japan to carry the costs of its own security, Japanese political leaders professed shock. In a dispatch from Tokyo, George Sherman reported the effect:[18]

> This straight talking may seem quite sensible to the Pentagon, harassed by a hostile Congress and post-Vietnam withdrawal symptoms in the American body politic. After all, Japan puts only eight-tenths of one percent of its soaring national income in defense (compared with six percent in the United States).
>
> But in Japan, it looks like a recipe for political suicide for any Japanese government willing to follow it. It bluntly raises the specter of renewed militarism and naked power politics which produced World War II in Asia and which the Japanese and their neighbors—including Korea—have spent a generation overcoming.

232

Diplomatic repudiation of the American initiative is more testimony that the Nixon doctrine was a facade for withdrawal from Vietnam. It is not applied to allies which have the financial and industrial capacity to assume more of their own security costs. American workers should be asking how long their products must carry a defense charge of six percent while the products of Japanese workers carry a defense charge of less than one percent.

CONSEQUENCES OF DÉTENTE POLICY

If a policy of détente were monitored by criteria measuring the effect of our peaceful initiatives, it would long ago have been established as an emotional exercise. The record would show that the vast concessions of the United States not only have been unrequited but have strengthened the intransigence of the Communist powers. The accommodation of the United States to Communist pressures confirms Communist conviction and purpose.

Alas, U.S. policy is not framed in any such objective self-examination. It is guided by a possessed error which makes all considerations of objectivity irrelevant. That error, moreover, is at root an error of cowardice, not of good will. It is based on self-interest, not on generosity. It marks a degeneration of the American spirit. Though a sycophant press clothes the error in high purpose, it deceives only itself. Our allies are more perceptive:[19]

> The people most like ourselves in all countries, but especially in Europe, are utterly dismayed by our moral posture. In practice, we act as if we believed that international communism is the great enemy of the free peoples and that the governments of free peoples must be strengthened to resist the extension of the conspiratorial tyranny in our statements of national goals, on the other hand, we propose to persuade Russia to join us in our way of toppling the established regimes of the civilized world in favor of revolutionaries. The European statesmen have read our *Blueprint for the Peace Race,* and they know the old Rostow argument about how nobody is gaining any relative advantage or losing anything of value in the process of convergence. But they imagine that they know a little more than our Rostows and Fulbrights about how great powers are forced to behave when the chips are down. . . .

Whittaker Chambers knew the Communist mentality well:[20]

> The notion that communism could be lured or bribed into peace was as wildly fanciful as the notion that communism would honor the terms of any agreement which it found in its interest to break. It makes no sense to say that the statesmen of the West could not foresee this turn unless we assume that the word "statesman" has no meaning. For many minds in the West who were not statesmen did foresee and warn of it. The insight required no illuminating genius; was, indeed, less an insight than a habit of pointing to communism's invariable record. However certainly opinion in the West prefers to rationalize the Yalta effect, the satellite peoples have no need to. To them it is a simple fact which they daily live: They were abandoned.

233

Hope is like a drug working on the merchant mentality:[21]

On one hand, the disclosures lead to a hue of moral outrage. On the other hand, the West continues to deal with the Communist center as if this were not true. Thus the West itself engages with respect to communism in a kind of double-think which it supposes to be one of communism's distinctive faculties. This singular behavior is paced by another even more singular. This is the cherished notion, constantly blighted, ever ready to flower anew, that communism and Communists are about to undergo a change of mind (or heart) so that henceforth they will no longer act like Communists; they will be like us.

The Marxist-Leninist mind is not a mystery. It is at work in the world all around us. It publishes its views daily in hundreds of newspapers. For example, November 19, 1972, *Pravda* published a quite ordinary compliment to M. A. Suslov of the Politburo: "M. A. Suslov profoundly demonstrated the international character of Leninism. Marxism-Leninism does not recognize international boundaries and is the ideological, theoretical basis of the international unity and fraternity of the workers in all countries."[22]

There is no evidence whatsoever that four decades of U.S. political and economic appeasement have in any degree softened Soviet ideology or practice. Party Secretary Brezhnev does not depart in any degree from the teachings of Lenin. The spirit of convergence exists only in the illusions of the West.

There is a shrivelling of the human spirit nurtured by our obsession with "peace" as a symbol of survival:[23]

So baffling has the problem of our national purpose become that it is now the fashion to say that our purpose is simply "survival." The statement, I think, indicates the depth of our political bankruptcy. This is not a purpose worthy of the world's most powerful nation. It utterly fails to measure the meaning of the historical moment or to estimate the opportunities for greatness inherent in the moment. Worst of all, if we pursue only the small-souled purpose of survival, we shall not even achieve survival.

Our obsession with peace fosters the self-deception that there is some way to exist without taking risks. We withdraw from every confrontation in the vain hope that peace is so served:[24]

We may expect that Soviet doctrine will continue to dictate the same policy of maximal security and minimal risk. This expectation furnishes a measure by which to decide the gravest and most pervasive problem of foreign and military policy, namely how to balance the elements of security and of risk. Only by such a policy can we seize and retain the initiative in world affairs. And it is highly dangerous not to have the initiative. On the premise of this balance we did, in fact, enter the Korean War, which was right. But then we retreated from the premise to a policy of minimal risks, which was a mistake . . . Moreover, it would be prudent even to create situations of risk for the Soviet Union—situations in which the risk would be too great for it to take. We may be sure that the Soviet leadership will not risk the debacle of the World Revolution through a major war for the sake of anything less than the soil of the homeland of the revolution. We may expect that it will yield tactical ground or refrain from going after tactical ground if the risk of holding it or going after it becomes serious. But if there is no risk, or only a minimal risk, aggressive policies will be carried through, as they were in Hungary, where nothing was done to create a risk.

But this posture of cowardice is found only in our ruling elites, not in the people:[25]

> One has only to look into the face of its soldiers—one astute commentator has observed—to grasp that, when the chips are down, Americans generally will be readier than any other people on the face of the earth today to give up material well-being and life itself. The Academicians talk, and they encourage what Pareto calls the rule of the foxes, who get their way, for a time, by cunning and public bribery, but it would be a grave error, the same commentator warns, to mistake what the upper-class intellectuals say for what the great mass of Americans are prepared to do when their real interests are endangered or when they feel themselves being thoroughly humiliated in foreign relations. When the great crises come and decisions of life and death have to be faced, "one gazes with amazement," as Pareto observed, "on the energies that are suddenly manifested by the masses at large, something that could in no way have been foreseen by studying the upper classes only.

BETRAYAL OF CAPTIVE NATIONS

Although the American people were little aware of it, a drastic change in U.S. foreign policy occurred during the administration of Franklin Roosevelt. Before that time, our policy had been forthright, friendly and fearless. Thereafter it became increasingly slavish to British policy. The Anglo-American financial axis, which had been frustrated after World War I by U.S. rejection of the Versailles Treaty and the League of Nations, invaded the government in force in 1933. Its disciples displaced older diplomats in positions of influence to give the country a "New Deal." Thenceforth, they dominated U.S. foreign policy.

Franklin Roosevelt was a self-confident person who could be influenced but not intimidated by his British friends. They could only cultivate his vanity while pressing their policy judgments upon his subordinates. The real disaster to U.S. interests came at the close of World War II. That was when President Roosevelt decided that bringing the Soviet Union into the United Nations was more important than fulfilling our promises to the peoples of Eastern Europe. He began the policy of appeasement which delivered those peoples to Communist rule.[26]

> It was never a question of comparative physical strengths. Power, on the part of the West, was never lacking. *Will* was lacking. And the failure of will has been matched by a failure of intelligence. In general, this has taken the form of an ageless complacency that neither knows, nor really wishes to know, the meaning, motives, or methods of communism. But it runs off recurrently, too, into mass delusions that communism, if coddled, is about to change into the opposite of itself, of all that has given it power and empire, and to become something more like the image that the West cherishes of the West— something more eligible for the garden-party guest list. This of the most implacably purposeful revolutionists in history.

Those who created the new policy had to defend themselves against the

235

recurring testimony of refugees who had suffered the reality of communism. A massive propaganda was spread by an obedient press:[27]

> It is a rejection, by the enlightened mind of the West in the name of a superior intelligence and reason, of the truth which some have struggled back to warn them of while there is still time, usually, in one way or another, from the margin of life. That rejection is life- and soul-destroying. But it does not kill simply. It slowly suffocates those against whom it is directed as if they were buried alive. It is invisible and intangible, nobody really does anything. All that is necessary to maintain that silence is a glance, a tone of voice, the lilt of an impermeable, dismissing complacency, or someone to say from time to time: "No one can believe a former Communist."

The peace people cherished their illusions and bitterly resented the testimony of those who had suffered Communist persecution.[28]

> As his health improved, Bishop O'Gara began to try to tell public groups what communism had done to him and his life, the urgent danger that he felt it posed to the lives of his listeners, and what he feared it might presently do to them. After one such talk, an intelligent, authoritative woman, whom Bishop O'Gara took to be an educator, came up to him: "Bishop," she said, "that just isn't true." The ailing Bishop told me: "I said to my companion: 'Get me out of here. Get me out of here. Get me out into the air.' I thought I was simply going to faint." Bishop O'Gara set the heel of his palm on his chin and pressed his hand hard across his face to his forehead in a gesture that has become an unconscious habit. "And then," he said with a wry smile, "they expect us to remain sane."

Briefly, just for a few years, President Eisenhower acted as though he were ready to reverse the Roosevelt policy and resume America's dedication to freedom. His administration talked of freedom for the captive nations. But that purpose, if he ever held it, was short-lived. A test came in 1956 when Hungarians fought for freedom from Soviet domination. President Eisenhower, fearful of conflict, gave no help when help was possible:[29]

> At that point the station Radio Budapest went off the air and the silence was more stunning than the words. We must remember who these revolutionists are. They are those whom the West abandoned to communism. They are the human herd of one of history's greatest cattle deals. Unless a man's good sense is inflamed by a partisan political need to justify that deal, is there really anyone who does not know that the West traded these populations to communism as the price of something that the West held more important than freedom? The West called that something "permanent peace" and sought to safeguard it through the agency of the United Nations. Therefore, these populations were bound over to communism. Under all the verbiage, that was the reason these populations were the bait with which we meant to lure communism into the United Nations—as if anything could have kept communism out. It is nonsense to say that this was wisdom then, and these peoples were subsequently enslaved because communism welshed on its pledges safeguarding their freedom. A village banker would have hesitated to draw a $100 mortgage in such terms, not only because (as many knew and warned) the pledges were patently worthless, but also because they were unenforceable. So, in the name of peace, the West abandoned these mil-

lions to communism and watched them run into its pens, roped and thrown and branded with its brand.

Many a Polish and Hungarian child was too young to know that the whole course of life on earth had been sealed irrevocably at the moment when the wise men of the West set their signatures to that deal beside those of the cunning men in Moscow. A round twelve years later, those children knew it well enough when, in the streets of Poznan and of Budapest, they went with bottle-bomb and revolver against this or that Communist monster. They knew then that they had been abandoned by the West. And when they rose and fought outmatched, against that fate, and the West approved and watched, they knew something else. They knew that they had been abandoned twice.

And even though the fight for freedom was in that engagement lost, the Hungarian people had shown again that the human spirit was uncowed by tyranny:[30]

Those miserable human forces in the satellites—and they alone in the world first dared to rise against the dictatorship. They—and not the immensely rich, deployed, embattled West—dared defy and make effective headway against outmatching communism. Now in defeat and captive still, they must nevertheless feel stirring in themselves the force of something like Lucretius' meaning: "When all mankind lay groveling in the dust, one man stood up and walked at length along the flaming walls of the world."

There is doubt that the United States can free itself from its bankrupt foreign policy while the Fabian elites who made it continue to hold power in both political parties:[31]

I no longer believe that political solutions are possible for us. I am baffled by the way people still speak of the West as if it were at least a cultural unity against communism though it is divided not only by a political, but an invisible cleavage. On one side are the voiceless masses with their own subdivisions and fractures. On the other side is the enlightened, articulate elite which, to one degree or other, has rejected the religious roots of civilization—the roots without which it is no longer Western civilization, but a new order of beliefs, attitudes and mandates.

Is there any possibility at all that the policy of seeking detente could be successful?[32]

It is, of course, not impossible that some basic change may take place in Soviet doctrine. But if it did the repercussions would be felt all through the edifice of power erected on the doctrine; and if they were not checked, the edifice could not long survive. The basic Soviet structure is an indivisible and interlocking whole. It cannot permit itself to be tampered with at any point, save on peril of destruction. Still less can it contemplate changes in the dogmas that sustain the edifice of imperialistic power.

Of course the Communist states are highly vulnerable to the subversive force of freedom. But how can a country act which has abandoned freedom as an aim of its foreign policy?[33]

But suppose the United States were to come out of the international delirium in which its policy planners have been lost for the past several decades, could the Soviet Union and Red China be led or maneuvered into abandoning their designs for a final solution? How would the Soviet Union have responded, for instance, had we pressured her immediately after World War II to deal with us as a true nation-state, threatening to withdraw our recognition, and urging our allies to do the same if she did not abandon publicly her professed ambition to impose a classless, stateless Communist peace on the world? The historical fact is, of course, that while we have acted more or less consistently as a nation-state in attempting to contain the aggressive force of international communism, we have no less consistently defined our ultimate foreign-policy objectives in terms that could only obstruct every tendency of the Communist powers to accept our deeds at their face value.

In their adamant rejection of reality, American Fabians displayed an invincible pro-Soviet bias that some socialists had overcome. Though socialists everywhere are tempted to make alliance with the Communist parties for mutual advantage, the real danger of that course has been known to the experienced socialist leaders of European political parties:[34]

> The Communist Party is the sworn inveterate enemy of the socialist and democratic parties. When it associates with them it does so as a preliminary to destroying them. . . . The Communist does not look upon the socialist as an ally in a common cause. He looks upon him as a dupe, as a temporary convenience, and as something to be thrust aside when he has served his purpose.

THE NIXON FOREIGN POLICY

The Nixon policy, pretentiously displayed in heavy tomes from the Kissinger staff, is the same policy of appeasement which Richard Nixon had so often condemned. And whereas his predecessors had pursued the policy with some caution, aware of the basic thrust of Soviet power and interest, the Nixon Administration has shown great zeal for error, as though it could succeed by its very enthusiasm for the old cause. But this zeal seems more the academic imagination of Professor Henry Kissinger than the cautious politics of Richard Nixon.

Richard Nixon had long been a hardliner about Red China before he took Henry Kissinger as foreign-policy adviser. In 1968, candidate Nelson Rockefeller, with Henry Kissinger as his foreign-policy adviser, offered a foreign policy to America:[35]

> New York Governor Nelson A. Rockefeller says as president he would work toward international creation of "a new world order" based on East-West cooperation instead of conflict. The Republican presidential contender said he would begin a dialogue with Red China, if elected, to "improve the possibilities of accommodations" with that country as well as the Soviet Union.

This appears to be a good description of the policy which President Nixon has adopted in practice. But it is also a description of the policy the Americans for Democratic Action have been pressing for two decades.

The Nixon policy has had an appearance of success because of the prevailing distress in the Soviet Union and Red China. Those two powers desperately needed the wheat of the United States and its technology.

U. S. industry might build the modern, efficient plants which both powers needed to improve production. Moreover, these opportunities could hardly be refused when the United States financed the major sales at below market prices.

President Nixon arranged the withdrawal of U.S. troops from Vietnam, not through the good offices of Moscow or Peking but through his December 1972 intensive bombing of Hanoi. That was a small achievement. Because he had failed to support aggressive military action against the North while he negotiated at Paris in the Spring of 1972, he was forced in his "peace with honor" to leave the bulk of the Army of North Vietnam in occupation of the South. In reality, this was another retreat in the face of Communist pressures, motivated by the same policy which courted disaster in Mainland China after World War II, in Korea, and in Cuba. It was a policy of losing.

Richard Nixon was not the first President to make political capital out of willingness to negotiate. It was an old ploy.[36]

> It is time we, too, learned not to fix our policy by negotiations but to conduct negotiations in order to fulfill our policies. It is time, too, that we laid aside completely the concept of "sincerity" as a category of political morality even though it is so dear to a type of Eastern seaboard political mind that believes in nothing else. To inquire into Soviet "sincerity" or to require "sincerity" of the Soviet Union is a complete waste of time.

When Mr. Suslov was questioned by his comrades about the Soviet policy of detente, he replied that the Soviet Union was gathering its strength for a new offensive against the capitalist world. If President Nixon continues to retreat at an acceptable rate while American businessmen seek new profits in trade, the new offensive may be delayed awhile. Timing is in the hands of the Soviet leaders. The accumulation of a huge debt to the United States will be an additional incentive to resuming the cold war and suspending payment.

For years, Western strategists speculated that when Stalin died, the real test of the Soviet system would occur. That would be the time for a leader offering liberation to the Russian people to capture their support and put an end to the repressive Communist regime. When Stalin died, the West then decided that this was a delicate period in which any Western call for freedom might lead the Communists in power to turn to war as a measure to unite the people. So Western leaders did nothing; and the Communist leaders consolidated power under Khrushchev. There is some strange hypnosis which persuades Western leaders that they must not act against the Communist powers. A pretext for inaction can always be found.

The posture of the West seems especially tragic at a time when the cultural leaders of the Soviet Union, all loyal socialists, are rebelling at the political barbarity of the ruling regime. Men of great talent are risking prison and persecution in valiant efforts to win elementary human rights for their people. Thus, Yuri Daniel and Andrei Sinyavski, well known Soviet writers, published works in the West for five years under pen names of Nikolai Arzhak and Abram Tertz before they were discovered by the KGB and sentenced to five and seven years of hard labor respectively.[37] On release from prison, they were non-persons, at the mercy of state institutions for enough work to earn a meager livelihood.

The cry of Solzhenitsyn against the cowardice of the West, in his acceptance of the Nobel Prize for literature and in other criticism of the repressions of the Soviet police state, has been noted. There is no response from Western leaders, nor from Western intellectuals who seem hypnotized by the persistent liberal extenuation of Communist barbarism.

In a dispatch from Moscow on August 9, 1973,[38] Theodore Shabad reported the circulation of an open letter written by Vladimir Maksimov protesting Western policies of detente with the Soviet Union at a time when the Soviet regime was intensifying the repression of its own people. Western powers, which should have been working to liberalize internal Soviet policies, were being used to worsen conditions. Mr. Maksimov condemned especially the role of Chancellor Brandt in Germany, which had won favor with President Nixon. He characterized Chancellor Brandt as a "mediocre apologist for a new Munich who takes himself for a great politician," and deplored the course of the free countries: "Only the Almighty can know what price in blood we are going to pay for the diabolical games of the blockheads of modern diplomacy."

From the voices of the damned came cries of anguish, but the West was too deeply involved in its quest for profits to heed the call.

The Kissinger contribution to the Nixon foreign policy has been in large measure dramatic acting. While he faced three years of intransigence in Paris negotiations, Dr. Kissinger managed to convey to the American press an impression that a breakthrough might occur at any moment. That manufactured suspense made the long delay politically tolerable. When it finally arrived, the truce agreement was a bad settlement. It achieved the withdrawal of known U.S. prisoners but it left the free countries of Southeast Asia in a precarious condition. With fewer casualties than it sustained under United States restraints, the Army of South Vietnam could have seized Vinh and the southern provinces of North Vietnam, closed the Ho Chi Minh Trail, forced the withdrawal of North Vietnamese forces from Cambodia and southern Laos and established a negotiating position for the return of all war prisoners in a peace settlement. That kind of action to defeat a socialist aggressor was outlawed by the Nixon policy of giving no offense to the Soviet Union and Red China.

In their rapprochement with Red China and the Soviet Union, President Nixon and Dr. Kissinger pursued a policy of gradual retreat. Their task was to limit the rate of retreat to a scale tolerable for the American people, yet fast enough to win some superficial agreement from the Communist powers. Apparently the Communist leaders understood the signals and agreed to appearances of detente in reward for substantial concessions. Richard Nixon became a Soviet favorite, taking a position heretofore reserved for cooperating Democratic Presidents.

The cost was heavy. In the Vietnam War, a pretentious cease-fire which was never respected by the enemy became the pretext for sanctioning North Vietnam's occupation of the South. The United States imposed on its allies in South Vietnam, Laos and Cambodia compliance with terms which were contemptuously violated by the North Vietnamese. Explaining this fraudulent peacemaking to an Armed Forces Day assembly at the Norfolk Naval Base in 1973, President Nixon said: "We want a peace agreement that is adhered to. We are adhering to the agreement. We expect the other side to adhere to the agreement." How could he say this after six months of blatant violation of the agreements by North Vietnam, violations which the United States had documented and protested?

The President continued: "It should be clearly understood by everyone concerned in this country and abroad, that our policy is not aimed at continuing the war in Vietnam or renewing the war that has been ended. Rather the aim of our policy is to preserve and strengthen the peace, a peace which we achieved at great cost in the past, which holds such promise for the future." How could Richard Nixon talk about "peace" when the casualties of our South Vietnamese allies had actually *increased* after the putative cease-fire? He seemed determined to maintain a pretense of peace to obscure the steady deterioration of our position under the advantages he was allowing to the enemy.

A TIME FOR CHANGE

The sound basis for foreign policy, now as then, was stated by President Washington in his farewell address:

Observe good faith and justice towards all nations. Cultivate peace and harmony with all. Religion and morality enjoin this conduct; and can it be that good policy does not equally enjoin it? . . .

In the execution of such a plan, nothing is more essential than that permanent, inveterate antipathies against particular nations and passionate attachments for others should be excluded: and that in place of them just and amicable feelings towards all should be cultivated. . . .

So likewise a passionate attachment of one nation for another produces a variety of evils. Sympathy for the favorite nation, facilitating the illusion of an imaginary common interest in cases where no real common interest exists, and infusing into one the enmities of the other, betrays the former into a participation in the quarrels and wars of the latter, without adequate inducement or justification. It leads also to concession to the favorite nation of privileges denied to others, which is apt doubly to injure the nation making the concessions, by unnecessarily parting with what ought to have been retained, and by exciting jealousy, ill-will, and a disposition to retaliate in the parties from whom equal privileges are withheld; and it gives to ambitious, corrupted, or deluded citizens (who devote themselves to the favorite nation), facility to betray or sacrifice the interests of their own country without odium, sometimes even with popularity; gilding with the appearances of a virtuous sense of obligation, a commendable deference to public opinion, or a laudable zeal for the public good, the base or foolish compliances of ambition, corruption, or infatuation.

The imperative of a sound foreign policy is realism. No person can mobilize his resources and use them intelligently while he lives in the fancies and wishful thinking of his own imagination. It has been established by voluminous records of actual experience that present U.S. foreign policy is anchored not in reality but in utopian preconceptions divorced from reality.

In an era of conflict, the first requirement of sound planning is to identify the enemy. The enemy of freedom is tyranny. Tyranny in the world today is communism. A sound foreign policy for the free world must confront the problem of ending tyranny.

A sound policy ranges the free world on the side of the people against the tyrants. This means that our political and economic powers are committed to liberating the people. One possible use of this influence is the complete severance of diplomatic and trade relations with the Communist regimes and the restoration of these relations only under conditions conducive to the freedom of the subject peoples.

For example, we would not have cultural exchanges in which Soviet spies are free to roam America but American tourists are admitted to the Soviet Union only under strict and continuing surveillance. The time to require new Soviet policy is in the negotiating stage. We should not make unbalanced agreements in the belief that they will be improved later, or that something is better than nothing. It is often much better for our side to adhere to nothing.

To be effective, our foreign policy should frankly state the true aims and methods of the enemy and describe how we propose to achieve our aims. The nature and aims of the Communist regimes have been accurately analyzed in congressional publications. These analyses should provide the foundations of a policy to advance our purposes in the world. Then we must have men and women in our diplomatic service who know the enemy, who know how to cope with him and who are oriented to aggressive measures to discredit and defeat the Communist tyrannies.

When a right foreign policy is stated, right programs to support it will flow naturally from the genius of our people. There is no need to detail them here. We can be certain, however, that with the cooperation of the subject peoples, the attainment of their freedom and self-government will not be a difficult or lengthy task. The Communist tyrannies survive only with the approval of the free world. When that approval is withdrawn, they will collapse altogether. The critical pressures will be applied in the Soviet Union and Red China against the governing regimes in those countries.

Behind this foreign policy we must have strong military forces for the security of the free world. Their role is to make political and economic activism both prudent and safe.

In short, we must turn about and march in the opposite direction. Our present foreign policy is designed to destroy America.

Chapter 21

THE NIXON TENURE

THE TRIALS AND TROUBLES of the Johnson presidency brought the country to unprecedented internal strife—the burning of our cities, including the second burning of Washington, and urban vandalism protected by public officials. If Johnson's reign demonstrated the bankruptcy of the liberal pretensions on which he sought so diligently to serve, surely the Nixon presidency has demonstrated a similar bankruptcy of the conservative political pretensions which he rode into office. The people repudiated the Johnson management, and got in Richard Nixon a proconsul of the same stripe. Our political system could not produce an alternative. The event confirmed the survival of that controlling direction of policy which Professor Quigley had found in the hands of J. P. Morgan.

After his defeat for the presidency of the United States in 1960 and for the governorship of California in 1962, it appeared that the political career of Richard Nixon was finished. But more prescient observers were not blinded by appearances. Richard Nixon was lifted out of his despair and installed in a New York law partnership, where his extensive political experience and wide international contacts could be put to good use. He was given a handsome income and commissioned to sustain the political interests of the Dewey-Rockefeller Republicans. In 1964, he opposed the nomination of Senator Barry Goldwater for the presidency; but after the

244

convention, he worked loyally in the Goldwater campaign, keeping his contacts with the party professionals. That is why he, and not Governor Rockefeller, became President in 1968.

The Rockefeller blunder was one of those unaccountable misjudgments to which the best of politicians are somehow prone. He should have realized that in the aftermath of the Kennedy assassination, Goldwater could not win. The Rockefeller repudiation was not necessary to assure that defeat. To assure his own nomination in 1968, Rockefeller had a magnificent opportunity to win the loyalty of party conservatives by working openly for the Goldwater election. It would cost nothing but the suppression of his own pique—but he could not bring himself to that healing act. Had he been loyal to the party nominee, he would have commanded the nomination in 1968. A defeated Vice President could not have competed with the Governor of the Empire State.

The Rockefeller defection of 1964 made him an unacceptable candidate in 1968. There was no other Republican Senator of merit to bid for the Goldwater mantle. The outstanding Governor was Ronald Reagan of California, a newcomer to politics who held his first public office in the governorship. Reagan had won national attention by a last-minute fighting speech for Goldwater in the 1964 campaign. He had gone on to win the California governorship in 1966, an endeavor at which Richard Nixon had failed. In office he had demonstrated an open and forthright address to public questions which won public confidence. He had shown courage in challenging a profligate and hostile legislature. He seemed to represent the antithesis of the Johnson liberalism which had torn the country apart.

Governor George W. Romney of Michigan, who had been reelected in 1966, was another promising candidate. But the burning of Detroit in the riots of July 1967 dimmed the Governor's lustre as a leader, and his confused rhetoric about Vietnam virtually eliminated him from the competition.

There was also Richard Nixon. He had mended his fences. He had helped party pros all across the country. He commanded necessary financial support. He moved early to cash in on the IOUs of the Republicans he had helped—and not the least of these, Barry Goldwater.

Could this twice-defeated candidate for public office make a comeback? It all depended upon the handling of the Reagan campaign. Cliff White, who had done an impressive job of managing the Draft Goldwater movement of 1964 and had then been shelved by Goldwater in the main campaign, was commissioned to do the job. He chose to hold back the Reagan candidacy, making no announcement before the opening of the National Convention in Miami.

Reagan's strategy and the Romney default left the field to Rockefeller and Nixon. The unforgiving conservative Republicans gave Rockefeller short shrift, leaving Nixon a front runner. Unless Reagan entered the lists, the Nixon nomination was assured.

All politicians want to win. Commitments must be made. Delegations preferring Reagan could not commit themselves to a non-candidate. With Reagan undeclared, they could only vote for Nixon.

The conservative leaders—Goldwater, Thurmond, Tower—endorsed Nixon. Even then, Reagan held back. At the convention, it was too late. The contest had been lost.

Early in the campaign, while there was a possibility of a Rockefeller-Nixon deadlock in the convention, holding Reagan back as a compromise candidate might have been a practical strategy, if the conservative leaders could have been held in line. But to hold Reagan out of the race until convention time was an inexplicable political decision.

YEAR OF DECISION—1968

Governor Reagan of California was the logical heir to the Goldwater mantle. In two years as Governor of the country's largest state, he had demonstrated a political skill and statesmanship which made professional politicians look dull and inept. He had carefully maintained a cordial relationship with Governor Rockefeller of New York, the representative of the liberal wing of the party. In his own 1966 campaign, he had successfully united liberal and conservative Republicans to win the governorship.

In his endorsement of Richard Nixon, Barry Goldwater may merely have been stating his rejection of Rockefeller. He rationalized his choice of Nixon over Reagan by noting Reagan's limited political experience. That was strange reasoning—preferring a defeated gubernatorial candidate to the successful Governor of the most populous state of the Union. It did accommodate the preference of the Republican king-makers of New York for a man responsive to their own interests, and in this respect it was consistent with the Goldwater position following his 1964 defeat for the presidency, when he turned the Republican Party back to the Eastern liberals who had repudiated him.

When the people were ready to turn away from the great liberal debacle of the Johnson presidency, conservatives turned away from the people. They accepted the Goldwater defeat of 1964 as a sign that the people would not support a conservative candidate. (This was the old liberal ploy for defending its own claims to party leadership.) They swallowed the thesis that Governor Reagan lacked political experience, though the Governor was filling—successfully—a more responsible office than Richard Nixon had ever held.

After the assassination of President Kennedy, 1964 was not a time when Republicans could win the presidency. In contrast, 1968 was a time of revulsion against the Democrats. There was a good prospect that with Reagan as candidate, Governor George Wallace of Alabama would not head a third-party ticket and the full effect of the people's revolt would be reaped by the Republican candidate. This was the time when Republican conservatives supported Nixon and congratulated themselves on defeating Rockefeller, a scarecrow target posted for their hostility.

THE 1969 PRESIDENTIAL CAMPAIGN

Richard J. Whalen, the disillusioned Nixon speechwriter, has given us some insight into the Nixon character and campaign organization.[1] What candidate Nixon said to his speechwriter did not necessarily reflect his real judgment of the issues. As a shrewd politician, he presumably said what was needed to keep Mr. Whalen writing the kind of speeches Mr. Nixon wanted. Even with that discounting, the Nixon grasp of the issues is hardly that of a competent statesman.

Whalen's area of responsibility was defense and national security. His appraisal of the war showed how thoroughly the liberal war propaganda had confused the conservatives:[2]

A couple of days later I saw columnist Robert Novak, just back from a swing through California. He reported a sharp turn against Vietnam even among conservative and publicly hawkish Republicans. John McCone, former CIA Director and a pillar of the GOP establishment, had declared to him that the U.S. must get out of Vietnam. . . .

Vietnam, a war sprung from reckless globalism, was pushing us toward the other extreme of isolationism. The answer, it seemed to me, was to withdraw from Southeast Asia as quickly as we could, on the terms we could obtain. A firm stance vis-à-vis the Soviets would cover that retreat and prepare public opinion for possible tests elsewhere.

No doubt Nixon's talks with Whalen reflected his awareness of the Whalen view of Vietnam.[3]

I realized that he was thinking aloud and kept silent. "Militarily and diplomatically, we've stuck on dead center. The greatest danger of escalation into a big war is through a long, drawn-out war. Our national interest requires ending the war. . ." He paused, "I've been saying, 'an honorable end to the war,' but what the hell does that mean? What about, 'the war must be ended promptly on a basis consistent with the strategic interests of the United States and the free Asian nations? . . .'"

Paraphrasing Nixon: "Do we want to take big risks? We can't send another three hundred thousand men. We can't invade North Vietnam. The only thing left is Haiphong, and that involves risks with the Soviets. . . ."

Quoting Nixon: "I've come to the conclusion that there's no way to win the war. But we can't say that, of course. In fact, we have to seem to say the opposite, just to keep some degree of bargaining leverage."

Pushed to capture public attention in the New Hampshire primary, Nixon turned to vague promises:[4]

"If in November this war is not over," he declared, "I say the American people will be justified in electing new leadership, and I pledge to you that new leadership will end the war and win the peace in the Pacific."

Whalen reported the result of the ploy:[5]

This promise, implying a plan to fulfill it, splashed across the front pages and brought the reporters and TV crews rushing back to the Republican side of the New Hampshire campaign, eager for details. There weren't any. Nothing lay behind the 'pledge' except Nixon's instinct for an extra effort of salesmanship when the customers started drifting away.

This most intimate picture of the Nixon campaign by a sympathetic conservative was a perceptive forecast of things to come. It confirmed what others had said about the reserved quality of the Nixon personality, his ability to be all things to all people, using conservative and liberal speechwriters according to the demands of the situation, adapting his image to the mood of his audience. Whalen also revealed the arrogant quality of the Mitchell-Haldeman-Ehrlichman triumvirate which dominated campaign activities with the apparent approval of the candidate. This was the quality of administration, then discreetly shielded from public view, which was to become well known to Washington critics long before the Watergate incident achieved the status of a national scandal.

THE NIXON ADMINISTRATION

Having elected "their" candidate, conservatives sat back and waited for Richard Nixon to give them a conservative administration. When instead he brought Henry Kissinger, a Rockefeller foreign policy adviser, and Daniel P. Moynihan, a Humphrey supporter, into his most intimate cabinet relationship, conservatives explained that the President had to keep tolerable relationships with a Democratic Congress. They were sure Nixon would keep the administration on a conservative course.

A companion thesis explaining the Nixon liberalism was, "You can't expect him to antagonize a Democratic Congress in his first term—but just wait until the second term." Conservatives seemed not to realize how insulting to Nixon this thesis was—postulating that he could not serve the national interest if to do so would jeopardize his prospect for reelection.

The Nixon political technique was ambivalent. He talked about fiscal restraint and fighting inflation even as he courted unprecedented deficit spending. He talked of a secure national defense even as he poured billions into social welfare programs and seriously cut security programs. He spoke out against forced school busing, even as his Attorney General and his Secretary of Health, Education and Welfare worked assiduously in the courts to extend forced busing programs.

These are but examples of a political method which obscured the real course of his administration with a rhetoric comforting to conservatives. It was a surprisingly effective technique which accommodated the preoccupation of conservatives with rhetoric and of liberals with deeds.

The general tactic was not new. Most politicians adjust their correspondence to please both conservative and liberal constituents. But Richard Nixon had achieved a skill at the practice and a cold-blooded efficiency which few politicians achieve. A desire to please constituents is natural for politicians, but not many can make such a mockery of sincerity as Richard Nixon did.

A President is elected on a party platform which invites the public to support certain general principles and policies. The platform seeks especially to define its differences with the other party. The people make a choice.

If the President-elect adopts the programs and policies of the opposition, he can win opposition support of his programs. If he can then, through party discipline, quiet any dissent in his own party ranks, he can create a public impression of national unity and harmony. If, as in the Nixon ploy, this betrayal of party principles and programs has the warm approval of the dominant news media, a widespread aura of successful administration can be created.

In holding the acquiescence of conservatives, President Nixon repeated the ploy of the Eisenhower administration. Just as Nixon played the conservative villain to Eisenhower's liberal role, Vice President Spiro Agnew was given the role of conservative villain to Nixon's "man of peace." The change of Spiro Agnew from a Rockefeller liberal to a Taft conservative was easily accomplished. Richard Nixon merely assigned his conservative speechwriter, Patrick Buchanan, to mastermind the transformation. This was a matter of words, not of deeds.

The contentment of conservatives with the Agnew rhetoric revealed the shallow quality of conservative politics. The Vice President has no power whatsoever in an administration except to break tie votes in the Senate. What the President does is the issue. Conservatives did not like what the President did, but they were easily mollified by the Vice President's talk.

The Nixon administration has used the alleged conservative principles of the President as a cover for his steady enlargement of the government in service to liberal demands. As one example of a continuing practice, Congressman H. R. Gross of Iowa described the Nixon program of decentralizing authority to the states:[6]

On June 7, the House of Representatives had before it a "reorganization plan," advocated by the Nixon administration, which would create still another agency in a government which is already overrun with agencies and employees.

This one proposes establishment of a Drug Enforcement Administration under which would be combined the personnel and funds of the existing Bureau of Narcotics and Dangerous Drugs, Office of Drug Abuse Law Enforcement, Office of National Narcotics Intelligence, Law Enforcement Assistance Administration and parts of the Bureau of Customs as well as Immigration and Naturalization Service.

No one is opposed to a consolidation of agencies that means greater efficiency and economy, but we predict that this one—as with others that have gone before, such as creation of the Defense and Transportation Departments—will only mean more higher paid executives, and more millions of expenditures. The Defense Department simply created another layer of expensive fat in the Pentagon and the Transportation Department has provided no solutions to the age-old problems of adequate rail and other transportation services. Farmers, for instance, can attest that the rail car shortage was more acute this year than ever before.

But what the general public doesn't know is that in order to get this alleged "reorganization" legislation approved in the House, the Nixon administration entered into an underhanded agreement with the labor bosses to secure their support—a "sweetheart contract" assuring that federal employees would have job protection. This was engineered by Fred Malek, Deputy Director of the Office of Management and Budget, with leaders of the AFL-CIO who, for their part, agreed to change from opposition to support.

In exchange for the union bosses' promise to lobby in the House and Senate for the "reorganization," the White House agreed to ignore and thus nullify a section of the very same plan it had sent to Congress for full approval. Moreover, few members of the House knew, until only hours before the legislation was called for a vote, of the secret dealings between the administration and labor leaders.

It is one of the most contemptuous acts ever perpetrated by the White House upon the House of Representatives and the fact that a majority of the members approved it is further evidence of the low estate to which at least one branch of the national legislature has sunk.

As evidence mounted that President Nixon was in fact giving a more liberal administration than Hubert Humphrey could have given, conservatives swallowed the Nixon course and consoled themselves with patronage. Like the Southern Democrats in the Roosevelt-Truman years, they took the spoils of office as salve for their exclusion from policy-making.

Richard Whalen reported the Goldwater response:[7]

The philosophy that the electorate had repudiated still held sway," said Goldwater sorrowfully. . . . Instead of bellowing his wrath, as he had every right to, the spokesman for the Republican conservatives all but apologized for this muted criticism of the White House. It was no wonder that the self-styled pragmatists and Ripon Society liberals on the President's staff were contemptuous of conservatives.

How true this commentary was! Conservatives seemed to regard politics as a football game in which every player was obligated to obey the signals from the White House. Liberals knew better. Politics is a pressure game in which the President gives where he must and takes what he can. He compromises party differences to maintain party support. Even before Richard Nixon took office he was besieged by liberal pressure groups urging their solutions to current problems.

If the conservatives were content with a few crumbs of patronage, that is what they would get. But the liberals demanded more. They wanted domestic and foreign policies which would accelerate the centralization of power in the federal government and accommodation with the Communist great powers. They prevailed because there was no countervailing pressure for conservative policies.

The reality of politics seems to be that liberals are devoted to their programs and will support any party which serves those programs, while the conservatives, who prate so much of principle, are really slaves of party politics.

During the Nixon first term, when reporters asked if the liberal Nixon policies would not antagonize Republican conservatives, White House exec-utives responded that "they have no place else to go." It was clearly the Nixon gambit to preempt all the liberal positions and to gather as many as possible of the unhappy Democratic voters to his side. He could do this with confidence that Republican conservatives would "go along."

A gambit to lure conservative Democrats into a national coalition was not considered possible. Liberal Republicans were so committed to their policy lines that they would violently oppose any presidential move to the Right. When the President did send up the Supreme Court nomination of Chief Judge Clement Haynesworth of the Fourth Circuit Court of Appeals, the nomination was opposed in the Senate by the Minority Leader and Minority Whip.

If in the Sixties, conservatism seemed to be a fighting opposition to the spreading socialization of society, the Nixon Administration destroyed that promise. It demonstrated that conservatism within the existing parties was a negligible political force. It was merely a sentiment of the people to which appeal should be made at election time, not a force to be reckoned with in the politics of power.

Conservatism had been reduced to a mere choosing of alternatives. It had no political program and no political following. Thus, throughout the long Vietnam war, conservatives had no alternative to the policies of Lyndon Johnson. By preferring the policy of Johnson to that of Senator Fulbright, they had expressed their judgment. They were content with the lesser of two evils. It never occurred to them that they had a duty to chart a course that would end the war quickly by using allied military power to end the aggression.

Richard Nixon knew his conservative constituency well. If he could be only slightly more conservative than his prospective Democratic opponent, he would hold the conservative vote. As the Democratic Party moved to the Left, so did Richard Nixon. He put across programs which a liberal Dem-ocrat could not have managed. He silenced the Republican criticism which would have attacked these measures from Democratic hands.

Ever since the Roosevelt years, the Republican Party had been identified in principle with limited government, fiscal conservatism, a strong national security posture and individual responsibility. In his first administration, Richard Nixon betrayed all these principles. He increased the federal bu-reaucracy and extended its powers. He incurred unprecedented deficits which in turn provoked rampant inflation, two devaluations of the dollar and a crisis of confidence in American fiscal integrity. He inaugurated Strategic Arms Limitations Talks at a time when the Soviet Union was en-gaged in a great building program and U.S. weapons production was nil, thus enabling the Soviet Union to take a critical lead in strategic weaponry and preeminence in all military forces. He proposed a "Family Assistance Plan" which would double the welfare rolls, and which was blocked only through the leadership of Senator Russell B. Long of Louisiana and his Senate Finance Committee, after the House of Representatives had approved the proposal. And yet, with few exceptions, Republican conservatives in both houses of Congress supported the Nixon programs.

Conservative Republicans in the Congress had no reason to fear a loss of patronage. They had a large enough bloc to prevent such infringement of their privileges by the President. Rather, they seemed to suffer a failure of wit. They could not adjust to the reality that they must bring pressure to bear on "their President" if they were to have any influence on policymaking; they tried instead to defend their behavior by apologizing for administration policy.

There were a few exceptions. Some Republicans, like Congressman John Ashbrook of Ohio, regarded office as a contract to serve their constituents and to practice the principles they had advocated as candidates. It was a revealing view of political conservatism which showed so few Republicans in this category.

CREEP

The Committee to Re-Elect the President, organized in 1972 by John Mitchell, the Attorney General and 1968 Campaign Manager, raised the art of political fund raising to new heights of achievement. Mitchell left the cabinet to take the chairmanship of the committee.

The committee selected Senator George McGovern, the least prestigious of the Democratic candidates, as the optimum opponent and worked for his nomination. With that goal achieved, it was possible to raise unprecedented contributions from wealthy citizens fearful of a McGovern presidency.

The flood of contributions made it possible for the committee to finance radical political ventures which might otherwise have received more critical examination. Creation of the "plumbers" group in the White House staff, to conduct counterespionage activity which the Federal Bureau of Investigation shunned as unlawful, reflected the arrogant quality of the Nixon staff. The venture to tap the telephones of the Democratic National Committee in the Watergate building complex in Washington, D.C., was the gesture of a political cabal too well heeled.

In raising $60 million for the presidential campaign, where it was hardly needed after the nomination of Senator McGovern, and in keeping Republican campaign contributions from the congressional races where the funds were urgently needed, the committee achieved the combination of a Nixon victory and Republican Party failure. The presidential sweep accompanied a loss of two seats in the Senate and a gain of only 13 seats in the House, leaving the party outnumbered 57 to 43 in the Senate and 255 to 179 in the House.

The Nixon brand of politics was handsomely rewarded in the 1972 election, just as the Johnson politics had triumphed in 1964. But winning elections is one thing and sound policy is another. Election did not help President Kennedy steer a sound course for the country. Election did not keep Lyndon Johnson from mounting disaster at home and abroad. Election did not overcome the flaws in the Nixon character, nor save the country from the folly of his policies.

WATERGATE

During the 1972 political campaign, President Nixon was able to keep the Watergate break-in in the background. The law violators pleaded guilty to avoid giving testimony. Presidential trips to Peking and Moscow, the intensified war in Vietnam and the peace negotiations occupied the front pages of the national news media.

In March 1973, Judge John Sirica announced an extremely severe sentence for G. Gordon Liddy, and thereafter withheld sentencing of James W. McCord, Jr., pending his decision to cooperate with the court in revealing the ramifications of the crime. When Mr. McCord agreed to give testimony, he triggered confessions of other administration officials about the conduct of the political campaign and the internal operations of the White House staff. The Senate authorized an investigation of campaign activities by the Ervin Committee.

White House Chief of Staff H. R. Haldeman and Domestic Policy Coordinator John Ehrlichman, two of the President's closest confidants, resigned. Former cabinet officers John Mitchell and Maurice Stans were indicted for fund-raising irregularities. Other members of the Committee to Re-Elect the President were drawn into the Watergate trial. Attorney General Richard Kleindienst resigned and was replaced by Elliot Richardson, who then appointed Professor Archibald Cox as a special prosecutor to handle the Watergate case.

It was revealed that President Nixon had taped White House interviews with staff and visitors. When Prosecutor Cox demanded the tapes to check upon the veracity of other testimony revealed in the trial, the President claimed executive privilege. When Judge Sirica ordered the tapes delivered for his examination, the government appealed. The Appellate Court sustained Judge Sirica, with some added conditions. After the President dismissed Special Prosecutor Archibald Cox, a storm of public criticism caused the President to release the tapes to Judge Sirica, as ordered by the Appellate Court.

Meanwhile, the Ervin Committee conducted televised hearings with a parade of witnesses confessing to the dastardly deeds of CREEP. But the aimless questioning of the committee, which seemed directed more to tarnishing reputations than to any legislative purpose, soon wearied the viewing public. This was just another aspect of the astonishing behavior of public officials.

That one political faction would attempt to discover the political plans of another faction seemed unremarkable. That any administration could so confound the national security interest with its own partisan political interests was more unusual. That a judge would use extraordinary and grossly unreasonable sentences to blackmail defendants into giving testimony was remarkable. That a Republican administration would appoint a Democratic special prosecutor to prosecute itself bordered on the irrational. That Republican members of the Senate Watergate Committee would concur in open, televised hearings parading Republican aberrations not pertinent to the committee purpose was a noteworthy lapse of political sophistication. In the whole Watergate gambit, the Nixon administration and the Republican leadership seemed to have taken leave of their senses.

The basic immorality of Watergate derived from the sin of self-righteousness. Responsible members of the Committee to Re-Elect the President and of the White House staff could, in their own minds, justify criminal trespass as warranted for the greater good of keeping Richard Nixon in office. Self-righteousness is a common human fault which in persons like Robespierre, Lenin and Mao could have devastating consequences for humanity.

But in Watergate, the greater immorality was that of the news media which, zealous to protect the greater corruption of their own dishonesty, posed as the defender of civic virtue. Rev. Daniel Lyons editorialized that "the networks, *The New York Times*, and the mainstream of our press have been corrupted much longer and much deeper than has the Nixon team. Example: the media reported very prominently last year that President Nixon had made $60,000 on a real estate transaction. Yet it had no comment when it learned that President Johnson left a personal fortune of more than $25 million . . . His leaving $25 million is one of the greatest scandals of our time. But few if any columnists or commentators have said a word of criticism."[8]

The news media live by a double standard. They have their own self-righteousness, but unrelated to money.

In another commentary on Watergate, Father Lyons remarked:[9]

> . . . we should remind ourselves that the media is free only to be responsible. It is not free to be dishonest, to distort, or to be irresponsible . . . as you travel around the United States you see the enormous effect of a huge paper like *The New York Times*, which sets the pace and tone and supplies information to other papers all around the country . . .
>
> Now in regard to Watergate, the interesting thing is the way the press is constantly bringing in all non-related issues. For example: *Newsweek*, twice in one issue, referred to Vietnam and Watergate. So what is really bothering *Newsweek* is not so much Watergate as the fact that President Nixon refuses to surrender South Vietnam.

THE AGNEW SCANDAL

Even as the Watergate investigation and trial were obsessing public attention, the U.S. Attorney at Baltimore, Maryland, was uncovering evidence of a cozy relationship between public officials and the architect-engineer beneficiaries of public contracts. Soon the testimony involved Vice President Spiro T. Agnew, who was notified of the investigation. After some plea bargaining and much publicity, the Vice President resigned, pleading *nolo contendere* only to knowing failure to pay income taxes. But the prosecution spread on the record its account of substantial and long-continued payments to Mr. Agnew by Maryland state contractors while he was Baltimore County Executive, Governor of Maryland and Vice President.

The event raised many questions. Governor Agnew had been a minor official, a county executive, when a division in the Democratic Party in the 1964 election made possible his election as Governor. He was a Rockefeller supporter in the 1968 campaign until it became clear that Rockefeller would not be the convention choice. Why did Richard Nixon pick Agnew to be his running mate, putting aside better known leaders of the Republican Party? Was the selection urged by someone who knew the Agnew past? The Maryland practice of paying public officials was widely known to the initiated; and a most effective way of controlling politicians is to possess information of their crimes or sins.

The procedures for his removal were highly irregular. Law and custom require that high public officials be impeached and removed from public office before they become subject to prosecution. This procedure is a protection of public officers against harassment in the courts. Congress neglected its responsibility in failing to take jurisdiction for impeachment, and the President compounded the disorder by inaugurating prosecution prior to impeachment. The consequence was plea bargaining, which allowed Vice President Agnew to resign and to escape with a $10,000 fine and three years probation for his acknowledged crime.

The claimed justification of this settlement was the avoidance of an extended public trial of the Vice President. But that prospect would have been avoided if proper procedure had been followed. If the evidence had been presented to the House of Representatives for impeachment and then to the Senate for conviction, and if the Vice President did not sooner resign, the removal could have been accomplished expeditiously without plea bargaining. Mr. Agnew would then have been in the courts like any other tax evader, without protection of his former office. Why indeed did President Nixon choose this irregular procedure to arrange so favorable a release for the Vice President?

There were some plausible excuses. Congress was reluctant to inaugurate impeachment proceedings, preferring to have the alleged criminal action tried in the courts without prior legislative action. Thus, the reluctance of the Congress to perform its duty caused it to delegate its powers, de facto, to the courts. The important public policy of securing public officials against court harassment was abandoned.

Some congressional leaders, in this derogation of law, pontificated that "no man is above the law." This is of course a misleading cliche. When the law itself provides exemption from prosecution for an official, the lawlessness is in attempting prosecution before removing him from office.

It seemed as though someone had decided that the time had come to end the Agnew charade.

THE PRESIDENTIAL RETREATS

As President, Richard Nixon had the White House and a comfortable retreat at Camp David supplied by the people. He had at his service all the ships of the U.S. Navy and the installations of the armed forces as secure retreats from the burdens of Washington. After his election, he chose to buy homes at Biscayne Beach, Florida, and at San Clemente, California, and to equip them at government expense amounting to about $10 million as alternate White Houses. This action reveals much about Richard Nixon, and about his administration.

According to available estimates of his net worth, Richard Nixon is not a man who would need or who could afford to maintain two such homes after his presidency. The reasonable explanation of his purchases is that they are investments—that his friend Rebozo persuaded him that, given a continuation of high rates of inflation, the homes would increase in value, aided by identification as former presidential "White Houses." The gambit uses two cornerstones: first, it exploits the presidential office for personal aggrandizement; second, it commits the President to a policy of continuing inflation. The impropriety of such action seems apparent.

Should the President use the prestige of his office to increase his personal wealth, much as Miss America does, but more subtly? There are legions of opportunists ready to help him do so, but no such pursuit of personal gain can be reconciled with his duties as President. In accepting the office, he is bonded to the people and to no other cause or interest. To maintain the objectivity which the office requires, he can have no other interests of persons or causes.

Perhaps he could plead that inflation was already a fact of U.S. policy, that neither he nor anyone else could restrain the Congress, and that his investment merely recognized a condition which he could not control. Whatever merit such a thesis might have had, it was destroyed by his commitment. A President must not make an investment to take advantage of a condition which he is duty bound to terminate. The appearance, and perhaps the reality, is that Richard Nixon had given his bond to maintain a continuing inflation as the price of political support of his election.

What manner of man, having reached the presidency and the substantial income it assured, would use the office to further schemes for his personal aggrandizement?

This exploitation of public office for personal advantage by President Nixon may indeed seem trivial compared with the record of President John-

256

son who, in a lifetime of public service, amassed a fortune of $25 million. No doubt the Johnson fortune was a very small payment on the service he rendered to industry in his exercise of public authority. That he served the public interest must forever be in doubt.

The reality we face is that government is vastly corrupted by the readiness of some public officials to use public authority for personal gain. It is in the interest of the great lobbies, often unregistered, to have such men in public office. Being corrupt, these officials are at the mercy of their paymasters, for public exposure could destroy and perhaps jail them.

The Nixon investments, so trivial in the perspective of his office, nevertheless compromised his integrity as President of the United States.

GROWING DISCORD

As 1973 moved to its close, the Nixon administration was in sad disarray. His liberal foreign policy still enjoyed a good press, but credit for that success was accorded to Henry Kissinger, now Secretary of State. Gross mismanagement of wheat sales, to the great benefit of the Soviet Union and the cost of the American people, was for American liberals an acceptable cost of detente, though altogether unnecessary for that purpose. The outbreak of war in the Middle East seemed a strange fruit of detente, but the peacemakers never recognize war as the logical fruit of their endeavors.

On the home front, the administration's bizarre prosecution of itself reflected an abject deference to political pressures, a crisis of purpose as those who had been the mainstays of the administration battled to stay out of jail. Court trials in Washington, New York and Los Angeles pilloried the erstwhile rulers of the country.

Events had taken the measure of Richard Nixon. He was in many respects a typical product of the age. A man of considerable talent but limited means, he was launched into politics in the aftermath of World War II. He lacked the gregarious, outgoing temperament which is so important to political success, and remained throughout his career much the loner. He lacked the leadership capacity which could attract men of talent to his banner. He was more comfortable with men of limited talent and unquestioning loyalty, as though that loyalty were essential for his own inner security. Thus, he was thrown into dependence on his own limited talents, talents inadequate to the great enterprise he was called to lead.

Although Richard Nixon adhered in his personal life to traditional Christian morality, he seemed to lack any defined sense of civic morality. He was facile in using the cliches of honor and high purpose, regarding them as John Kennedy did, as the ordinary tools of politics. His political morality seemed to flow from the same view of politics as amoral. The task was to win, and morality had nothing to do with it. Thus, he was led by his subordinates into schemes which promised political advantage, without regard to their immorality.

257

His association with Nelson Rockefeller seemed to be entirely an arrangement of convenience. He did what was necessary to become President, not thereby gaining any respect or affection for the man who had lifted him out of the 1962 defeat in California and provided a lucrative law partnership for his rehabilitation. It did no violence to his political convictions to be either liberal or conservative. He had no political convictions and could therefore adapt his policies to the prevailing expediency. He was a manageable instrument of the Fabian elites.

Chapter 22

THE CONSERVATIVE DEFAULT

WE HAVE NOTED many of the forces committed to altering the basic structure and ethic of our society and some of the responses to challenge. It remains to explain why an ancient order which was so admirably suited to service in our modern world should have been forsaken just when its values were critically needed.

We have seen that the political party, being essentially a power-seeking apparatus directed by expediency and lacking national wisdom or purpose, is necessarily destructive unless it is controlled by some higher purpose. But the party can be controlled only by political purpose because it responds to no other appeal. Why, then, has the nation failed to provide a political mechanism that reflects the national will and restrains the destructive tendencies of the political parties?

We could turn to Oswald Spengler and conclude that in a free society, the domination of money and the consequences of that domination are inevitable. There is no way to prevent the corruption of such a state and no way to cure the corruption except by dictatorship. His thesis has been demonstrated so often in history that we must with caution put it aside.

There are two possible alternatives to the Spenglerian outcome. One is to have a rule of money which is informed and politically astute; the other is to divorce money from politics so that the state will reflect the will not of the few but of all the people. Neither alternative is operative in the United States today.

The power of wealth is directed toward a futile and wasting effort to reconcile freedom and communism. The political forces which should be severing the moneyed control of politics are weak and ineffectual. The condition is related to the difficulty of arousing a free people to common danger in the absence of alert and vigorous leadership.

One of the luxuries of a free society is freedom from politics. The citizen can go about his work, building his business or doing his job, free from interference of government. He can spend his leisure time according to his heart's desire, playing golf, tending his garden, visiting with friends. Politics is the province of people who specialize in public office and who come around every two years to ask for a vote. In sum, the citizen develops a sense of political security which insulates him from public affairs. An increase in taxes may cause some concern but he soon adjusts to the new condition.

With this condition of the public psyche, it was easy for a political elite to take over the public authority and exercise it for the benefit of the few. It is a far cry from the protective tariff to the profligate subsidies the Congress grants today. The political hand in the public treasury has made many a fortune in the United States in recent decades.

In the beginning, Americans appreciated the merits of the decentralized constitutional order as the guarantor of their liberties. But as the Fabian promise of utopian achievement through centralized government made inroads, first in higher education and then in public education, public loyalty to the Constitution faded. A remnant of scholars and of older citizens preserved the heritage of freedom, fought the socialist encroachment, adhered to the rhetoric of the free-market economy and resisted the centralization of political power. For a while in the postwar years, this remnant was represented in the Congress by a coalition of Southern Democrats and conservative Republicans who restrained the more extreme demands of the dominant liberals. For this coalition to be effective, one element had to vote against the party leadership and its own President, an action increasingly hazardous as presidential power expanded. The coalition could therefore be called to action only on extreme measures.

In the public information field, in both press and broadcast media, liberal schools of journalism produced a flow of university graduates indoctrinated with visions of the planned society and the utopia they would help to achieve. Gradually but steadily, the temper of our news media changed from our traditional American cultural pattern to a zeal for change. That the change was in character a move from individualism to paternalism, from freedom to socialism, seemed of scant concern to the advocates. They just wanted the government to do more for everyone.

260

CONSERVATIVE RESPONSE

Conservative rhetoric, essentially dedicated to adherence to sound principle under changing conditions, was defensive in character. It expressed a sense of values which had once inspired men to combat, but their reiteration bore no aura of combat. The literature was of protest against old errors resurrected and clothed in modern garments, but it lacked vitality and purpose.

Principles must be translated into programs before they can become effective politically. This is the work conservatives didn't do. They were forever talking and writing about principles violated in the programs of the Left, but they had no alternative programs to offer except to maintain the status quo.

The status quo may indeed be the right position on a particular issue, but it then requires a vigorous exposition to show the people that it is the best of all choices. Thus, we oppose the centralization of control of education in Washington not merely because local control is in principle sound, but because we can demonstrate that national control both increases the cost and reduces the quality of the education which the worker receives for his investment in taxes. If we compare the two programs, we can show the worker that no sensible person could choose centralization of educational control in a federal bureaucracy.

As we survey the political campaigns of the last forty years, we find very little programmatic support of conservative principles. The prevailing tactic has been to attack the more extreme programs of the Left while accepting more moderate programs of the Left. The programs for which conservative legislators have voted have been introduced by liberals and occasionally modified to meet some conservative objection. There have been no positive conservative programs in the Congress in four decades.

As we have noted, from 1936 to 1960 the Republican Party offered only liberal candidates for the presidency. In terms of dedication to the American political system it could not by any stretch of language be called a conservative party. It was only less liberal than the Democratic Party. Governor Alfred Landon was the fall guy for liberal Republicans who liked Franklin Roosevelt. Wendell Willkie was a blocking candidate to keep the people from voting for Senator Taft. Governor Dewey was a spokesman for Wall Street. General Eisenhower was an amiable and docile exponent of the prevailing liberalism.

Richard Nixon was defeated in 1960, in part because he bore a false image of conservatism derived from his duties for President Eisenhower. When the party convention of 1960 seemed inclined to adopt a strongly conservative platform, Vice President Nixon, after consultation with Governor Rockefeller, intervened to guide the platform committee to more liberal positions. Vice President Nixon's choice of Ambassador Henry Cabot

Lodge as running mate, the very has-been whom candidate Kennedy had unhorsed in a Massachusetts Senate race eight years earlier, may have been deferential to the party liberals but it was not a choice to inspire popular enthusiasm.

By 1964, the national climate had changed. The liberal Democratic policies which had embroiled the country in one tragic war in Korea and had then been repudiated by the people, were leading the country into a similar quagmire in Vietnam. The Kennedy-Johnson administration had been one unending sequence of defeat and retreat before Khrushchev's belligerency. Opposition crystallized around the person of Senator Barry Goldwater, who might have defeated President Kennedy but could not defeat his ghost.

As Lyndon Johnson pushed the liberal programs to their logical ends in his second term, national disaster mounted, at home and abroad. The bankruptcy of the Democratic Party was public knowledge. Voters were prepared for one of the great switches of the century. Where were the conservatives who should have been offering programs to save the country?

As the urban news media turned in mid-century to an overwhelming liberal bent, new publications were launched to serve the conservative remnant. In 1944, Frank Hanighen launched *Human Events* as a weekly journal of conservative comment on current issues. This new journal undertook a continuing analysis of congressional and other governmental action to keep conservative citizens informed of the course of politics in America. It soon became an important national journal of conservative opinion.

William F. Buckley, Jr., had done a notable analysis of the liberal indoctrination of college students in his book, *God and Man at Yale*. In 1955, he launched *National Review* as a voice for the conservative philosophy in the United States. The magazine, with such established authorities as James Burnham and Frank Meyer on its editorial board, became a forum of conservative thought on current issues.

In 1958, Admiral Ben Moreell, the retired chief of the U.S. Navy Bureau of Yards and Docks and founder of the famed Seabees of World War II, joined with leading conservative members of Congress to organize Americans for Constitutional Action, with a purpose of doing for conservative politics what Americans for Democratic Action had done for liberal politics. As a political action agency without tax exemption, ACA was never able to raise the funds required for its full mission. With true conservative prudence, Admiral Moreell adjusted his program to his funding and concentrated upon the election of conservatives to Congress. He reasoned that the restoration of Congress to its proper constitutional role was the key to all political reform in America.

In 1964, another effort to bring all conservatives into concerted political action was made with the organization of the American Conservative Union. This movement reached a peak of political independence and rhetorical honesty under the chairmanship of Congressman John M. Ashbrook of Ohio.

In these references to conservatives, we have mentioned only the clientele of *National Review* and *Human Events* and the politicians who subscribe to the general tenets of those journals. But this is the effete element of conservatism, aligned generally with the Republican Party.

The other branch of conservatism consists generally of Democrats in revolt against the liberal directions of their party. They have voiced their dissent by joining groups such as the John Birch Society and supporting a plethora of associations dedicated to constitutional government, fiscal responsibility, anti-communism and victory in Vietnam. In 1968, they were gathered into the American Party by Governor Wallace. They then polled about one-half of the 1964 Goldwater vote, indicating roughly the conservative split between hardliners and softliners.

Within this group, there is a literature of vigorous opposition to the socialist trend of American politics. But this literature circulates only to a small band of perhaps a million Americans. It is excluded from fair notice in the national news media, and is rarely mentioned on television or by the wire services except in some disdainful reference to "extremism." Radio has offered a better medium for this message. It has been used extensively by such conservative radio churchmen as the Reverend Billy James Hargis, the Reverend Stuart McBirnie and the Reverend Carl McIntire.

THE HOSTILE MEDIA

One of the most successful propaganda operations since that of Goebbels in Nazi Germany has been that of the liberal news media in the United States. *The New York Times* reflects the general trend and method. It cultivates the complacency of a snobbish elite satisfied with its own shibboleths and contemptuous of opposing views. It uses the smear tactic to discredit opposition and reinforce the faith of its own adherents. It has created a near monopoly control of public information.

Popular liberals like Malcolm Muggeridge and the late John Dos Passos who turned away from the anti-intellectualism of liberalism to resume the ancient search for truth were suddenly ignored, cast into oblivion. Only newsmen who repeat faithfully the liberal propaganda for peace, poverty and big government are favored with advancement in the big corporate news monopolies.

William F. Buckley, Jr., learned about the obstacles which confront every attempt to illuminate the liberal shadows. He made his peace with the liberal powers by launching an attack on the John Birch Society, bracketed with "McCarthyism" as the bogeyman of liberals. He created a cleavage between Republican highbrows and Democratic commoners which effectively destroyed all prospect of concerted conservative political action. He was rewarded with liberal acceptance as the spokesman of "conservatism." He was given a television program by Public Broadcasting Service, nominally to represent the conservative ethic but actually to interview prominent liberals. Thus he fulfilled the liberal mission of publishing the liberal philosophy, with only a mild Buckley dissent. The networks would not of course do the reverse. They would not commission Howard K. Smith to conduct a program of interviewing conservatives, for that would put conservative views before the people.

The liberal smear has effectively divided those Americans who oppose the march into socialism. One branch seemingly accepts liberal toleration as the limit of its political action and is therefore ineffectual. The other proclaims a forthright adherence to the American political ethic as the only acceptable standard of politics and is roundly smeared. Divided, they are unable to sound a persuasive voice or to organize a political party which can oppose effectively the liberal two-party monopoly of political power.

In 1972, a million Americans voted for Congressman John Schmitz of California, former Republican and candidate of the American Party for the presidency. The total included conservative Democrats and Republicans who rejected the adherence of their conservative leaders to the Nixon banner. There is no doubt that most of the 27,000,000 Goldwater-conservative votes went to Richard Nixon, not for his conservatism but in fear of Senator George McGovern. The national resistance to Nixon liberalism was pitiful.

The experience of these years demonstrates how effectively money controls politics in America. In the 1972 primary campaign, Senator McGovern, who was the least popular and least promising of the Democratic candidates, had generous funding and a fine press. Senators Muskie, Humphrey and Jackson had limited funding and a hostile press; they seemed to be continuously in trouble. After the McGovern nomination, his campaign faltered. President Nixon had the money and the good press.

This operation was not essentially different from the Morgan control of party nominations in the 1880s, described by Professor Quigley. The task in 1972 was in some degree to influence party primaries rather than party conventions, but money and the skills it commanded still did the job.

On this scene, the conservative citizens were part of the manipulated public, whipsawed by the contrived dramatics of party conflict. It was impossible for them to command public respect unless they stood for something—and they did not. Conservative politicians violated their principles routinely on the plea that prudence required a choice of liberal alternatives.

Perhaps the best example of the faithlessness of conservative politics was the action of the Conservative Party of New York in giving its 1972 endorsement to President Nixon. The Conservative Party had been formed in New York State in rebellion against the liberalism of Governor Rockefeller and the state Republican Party. It had prospered because it provided a rallying point for public opposition to the liberalism of the two major parties.

But in office, Richard Nixon had made a record of arrant liberalism which in every aspect showed the Rockefeller brand. How could a political party espousing conservative principles endorse such a record? The New York Conservative Party had a great opportunity to declare its principles and deny endorsement to both McGovern and Nixon. Instead it panicked in fear of McGovern and declared for Nixon. It joined the mass of leaderless "conservative" voters in accommodating the plans of the liberal Republicans by turning to Nixon.

It was not that the conservatives had nowhere else to turn, as liberals in the White House had predicted, but that they lacked the wit and gumption to lead in any direction. How could anyone believe in the principles proclaimed by the New York Conservative Party after it had endorsed the record of Richard Nixon? The lure of patronage and of a less offensive liberalism destroyed the New York Conservative Party as a force in American politics.

The country approaches its 200th birthday in a remarkable state of distress. It is returning to the paternalism and authoritarianism which the Founding Fathers rejected. It is beset by a sea of troubles related to that erroneous course. And yet, there is not in sight a political consensus capable of presenting to the people the rational alternatives to their present troubles.

Because **both** political parties are committed to the socialist course, the people **have no** voice representing their traditional political ethic. Is the cause dead, or is it merely neglected?

Chapter 23

IN TIME OF CRISIS

The Nixon Administration epitomizes the weakness of Western civilization in this time of challenge. It is bemused with the tactics of domestic political conflict and incapable of addressing—perhaps even of comprehending—the relentless war which is being waged against our country and our culture.

By every objective measure of relative strength the Communist powers are expanding and the Free World nations are declining. Territorially, this has been so for fifty years. Militarily, it has been so for a decade. But strength is not measured alone by territory and military power; the disintegration of the integrity and commitment of the free nations to freedom is the basic threat to their survival.

This is not to blame all our troubles on militant communism. Wealth, ease, and luxury would have taxed the moral fiber of the productive capitalist societies even without the planned exacerbation of their corrosive influences by the Communist powers. Human character is at its best in fighting evil, at its worst in resisting luxury. And resistance to luxury is weakest in capitalist politicians. The Communist achievement has been to give purpose and direction to the natural forces of decay in capitalist societies and to reinforce those material influences with its own considered programs.

Indulgent parents do spoil their children with too much unearned money. Spoiled children do conceive illusions of power and righteousness, unrestrained by experience, victimized by unscrupulous elders. Criminal activity is increased by the availability of easy money. Social conflict is encouraged by weak government. But these and similar factors do not of themselves create a solicitude for the preservation of socialist systems which arrests our response to their aggressions.

There is no better index of the American decline than the Nixon settlement in Vietnam. This accommodation of defeat is deeply immoral. It necessarily has devastating consequences for the nation which so dishonors itself.

The United States moved into Vietnam to replace the French as the chief support of local government against Communist aggression after the division of the country at Geneva in 1954. Within a year, the people of South Vietnam had established a secure and successful government which was the boast of the Free World. President Diem was honored with a reception by President Eisenhower in Washington.

Then, as Eisenhower's second term moved to its close, the campaign of subversion against South Vietnam was inaugurated. By 1960, it was estimated that Vietcong forces had been increased to 20,000—still not a formidable problem for a country of 14,000,000 people with an army of 150,000 men. But President Kennedy brought to power an administration with the same instincts that produced the Democratic errors of Korea. It thought a settlement could be negotiated before the military conflict was resolved. In pursuit of that chimera, it denied South Vietnam its clear right in international law to strike on the ground at the North Vietnamese bases illegally developed in Laos, and it thereby rendered the defense of South Vietnam impossible. The course of the war was foreordained by that decision.

As the slaughter mounted, no Democratic leader—not President Johnson, not Senator Russell, not Senator Stennis—ever summoned the courage to advocate attacking the immediate sources in Laos and North Vietnam of the enemy buildup in South Vietnam. Lesser members of the party did so, but they were ignored. A self-imposed delusion that such response by South Vietnam would bring Red China into the war combined with fatuous hopes that the cooperation of the Soviet Union would bring its good offices to bear for peace, and in this mental prostration, political leaders wrestled with the Sisyphean task which Soviet strategy had set before them—to defend South Vietnam while allowing sanctuary to the enemy in Laos.

By 1968, the utter futility of the Johnson strategy was obvious to all. Most Americans believed our forces should defeat the enemy and end the war; but others, confused by claims that the enemy could not be defeated, wanted to withdraw.

When President Nixon took office and enunciated a policy of "negotiation, not confrontation," his conservative followers, who knew very well what action was required on the war front, extenuated his soft position with claims that public sentiment had so far turned against the war that it was too late for decisive action on the military front. The very persons who had been urging the Democrats to action now concluded that Nixon, with an overwhelming mandate against the Democratic war policy, could not take the action.

President Nixon adopted the policy inaugurated by Secretary of Defense Clark Clifford of building up South Vietnamese forces to assume the full battle responsibility and withdrawing U.S. military forces from South Vietname—the policy that came to be known as Vietnamization. This policy represented an unprecedented deterioration of America's moral position. It was an acceptance of defeat, the abandonment of an ally in the heat of battle, a refusal to use our mobilized military superiority in the field to secure our ally against continuing, powerful, external assault. It transferred to a small ally the burden of a war the United States was unable to resolve because of the inadequate moral and intellectual stature of its political leadership.

President Nixon did take action against the sanctuaries in 1970 when he sent U.S. forces into Cambodia. Because his political rhetoric had misled people to expect negotiation, not confrontation, his political enemies could and did depict the invasion of Cambodia as a betrayal of presidential promises. They aroused a furor of student clamor in the colleges.

In 1971, the President supported a South Vietnamese attack on the enemy bases in Laos. A hostile press decried the move, belittling the South Vietnamese performance. A year later, when South Vietnamese forces were stronger and battle-hardened, no invasion of Laos was permitted. By this time, the President was embroiled in ping-pong diplomacy with Red China. The Red Chinese diplomacy paralyzed U.S. initiatives in Southeast Asia.

In 1972, when the President was informed of the North Vietnamese concentration for an invasion of the South, he vetoed the plan of the Joint Chiefs of Staff to bomb these forces in their assembly areas, where they were already in violation of the bombing suspension terms which President Nixon had himself laid down. In consequence, South Vietnam suffered a smashing attack with widespread carnage and devastation, all of it avoidable by a simple exercise of prudence. But the Nixon mind was so deceived by Soviet and Red Chinese omens of detente that it had lost its powers of discrimination.

Angrily, the President responded with renewed bombing and a blockade of Haiphong—but it was too late to mend the damage done in South Vietnam. Virtually the whole army of North Vietnam remained in occupation of South Vietnam—and its presence was then validated by the Paris agreements of January 1973. South Vietnam, despite Nixon pretenses that "peace" had been achieved by a cease-fire, was left in a continuing war with a very high level of battle casualties. The cease-fire was imposed only on South Vietnam, for the U.S. had no way to force North Vietnam to comply with its provisions. As U.S. official protests made clear, the North Vietnamese violations were massive and continuing.

Instead of defeating the enemy and restoring peace, a task easily within the capacity of our assembled military forces, the Nixon administration thought to withdraw to fortress America and use our allies to fight America's battles. For these were our battles, in which the United States, controlling war policy through its supply of munitions, denied the right of South Vietnam to expel the enemy from its territory. The continuing sacrifice of Vietnamese lives on both sides of the conflict is a bloody tribute to the folly of American politics and to the superior, purposeful intelligence of the Communist leaders.

INTERNAL DECLINE

This debasement of American foreign policy came after decades of steady decline in the moral quality of American culture. In the worldwide war of militant atheistic materialism against the cultures of freedom, the Communist powers had the advantage of working in the Free World arena under cover of peace. Agents could be infiltrated into free institutions to change and redirect their policies in subtle and plausible ways. Money could be used to buy newspapers and publishing houses, to subsidize favorable propaganda and to support attacks on the moral structure of the law. Because every society has its lawless elements, Communist policy had only to foster surreptitiously the attack of this element on the foundations of the free order.

Under this attack, abetted in many aspects by the power of the Fabian elites, responsible officialdom felt compelled to adapt to change. It conceived new individual rights and construed the Constitution to allow them. The claim of traitors that they were only being loyal to a higher ethic received more currency than a few trials evidenced. Courts extenuated riotous attacks on government as though government were an enemy of the people. Officials acted as though attacks on legal process were matters of conscience rather than of law. The objective reality of law depreciated as courts and enforcement officers devised excuses for setting it aside. A society which once thrived on a strong work ethic was transformed through growing wealth and irresponsibility into a money-grubbing society of selfish forces contending for unearned advantage through political manipulation of law and public resources.

These conditions affected chiefly the leaders, only remotely the people. They did not develop a leadership capable of contending with the disciplined materialism of the Communist masters.

Because the political parties were aggregations of citizens with a common, selfish interest of holding public office, they became ready agents of the subversion of public integrity. Their game was to win elections, and that could be accomplished by taking the support of wealthy backers who had most to gain from the political control of society.

With political control exercised through the parties, government ceased to be representative. Its purpose was no longer to be responsive to the people but to render such service to the controlling power blocs as could be supplied without arousing a popular revolt. Government in its various elements functioned to provide such accommodation as the resources of the country could supply—and even to borrow against future income to placate immediate demands of the politically powerful.

The troubled elites of the Fabian dimension were finding their notions of the beneficent state illusory. Every ministration of political power to the problems of poverty and social conflict only exacerbated the national malaise. The increasing federal power had passed beyond management by Congress and would soon require a national dictator to direct the administration of government.

Our political parties have forsaken honor and integrity in public service to pursue power for personal and party aggrandizement. They have espoused dishonest policies of inflation which rob the working man of his savings. They have undermined the moral foundations of public order by suspending enforcement of the law against favored political blocs. They have used public office for personal and corporate enrichment. They have impoverished the national treasury and strained the national credit with profligate spending of the people's savings.

In our relations with other nations, our political leaders have retreated from our traditional stand for freedom to exhibit a cowering concern for peace at any price. Facing the most powerful and barbarous tyranny the world has ever known, they have sought to placate it with smiles and concessions. They have wasted our youth and our substance in wars of attrition which they lacked the wisdom and the courage to prevent or to win. They have demeaned our country with their personal fears and irresolution.

These events and conditions define a course of steady decline which has afflicted our society for forty years and has become apparent to the most casual observer since the close of World War II. Our government has misjudged the purpose and resolution of the Communist regimes, has resorted to ineffectual measures to protect our national interests, has shattered the hopes of the Captive Nations for recovery of their freedom and has strengthened the reigning tyrants in their seats of power. It has idled complacently while the Soviet Union, with only one-half of our industrial resources, has surpassed us in strategic nuclear armament.

One perceptive observer has noted the decline of liberty as a dynamic force in American life:[1]

> Even in the United States where men give lip service to liberty, it is not the dynamic force it once was. Now that our affluent society has savored its blessings, it has come to take them for granted. Ideas esteemed for their acceptability take precedence over ideas esteemed for their foundation in moral principle, and political leadership succumbs to expediency. In the face of an adversary who asserts supreme confidence in the superiority of his ideology, this is a fatal weakness.

NEW DIRECTIONS

It is clear that the charted course of our present political leadership courts

270

mounting disaster and ultimate disintegration or defeat. It is imperative that our people turn to the task of healing our divisions, restoring a vigorous moral tone to society, and addressing confidently the threat to our nationhood and to Western civilization. The outlines of such a new order and the measures required to inaugurate it are clearly defined in our own history and in the present condition of the world.

The first condition of a good society is the freedom and responsibility of the individual. This condition is preserved in our society by respecting the assertion of our Declaration of Independence "that all men are created equal, that they are endowed by their Creator with certain Inalienable Rights, that among these are life, liberty, and the pursuit of happiness. That to secure these Rights, Governments are instituted among Men, deriving their just powers from the consent of the governed."

Government must be supported by and be dependent upon its citizens. It must never become an institution upon which citizens are dependent.

Representative government is subverted chiefly by the power of money. Oswald Spengler said that democracy has historically foundered on the rule of money. It has disintegrated because money has neither the wisdom nor the spirit to bind a nation. A state must have other reason for its existence.

Ours was to have been a republic in which *money would not rule*. People would rule. And in the first century of our constitutional republic, the people did rule. But in the second century, money took over the levers of power and people became the pawns of politics. The critical question for America is whether it can drive the money power out of politics and reestablish the rule of the people. Because the legal power resides in the people, we need only a few changes of law and outlook to restore rule by the people. It should be clear to all citizens that the survival of the Republic requires the exclusion of big money from politics. Let citizens amass what wealth they can under our laws but do not let those who hold the wealth make the laws.

All the people, and especially all public officials, must understand that in our society money may not buy anything political. When that resolution of the people is established, the law will be respected. Then we shall have no corruption of the democratic process by such massive bribing of the people as Pompey and Caesar practiced in Rome.

Political campaigns should not be financed by public funds. Only money which comes voluntarily from the people should be allowed in politics. To accomplish this, appropriate laws should limit all campaign contributions to a sum which persons of modest means could be expected to give to a political cause without quid pro quo—say $500. Candidates, too, would be limited to such personal political expenditure so that no candidate could use his personal fortune for political advantage.

In such a system, all candidates for office would be financed by the contributions of their constituents, with so many contributors that no individual would have any claim on the candidate's service if he is elected. Equitable provision for free access of candidates to radio and television should be imposed by law as a cost of holding a public franchise.

When the election process is thus purified, it will be clear that the function of government is to serve all the people, and that the function of corporations, as with individuals, is to obey the law.

Because rule by the people has been neglected for a century, there is much to be done. In particular, there must be a general review of federal laws to assure that it does govern private and corporate interstate business activity which is beyond the capacity of any state to control, and that it does withdraw from jurisdiction which is properly governed by state law.

RESTORING THE AMERICAN SYSTEM

When the dictation of money is removed from politics, it will become possible to restore the integrity of the American republic. The massive propaganda for centralization of government will be stilled. Officials will be elected to give good government and will address that problem; and they will find that the separation of state and federal powers provided in the Constitution is the true basis of good government. The states will recover their full powers over local government. The federal government, divorced from its intervention into local affairs, will address solely the great national problems which have for so long been neglected.

Much of the restoration of the decentralized constitutional order can be done by Supreme Court reversals of the course of the Warren Court. But in the new order, the Congress must recover its place and exercise its authority, acting where necessary to restore the constitutional order in the absence of Court action. When Congress again represents the people, it will recover its integrity and attend to its constitutional responsibility.

When the Bill of Rights becomes again, as it once was, solely a restriction on the federal government, the states will recover full control of their police powers, including control of public morality, the right to spend money in support of public services rendered by religious bodies and the right to censor publications subversive of public order. We can with confidence expect the states to exercise these powers prudently and to restore a public morality and public safety which has been all but destroyed by the Supreme Court.

When the federal government is removed from welfare services and states are required to finance from their own taxation such services as they render, we shall have a reduction of waste and corruption in this field, new incentives to work, and a compassionate care for those truly in need. We shall have also a revitalization of religion through restoration of its responsibility for charity and for aid to the sick.

Individual independence requires that every citizen be able to obtain the work and income required for his own maintenance. This condition can be created and maintained only in a society in which the people are free to address their creative energies to the needs of the community. The proper contribution of government to that condition is a system of law and a stable

272

currency which foster citizen initiative, for government cannot create the condition by its own direct intervention in the economic process.

Relieved of the election pressures of the money powers, Congress must recover responsibility for maintaining a stable currency. Congress will not be responsible for full employment but it will have responsibility for maintaining a system of federal law which encompasses its responsibilities.

Maintenance of this climate of individual responsibility in freedom is a function of the whole society. All of the structures of society, public and private, must be geared to sustain it. The system of law and the exercise of governmental authority must contribute to it. The churches, the fraternal and patriotic orders, the business organizations, the health and recreational formations must all contribute to it. All must be in harmony with this central responsibility of society.

Because religion represents the most basic thinking of the people about their presence and purpose in this world, it is a vital element of every right political order. The close collaboration of all religious groups with government is an imperative of nationhood. Trends of the Supreme Court in recent decades to separate the state from religion must be reversed.

In our pluralistic society, the concept of a "wall of separation" between church and state has been abused in recent decades to postulate an hostility of government to religion which belies both the statement of Thomas Jefferson and the wisdom of George Washington. The Constitution clearly prohibits the national government from *establishing* a national church or interfering with the people's practice of religion. But these provisions are entirely consistent with cooperation of church and state in public service where that cooperation is offered impartially to all religious groups. In fact, the good of society requires such sensible cooperation in public service, for both government and religion have a duty to sustain the moral order of society.

CHANGE NEEDED

The chief threat to the independence of the citizen comes from a government that, in offering every free service, would make him its ward, inverting the order of sovereign and servant. As the agent of society for the enactment and enforcement of law, government is delegated a power which must be precisely defined and prudently limited. The best definition of limited government yet devised by man is contained in the U.S. Constitution, but it has not been good enough to preserve representative government and the sovereignty of the people.

There are two serious defects in the U.S. Constitution: (1) It does not adequately restrict the law-making authority of the national government in the fields of its delegated powers, and (2) it does not adequately limit the taxing authority of the national government. If the freedom of the individual is to be preserved, no government should be granted unlimited authority either to make law or to collect taxes.

Flagrant abuse of the interstate commerce clause of the Constitution by Congress and the Supreme Court in recent decades—a clause once considered to be clear and adequate—underscores both the difficulty and the necessity of strictly defining all delegations of power to government. Although the U.S. Constitution pioneered in limiting government, it did not go far enough.

The Constitution did prudently limit the taxing authority of the national government to direct taxes, but that limitation was unwisely nullified in the Sixteenth Amendment to the Constitution. Experience has shown the prudence of the original restriction. But that restriction alone was not enough. Congress should have been required to balance the federal budget annually except in time of declared war, a limitation which the Constitution of the Federal Republic of Germany imposes on the Bundestag.

The federal government must do more than balance the budget. It must begin to retire the national debt which now consumes in interest so much of current income. The annual expenditures of the Congress should provide regularly for debt retirement. By that action, Congress will restore confidence in itself and in the nation.

The prudent rule of limiting governmental authority has equal validity for state governments. Some states have constitutional limitations on the law-making and taxing powers of their legislatures, but others lack these restrictions or have generally inadequate provisions.

The logic and the urgency of limiting the law-making function of courts is even more compelling than that of limiting the legislatures. Legislative process provides some protection of the people's power and interest while court legislation provides no protection. All constitutions should provide rigorous definition of and limitation upon the judicial function.

Congress will have a major task also in restoring proper relations with the Executive. Delegated legislative powers must be recovered. The Executive must be only an executive, not a lawmaker. To accomplish this and other tasks, the Congress must reform itself.

The first task of reform is to get Congress functioning again. Congress is designed as the legislative body. It can be effective only when it acts as a body. The present dispersion of authority and power to committee chairmen fragments the power and influence of Congress in government. Each house must function as a unit addressing its constitutional duties, and this cannot be done through a congeries of committees. The House of Representatives must be organized as a unit under the Speaker, with a bipartisan Policy Committee directing the course of the whole body. This committee should assign the tasks of the various committees concerned with segments of the total task. It should determine what the budget will be and assign ceilings to the Ways and Means and Appropriations committees. It should determine which laws shall be passed and which laws shall be rescinded. The Senate should be similarly organized. These working committees of the Congress should have no policy-making functions but should have only the duty of detailing the policies of the whole body determined by the leadership.

The leadership represented on the Policy Committee would be elected by the total House membership and would be responsible to the whole body. It would bear the responsibility of shaping national policy and giving effect to that policy through laws and appropriations.

When Congress is properly constituted for its task, it will gather to it the talent and resources required to fulfill its duties. It will begin to shape government, to curb the Executive and the courts, to recover its delegated and neglected responsibilities.

Its most vital task will be to restore the decentralized constitutional order, to arrest and reverse the centralization of power in Washington. It is an elementary principle of organization that as size increases, authority and responsibility must be delegated to lower echelons for administration. The concentration of power in Washington in recent decades defies this sensible rule.

Some recognition of the gross ineptitude of centralized administration is made in the federal decentralization of departmental responsibilities into regional offices. But this measure attempts to make practical a seizure of local powers which the federal government should never have made in the first instance. The correct procedure organizationally is not to create a decentralized central government but to restore to the states full responsibility and authority for local affairs by divesting the federal government of authority in these fields.

Adherence to the principle of subsidiarity is the sensible guide to order in government. In the United States, this requires that the national government be divested of its assumed authority over individual health, education, welfare and local law enforcement and be restored to its former exclusive concern with national functions of maintaining a stable currency, conducting foreign policy, waging war and regulating interstate commerce. It requires that the states, including state judicial systems, be restored authority over the reserved powers, subject only to the constitutional limitations on those powers.

The restoration of decentralized government will require reallocation of tax income between national and state governments. However, the imperative need is for the reduction of all government spending and the concurrent restoration of responsibility to the people for spending their own money. Therefore, the revision of taxing authority requires a reexamination of the whole tax structure to strip nonessential functions from all government.

Individual freedom requires protection not alone from government but also from concentrations of private wealth and power which are inimical to a sound public order. Just as society limits the role of government, it must limit the size, authority and activity of private corporate or other structures to dimensions assuring responsiveness and subordination to law.

Care of the individual is a function not of government but of the individual. Management and labor must so order production that all persons are admitted to a share of work and income in accordance with their interests and talents.

Society in all its structures and activities must inculcate in youth and maintain in mature citizens the virtues of patriotism and courage upon which the safety of society depends. The institutions of society, including but not limited to government, must foster the development of individual character by contributing to a sense of the nation's history, achievements and responsibilities.

OUR WORLD OUTLOOK

Our experience in disregarding the advice of President George Washington has confirmed the wisdom of his precepts in foreign relations: "Observe good faith and justice toward all nations, cultivate peace and harmony with all. Religion and morality enjoin this conduct. . . . In the execution of such a plan nothing is more essential than that permanent, inveterate antipathies against particular nations and passionate attachments for others should be excluded, and that in place of them just and amicable feelings toward all should be cultivated. . . . The great rule of conduct for us in regard to foreign nations is, in extending our commercial relations we have with them as little political connection as possible."

This advice stands as a reproach to our special relations with Britain, to our illusions about preserving peace through political alliance and to the consequent squandering of our lives and resources in foreign adventures. Alliances for national security are as necessary and proper today as they were when the United States accepted French aid during the American Revolution. Prudence requires that such alliances be temporary in character and limited in scope to the mutual interest which warrants their inception.

The Bolshevist regime inaugurated by Lenin in Russia, and then extended to China and other countries, makes the most barbaric use of terror in the history of mankind. The calculated slaughter and starvation of their own peoples surpasses the cruelty of all other dictatorships since the beginning of time. It marks the Communist regimes as enemies of mankind.

For forty years, the United States has refused to face the reality of Communist power and purpose and to address itself realistically to the removal of this threat to Western civilization and to our own security. This policy has caused a perilous decline in the world position of the United States and a corresponding ascendancy of the Soviet Union to a position of world military leadership. Honesty and candor require the United States to adopt a new policy: To reaffirm its interest in the freedom of all peoples, to declare its solidarity with all peoples oppressed by communism and to condemn the dictatorial Communist regimes which now hold their own peoples and the Captive Nations in servitude. Only through internal revolution can these dictatorships be overthrown, their subjects liberated and their threat of world conquest aborted.

Pending the dissolution of the Communist dictatorships under political attack, the Free World must secure its own domain. In this mission, the role of the United States is to prevent or defeat any incursion of the Soviet Union or Red China upon the territory of our allies. It is the duty of our allies to assure their own internal security and to prevent or defeat any incursion upon their territories by lesser Communist countries. It is the duty of all free countries to fulfill these obligations according to their needs and means, with help from allies where necessary.

It is the duty of responsible political leadership to inform the people of our world interests and of the policies and means which will be used to serve them, so that measures taken may be truly national in character, bearing the full support of the people. To this end, Congress must decree an end of the news media monopolies which now inhibit the full dissemination of information to the people.

The people must maintain through government and through private institutions a continuing surveillance of the functioning of our society to the end that government may remain limited and efficient and that the private organization of society may be conducive to the higher development of the human spirit in peace and justice.

This enumeration of new directions for U.S. policy highlights the kind of change which is needed. When the new direction is taken, the initiatives of our people will be released to find prudent solutions to issues of foreign and domestic policy. It is, indeed, the function of policy to give sound direction to national purpose and effort so that supporting measures may be effective instead of being wasteful and frustrating. From this new direction, peace will flow and the confidence of our people will be restored.

It should be clear that these new directions will require a reconstitution of the political parties. They can no longer serve as the agents of Big Money, imposing on the people laws and policies destructive of the national interest and shattering the unity of our people. Perhaps the existing parties will simply die, to be replaced by other representatives of citizen interest structured more democratically and responsive to the will of the people. It will not matter what form the new political associations may take so long as they perform a useful function in upholding our American political order. That is the prize of great worth to which our Republic must cling if it is to reverse the law of history—and live.

Appendix I

"COME BACK
TO YOUR FATHER'S HOUSE"

ALFRED EMANUEL SMITH

*Address before the American Liberty League dinner, Washington, D.C., and a
national radio audience, January 25, 1936.*

Mr. Chairman, members and guests of the American Liberty League, and
my friends listening in, as I have been told by the newspapers, from all
parts of the United States: At the outset of my remarks let me make one
thing perfectly clear. I am not a candidate for nomination by any party, at
any time. What is more, I do not intend even to lift my right hand to secure
nomination from any party at any time.

Further than that, I have no axe to grind. There is nothing personal in
this whole performance in so far as I am concerned. I have no feeling
against any man, woman or child in the United States. I am in possession of
supreme happiness and comfort. I represent no group, and I speak for no
man or no group, but I do speak for what I believe to be the best interests
of the great rank and file of the American people in which class I belong.

I am here tonight also because I have a great love for the United States of America. I love it for what I know it has meant to mankind since the day of its institution. I love it because I feel that it has grown to be a great stabilizing force in world civilization. I love it, above everything else, for the opportunity that it offers to every man and every woman that desires to take advantage of it.

No man that I know of or that I ever read of has more reason to love it than I have. They kept the gateway open for me. It is a matter of common knowledge throughout the country, and I do not state it boastfully, because it is well known, that, deprived by poverty in my early years of an education, that gateway showed me how it was possible to go from newsboy on the sidewalks of New York to the Governorship of the greatest State in the Union.

I have five children and I have ten grandchildren, and you take it from me I want that gate left open, not alone for mine—I am not selfish about it—not for mine, but for every boy and girl in the country. And in that respect I am no different from every father and mother in the United States.

Now, think it over for a minute, figure it out for yourself. It is possible for your children's success to be your success.

I remember distinctly my first inauguration as Governor of New York, and I am not sure that the young folks understood it thoroughly, but there were three people at that inauguration that did understand it: One was my mother, and the other was my sister, and the third was my wife, because they were with me in all of the early struggles.

I am here for another reason. I am here because I am a Democrat. I was born in the Democratic party and I expect to die in it. I was attached to it in my youth, because I was led to believe that no man owned it. Furthermore, that no group of men owned it, but, on the other hand, that it belonged to all the plain people of the United States.

Now, I must make a confession. It is not easy for me to stand up here tonight and talk to the American people against a Democratic administration. It is not easy; it hurts me. But I can call upon innumerable witnesses to testify to the fact that during my whole public life I put patriotism above partisanship.

And when I see danger, I see danger. That is the stop, look and listen to the fundamental principles upon which this government of ours was organized. And it is difficult for me to refrain from speaking up. What are these dangers that I see? The first is the arraignment of class against class. It has been freely predicted that if we were ever to have civil strife again in this country it would come from the appeal to the passions and prejudices that come from the demagogues who. would incite one class of our people against the other.

In my time I met some good and bad industrialists. I met some good and bad financiers, but I also met some good and bad laborers. This I know—that permanent prosperity is dependent upon both capital and labor alike. I also know that there can be no permanent prosperity in this country until industry is able to employ labor, and there certainly can be no permanent recovery upon any governmental theory of soak the rich or soak the poor.

And let it be said to the glory of our educational institutions, that even the children in our high schools know that you can't soak capital without soaking labor at the same time.

The next thing that I view as being dangerous to our national liberty is government by bureaucracy instead of what we have been taught to look to: government by law. Just let me quote something from the President's message to Congress:

"In thirty-four months we have set up new instruments of public power in the hands of the people's government, which power is wholesome and appropriate, but in the hands of political puppets, of an economic autocracy, such power would provide shackles for the liberties of our people."

Now, I interpret that to mean that, if you are going to have an autocrat, take me. But be very careful about the other fellow.

There is a complete answer to that, and it rises in the minds of the great rank and file, and that answer is just this—we will never, in this country, tolerate any law that provides shackles for our people. We don't want any autocrats, either in or out of office. We wouldn't even take a good one.

The next thing that is apparent to me is the vast building up of new bureaus of government, draining the resources of our people, to pool and redistribute them, not by any process of law but by the whim of the bureaucratic autocracy.

Well, now, what am I here for? I am here not to find fault. Anybody can do that. I am here to make a suggestion. Now, what would I have my party do? I would have them re-establish and re-declare the principles that they put forth in that 1932 platform.

Even our Republican friends, and I know many of them, have all agreed that it is the most compact, the most direct and the most intelligent political platform that was ever put forth by any political party in this country.

The Republican platform was ten times as long. It was stuffy, it was unreadable, and in many points not understandable.

No administration in the history of the country came into power with a more simple, a more clear, or a more inescapable mandate than the party that was inaugurated on the 4th of March in 1933. And, listen, no candidate in the history of the country ever pledged himself more unequivocally to his party platform than did the President who was inaugurated on that day.

Well, here we are. Millions and millions of Democrats, just like myself, all over the country, still believe in that platform. What we want to know is, why wasn't it carried out?

There is only one man in the United States of America that can answer that question. It won't do to pass it down to an Under-Secretary. I won't even recognize him when I hear his name.

Let us take a look at that platform and let us see what happened to it. Here is the way it started out:

"We believe that a party platform is a covenant with the people to be faithfully kept by the party when entrusted with power and that the people are entitled to know in plain words the terms of the contract to which they are asked to subscribe.

"The Democratic party solemnly promises by appropriate actions to put into effect the principles, policies and reforms herein advocated and to eradicate the political methods and practices herein condemned."

My friends, these were what we called "fighting words." At the time that platform went through the air and over the wire, the people of the United States were in the lowest possible depths of despair, and the Democratic platform looked to them like a star of hope. It looked like the rising sun in the East to the mariner on the bridge of a ship after a terrible night. But what happened to it?

First plank: "We advocate an immediate drastic reduction of governmental expenditures by abolishing useless commissions and offices, consolidating departments and bureaus, and eliminating extravagance, to accomplish a saving of not less than twenty-five percent in the cost of the Federal Government."

Well, now, what is the fact?

No bureaus were eliminated, but the alphabet was exhausted in the creation of new departments. And—this is sad news for the taxpayer—the cost, what we refer to as "housekeeping costs" over and above all emergencies, that ordinary housekeeping cost of government is greater today than it has ever been in any time in the history of the Republic.

Another plank: "We favor maintenance of the national credit by a Federal budget annually balanced on the basis of accurate executive estimates within revenue."

How can you balance a budget if you insist upon spending more money than you take in? Even the increased revenue won't go to balance the budget, because it is "hocked" before you receive it.

It is much worse than that. We borrow. We owe something. We have borrowed so that we have reached a new high peak of Federal indebtedness for all time. Well, that wouldn't annoy me so very much ordinarily. When I was Governor of New York, they said I borrowed a lot of money. If it solved our problems and we were out of trouble, I would say, "All right, let it go." But the sin of it is that we have the indebtedness, and at the end of three years we are just where we started. Unemployment and the farm problem we still have with us.

Now, here is something that I want to say to the rank and file: There are three classes of people in this country. There are the poor and the rich, and in between the two is what has often been referred to as the great backbone of America. That is the plain fellow that makes from $100 a month up to the man that draws down five or six thousand dollars a year. There is that great big army.

Forget the rich; they can't pay this debt; if you took everything they got away from them, you could not pay it, there are not enough of them. There's no use of talking about the poor. They will never pay it, because they've got nothing. This debt is going to be paid by that great big middle-class that we refer to as the backbone and the rank and file. And the sin of it is, they ain't going to know that they're paying it.

It is going to come to them in the form of indirect taxation. It will come in the cost of living, in the cost of clothing, in the cost of every activity they enter into. And because it isn't a direct tax, they won't think they are paying it, but take it from me, they are going to pay it.

Another point: "We advocate the extension of Federal credit to the States to provide for unemployment relief when the diminishing resources of the State render it impossible to provide for them."

That is pretty plain. That was a recognition in the national convention of the rights of the States. But what happened? The Federal Government took over most of the relief problems. They started out to prime the pump for industry in order to absorb the ranks of the unemployed, and at the end of three years their affirmative policy is absolutely nothing but the negative policy of the administration that preceded it.

We favor unemployment and old age insurance under State laws. Now, let me make myself perfectly clear so that no demagogue or no crack pot in the next week or so will be able to say anything about my attitude on this kind of legislation. I am in favor of it, and I take my hat off to no man in the United States on the question of legislation beneficial to the poor, the weak, the sick or the afflicted, men, women and children. Because when I started out a quarter of a century ago, when I had very few followers in my State, during that period I advocated, fought for and introduced, as a legislator, and finally as Governor, for eight long years, and signed more progressive legislation in the interest of men, women and children than any man in the State of New York. The sin of this whole thing, and the part of it that worries me and gives me concern is, that this haphazard legislation is never going to accomplish the purpose for which it was designed. And bear this in mind—follow the platform—"under State law."

Here is another one: "We promise the enactment of every constitutional measure that will aid the farmers to receive for their basic farm commodities prices in excess of cost."

Well, what is the use of talking about that? "We promise every constitutional measure." The Supreme Court disposed of that within the last couple of weeks. And, according to the papers the other day, some brilliant individual has conceived the idea of how to get around the Constitution. We are going to have forty-eight AAA's, one for each State.

The day that the United States Supreme Court decided the case I left my office to attend a board of trustees meeting. I got in a taxicab to go down-town. The driver was reading the extra, "Supreme Court Declares AAA Unconstitutional." We rode along for a few minutes and then we got caught at a red light. The taxi fellow turned around and said: "Governor, ain't there any lawyers in Congress any more?" Just then the lights changed. I was afraid to answer him for fear I might disconcert him, but I was all ready to say: "Yes, son, but they don't function."

We got another plank! "We advocate strengthening and impartial enforcement of the anti-trust laws." What happened? The NRA just put a gas bag on the anti-trust laws and put them fast asleep. And nobody said anything about it. I don't know whether they are good or whether they are bad, but I know that they didn't work.

Another one: "We promise the removal of government from all fields of private enterprise, except where necessary to develop public works and national resources in the common interest."

NRA! A vast octopus set up by government that wound its arms around all the business of the country, paralyzed big business and choked little business to death. Did you read in the papers a short time ago where somebody said that business was going to get a breathing spell? What is the meaning of that? And where did that expression arise? I will tell you where it comes from. It comes from the prize ring. When the aggressor is punching the head off the other fellow, he suddenly takes compassion on him and gives him a breathing spell before he delivers the knockout wallop.

Here is another one: "We condemn the open and covert resistance of administrative officials to every effort made by Congressional committees to curtail the extravagance and expenses of government and improvident subsidies rendered to private interests."

Now, just between ourselves, do you know any administrative officer that ever tried to stop Congress from appropriating money? Do you think there has been any desire on the part of Congress to curtail appropriations? Why, not at all. The fact is that Congress is throwing them left and right, don't even tell what they are for. And the truth is that every administrative officer sought to get all he possibly could, to expand the activities of his own office, and throw the money of the people right and left.

As to the subsidy—never at any time in the history of this or any other country were there so many subsidies granted to private groups and on such a large scale. The fact of the matter is that most of the cases pending before the United States Supreme Court revolve around the point of whether or not it is proper for Congress to tax all the people to pay subsidies to a particular group.

Here is another one: "We condemn the extravagance of the Farm Board, its disastrous action which made the government a speculator in farm products, and the unsound policy of restricting agricultural products to the demands of domestic markets."

Listen, and I will let you in on something. This has not leaked out, so kind of keep it to yourself until you get the news. On the first of February we are going to own 4,500,000 bales of cotton. The cost is $270,000,000. And we have been such brilliant speculators that we are paying thirteen cents a pound for it when you add storage and carrying charges, and it can be bought in any one of the ten cotton markets of the South today for 11½ cents. Some speculators!

What about the restriction of our agricultural products and the demands of the domestic market? Why, the fact about that is that we shut out entirely the foreign market, and by plowing under corn and wheat and the destruction of foodstuffs, food from foreign countries has been pouring into our American markets, food that should have been purchased by us from our own farmers.

In other words, while some of the countries of the Old World were attempting to drive the wolf of hunger from the doormat, the United States of America flew in the face of God's bounty and destroyed its own foodstuffs. There can be no question about that.

Now, I could go on indefinitely with some of the other planks. They are unimportant, and the radio time will not permit it. But just let me sum up this way: regulation of the Stock Exchange and the repeal of the Eighteenth Amendment, plus one or two minor provisions of the platform that in no way touched the daily life of our people have been carried out, but the balance of the platform was thrown in the waste-basket. About that there can be no question.

And let us see how it was carried out. Make a test for yourself. Just get the platform of the Democratic party and get the platform of the Socialist party and lay them down on your dining-room table, side by side, and get a heavy lead pencil and scratch out the word "Democratic" and scratch out the word "Socialist" and let the two platforms lay there, and then study the record of the present administration up to date.

After you have done that, make your mind up to pick up the platform that more nearly squares with the record, and you will have your hand on the Socialist platform; you would not dare touch the Democratic platform. And incidentally, let me say that it is not the first time in recorded history that a group of men have stolen the livery of the church to do the work of the devil.

If you study this whole situation you will find that it is at the bottom of all our troubles. This country was organized on the principles of a representative democracy, and you can't mix socialism or communism with that. They are like oil and water. Just like oil and water, they refuse to mix.

Incidentally, let me say to you that is the reason why the United States Supreme Court is working overtime, throwing the alphabet out of the window, three letters at a time. I am going to let you in on something else. How do you suppose all this happened? The young brain trusters caught the Socialists in swimming and they ran away with their clothes.

It is all right with me if they want to disguise themselves as Karl Marx or Lenin or any of the rest of that bunch, but I won't stand for allowing them to march under the banner of Jackson or Cleveland.

What is worrying me is: Where does that leave us millions of Democrats? My mind is all fixed upon the convention in June in Philadelphia. The committee on resolutions is about to report. The preamble to the platform is: "We, the representatives of the Democratic party, in convention assembled, heartily endorse the Democratic administration." What happened to the recital of Jefferson and Jackson and Cleveland when that resolution was read out? Why, for us it is a washout. There is only one of two things we can do. We can either take on the mantle of hypocrisy or we can take a walk, and we will probably do the latter.

Now, leave the platform alone for a little while. What about this attack that has been made upon the fundamental institutions of this country? Who threatens them, and did we have any warning of this threat? Why, you don't have to study party platforms, you don't have to read books, you don't have to listen to professors of economics. You will find the whole thing incorporated in the greatest declaration of political principle that ever came from the hand of man—the Declaration of Independence and the Constitution of the United States.

Always have in your mind that the Constitution and the first ten amendments were drafted by refugees and by sons of refugees, by men with bitter memories of European oppression and hardship, by men who brought to this country and handed down to their descendants an abiding fear of arbitrary, centralized government and autocracy. All the bitterness and all the hatred of the Old World was distilled, in our Constitution, into the purest democracy that the world has ever known. There are just three principles and in the interest of brevity I will read them. I can read them quicker than I can talk them.

First, a Federal Government strictly limited in its powers, with all other powers except those expressly mentioned reserved to the States and to the people, so as to insure State's rights, guarantee home rule and preserve freedom of individual initiative and local control. That is simple enough. The difference between the State Constitution and the Federal Constitution is that in the State you can do anything you want to do provided it is not prohibited by the Constitution, but in the Federal Government, according that document, you can do only that which that Constitution tells you that you can do.

What is the trouble? Congress has overstepped its power. It has gone beyond that constitutional limitation, and it has enacted laws that not only violate that, but violate the home rule and the State's rights principle. And who says that? Did I say it? Not at all. That was said by the United States Supreme Court in the last ten or twelve days.

Second, the government with three independent branches: Congress to make the laws, the Executive to execute them, the Supreme Court, and so forth, and you all know that. In the name of heaven, where is the independence of Congress? Why, they just laid right down. They are flatter on the Congressional floor than the rug under this table here. They centered all their powers in the Executive, and that is the reason why you read in the newspapers reference to Congress as the rubber-stamp Congress.

We all know that the most important bills were drafted by the brain trusters and sent over to Congress and passed by Congress without consideration, without debate, and without meaning any offense at all to my Democratic brethren in Congress I think I can safely say without 90 percent of them knowing what was in the bills, what was the meaning of the list that came over.

And beside certain items was "must." Speaking for the rank and file of the American people, we don't want any Executive to tell Congress what it must do. We don't want any Congress to tell the Executive what he must do. We don't want Congress or the Executive, jointly or severally, to tell the United States Supreme Court what it must do.

On the other hand, we don't want the United States Supreme Court to tell either of them what they must do. What we want, and what we insist upon, and what we are going to have, is the absolute preservation of this balance of power which is the keystone upon which the whole theory of democratic government has got to rest, and when you rattle it you rattle the whole structure.

Of course, when our forefathers wrote the Constitution, it couldn't be possible that they had in their minds that that was going to be all right for all time to come, so they said, "No, we will provide a manner and method of amending," and that is set forth in the document itself. And during our national life we amended it many times.

We amended it once by mistake, and we corrected it.

And what did we do? We took the amendment out. Fine! That is the way we ought to do it. By recourse to the people.

But we don't want an administration that takes a shot at it in the dark and that ducks away from it and dodges away from it and tries to put something over in contradiction of it upon any theory that there is going to be a great public power in favor of it and it is possible that the United States Supreme Court may be intimidated into a friendly opinion with respect to it. But I found all during my public life that Almighty God built this country and He did not give us that kind of a Supreme Court.

Now, this is pretty tough for me to have to go after my own party this way, but I submit that there is a limit to blind loyalty. As a young man in the Democratic party I witnessed the rise and fall of Bryan and Bryanism, and in the memory of Bryan, what he did to our party, I know how long it took to build it after he got finished with it. But let me say this, for the everlasting memory of Bryan and the men that followed him, that they had the energy and the courage and the honesty to put into the platform just what their leaders told them.

They put the American people in the position of making an intelligent choice when they went to the polls. The fact of this whole thing is, I speak now not only of the Executive but of the Legislature at the same time—that they promised one set of things, they repudiated that promise, and they launched off on a program of action totally different.

Well, in twenty-five years of experience I have known both parties to fail to carry out some of the planks of their platform, but this is the first time that I have known a party, upon such a huge scale, not only not to carry out the planks, but to do directly the opposite thing to what they promised.

Now, suggestions—and I make these as a Democrat, acting for the success of my party, and I make them in good faith. Here are my suggestions:

Number 1—I suggest for the members of my party on Capitol Hill here in Washington that they take their minds off the Tuesday that follows the first Monday in November. Just take your mind off it to the end that you may do the right thing and not the expedient thing.

I suggest to them that they dig up the 1932 platform from the grave that they buried it in and read it over and study it, read life into it and follow it in legislative and executive action to the end that they make good their promises to the American people when they put forth that platform and the candidate that stood upon it 100 percent—in short, make good.

Third, I would suggest that they stop compromising with the fundamental principles laid down by Jackson and Jefferson and Cleveland.

Fourth, stop attacking the structure of our government without recourse to the people themselves, as provided in their own Constitution which really belongs to the people, and not to any administration.

Next, I suggest that they read their oath of office to support the Constitution of the United States and I ask them to remember that they took that oath with their hands on the Holy Bible, thereby calling upon God Almighty himself to witness their solemn promise. It is bad enough to disappoint us.

Sixth, I suggest that from this moment on they resolve to make the Constitution again the Civil Bible of the United States and to pay it the same civil respect and reverence that they would religiously pay the Holy Scripture. I ask them to read from Holy Scripture the paragraph of the prodigal son, and to follow his example, "Stop, stop wasting your substance in a foreign land and come back to your father's house."

In conclusion, let me give this solemn warning: There can be only one capital, Washington or Moscow. There can be only one atmosphere of government, the clear, pure, fresh air of free America, or the foul breath of communistic Russia. There can be only one flag, the Stars and Stripes, õr the flag of the godless Union of the Soviets. There can be only one national anthem, "The Star-Spangled Banner" or the "Internationale." There can be only one victor.

If the Constitution wins, we win. But if the Constitution—stop, stop there—the Constitution can't lose. The fact is, it has already won, but the news has not reached certain ears.

Appendix II

"ADDRESS ON THE PROPOSED CONSTITUTIONAL AMENDMENT TO GRANT INCOME TAX POWERS TO THE FEDERAL GOVERNMENT"

RICHARD E. BYRD, SPEAKER OF THE VIRGINIA HOUSE OF DELEGATES, ON MARCH 3, 1910

IT (THE 16TH AMENDMENT) means that the state must give up legitimate and long established source of revenue and yield it to the Federal Government.

It means that the state actually invites the Federal Government to invade its territory, to oust its jurisdiction and to establish Federal dominion within the innermost citadel of reserved rights of the Commonwealth.

This amendment will do what even the Fourteenth and Fifteenth Amendments did not do—it will extend the Federal power so as to reach the citizen in the ordinary business of life. A hand from Washington will be stretched out and placed upon every man's business; the eye of a Federal inspector will be in every man's counting house.

The law will of necessity have inquisitorial features, it will provide penalties. It will create a complicated machinery.

Under it businessmen will be hauled into courts distant from their homes.

Heavy fines imposed by distant and unfamiliar tribunals will constantly menace the taxpayer.

An army of Federal inspectors, spies and detectives will descend upon the State. They will compel men of business to show their books and disclose secrets of their affairs. They will dictate forms of bookkeeping. They will require statements and affidavits. On the one hand, the inspector can blackmail the taxpayer and on the other, he can profit by selling his secret to his competitor.

When the Federal government gets a strangle hold on the individual businessmen, state lines will exist nowhere but on the maps. Its agents will everywhere supervise the commercial life of the states . . . I am not willing by any voluntary act to give up revenue which the State of Virginia herself needs, nor to surrender that measure of states' rights which was, and the construction of the Federal courts have permitted to remain.

[Virginia did not ratify the Sixteenth Amendment.]

NOTES

CHAPTER 1   The Foundation of Politics

1. Jacques Maritain, *Man and the State* (Chicago: University of Chicago Press, 1951), p. 43.

2. John Courtney Murray, *We Hold These Truths* (New York: Doubleday and Co., 1964), p. 40.

CHAPTER 2   Organizing Society

1. John Courtney Murray, *We Hold These Truths* (New York: Doubleday and Co., 1964), p. 275.

CHAPTER 3   The American Revolution

1. John Courtney Murray, *We Hold These Truths* (New York: Doubleday and Co., 1964), pp. 8, 9.

2. Herbert Hoover, *The Challenge to Liberty* (New York: Charles Scribner's Sons, 1934), p. 31.

3. Murray, *op. cit.*, p. 91.

CHAPTER 4   Creating a New Order

1. Jacques Maritain, *Man and the State* (Chicago: University of Chicago Press, 1951), p. 140.

2. John C. Calhoun, cited in John Courtney Murray, *We Hold These Truths* (New York: Doubleday and Co., 1964), pp. 65, 66.

3. Maritain, *op. cit.*, p. 183.

4. Guy Hawthorn, Howard R. Penniman, and Mark Ferber, *Government and Politics in the United States* (Princeton: D. Van Nostrand Co., 1965), p. 6.

5. *The Federalist Papers*, No. 37 (New York: Washington Square Press, 1964), p. 85.

6. Frank S. Meyer, *The Conservative Mainstream* (New Rochelle, N.Y.: Arlington House, 1969), as cited in *America's Future*, January 5, 1973.

CHAPTER 5   A Competing Concept

1. Ludwig von Mises, *Bureaucracy* (New Rochelle, N.Y.: Arlington House, 1969), p. 17.

2. Whittaker Chambers, *Cold Friday* (New York: Random House, 1964), p. 68.

3. John Courtney Murray, *We Hold These Truths* (New York: Doubleday and Co., 1964), p. 205.

4. Chambers, *op. cit.*, p. 150.

5. Henry Paolucci, *War, Peace, and the Presidency* (New York: McGraw Hill Book Co., 1968), p. 186.

6. *Ibid.*, p. 187.

7. Ann Watson, *They Came in Peace* (Palos Verdes Estates, Calif.: TW Publishing Co., 1972), p. 95.

8. Jacques Maritain, *Man and the State* (Chicago: University of Chicago Press, 1951), p. 192.

9. Arthur Koestler, *Darkness at Noon* (New York: Random House, The Modern Library edition, 1941), pp. 98, 99, 152.

10. Antony C. Sutton, *National Suicide* (New Rochelle, N.Y.: Arlington House, 1973).

11. Chambers, *op. cit.*, p. 245.

12. Murray, *op. cit.*, p. 203.

CHAPTER 6   Of, By, and For the People

1. *Notes From FEE* (Irvington-on-Hudson, N.Y.: Foundation for Economic Education, September 1972).

2. Lyman A. Garber, *Of Men, Not of Law* (New York: Devin-Adair Co., 1966), p. 51.

3. Jacques Maritain, *Man and the State* (Chicago: University of Chicago Press, 1951), p. 11.

4. Cited in Garber, *op. cit.*, p. 107.

5. Quoted in Henry Paolucci, *War, Peace, and the Presidency* (New York: McGraw-Hill Book Co., 1968), p. 99.

6. Homer Lea, *The Valor of Ignorance* (New York: Harper and Brothers, 1909), p. 25.

CHAPTER 7   The Fabian Ascendancy

1. Cited by E. L. Wilkinson in a commencement address at Brigham Young University, May 28, 1965.

2. Rose L. Martin, *Fabian Freeway* (Chicago: Heritage Foundation, 1966), p. 11.

3. Cited by Wilkinson, *op. cit.*

4. Whittaker Chambers, *Cold Friday* (New York: Random House, 1964), p. 114.

5. *Ibid.*, p. 93.

6. Clarence B. Carson, *The Flight From Reality* (Irvington-on-Hudson, N.Y.: Foundation for Economic Education, 1969), p. 199.

7. Walter E. Weyl, cited in Carson, *ibid.*, pp. 209, 317.

8. Ludwig von Mises, *Bureaucracy* (New Rochelle, N.Y.: Arlington House, 1969), pp. 113, 114.

9. Martin, *op. cit.*, p. 222.

10. Chambers, *op. cit.*, p. 79.

11. John Courtney Murray, *We Hold These Truths* (New York: Doubleday and Co., 1964), pp. 23, 24.

12. *Ibid.*, p. 23.

CHAPTER 8   The Two-Party System

1. Henry Paolucci, *War, Peace, and the Presidency* (New York: McGraw-Hill Book Co., 1968), p. 140.

2. *Ibid.*, p. 109.

3. *Ibid.*, p. 46.

4. *Ibid.*, pp. 115, 116.

5. Ludwig von Mises, *Bureaucracy* (New Rochelle, N.Y.: Arlington House, 1969), p. 118.

6. Arthur Krock, *Memoirs* (New York: Funk and Wagnalls, 1968), p. 382.

7. Paolucci, *op. cit.*, p. 114.

8. Phyllis Schlafly, *A Choice, Not an Echo* (Alton, Ill.: Pere Marquette Press, 1964), p. 30.

9. *Ibid.*, p. 40.

10. Krock, *op. cit.*, p. 360.

11. Homer Lea, *The Valor of Ignorance* (New York: Harper and Brothers, 1909), p. 232.

12. Edgar Ansel Mowrer, *Triumph and Turmoil* (New York: Weybright and Talley, 1968), p. 135.

13. Paolucci, *op. cit.*, p. 30.

CHAPTER 9   The Money Power

1. Oswald Spengler, *Decline of the West* (New York: Alfred A. Knopf, 1962), p. 414.

2. John Courtney Murray, *We Hold These Truths* (New York: Doubleday and Co., 1964), p. 104.

3. Carroll Quigley, *Tragedy and Hope* (New York: The Macmillan Co., 1966), p. 52.

4. *Ibid.*, p. 61.

5. *Ibid.*, p. 72.

6. *Ibid.*, pp. 950, 951.

7. *Ibid.*, p. 952.

8. *Ibid.*, p. 953.

9. *Ibid.*, p. 73.

10, *U.S. News & World Report,* January 15, 1973, p. 55.

11. Homer Lea, *The Valor of Ignorance* (New York: Harper and Brothers, 1909), p. 26.

12. Henry Hazlitt, *What You Should Know About Inflation* (New York: Funk and Wagnalls, 1968), p. 102.

13. *Ibid.,* p. 48.

14. Quigley, *op. cit.,* p. 945a.

15. *Ibid.,* pp. 939, 940.

16. *Ibid.,* p. 945b.

17. *Ibid.,* p. 941a.

18. *Ibid.,* p. 941b.

19. *Ibid.,* p. 937.

20. Cited in the *Washington Sunday Star,* June 10, 1973, p. E4.

21. Antony C. Sutton, *Western Technology and Soviet Economic Development,* cited in *Human Events,* July 31, 1971, p. 9.

22. Cited in the *Congressional Record,* October 16, 1973, p. H9149.

23. *The New York Times,* August 10, 1973, p. 31.

24. *Congressional Record,* October 16, 1973, p. H9150.

25. Spengler, *op. cit.,* p. 402.

26. Lea, *op. cit.,* p. 67.

CHAPTER 10   Industry—The Runaway Machine

1. Peter F. Drucker, *The New Society* (New York: Harper and Brothers, 1949), p. 351.

2. Cited by E. L. Wilkinson in a commencement address at Brigham Young University on May 28, 1965.

3. H. R. Gross, "On the Capitol Firing Line," May 23, 1973.

CHAPTER 11   The Rule of Law

1. 11 Am. Jur. Constitutional Law, Sec. 225, p. 987, cited in Charles J. Bloch, *States Rights, The Law of the Land* (Atlanta: The Harrison Co., 1958), p. 63.

2. *Barron* v. *Baltimore,* 7 Peters 243 (1833), cited in Bloch, *ibid.,* p. 28.

3. The slaughter house cases, 16 Wallace 36, 21 L. Ed. 394, cited in Bloch, *ibid.,* p. 82.

4. *Ibid.,* p. 250.

5. *Ibid.,* p. 88.

6. Constitutional Construction and Interpretation, U.S.C.A., p. 77 (U.S. Constitution, Art. 1, Sec. 1 to Art. 1, Sec. 9), cited in Bloch, *ibid.,* p. 96.

7. *Ibid.,* p. 201.

8. *Ibid.,* p. 175.

9. *Ibid.,* p. 204.

10. Rexford Guy Tugwell, "Reflections on the Warren Court," in *The Center Magazine,* January-February 1973, p. 62.

11. Bloch, *op. cit.,* p. 244.

12. Bloch, *op. cit.*, p. 245.

13. Arthur Krock, *Memoirs* (New York: Funk and Wagnalls, 1968), p. 44.

14. Tugwell, *op. cit.*, p. 61.

15. Ludwig von Mises, *Bureaucracy* (New Rochelle, N.Y.: Arlington House, 1969), p. 42.

16. Tugwell, *op. cit.*, p. 59.

17. Rousas John Rushdoony, in "Imprimis" (Hillsdale, Mich.: Hillsdale College, February 1943), p. 3.

18. *Ibid.*

19. "They Spoke Unanimously" (Buena Park, Calif.: Colonial Research Library, Knotts Berry Farm).

20. Krock, *op. cit.*, p. 416.

21. Guy Hawthorn, Howard R. Penniman, and Mark Ferber, *Government and Politics in the United States* (Princeton: D. Van Nostrand Co., 1965), pp. 1-8.

22. John Courtney Murray, *We Hold These Truths* (New York: Doubleday and Co., 1964), p. 308.

23. Robert M. Hutchins, cited in Lyman A. Garber, *Of Men, Not of Law* (New York: Devin-Adair Co., 1966), p. 96.

CHAPTER 12   Black and Marxist

1. Walter Bagehot, cited in Henry Paolucci, *War, Peace, and the Presidency* (New York: McGraw Hill Book Co., 1968), p. 80.

2. Jacques Maritain, *Man and the State* (Chicago: University of Chicago Press, 1951), p. 10.

3. Arthur Krock, *Memoirs* (New York: Funk and Wagnalls, 1968), p. 277.

4. Willmoore Kendall, *Willmoore Kendall Contra Mundum* (New Rochelle, N.Y.: Arlington House, 1971), p. 460.

5. *Ibid.*, p. 461.

6. Paolucci, *op. cit.*, p. 236.

7. *Ibid.*, p. 232.

8. Hanson W. Baldwin, "A Soldier's Reflections," in *Intercollegiate Review*, Winter 1972-73, p. 109.

9. Paolucci, *op. cit.*, p. 233.

10. *Palo Alto Times*, July 19, 1966.

CHAPTER 13   Freedom of the Press

1. Jacques Maritain, *Man and the State* (Chicago: University of Chicago Press, 1951), p. 146.

2. *Air Force*, July 1972, p. 12.

3. Arthur Krock, *Memoirs* (New York: Funk and Wagnalls, 1968), p. 93.

4. *Ibid.*, p. 375.

5. Richard J. Whalen, *Catch the Falling Flag* (Boston: Houghton Mifflin Co., 1972), p. 102.

6. Edgar Ansel Mowrer, *Triumph and Turmoil* (New York: Weybright and Talley, 1968), p. 141.

7. Oswald Spengler, *Decline of the West* (New York: Alfred A. Knopf, 1962), pp. 394, 395.

8. Adolf Hitler, *Mein Kampf,* as cited in Ann Watson, *They Came in Peace* (Palos Verdes Estates, Calif.: TW Publishing Co., 1972), p. 99.

9. Willmoore Kendall, *Willmoore Kendall Contra Mundum* (New Rochelle, N.Y.: Arlington House, 1971), p. 549.

10. Whittaker Chambers, *Cold Friday* (New York: Random House, 1964), p. 44.

CHAPTER 14   Law Enforcement

1. Homer Lea, *The Valor of Ignorance* (New York: Harper and Brothers, 1909), p. 87.

2. *Ibid.,* p. 57.

3. John Courtney Murray, *We Hold These Truths* (New York: Doubleday and Co., 1964), p. 48.

4. Henry Paolucci, *War, Peace, and the Presidency* (New York: McGraw Hill Book Co., 1968), p. 31.

5. Herbert Hoover, *The Challenge to Liberty* (New York: Charles Scribner's Sons, 1934), p. 197.

6. Murray, *op. cit.,* p. 157.

7. Lyman A. Garber, *Of Men, Not of Law* (New York: Devin-Adair Co., 1966), p. 123.

8. *Ibid.,* p. 129.

9. Arthur Krock, *Memoirs* (New York: Funk and Wagnalls, 1968), p. 326.

CHAPTER 15   The Moral Climate

1. John Courtney Murray, *We Hold These Truths* (New York: Doubleday and Co., 1964), p. 41.

2. *Ibid.*

3. *Ibid.,* p. 88.

4. *Ibid.,* p. 67.

5. *Ibid.,* p. 32.

6. Jacques Maritain, *Man and the State* (Chicago: University of Chicago Press, 1951), p. 159.

7. Whittaker Chambers, *Cold Friday* (New York: Random House, 1964), p. 99.

8. Cited by Alan Courtney in the *Greater Miami Journal,* July 27, 1972, p. 1.

9. Maritain, *op. cit.,* p. 174.

10. *Washington Evening Star,* July 4, 1973.

11. Herbert Hoover, *The Challenge to Liberty* (New York: Charles Scribner's Sons, 1934), p. 193.

12. *The Ayn Rand Letter,* July 3, 1972.

CHAPTER 16   The Education Empire

1. Willmoore Kendall, *Willmoore Kendall Contra Mundum* (New Rochelle, N.Y.: Arlington House, 1971), p. 550.

2. Oswald Spengler, *Decline of the West* (New York: Alfred A. Knopf, 1962), p. 390.

3. John Courtney Murray, *We Hold These Truths* (New York: Doubleday and Co., 1964), p. 308.

4. *Ibid.*, p. 135.

5. Jacques Maritain, *Man and the State* (Chicago: University of Chicago Press, 1951), p. 121.

CHAPTER 17 The Politics of Poverty

1. *Notes From FEE* (Irvington-on-Hudson, N.Y.: Foundation for Economic Education, May 1972).

2. *Ibid.*

3. Henry Paolucci, *War, Peace, and the Presidency* (New York: McGraw Hill Book Co., 1968), p. 149.

4. *Ibid.*, p. 168.

5. *Ibid.*, p. 39.

6. Whittaker Chambers, *Cold Friday* (New York: Random House, 1964), p. 15.

7. Paolucci, *op. cit.*, p. 93.

8. *Ibid.*, p. 198.

9. Chambers, *op. cit.*, p. 87.

10. Rexford Guy Tugwell, "Reflections on the Warren Court," in *The Center Magazine*, January-February 1973, p. 61.

11. John Courtney Murray, *We Hold These Truths* (New York: Doubleday and Co., 1964), p. 206.

12. Guy Hawthorn, Howard R. Penniman, and Mark Ferber, *Government and Politics in the United States* (Princeton: D. Van Nostrand Co., 1965), p. 8.

13. *Ibid.*

14. *Ibid.*, p. 61.

CHAPTER 18 Building the Welfare State

1. Alfred E. Smith, "Come Back to Your Father's House," an address to the American Liberty League dinner in Washington, D.C., January 25, 1936. It is included in this volume as Appendix I.

2. David S. Broder, *The Party's Over* (New York: Harper and Row, 1971), p. 5.

3. Henry Paolucci, *War, Peace, and the Presidency* (New York: McGraw Hill Book Co., 1968), pp. 201, 202.

4. Arthur Krock, *Memoirs* (New York: Funk and Wagnalls, 1968), p. 403.

5. Excerpt from the address of Richard E. Byrd, Speaker of the Virginia House of Delegates, on the proposed constitutional amendment to grant income tax powers to the federal government, March 3, 1910. It is reproduced in this volume as Appendix II.

6. *U.S. News & World Report*, August 7, 1972, p. 46.

7. Broder, *op. cit.*, p. 235.

8. Krock, *op. cit.*, p. 406.

CHAPTER 19 War

1. Homer Lea, *The Valor of Ignorance* (New York: Harper and Brothers, 1909), p. 42.

2. Edward Geary Lansdale, *In the Midst of Wars* (New York: Harper and Row, 1972), p. 161.

3. Cited in Arthur Krock, *Memoirs* (New York: Funk and Wagnalls, 1968), pp. 477, 431, 477, 479, 478, 480, 482.

4. *Ibid.*, pp. 480, 482.

5. Isaac Don Levine, *Eyewitness to History* (New York: Hawthorn Books, 1973), p. 283.

6. "United States Military Aid and Supply Programs in Western Europe," House Report No. 1371, February 20, 1958, Committee on Government Operations.

7. Hanson W. Baldwin, "A Soldier's Reflections," in *Intercollegiate Review*, v. 8, no. 3, Winter 1972-73, p. 109.

8. Lea, *op. cit.*, p. 230.

9. Maxwell D. Taylor, *Swords and Plowshares* (New York: W. W. Norton and Co., 1972), p. 135.

10. *Ibid.*, p. 157.

11. Lea, *op. cit.*, p. 57.

12. Hanson W. Baldwin, *Strategy for Tomorrow* (New York: Harper and Row, 1970), p. 13.

13. Baldwin, in *Intercollegiate Review, op. cit.*, p. 112.

14. Baldwin, in *Strategy for Tomorrow, op. cit.*, p. 21.

15. Henry Paolucci, *War, Peace, and the Presidency* (New York: McGraw Hill Book Co., 1968), p. 141.

16. *Ibid.*, p. 32.

17. *Ibid.*, p. 38.

18. *Ibid.*, p. 42.

19. *Ibid.*, p. 130.

20. J. A. Williams, "Korea and the Malayan Emergency—The Strategic Priorities," in *RUSI* (London: Royal United Services Institute), June 1973, p. 60.

21. Douglas MacArthur, *Reminiscences* (New York: McGraw Hill Book Co., 1964), p. 375.

22. October 1972.

23. *The New York Times*, July 9, 1973, p. 33.

24. Baldwin, in *Strategy for Tomorrow, op. cit.*, p. 292.

25. Lea, *op. cit.*, p. 242.

CHAPTER 20   An American Foreign Policy

1. Henry Paolucci, *War, Peace, and the Presidency* (New York: McGraw Hill Book Co., 1968), p. 205.

2. *Human Events*, September 30, 1972, p. 14.

3. *Ibid.*

4. *Ibid.*, p. 20.

5. Paolucci, *op. cit.*, p. 131.

6. *Ibid.*, pp. 194, 137.

7. *Ibid.*, p. 71.

8. *Ibid.,* p. 63.

9. *Ibid.,* p. 135.

10. *Ibid.,* p. 152.

11. *Ibid.,* p. 199.

12. *Ibid.,* p. 191.

13. "Debate on the ABM," in *Bulletin of the Atomic Scientists,* June 1967. Scientists, June 1967.

14. Jerome D. Frank, M.D., in C. A. Barker (ed.), *Problems of World Disarmament* (Boston: Houghton Mifflin Co., 1963), p. 96.

15. Robert M. Slusser, in Barker, *ibid.,* p. 120.

16. Whittaker Chambers, *Cold Friday* (New York: Random House, 1964), p. 72.

17. *The New York Times,* July 9, 1973, p. 33.

18. *Washington Star News,* June 8, 1973.

19. Paolucci, *op. cit.,* p. 183.

20. Chambers, *op. cit.,* pp. 310, 311.

21. *Ibid.,* p. 75.

22. Cited in "Foreign Report," *The Economist,* November 22, 1972.

23. John Courtney Murray, *We Hold These Truths* (New York: Doubleday and Co., 1964), p. 93.

24. *Ibid.,* pp. 229, 230.

25. Paolucci, *op. cit.,* p. 217.

26. Chambers, *op. cit.,* p. 294.

27. *Ibid.,* p. 59.

28. *Ibid.,* p. 58.

29. *Ibid.,* p. 291.

30. *Ibid.,* p. 310.

31. *Ibid.,* p. 225.

32. Murray. *op. cit.,* p. 223.

33. Paolucci, *op. cit.,* p. 191.

34. Aneurin Bevan, in the foreword to Dennis Healey, *The Curtain Falls,* cited in *East-West Digest,* January 1973, p. 55.

35. Associated Press dispatch of July 26, 1968, cited in *American Opinion,* June 1972, p. 59.

36. Murray, *op. cit.,* p. 225.

37. Ivan Golomstock, in the *London Sunday Times,* April 15, 1973.

38. *The New York Times,* August 10, 1973, p. 4C.

CHAPTER 21   The Nixon Tenure

1. Richard J. Whalen, *Catch the Falling Flag* (Boston: Houghton Mifflin Co., 1972).

2. *Ibid.,* pp. 17, 29.

3. *Ibid.,* pp. 26, 131, 137.

4. *Ibid.*

5. *Ibid.*

6. H. R. Gross, "On the Capitol Firing Line," June 27, 1973.

7. Whalen, *op. cit.*, p. 227.

8. *Twin Circle* magazine, June 8, 1973.

9. "Manion Forum" broadcast, June 17, 1973.

CHAPTER 23   In Time of Crisis

1. Eugene E. Wilson, *Kitty Hawk to Sputnik to Polaris* (Palm Beach: Literary Investor's Guide, 1967), microfilm edition, p. 188.

Index

Reston, James, 209
Rhodes, Cecil, 75
Rhodes Trust, 75, 76
Richardson, Elliot, 253
Roberts, Owen, 99
Robespierre, Maximilien, 32, 33, 254
Roche, Dr. George C., III, 171
Rockefeller, David, 85, 164
Rockefeller, John D., III, 159
Rockefeller, Nelson, 71, 78, 82, 161, 164, 238, 244-249, 255, 258, 261, 264
Rockefeller, William, 74, 75
Rockefeller Foundation, 87
Roman Empire, 16, 17, 88, 175, 179, 271
Romney, George W., 245
Roosevelt, Franklin D., 44, 54, 60-66, 83-85, 97, 100, 109, 115, 177, 184, 185, 191, 194, 204, 211, 212, 214, 224, 229, 235, 250, 261
Roosevelt, Theodore, 44, 50, 51, 58, 78
Root, Elihu, 74
Rosenberg, Arthur, 35
Rostow, Walt, 62, 227
Rothbard, Murray, 81
Rough Riders, 44
Round Table Groups, 75, 76
Rousseau, Jean Jacques, 150
Royal Institute of International Affairs, 75
Rushdoony, Rev. Rousas John, 103, 104
Russell, Lord Bertrand, 59, 216, 227
Russell, Richard B., 267

St. Augustine, 176
St. Louis Post-Dispatch, 209, 210
St. Paul, 17
Sakharov, Andrei G., 85
Saturday Review, 82, 215
Schmitz, John, 264
Seymour, Charles, 75
Shabad, Theodore, 240
Shaw, George Bernard, 48
Shepardson, Whitney, 75
Sherman, George, 232

Shotwell, James T., 75
Shriver, Sargent, 124
Singer, 84
Sinyavski, Andrei, 239, 240
Sirica, John, 253
Smith, Alfred E., 184, 278-287
Smith, Howard E., 185
Smith, Howard K., 264
Smith v. *Allwright*, 99
Socialism, 35-39, 44, 46-56, 144, 154-156, 158, 163, 168, 169, 173, 182, 284; *see also* COMMUNISM, FABIAN SOCIALISM
Socialist Party (U.S.), 54, 64
Solzhenitsyn, Aleksandr, 85, 224-226, 240
South Africa, 75
Soviet Union, 8, 23, 32, 35-37, 59, 60, 63, 83-87, 95, 136, 160, 203-208, 210, 211, 215-217, 219, 220, 223, 224, 226-242, 247, 251, 253, 267, 268, 276, 277, 287; *see also* COMMUNISM
Spain, 44
Spengler, Oswald, 73, 87, 88, 90, 132, 171, 259, 271
Stalin, Joseph, 35, 62, 63, 83, 85, 156, 204, 205, 207, 224, 239
Stans, Maurice, 253
Stennis, John C., 267
Stevenson, Adlai, 215
Straight, Dorothy, 81
Straight, Willard, 74, 81, 82
Strategy for Tomorrow, 213
Supreme Court, 29, 30, 51, 67, 96-111, 116, 117, 125, 126, 141, 142, 146, 147, 153-159, 161, 162, 177, 184, 193, 197, 198, 251, 272-274, 282-286
Suslov, M. A., 234, 239
Sutherland, George, 98
Sutton, Dr. Antony C., 37, 84, 86
Sweatt v. *Painter et al.*, 99
Swords and Plowshares, 212, 214

Taconic Foundation, 116
Taft, Robert A., 64, 65, 185, 249, 261

307